D0221478

The end of empire in the Middle East is an original and perceptive study of Britain's withdrawal from her last Arab dependencies – the Sudan in 1955, South West Arabia (Aden) in 1967 and the Gulf states in 1971.

Glen Balfour-Paul opens by outlining Britains' position in the Middle East at the end of World War II. He then presents in three separate chapters a detailed account of the forces that culminated in withdrawal from each of the countries, demonstrating how each time it occurred against different constitutional backdrops and for different reasons. In the final chapters, the author compares and contrasts the three episodes in terms of Britain's evolving attitude to empire, public pressures from within and outside the territories, the tensions that arose between policy-makers in London and those executing their decisions, attitudes of British officials to their task and the political and economic aftermath of independence.

This study is based upon a combination of first-hand experience and extensive research. Glen Balfour-Paul has used official material that has only recently become available to the public and a large number of private papers, including those of Sir William Luce, who played a central role in all three episodes. This book will be essential reading both for students and teachers of modern Middle East and Imperial History and for anyone interested in the end of the empire in the Middle East.

THE END OF EMPIRE IN THE MIDDLE EAST

Cambridge Middle East Library: 25

Editorial Board

The *Cambridge Middle East Library* aims to bring together outstanding scholarly work on the history, politics, sociology and economics of the Middle East and North Africa in the nineteenth and twentieth centuries. While primarily focussing on monographs based on original research, the series will also incorporate broader surveys and in-depth treatments.

Cambridge Middle East Library

THE END OF EMPIRE IN THE MIDDLE EAST

Britain's relinquishment of power
in her last three Arab dependencies

GLEN BALFOUR-PAUL

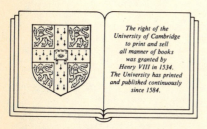

The right of the
University of Cambridge
to print and sell
all manner of books
was granted by
Henry VIII in 1534.
The University has printed
and published continuously
since 1584.

CAMBRIDGE UNIVERSITY PRESS

CAMBRIDGE
NEW YORK   PORT CHESTER   MELBOURNE   SYDNEY

Published by the Press Syndicate of the University of Cambridge
The Pitt Building, Trumpington Street, Cambridge CB2 IRP
40 West 20th Street, New York, NY 10011, USA
10 Stamford Road, Oakleigh, Melbourne 3166, Australia

First published 1991

Printed in Great Britain at the University Press, Cambridge
Typeset by Wyvern Typesetting Ltd, Bristol

British Library cataloguing in publication data
Balfour-Paul, Glen
  The end of empire in the Middle East: Britain's
  relinquishment of power in her last three Arab
  dependencies.
  1. Middle East. Political events. Role of Great Britain,
  1945–1980
  I. Title
  956'.04

Library of Congress cataloguing in publication data
Balfour-Paul, Glen.
  The end of empire in the Middle East: Britain's relinquishment of
  power in her last three Arab dependencies/Glen Balfour-Paul.
     p.   cm. – (Cambridge Middle East library: 25)
  Includes bibliographical references.
  ISBN 0 521 38259 9
     1. Middle East – Foreign relations – Great Britain.   2. Great Britain –
  Foreign relations – Middle East.   I. Title.   II. Series.
  DS63.2.G7B34   1990
  327.41017'671 – dc20   89–77371 CIP

ISBN 0 521 38259 9 hardback

But what is Freedom? Rightly understood,
A universal licence to be good.

Hartley Coleridge

Contents

Illustrations

Maps

Foreword

by Sir Anthony Parsons, GCMG, MVO, MC

When World War II ended in 1945, Britain had emerged supreme in the Middle East from Libya in the West to the frontier of Afghanistan in the East. Her old rivals in the Eastern Question – France, Russia, Germany and Italy – had been driven from the field by defeat in war or revolution at home. The mantle of the Ottoman Empire, so long sustained by the competition of the Great Powers but destroyed through choosing the wrong competitor in World War I, had been assumed by the British Empire. Only twenty-six years later, a mere flicker of the eyelid of history, Britain too had passed from the scene. Both the author of this book and myself were involved for the greater part of our professional careers in this rearguard action which culminated in the termination of British protection over the small Arab states of the Southern Gulf in 1971. However history may view it, to me it was a long pilgrimage, sometimes frustrating, sometimes bitter, sometimes tragic, sometimes over-stimulating, but never boring. Britain's relationship with the Arab world has now moved into calmer waters than at any time since the Arab Revolt was launched in 1916 – apart from other considerations each side is less important to the other – and it is timely that those who lived through stormier seas should look back at the strange eventful history of Britain's last moments before they too leave the ship.

To me Glen Balfour-Paul's book is remarkable in many ways. First it is elegantly written and thereby very readable. That was to be expected. He has eschewed resort to the leaden lexicon of social sciences, thus sparing me the necessity to turn to the dictionary to confirm hazy impressions of the meaning of words rarely if ever used outside academic seminars and theses. Secondly, it is widely and meticulously researched, going far beyond the scope of a personal memoir. Thirdly, it is impartial and objective almost to a fault: it in no way stresses the fact, for example, that the author himself was an active participant in two of the three episodes which he describes and analyses.

The three episodes in question are the end of the Anglo-Egyptian Condominium in the Sudan (1956), the British withdrawal (if that is not too polite a word) from South West Arabia (1967) and the termination of British protection in the Gulf (1971).

Successive British governments do not come well out of the study. I have neither the talent nor the education to compete with Glen Balfour-Paul's metaphorical and stylistic skills. But he will forgive me, I hope, for joining him in the use of cricketing metaphor. Governments, Labour and Conservative, were like teams embarking on what they believed to be a timeless, at least a five-day, Test Match. Suddenly they discovered that the rules had been changed: they were playing a limited-overs game and, at the beginning of each session, the umpire reduced the number of overs remaining. Long term strategy and planning, if any, gave way to hasty improvisation, the important lost priority of the urgent, decisions were made for the wrong reasons, or were not made at all, advice from the region was ignored or rejected.

I accept the Balfour-Paul thesis that 'people in authority (despite obvious exceptions) do things they believe to be right' as qualified by the rider that 'most human activities – in their motivation as in their execution – are a mixture of good and bad, in part praiseworthy, in part repellent'.

But, despite all the constraints on post-war Britain, should we have treated the future of the people of the Sudan as a function of Anglo/Egyptian relations? Should we not have made greater efforts to integrate the non-Arab South with the Arab North (the civil war in that region has now been going on for 30 years)? In South West Arabia, Britain in the 1950s and 1960s could not do much to make up for a century of neglect of the hinterland, but in 1960 many of us (I was in Cairo at the time) knew it to be ludicrous to embark on federating the prosperous, cosmopolitan Crown Colony with the anarchic and primitive Protectorates in the teeth of virulent opposition from pan-Arab Nasserism, then at the crest of its wave. We ended up with substantial British casualties, the collapse of our construct and the assumption of power by the only Marxist–Leninist tyranny in the Arab world.

Then, in the Gulf, no serious attempt was made by Whitehall to grasp the nettle of the necessity to modernize our archaic relationship with the shaykhdoms. Instead, when they all expected us to announce our withdrawal in November 1967, we sent out a minister to tell them we had decided to stay. Two months later, when they all expected us to stay, the same minister returned to tell them that we had after all decided to withdraw. As I recall, the volte-face was to do with the need not to have to raise prescription charges in the National Health Service. I also recall that two of the Rulers offered to pay out of their own pockets the cost of maintaining British protecting forces in the Gulf. Their gesture was rejected! I have often wondered what Lords Curzon, Cromer and Kitchener, observing the incident from whatever region of the Elysian Fields they inhabit, must have said to each other.

Add to these events the humiliating denouement in Palestine, Britain's futile opposition to pan-Arab nationalism culminating in the Suez fiasco, and the collapse of our politico/strategic structure in Iraq with the bloody revolution of 1958, and it is difficult to conclude that British withdrawal from our imperial sphere of influence in the Middle East was other than messy, compared to the end of Empire elsewhere in the world. The author's comments are measured, carefully excluding value judgements, and fair to all concerned. I admire his restraint.

More often than not, in this part of the world where individual personality counts for so much, it was left to the man on the spot, his advice frequently disregarded when it would have counted most, to pick up the pieces. In his concluding chapter Glen Balfour-Paul has reflected sympathetically and perceptively on the nature and character of those individuals who carried the burden on the last lap of the pilgrimage. He makes, among many others, the important point that it was possible to combine a dedicated concern for one's job with a lighthearted awareness of the irrationality of the whole business. This, the combination of conscientiousness with hilarity, is, I believe, a very British national characteristic of the twentieth century, one which frequently deceives foreigners, also the more humourless of our politicians, into believing that its possessors are frivolous defeatists, empty of serious purpose, not, to use a current phrase, 'one of us'. I can for example recall many occasions in New York when the buffooneries of the United Nations left the British (but only the British) Delegation helpless with laughter; and I had to explain to my colleagues, including Americans, that we were also capable of working hard and competently to produce the results we wanted, even though we knew that the resolution we were seeking would, more often than not, leave the world outside unchanged.

In my judgement, no one combined these attributes of seriousness and lightheartedness more perfectly than the man who played a leading part in all the three episodes recorded in this book, Sir William Luce. Britain was fortunate to have someone with his personality and abilities available for her service as we extracted ourselves from our last footholds in the Arab world. The author records how, as Governor of Aden, Luce saw immediately that it was of no use trying to weld a Crown Colony with a clutter of Protected States; that all should first be put on the same footing; and that a massive developmental effort had to be made in the backward Protectorates. His advice was not taken, more is the pity. As Political Resident in the Gulf, he realized that it would be futile to try to dragoon the nine small states into a federation for which they at the time showed no enthusiasm; and that the future lay in Peninsula Solidarity, under the benevolent aegis of Saudi Arabia. Again his advice was not taken but, as the author notes, today's Gulf Co-operation Council is close to Luce's vision. Finally he was given the difficult task of negotiating with the Gulf States, Iran and Saudi Arabia, in the process of British withdrawal, having first advised the new Conservative Government in 1970, to the annoyance of some members of the Party, that it was no good thinking of reversing the decision made by the Labour Government in 1968. His personal contribution to the success of this complex and delicate exercise was enormous.

I was Political Agent in Bahrain during part of Luce's time as Political Resident and worked with him on the last stages of the withdrawal negotiations throughout 1971. He used to stay with my wife and me in Tehran in the mid-1970s after his final retirement, the last occasion only a few weeks before his death. Most of all, I remember his personality. This book quotes the rubric of a ferocious District Commissioner in Omdurman as being 'Severity tempered with justice'. Bill Luce's should have been 'Firmness tempered with sympathy and humour'. I have met Arabs, who never knew him, who regard him as an old-fashioned imperialist. His appearance and background could give this absurdly false impression. He had a remarkable gift of persuading other people to adopt his point of view without their feeling either that they had been coerced or humiliated. This was where the lightheartedness came in. I can recall staff meetings in the Residency in Bahrain punctuated by roars of laughter, but I do not remember feeling that his ultimate decisions were wrong or had been taken without everyone having had a chance to put his or her view. I remember accompanying him to call on Arab dignitaries whom he wished to persuade either to change a course on which they were set or to embark on one which they were reluctant to follow. Again the meetings generally ended with high good humour and agreement with his arguments. This ability – to get his way without giving offence or leaving an aftertaste of resentment – was nowhere more skilfully deployed than in the year of negotiations which ended in December 1971. Luce had to deal with the vain and arrogant Pahlavi government in Iran, with suspicious Saudis and anxious Gulf Rulers, not to mention his political bosses in London, some of whom were far from committed to the decision to terminate the British protective presence in the Gulf. He charmed everybody, he persuaded everybody, he was patient, good humoured (with occasional explosions) and skilful. The overall conjuncture was favourable and Britain's last act closed with less trouble and more residual goowill than was the case with any of the other episodes in the Middle Eastern retreat. Bill Luce must take great credit for this and I regard this book as being in a way a tribute to his memory.

Preface

The approach to transliteration from Arabic used in this book, bearing in mind that a scrupulous uniformity which ignores common or local usages repels the ordinary reader, while the absence of a scholarly system offends the purist, is something of a compromise and will therefore please no-one. As a general rule I have departed from the uniform system nowadays in widespread use only when I saw good reason, for example when maps, the media or local habit have made the 'irregular' spelling of a place name or personal name familiar in the English-speaking world (Khartoum, Nasser, Naguib, etc.). With composite names I have preferred Abdulrahman and Abdulnasser for instance to the more correct ʿAbd ul-Rahman and ʿAbd ul-Nasir, which have a fussy and sometimes unfamiliar look. I have followed the current custom of representing the Arabic 'ayn' by ʿ, but when it figures at the beginning of a proper name I have omitted it altogether; and I have not bothered with the 'hamza' at all. Diacritical marks, which are caviare to the general as well as unappetising in appearance, have not been served up. Apologies are offered to the gourmet.

Compromise has also been sought in footnoting. To avoid overloading, the identification of sources for much historical background and for most statements believed to be non-controversial has been restricted. The source of information communicated personally has only been named with the person's agreement, and in omitting the names of sundry informants I have been influenced by the fact that ex-colleagues of whom they spoke disparagingly are still alive. The writer's own personal experience in two of the three episodes discussed will obviously have influenced, consciously or not, his interpretation of what happened; but objectivity has been the aim, and value judgements as far as possible have been eschewed. Perhaps I should add that the title originally proposed for the book was *A Universal Licence*, since Hartley Coleridge's couplet from which the words were borrowed encapsulates the philosophy of many of those involved in the transmission or surrender of British power. A less ambiguous wording of the title has replaced it. But the couplet remains a valid clue to the acrostics of decolonization.

Those to whom my thanks are due are too many to list. They include in particular Mr Albert Hourani for much initial encouragement and guidance, the Rt Hon. Richard Luce, MP, for making available the personal papers of his father, Lady Luce for her constant interest, Lady Robertson for letting me see her husband's diaries and other papers, Ms Lesley Forbes of Durham University for her help with the Sudan Archive, Sir Anthony Parsons for contributing a Foreword, Mr Paul Auchterlonie for compiling the index, Mr Terry Bacon of Exeter University for his work on the maps, and by no means least Mrs Jennifer Davies for reproducing the whole palimpsest with its end-less emendations on her word processor.

Acknowledgement is gratefully made to the Leverhulme Trust for the award of a Research Grant to enable me to complete the book; to Messrs Faber and Faber for permission to quote Philip Larkin's 'Homage to a Government' from *High Windows*, the lines by W. H. Auden from 'If I could tell you' and 'Moon Landing' in his *Collected Poems* and the lines by T. S. Eliot from 'Little Gidding' in his *Collected Poems* 1909–1962; to the Editor of *The Observer* for permission to reproduce Abu's cartoon, and to those named for permission to reproduce photographs.

Finally, the book would not have been started, let alone finished, without the encouragement of my wife.

Abbreviations

General

CAB   Cabinet papers as assembled in numbered volumes in the Public Record Office in London. Each document bears a Cabinet Office reference, e.g. CN 96(46)3, consisting of a group prefix, the consecutive number in that group, the year in brackets and the number of the relevant Cabinet meeting in that year.

CENTO   Central Treaty Organization was the title adopted in 1959 by the signatories of the 1955 Baghdad Pact; Iraq, Turkey, UK, Iran and Pakistan

Cmd   (e.g. Cmd. 8767 of February 1953) White paper presented to Parliament 'by Command of Her Majesty' and published with consecutive numbers by HMSO. Cmd. was replaced by Cmnd. in a new series beginning in November 1956

CRO   Commonwealth Relations Office

FCO   Foreign and Commonwealth Office, formed by the merger in 1968 of the Foreign Office (FO) and Commonwealth Relations Office (CRO)

FO   Foreign Office

FO 371   Initial reference symbol of FO/FCO General Correspondence (Political) as deposited in the Public Record Office

GOC   General Officer Commanding

HC Deb. House of Commons debate. Citations show the date of debate and the column(s) of the passage concerned in the official record, *Hansard*

HMSO   Her Majesty's Stationery Office

HQ   Headquarters

List of abbreviations

ICS	Indian Civil Service
IOR	India Office Records. Initial prefix of reference numbers of documents in the India Office Library in London
ME	Middle East
MOD	Ministry of Defence, London
NCO	Non-commissioned Officer
PA	Political Agent
PO	Political Officer
PRO	Public Record Office, London
RIIA	Royal Institute of International Affairs, London
Tel.	Telegram
UAE	Union of Arab Emirates

Sudan Episode

NUP	National Unionist Party
PDP	People's Democratic Party
SPS	Sudan Political Service
SRP	Socialist Republican Party

South West Arabian Episode

ATUC	Aden Trades Union Congress
BFAP	British Forces, Arabian Peninsula
CD & W	Colonial Development and Welfare (Act)
EAP	Eastern Aden Protectorate
FLOSY	Front for the Liberation of South Yemen

xxii

NLF	National Liberation Front
OLOS	Organization for the Liberation of the Occupied South
PDRY	People's Democratic Republic of Yemen (title changed from PRSY in 1970)
PORF	Popular Organization of Revolutionary Forces (FLOSY's military wing)
PRSY	People's Republic of South Yemen
PSP	People's Socialist Party
SAL	South Arabian League
UAS	United Arab States (ephemeral union of Egypt, Syria and North Yemen)
UNF	United National Front
WAP	Western Aden Protectorate
YAR	Yemen Arab Republic

Gulf Episode

GCC	Gulf Cooperation Council
PFLO	Popular Front for the Liberation of Oman
PFLOAG	Popular Front for the Liberation of the Arabian Gulf
PR	Political Resident in the Persian Gulf, under whom served PAs and POs
TOL	Trucial Oman Levies (later Trucial Oman Scouts)
UAE	United Arab Emirates

Introduction

Suppose the lions all get up and go
And all the brooks and soldiers run away;
Will Time say nothing but I told you so?
If I could tell you I would let you know.
                    W. H. Auden

The means by which Britain acquired control, at various times and in divers forms, of much of the Arab World lies outside the theme of this essay. Its concern is with the manner in which that control was ended in the last three of the eight Arab countries or communities over which Britain exercised empire during her 'Moment in the Middle East'.[1] Colonialism, though used in common parlance as the name of the game and for that reason employed occasionally here, is barely the right term. Britain's only Arab colony in the strict sense was Aden, and even there the complications of 'white settlement' were absent. Semantic niceties, however, do not affect the main point, that the rights of national sovereignty in all these territories were denied by Britain throughout her exercise of power. Indeed in many of them, even after power had been formally surrendered, limitations of that sovereignty survived. But by the time of our three final instances of Arab 'de-colonization', such residue of Britain's old dominion as lingered on elsewhere in the region displayed a different chemistry from the original formula. Prominence was not the same as dominance.

Be that as it may, formal independence had been secured by Egypt in various stages between the two World Wars; Britain's San Remo Mandate for Iraq had been surrendered in 1932; her domination of Transjordan had formally ended on the Emirate's conversion into the independent Kingdom of Jordan in 1946; her Mandate for Palestine had been shuffled off in 1948; and her responsibilities in Libya, briefly exercised as a spin-off from World War II, were progressively reduced before the creation of the Libyan State in 1951. This left (since we may ignore Oman, which was never directly or constitutionally under British administrative control[2]) only the three territories examined here: the Sudan, South West Arabia and the Shaykhdoms of the 'Persian' Gulf.[3]

In each of these three areas Britain's writ ran under a different rubric. In the Sudan it did so under the guise of an Anglo-Egyptian Condominium. South West Arabia comprised the Crown Colony of Aden and the two Protectorates in its hinterland, the former under close administrative supervision, the two latter barely administered at all. The ten Gulf Shaykhdoms from Kuwait to

Fujairah (treated for convenience here as a single community), though formally responsible for their own internal government, were tied to Britain as protecting power by Exclusive Treaties of nineteenth century origin.

Just as the nature of the responsibilities assumed by Britain differed in each case, so did the value in British eyes of prolonging control and the pressures, internal and external, for its surrender. The present study, while analysing those factors in each of the three cases, will summarize the processes by which power was successively relinquished in them and the attitudes along the way of those exercising responsibility on the spot. The interaction – tension would seldom be too strong a term – between London and its proconsuls in the framing of policy will be a recurrent leitmotiv. The ending of empire should, in the nature of things, be no less humbling for those exercising it than inspiring for those subjected to it. In that respect too the three cases differed, displaying not only bangs and whimpers but a range of more thoughtful and phlegmatic responses.

This is of course just one more exercise in 'Imperialism Revisited', a journey along tracks already pretty well worn. It may, however, offer the traveller occasional new views of the passing landscape. What the book is not is either a defence of the imperial ethos or an attack on it. Certainly it will seek to disinter something of that ethos (as represented in the area), if only because its semantics are by now as indecipherable as cuneiform to today's generation. It contains, however, few conscious value judgements – though the adoption of so self-denying an ordinance will not preclude criticism of policies or postures from which pragmatism or good sense were unquestionably missing. At the risk of appalling *naiveté* the view will be implicit that people in authority, despite obvious exceptions, do things they believe to be right. The fact that the beliefs of one lot often clash with those of another is what makes history interesting – if usually tragic. One is reminded by Auden that

> Our apparatniks will continue making
> The usual squalid mess called history.

But Auden's prognosis is perhaps excessively gloomy. It has in any case long been generally agreed that the making of history would be even messier if entrusted to philosophers.

The promptings of an impersonal *zeitgeist* – in the present context the 'wind of change' was to become the much-bandied equivalent – do also of course have a bearing on the course of events. But the efforts of personal operators to bend the course of events their way or stop it being bent some other way furnish, it is hoped, at least as much interest to the study of the past, particularly so recent a past, as does a more Tolstoyan (or Marxist) approach. It is at any rate in that belief that this essay has been ventured.

The three episodes in de-colonization here scrutinized were each, like every

2

episode in history, *sui generis*. The Anglo-Egyptian Condominium in the Sudan had no precedents. Egypt, moreover, was virtually excluded from any share in the exercise of power, so much so that the arrangement latterly became known to the wags as the 'Condominimum'. Nonetheless the formal answerability of the Governor General to both Co-domini – appointed, as he was, by the Khedive on the recommendation of His Majesty's Government – paradoxically gave him a singular measure of autonomy. A contrary oddity is that following the Anglo-Egyptian Treaty of 1936, when Britain's representative in Cairo became ambassador to a formally independent Egypt but remained for ten years High Commissioner for the Sudan, the Governor General was obliged to channel policy communications with London through the man in Cairo; and since throughout that decade the man was Lampson (later Lord Killearn), the last of the Cromerians, the Governor General's autonomy and his ability to call the tune suffered some dilution – even with a Governor General of Sir Hubert Huddleston's calibre. An entry in Killearn's diary for 11 September 1945, when the revision of the 1936 Treaty was in the offing, provides an engaging illustration. He and Huddleston were together in London and the latter was pleading for a public statement by the new Foreign Secretary of Britain's policy towards the Sudan. 'Huddleston', so Killearn recorded, 'wants a declaration. I put him firmly off it on grounds of higher policy'.[4] Huddleston, incidentally, was not put off.

The Governor General did of course enjoy the services of a sort of personal ambassador in London in the shape of the Sudan Agent, a top member of the Political Service able to lobby the Foreign Office and others under, as it were, Killearn's counter and that of his successors. The tensions generated in the process, as revealed by the Sudan Agent's weekly Top Secret exchange of correspondence with the Civil Secretary in Khartoum, make splendid reading.[5]

There is another unique and more fundamental feature of the Sudan episode. No parallel exists elsewhere for that country's entrapment throughout its approach to statehood in a dispute on an ostensibly quite different issue between two outside parties. There was no good reason in British eyes why Anglo-Egyptian arguments about the nature of Egyptian sovereignty over the Sudan should be tangled up in their debate about the ending of Britain's military occupation of Egyptian territory after World War II. But the Egyptian negotiators in the eight years before the 1952 revolution and the ouster of the monarchy insisted that the two were inseparable and that the resolution of the military issue (which was itself soluble) was dependent on the resolution of the unrelated Sudan sovereignty one (which was not). The frustrations thereby generated were galling enough for Britain's negotiators in London and Cairo; they were even more galling for the Governor General in Khartoum.

3

A third feature of the Sudan which set it apart from South West Arabia and the Gulf was strictly internal, namely the long-standing tug-of-war between the Sudan's two powerful sectarian rivals for supremacy, the Mahdist Ansar of Sayed Abdulrahman al-Mahdi and the anti-Mahdist Khatmiyya of Sayed Ali al-Mirghani. 'They divide and we rule', so Sir James Robertson, the Civil Secretary, wrote in his diary – though by the time he did so (December 1951) he must have been wryly conscious of gilding a fading imperial lily. With the Khatmiyya looking to Egypt for protection from the Mahdists and the Mahdists, by an irony of history, looking to Britain for protection from the Egyptians, the old sectarian division was translated into a different dimension – one from which Robertson and the Political Service could not in good conscience hope to benefit.

In South West Arabia and the Gulf there was no parallel for any of these Sudan peculiarities. South West Arabia presents in retrospect an imperial design tailor-made for disaster. It now looks obvious that the pressure-cooked Crown Colony of Aden and the raw joints of hinterland long left carelessly on a low back-burner could never serve up a savoury composite dish for the imperial gourmets or gourmands. Some resemblance between the circumstances here and those in the Sudan might parenthetically be detected by comparing the South West Arabian dichotomy (prosperous Aden and chaotic hinterland) with the Sudan dichotomy (aspiring Muslim North and primaeval non-Muslim South): but the resemblance cannot safely be carried far.

It was not only by her totally different treatment throughout history of Aden and of the interior that Britain created for herself an insoluble imperial problem. For even in the interior, treated as a composite organism in itself, the peculiar nature of the Protective – and later the Advisory – treaties signed over the years with the self-absorbed and jealous shaykhs and sultans afforded, or presents in retrospect, a wholly inadequate formula for constitutional progress towards any cohesive structure within the Protectorates (as the two groups of shaykhdoms were latterly styled), let alone for a happy partnership between them and the equally self-absorbed Crown Colony. On this reading, in short, if the British in the Sudan always took too much responsibility for good administration, the British in the Aden Protectorates never took enough. But if this is obvious to hindsight, it was scarcely recognized by Britain's earlier representatives on the spot, much less by governments in London – not, at least, until the faint chance of squaring the circle had slipped irretrievably by. Sir Charles Johnston, writing as late as 1964 following his three years as Governor of Aden, was still able to hope that his book on the subject would 'give the reader a glimpse of a colonial power withdrawing in good order'.[6] One has of course to appreciate that the pace of Britain's relinquishment of empire was nowhere foreseen. At the time of the Sidki-Bevin discussions on the future of the Sudan in autumn 1946 (see chapter 2), the Egyptians them-

4

selves expressed the view that the Sudan would not be ready for self-government for twenty years (and would not want it even then). A similar sort of time-scale (but not the parenthesis) was envisaged by the British. Nor did they later foresee the pace of history in South West Arabia or in the Gulf – the speed at which Britain's moment in the Middle East would come to an end.

Three other complications of an external kind obstructed a satisfactory solution to the British problem in South West Arabia. Firstly, the unabated claims of the Imams of North Yemen to sovereignty over the South and the steps they took to advertise and advance these claims made difficult the maintenance of the *Pax Britannica* in the South – let alone the merger of its centrifugal shaykhdoms into a cohesive unit, whether as a counter to the ideas of an all-Yemen union or as a prelude to independence. Secondly, Gemal Abdulnasser's inspirational malevolence and his use of Cairo radio during the critical decade were a plague to the British, for which Britain could find no remedy. Their impact on the educated young in Aden and their part in the politicization of the trade unions there (of whose establishment the British were initially rather proud) were irresistible. Thirdly, the task of the Governor in Aden was complicated by the obsession in Westminster, at least as long as Attlee's immediately post-war Government and its Conservative successors were in power, with the paramount strategic necessity of retaining control of Aden Colony indefinitely. Ironically, it was the next and differently motivated Labour Government that sacked in 1965 the one Governor, Trevaskis, who sought to switch the focus of attention to the hinterland. For all these reasons a happy issue out of Britain's mounting afflictions in South West Arabia was surely never on the cards.

In the Gulf, the problem was unique in a different way. In a sense the political fragmentation of this area – the outcome of Britain's nineteenth century treaties with whatever shaykhs they found locally in charge at the time, whereby their separate authority was legitimized and perpetuated – might have seemed superficially to resemble the fragmentation of South West Arabia. Indeed Britain's dispiriting experience of promoting (too late and too hesitantly) the federating of the latter was sometimes perceived as ruling out any prospect of a successful drive to federate the Gulf States. But to the extent that endeavours to that latter end were unsuccessful, this was not due – as chapter 4 will argue – to any genuine parallel between conditions there and conditions in South West Arabia.

Even more conspicuously than was the case with her South West Arabian treaties, what Britain's treaties in the Gulf did not do was to confer on Britain any rights of intervention in the internal affairs of the shaykhdoms. This deliberate avoidance of internal responsibility was convenient enough when the only relevance of the shaykdoms to British interests lay in the geography of imperial communications with India and the Far East; but it became a serious handicap once the area's oil potential became apparent and backwater isolation began to give place to international limelight.

Britain, in fact, found herself harnessed in the Gulf to a political equipage which outsiders at least regarded as an anachronism and debarred from pulling it in new directions by the flimsy nature of the harness she had herself designed. There were to be sure some observers in London, Foreign Secretary Eden amongst them, who thought that Britain's representatives simply needed to pull harder. The outside world may have assumed that Britain, for all her disavowals, covertly exercised internal power in much the same way as she overtly did in other bits of her shrinking empire proper. But this was to misunderstand the peculiar facts. For in practice, while Britain could release the Gulf States (as she first did with Kuwait in 1961) from the isolation which she had imposed on them through the treaties, she could not enforce changes in the internal political system which the same treaties had legitimized.

Pressures for change, from outside more than from within, certainly existed: ideological from Iraq, expansionist from Saudi Arabia, domineering from Iran and, more important, Arab nationalist in the Nasserist sense from Egypt. None of these pressures was regarded by the British as irresistible. They themselves, both at home and in the field, would have welcomed change of a gradual kind, a loosening of traditional autocracy and a more formal measure of democratic participation. But their hands were tied, whatever the world assumed, by a fairly strict observance of the treaties; and their search for other modes of ensuring the future stability of the area – before and even after the Labour Government, as part of a wider policy of retrenchment, opted in 1968 for withdrawal – found little to grasp hold of in the shifting sand. For all that, and despite the evidence that the winds of change were by this time blowing at gale force, the sense of imperial purpose amongst those in the field died curiously hard.

Our three dramas of the relinquishment of empire took place, therefore, against totally different constitutional backdrops and under noticeably different compulsions. Withdrawal from the Sudan was dictated initially by the private requirements of Britain's policy towards Egypt. Withdrawal from South West Arabia was forced upon Britain by a crescendo of much more public pressures. Withdrawal from the Gulf was determined less by political hustling (whether external or internal) than by Treasury calculations and a fading of the imperial will in Westminster.

Since the three cases were so different, it may seem illogical to examine them together. There are, however, linkages. Collectively they represent the final chapter in Britain's relinquishment of constitutional status in the Arab World; and though the period covered by the three separate episodes extended over more than two decades, this has the advantage of enabling us to follow the progressive change in attitudes to empire which the episodes reveal. An additional linkage is that one prominent actor, Sir William Luce, played a central role in all three episodes; and so far as the proconsular end of the business is concerned, the evolution visible in his personal approach to the ending of empire provides a valuable touchstone throughout.

1 The Regional Consequences of World War II

I did not even know that the British Empire is dying, still less did I know that it is a great deal better than the younger empires that are going to supplant it.

George Orwell (1936)

As World War II ended, the enormity of its economic consequences for Britain were neither instantly nor widely recognized, there or elsewhere, though recognition of her exhaustion in the economic field did in the nature of things come much quicker than recognition of the war's political consequences. The two of course were closely related. Political power can only be exercised on the world stage from a powerful economic base; and this, in the aftermath of war, Britain no longer enjoyed. Her treasury was empty. The saving grace of Lend Lease had stopped when the war with Japan ended; and the still greater benison of the Marshall Plan was not to descend for another three years. Britain's overseas debts incurred in the war, not least to certain Middle Eastern governments, were formidable and were soon to be increased when negotiation of a tough US loan was found inexorable. Britain's industries, after six years' concentration on the toys of war, could not without costly restructuring be geared back to the toys of peace; and in any case the need, both at home and abroad, for new arms production had by no means ended. The reintegration of her demobilized manpower into civilian employment was a giant task. The understandable demands from subject peoples who had stood by her for help with the refurbishing of their own economies could not honourably be ignored. The revitalization of the economic mess in Europe, a priority regarded as distinctly higher, imposed further obligations. In later retrospect Britain's newly elected Labour Government was to give a sympathetic American observer 'the sense of men struggling against overwhelming odds with an acute awareness of moral purpose'.[1]

Neither the odds nor the moral purpose were much apparent at the time to Middle Easterners. Nor as yet was the extent to which Britain's dominance of the region had been dented by other and largely local developments. These will be described later. The preliminary point to be established is more general and flows from Britain's own inability or disinclination to recognize quickly the extent to which the world and her own commanding role in it were irreparably changed. Even those at the top who were conscious of Britain's enfeeblement saw it in the immediate aftermath of the War as temporary. The Middle East still took its cue from Britain; and if the war's effect on Britain's ability to continue the exercise of empire there was not easily digested in Britain herself, nor was it in the metabolisms of the Middle East. Habits of mind die hard, habits of practice even harder. It would have been unnatural for the British Government to have publicly advertised their doubts, if they already had any, of their ability to maintain a pre-eminent role in the Middle East. If governments in that region continued to hold Britain responsible for most things that happened there, this was for a time a myth to which Britain's own reluctance to swallow her loss of power gave obvious encouragement.[2] Indeed, the Middle Eastern belief in Britain's habits of manipulation long survived even the humiliation of Suez and the final replacement of Britain's influence by that of America.[3] But this is to jump ahead: its relevance here is simply to illustrate how hard habits die.

Be that as it may be or was going to be, in 1946 Britain still bestrode the Arab World. This Colossus posture may have been deceptive and increasingly resented but it was nowhere denied. And whatever the writings on the wall, the Middle East retained in British perceptions a key importance. Indeed its importance was now magnified by the conviction in Britain that her wartime ally, the Soviet Union, was malevolently bent on expansion southwards into British preserves. This conviction was not of course universal and was not shared by Britain's Prime Minister, but Attlee's resistance was finally over-borne by such heavyweight pressures as those of Foreign Secretary Bevin and the Service chiefs.[4] Egypt, or more specifically the Suez Canal, was still seen as the empire's jugular vein, despite the imminence of Indian independence; and Egypt was not only the British corridor to India, it was also the Soviet corridor to Africa. The security of the Middle East as a whole was seen in London as a vital British interest – indeed a vital Western interest – in other contexts too, notably as the main source of oil, a commodity which the reconstruction of Europe's industrial base would clearly need on a larger scale. The idea of abandoning her role as the political and military protector of the region as a whole was not, in the Britain of 1946, remotely entertained.

It would of course be absurd to ignore the potent strain of anti-imperialism which had been at work in Britain, on the political left and amongst prominent intellectuals,[5] since at least as far back as the Boer War. But though this strain would soon manifest itself afresh, it had been much weakened in the late thirties by the Western world's confrontation with the menace of Hitler and Mussolini and had accepted the necessity of silence during World War II. When the war ended, what disturbed the British establishment more than any immediate recrudescence of such anti-imperialism was the admiration at large in the same (and wider) sections of the British populace for the Soviet Union, both for its signal contribution to victory over the Germans and on philosophic grounds.

Such considerations barely affected as yet Britain's position in the Middle

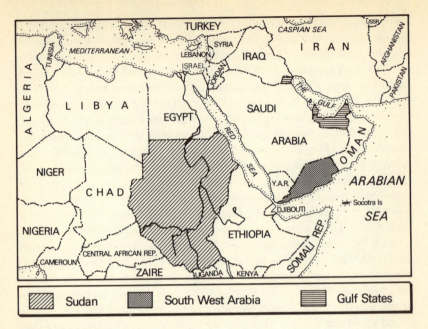

The Middle East: the regional context.

East, though communism itself had already attracted adherents there, the supposed barrier of Islam notwithstanding. Other developments, of a regional nature, were of more immediate relevance. Of these, the most damaging to Britain's reputation, both before and during the war, had been her policies in Palestine, seen throughout the area as a deliberate affront to all Arabs. When resentment at this affront was coupled with the probability in the early years of the War that the victor in it would be Germany and not Britain, it is remarkable how few Middle Eastern governments or organized groups sought at the time to climb on the German bandwagon or even covertly to reinsure in that direction. Certainly the Mufti of Jerusalem, Haj Amin al-Husayni, went the whole hog and 'defected'; certainly Rashid Ali in his briefly successful revolutionary take-over in Iraq in 1941 looked openly for German backing (though curiously little was forthcoming); certainly King Farouk and one or two other top Egyptians entered into correspondence, more or less privily, with the Axis when its military successes were echoing round the world; and there were Syrians too who, for rather different reasons, played along with the Germans. Though the mood changed after Alamein, such inclinations before that turning-point were perhaps understandable. What does need explanation is why Britain was able to keep the Arabs by and large on her side, particularly since the British were using their territory without scruple to fight a European war on, were restricting (as it must have seemed) their food supplies, were censoring their mail and publications and were generally causing inconvenience.

The most obvious, but insufficient, explanation of Arab loyalty was doubtless that the British were there, militarily and politically, and disaffection was risky. The French were at the time neither in a position nor in a mood to provide any counter-attraction. A second clue may lie in the nature of the Arab governments then in power, composed as they were of old-guard oligarchs whose own tenure depended at least in part on British favour. For the British the point was not so much that such regimes were (if only for that last reason) traditionally biddable as that they were traditionally able to exercise local control better than any visible alternatives; and by that token their undemocratic complexions had to be overlooked. Thirdly, the British were well aware, in view of the widespread Arab resentment over what was happening in Palestine, of the need to demonstrate their sympathy with less awkward Arab aspirations. In 1940–1941 these included, at least in the Fertile Crescent where it was by no means new, the movement in favour of unification of some kind.[6] Britain's response (adopted with difficulty in the light of known French objections) was Eden's Mansion House Speech of 30 May 1941, in which he declared Britain's 'full support for any scheme of [Arab] unity which commands general approval'. The fact that general approval for any specific scheme was improbable made the declaration easier. But the verbal purpose was served, and Eden repeated the text more effectively two years later. It is of interest that the prevailing view of top diplomats in the area, when consulted by Eden about the value of backing the idea of unification or federation as a counter to Axis propaganda, was that the implementation of the abortive 1939 White Paper on Palestine 'would do Britain far more good with the Arabs than any other initiative'.[7] That, however, was not to be: Churchill refused to yield to Foreign Office pressure. Whatever the explanation, the British war effort in the Middle East, before as well as after Alamein, met not only with singular tolerance from the Arabs as a whole but with much positive co-operation.

Three years after the Mansion House speech the formation of the League of Arab States was ostensibly to carry the movement towards Arab unity a major step forward. This too was not expressly ill-regarded in London at the time. But it significantly involved the transfer of the focus of Arab nationalism from Baghdad, where it had seemed to Britain manageable, to Cairo, where it was soon to prove a much more formidable challenge to British domination of the region. The Arab League itself may have progressively fallen into 'a chatter of shifting and quarrelsome cliques',[8] and an element of myth-making may always have underlain the gospel of Arab unity – a phenomenon 'as real to the Arabs (in Miles Copeland's happy phrase) as Santa Claus is to Marks and Spencers'; but the League's establishment under Egypt's auspices marked a dramatic watershed in that country's role in the Middle East. Before World

War II Egypt had regarded herself either as a Mediterranean country, an appendage in a sense of European civilization or, more widely and more self-consciously, as a purely 'Egyptian' entity. There had long been Egyptian thinkers who rejected both these conceptions of their country's status; but the official discovery (if discovery is not too strong a word) that Egypt was Arab and that her destiny lay not only *with* the Arab World but as its leader, was a phenomenon of the early forties. Whether her wartime experiences and her sympathy for the Palestinians prompted this revolution in her self-image, or whether they simply provided a convenient purchase in her climb towards Arab hegemony is barely relevant here. What is important is that from the mid-forties onward, Egypt was to establish herself as the focus of growing Arab opposition to Britain's regional supremacy. The possibility of liberation from British control received a modest boost from the withdrawal of British and French troops from Syria in 1946 and a more potent one from the resonant ending of the Raj in India the following year.

None of these developments, however, were seen by Britain in the early aftermath of the war as portending any basic change in her Middle Eastern responsibilities, her rightful role as the protecting supervisor of the whole region. Formally dependent territories – the Sudan, South West Arabia and the Gulf shaykhdoms – were by definition under British control; Palestine itself was still, however awkwardly, a British preserve; and as for formally independent territories, whatever the restiveness of Egypt, the regimes in Iraq, in Saudi Arabia, in Jordan and even in Syria (for which the enemy was France) were seen as reasonably well-disposed. Where treaties securing British military and political privileges were recognized as obsolescent or unequal, their simple revision was, in Britain's eyes, the most that would be needed to preserve the fundamentals of a *status quo*. The fate that would instantly over-take the 1948 Portsmouth Treaty with Iraq – the prime illustration of Britain's belief in the sufficiency of revision, Egypt being a case apart – lay two years in the future.[9]

Nor was Britain conscious of any growing disaffection amongst the Arab masses – those in Egypt perhaps excepted, though even there the hostility of the common people was largely regarded as a contrivance of power-seeking politicians. But in this general field too British confidence was already at fault. In the past, educational progress in all these countries had produced something of a divergence between the perceptions of the élite and of the masses. This had earlier been the case under the Ottoman Empire, amongst whose educated Arab subjects the syndrome of the sorcerer's apprentice had made itself felt. Under the successor empires of Britain and France the number of such apprentices in the more advanced Arab territories had greatly multiplied and their aspirations had conspicuously sharpened. But it was only after World War II, and partly as a consequence of it, that the gap between the perceptions of the few and of the many began to narrow visibly. The ordinary tribesmen, particularly in less developed areas where the British writ ran more emphatically, had previously shown little interest in nationalist politics and little resentment at foreign paternalist domination. Indeed there were many who welcomed protection from indigenous misgovernment. But now, thanks to the spread of basic education, to the development of mass media and in part to direct wartime experience of Britain's military pregnability, things were changing. A wider cross-section of society even in less developed countries began to share in the questioning, long current amongst the élite, of Britain's right to dominate their horizons.

The growing desire to be released from foreign control, and more specifically from foreign military occupation, obviously varied from country to country, the circumstances in each being different. But the diffusion of anti-British resentment from countries where it was strongest to those where it had not yet bitten deep was helped by new means of inter-communication. Some of these, notably the expansion of radio transmissions and the proliferation of receivers, had indeed been fostered by Europe's wartime propaganda techniques. Increased facilities for the production and distribution of newsprint also simplified the dissemination of ideas, and frontiers were barely an obstacle. Indeed, the movement of men as well as of ideas from country to country had grown easier. During the war itself the citizens of more backward Arab territories had, as enlisted volunteers, found themselves serving in homelands more advanced than their own and had learnt lessons in the process. The converse was also true: the backwardness of remoter areas was revealed to servicemen from the major Arab countries, fuelling criticism there of Britain's colonial policies.

For all these reasons increasing numbers of ordinary Arabs were growing politically aware and receptive to the trends of thinking amongst the more sophisticated minority. British reactions to this phenomenon, as and when the facts in different territories were recognized, were by no means uniform. As a general rule Britain's attitude to signs of incipient disaffection varied from country to country depending on the strategic or other importance of each in the British scheme of things and of course on the extent of the disaffection perceived.

Three other considerations of a non-Arab nature affected the tactics adopted by Britain for the maintenance of her regional hegemony. The most overriding of these was the fear, already mentioned, of Soviet aspirations in the area. Of the other two, the less important but in a small way equally compelling was the renewed need to foster an understanding with France which still regarded Syria and the Lebanon as her preserve. The ouster of Vichy France from her foothold there during the war barely alleviated this age-old problem, for Free French sensitivities on the subject of French rights in the Levant were equally acute. All Frenchmen suspected the British, as they had between the Wars, of seeking to undermine in their own interest France's standing in that area of the Middle East. British protestations to the contrary were never accepted as genuine. Yet Britain's official archives indicate that, whatever criticisms were voiced of French – including Free French – behaviour in the Levant, the importance of an *entente* with France often outranked in British valuations even the importance of an understanding with the Arabs. There were of course influential Englishmen, now as in the aftermath of World War I, who took a contrary view: General Sir Edward Spears (British Minister in Damascus from 1942 to 1944, whose criticisms of French activities in the Levant did not stop on his retirement in 1944) figures prominently in the gallery of French *bêtes noires*,[10] as T. E. Lawrence had done at the end of the previous one. But such personal opposition to French aspirations in the Levant, whatever substance it gave to France's belief in British duplicity, did not affect the main drift of British policy.

The third and more potent external restraint on Britain's freedom of manoeuvre was of American origins. In terms of global policy when the War ended – not least in their shared fears of Soviet expansionism and in their shared concern for the reconstruction of Europe – there was no conflict of purpose. But in the Middle East British and American policies were less harmonious. Friction arose from two main sources: America's continuing anti-colonial sentiment and Washington's support, despite misgivings in the State Department, for Jewish aspirations in Palestine. It is true that the US had as yet no desire to undertake military or other direct responsibilities themselves in the area – and Britain would have actively opposed their doing so.[11] But American misgivings about Britain's imperial practices and America's attitude to the Palestine *imbroglio* (more especially President Truman's undeniable duplicity in the handling of it) made for an uneasy partnership between the two Governments where the Middle East was concerned. It was not until the birth of NATO in 1949 that the US began to see virtue in the maintenance by Britain of what was left of her Middle Eastern hegemony; and even then their perspectives did not wholly converge.[12] While it suited Washington that British influence should exert itself to shore up Arab resistance to the perceived Soviet threat, the Americans, who had in those days little experience of the complexities of the Arab World, expected this to be done without old-fashioned coercion.

In sum, the problems of peace were as challenging in their own way as the problems of war. Britain herself remained convinced that the maintenance of controlling influence in the Middle East was essential to the imperial mission in which she still took pride and was as much in the interests of the Arabs themselves as it was in those of herself and her allies. Arab governments might have been willing to make or renew strategic concessions and provide political privileges in exchange for financial and material compensation; but this was something Britain, economically crippled as she was, no longer had in her gift. Her difficulties were compounded not only by the ripening of Arab resentments at foreign domination but also by the need to conciliate French sensitivities and by disharmony over regional tactics with her powerful transatlantic ally, on whose economic and therefore political support she was now dependent.

The rest of this book will only be concerned with the region as a whole to the extent that the Sudan, South West Arabia and the Gulf Emirates were part and parcel of it. These three territories were still directly under British tutelage in a way that set them apart, but only partially apart, from the rest of the Arab East. In much of the latter Britain still exercised authority of an informal kind; but this was increasingly under strain and would finally wither away by processes less visible and less traumatic – the Suez blunder and the 1958 Iraqi revolution apart – than was to be the case with the relinquishment of power in her three remaining formal dependencies. Nonetheless, the episodes now to be examined are all parts of a single inter-connected Anglo-Arab story. In hindsight their unfolding may seem inexorable; it did not seem so at the time.

The stages, often painful, by which Britain's residual dominance of the Middle East was finally extinguished are better remembered in the countries concerned, where they are matters of pride, than in Britain herself. The chapters which follow are a modest attempt to set down afresh three fragments of British history and to survey the attitudes, now almost forgotten, of those involved in them.

2 The Sudan episode

By slow prudence to make mild
A rugged people and through soft degrees
Subdue them to the useful and the good.
                    Tennyson, *Ulysses*

The drama which led to the setting up in 1899 of an Anglo-Egyptian Con-dominium in the Sudan, a device without historical precedent, engaged public interest in Britain more forcibly perhaps than the drama which led to its abrogation half a century later. As an episode of history, however, it occurred when the propriety of Britain's imperial mission was still, in Britain at least, unquestioned. Its ending, on the other hand, took place when Britain's right to dominate much of the Arab world was increasingly under question, though less in Britain than elsewhere. Even in Britain the Olympian certainties which had guided Cromer and his generation were already, by the end of World War II, nibbled by introspection.

Nonetheless, the Empire's rapid dismemberment was still, even after India secured its independence in 1947, regarded by most Englishmen as unthink-able; but the realization that the practice of empire needed justification had dawned even amongst its devoted practitioners. And what makes the Sudan episode fascinating in retrospect is that in the minds of those involved a passionate belief in the rightness of Britain's evolving imperial philosophy was combined with a degree of ironic self-observation of a kind which never troubled Cromer or Curzon, barely even Killearn (the last of that species). This gives the behaviour of the performers in the drama an engaging quality not present in their predecessors. Of these performers, so far as they were British, there were three main groups: those responsible for overall policy in London, those executing but seeking to influence it in one direction in Cairo, and those executing but seeking to influence it in a different direction in Khartoum. The pressures under which these three groups operated and the tensions generated between them will be given rather greater attention in this study than the formal expressions of an 'agreed' policy along the way, these last being fully documented elsewhere.

But the British formed only one side of the triangular story. The Egyptian actors and the Sudanese actors, both of whom were increasingly able to outmanoeuvre the British as the climax approached, were themselves divided. The compulsions internally dividing them and mutually separating them will equally be examined.

The nature of the Condominium, the setting within which the players moved, needs here only a summary description. For most of the nineteenth century the Sudan, in shape larger and more unnatural even than now, was formally part of the Ottoman Empire, brought within it by the ambitious and largely autonomous Khedives of Egypt and administered by them on the Sultan's behalf. The Mahdist revolt of 1881 was provoked primarily by the oppressions and inadequacies of this Khedivial administration but can now be seen – indeed it quickly took that form, consciously or unconsciously – as an early 'independence movement'. Meanwhile Egypt, already regarded in Europe as a key target in the sights of nineteenth century imperialism, had been falling increasingly into Britain's prospective sphere of influence and, following Urabi's revolt against the Khedive Ismail, was subjected in 1882 – not without Gladstonian misgivings – to British military occupation and administrative control.

Britain, however, refused to intervene on the Khedive's behalf in his initial eagerness to suppress the Mahdist uprising in the Sudan, beyond sanctioning the return there of the experienced Charles Gordon to 'report on the military situation' with a view to evacuating the remaining garrisons. The despatch of Wolseley's unsuccessful expedition at the end of 1884 to rescue the beleaguered Gordon from Khartoum did not imply any change in the policy of Gladstone's government to abandon the Sudan to the Mahdists. Nor did the widespread outcry over the 'betrayal' and death of Gordon, a popular hero but himself a pronounced critic of imperialism, impair Gladstone's opposition to any territorial expansion of empire. It needed the change in June 1885 to a Tory government, enflamed by a new jingoist mood, to set about re-shaping Britain's imperial control of Egyptian affairs and finally to determine upon the Sudan's reconquest – in the name of a now reluctant Egypt, partly with Egyptian troops and largely with Egyptian money.

Reconquest achieved, the novel status of a condominium under two flags was imposed on the Sudan by the Anglo-Egyptian Agreement of 1899. Though the exhausted Sudanese resigned themselves to it with varying degrees of approval, the main immediate beneficiary was Britain, Egypt playing as subordinate a role in its drafting as she was to do in the resulting administration of the Sudan. But the Egyptian Foreign Minister signed it: the protests of the nominal landlord in Istanbul were half-hearted: outside powers, though uneasily aware of its relevance both to the Eastern Question and to the continuing scramble for Africa, gave it *de facto* recognition, and its validity by the criteria of the time is not easily questioned. In the overt sense, it was much less over the virtual British monopoly of power in the Condominium (which the Agreement sanctioned) than over the question of where sovereignty lay (on which the Agreement was equivocal) that Egypt and Britain were to become over the next fifty years increasingly at odds.

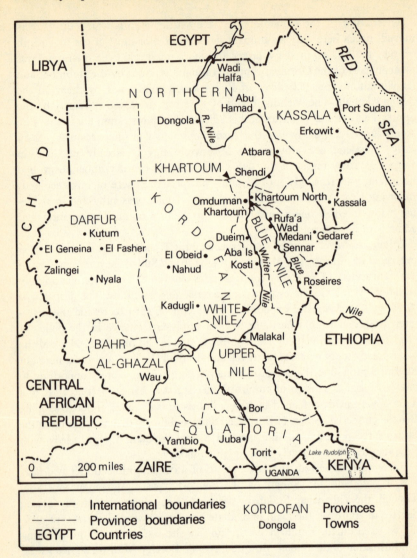

The Sudan

The Turkish decision to side with Germany on the outbreak of World War I and Britain's consequent decision to reinforce her position in Egypt by declaring it a Protectorate, may have held few practical implications for the Sudanese. But it served to reinforce the growing Egyptian clamour for independence – as did the formal dismemberment of the Ottoman Empire when the war ended and such concomitants as the Anglo-French Declaration of November 1918 promising emancipation to its former subject peoples. Outbreaks of violence illustrated Egyptian impatience. Negotiations for a new Anglo-Egyptian understanding followed, the main stumbling-block, for reasons that will shortly be discussed, proving to be the Sudan. Even when 'independence' was conferred on Egypt in February 1922, the Sudan was one of the subjects explicitly reserved to Britain.

Further Egyptian attempts to secure recognition of her formal sovereignty over the Sudan – as for instance in the draft Egyptian constitution of 1922 – were repressed. Britain, proud of the progress achieved in the Sudan with the minimum deference to Egyptian partnership, was convinced of her moral responsibility for ensuring its progressive development. A public tendency had furthermore manifested itself, even under the premiership of the previously anti-imperialist Ramsay Macdonald, of regarding the Sudan as effectively part of the British Empire. This tendency was strengthened not only by the Sudan's strategic relevance to the security of the vital Suez Canal but also by the value to British industry of its growing cotton production. The Egyptians saw things in an understandably different light.

The stage for part two of the drama of Anglo-Egyptian conflict over the Sudan was indeed already set. Its presentation simply awaited the formulation of a precise text. The probable direction of events was soon luridly illustrated. In November 1924 Sir Lee Stack, the Governor General of the Sudan (who was also Commander-in-Chief of the Egyptian army), was assassinated in Cairo by impatient Egyptian nationalists. Vindictive retribution was instantly imposed on Egypt by Lord Allenby, the High Commissioner, in the name of His Majesty's Government.[1] Egyptian resentments were reinforced: the Egyptian Prime Minister, Zaghlul, resigned. The irreconcilable nature of Britain's and Egypt's interests in the Sudan, already heavily pencilled, was inked in. It was basically over the Sudan that a series of negotiations over the next decade to resolve Anglo-Egyptian differences effectively foundered. In the third, Ramsay Macdonald, now in his last term of office, was as little disposed to compromise with Egyptian demands for control over the destinies of the Sudan, advanced on this occasion by his old friend Zaghlul,[2] as the next Labour leadership was to prove.

By 1936 a new stimulus to agreement, generated most directly by Fascist Italy's occupation of Abyssinia, had emerged. Coupled with his alignment with Hitler's Germany, Mussolini's action was seen in Britain as threatening her whole Middle Eastern position. Coupled with Italy's colonial presence on Egypt's Libyan borders, it was recognized in Cairo as a potential threat which Egypt, unassisted, would be too weak to repulse. The arguments for a military and therefore political understanding were compelling to both London and Cairo. In December 1936 a new twenty-year agreement was successfully negotiated by High Commissioner Lampson, the later Lord Killearn, and significantly, the Wafdist premier Nahas. But this was only achieved, despite minor concessions to Egypt's heightened sensitivities over the Sudan since the Allenby *diktat* of 1924, by again leaving the basic Sudan issue unresolved. Since the Treaty at least recognized Egypt as a sovereign state and imposed certain limits on Britain's military occupation, it was a cause of celebration there. But so far as the Sudan was concerned, the beneficiary was Britain.

World War II, while confirming more strongly than ever the strategic value to Britain of the Sudan and even more, of course, that of Suez, raised to an intense pitch Egyptian expectations of a reward for her wartime collaboration with Britain. This collaboration had only been secured during the dark days of February 1942, when Axis armies were at Egypt's gates, by Lampson descending on the Palace with an escort of tanks and demanding from Farouk, whose loyalty was at best dubious, the instant appointment of the 'reliable' Nahas as Prime Minister – roughshod treatment which, however defensible in the circumstances, had certainly sharpened Egypt's resentment at the adulterated nature of her sovereignty. But this was beside the point. Egypt's services to the allied cause during the war were undeniable; and Britain's public recognition of them when it ended was seen there as encouraging. The election of a Labour government strengthened Egyptian hopes of a new deal. Egypt's formal request in December 1945 for revision of the 1936 Treaty, though this still had ten years to run, was therefore predictable. The concluding words of the Egyptian Note – 'It goes without saying that the negotiations will include the question of the Sudan' – were by no means as throwaway as the inexperienced British reader might have assumed.

At this point we may pause to summarize just what the 'Question of the Sudan' then meant in Cairo and in London. Egypt's ambitions, imperialist or not, were to establish her historic rights of sovereignty over the Sudan, through which the Nile conveyed her life-blood, in which her surplus population might be resettled, and with half of whose people she could claim plausible bonds of affinity. Of this sovereignty Farouk's entitlement to be recognized as King of the Sudan as well as of Egypt – explicitly voiced in Cairo since 1922 at least – was a convenient symbol. For, despite an emerging distaste amongst many Egyptians for the monarchy itself, British disregard for Egypt's historic rights in the Sudan was widely resented. For Britain, however, the sense of paternalist responsibility for the evolution and welfare of the Sudan was a potent moral factor, while in terms of *real politik* the Sudan's strategic importance had been increased rather than diminished by the outcome of the war. The latter had brought with it both fear of Soviet expansionist aspirations in the Arab world and Africa and related uncertainties about the security of Britain's military domination of the Near East. It must also be remembered that in the immediate aftermath of the war there was simply no other 'free world' power qualified to protect the vital Near East region. This, and the need for its protection, were not disputed in anti-colonialist Washington.

But what meanwhile had been happening in the Sudan itself? The first significant sign of political disaffection amongst the products of the Government's measured educational initiatives had been the foundation of the White Flag League in the early twenties, which proclaimed the Unity of the Nile Valley. The League's activities and the associated mutiny of certain Sudanese troops, both of them decipherable as Egyptian-inspired, were firmly dealt with. The next decade – perhaps because the main feature of Allenby's 1924 *diktat* had been to curtail Egyptian presence in the Sudan – was quiet. While Britain's adoption in the late twenties of the then fashionable technique of 'Indirect Rule', in which politically unassertive tribal leaders were used as her main collaborative instrument,[3] was partly inspired by disenchantment with educated townsmen, a sense of national identity was gestating amongst the latter. Their adoption of the slogan 'The Sudan for the Sudanese' in the thirties was not initially discouraged by the British, since it had apparently the merit of being anti-Egyptian. One or two political newspapers were licensed; the expression of political opinion became less cautious; there was criticism of both co-domini for drawing up their 1936 Treaty without consulting Sudanese opinion. But the next formal move by the educated was the establishment in 1938 – with the Sudan Government blessing and consequently Egyptian misgivings – of the Graduates' Congress. Ostensibly a forum amongst schoolleavers for non-political and non-sectarian activities, its rapid transformation into a political (and ultimately sectarian) urban pressure group was doubtless inevitable. The resulting challenge to the authorities was soon presented. In a Memorandum of April 1942, explicitly in the name of 'public opinion in the country', Congress called amongst other things for Sudanese self-determination after the war. Even so liberal a Civil Secretary as Sir Douglas Newbold felt obliged to reject the Memorandum outright, though he sought in vain to reach an understanding privately with the leaders of Congress.[4] Amongst these a certain Ismail al-Azhari, soon to achieve prominence, figures as the most outspokenly critical.

More damaging than the Graduates' Congress to the stable evolution of the country – so most of its British administrators had been trained to believe – was the long-established rivalry between its two main Muslim sects, the followers of the Mahdi's posthumous son Sayed Abdulrahman, and the anti-Mahdist Khatmiyya led by Sayed Ali al-Mirghani. The threat to stability from the isolated negroid and non-Muslim south was barely yet discernible on the horizon. In the early years of the Condominium, neo-Mahdism had understandably been repressed and support given to the principal anti-Mahdist *tariqa*.[5] Sayed Abdulrahman's rehabilitation – a policy adopted by the British on the outbreak of war in 1914 as a potential counter to the Ottoman call for *jihad* – and his own astute self-advancement progressively brought the two sectarian leaders and their followers into conflict. Suspicions – not entirely unjustified, indeed they were shared by the Sudan Government – that Sayed Abdulrahman harboured ambitions of kingship were a perpetual nightmare to his opponents and the prime reason for Sayed Ali al-Mirghani's gradual if uneasy alignment with the pro-Egyptian activists. Sayed Ali al-Mirghani had previously shown little enthusiasm for Egypt. Indeed in 1929 he had been quoted as shrewdly hoping that 'an Anglo-Egyptian treaty would be concluded, as the demands of the Egyptians seemed to increase every time the Sudan question came up for settlement'.[6] The growing influence of Sayed Abdulrahman alarmed the Sudan Government too, but plans to check it had to be scrapped when the outbreak of World War II obliged the Palace to recognize (just as had been the case on the outbreak of World War I) that his collaboration could not be dispensed with. From 1943, when Sayed Abdulrahman broke with the Graduates' Congress, the main pro-Egyptian group, the Ashiqqa, was able to count on the support of the Khatmiyya in their joint hostility to neo-Mahdist pretensions – a situation of which the government's increasing cultivation of Sayed Abdulrahman was both cause and effect. Congress, with Egyptian encouragement and Azhari at the controls, turned into an anti-Mahdist as well as an anti-British instrument, opposed to collaboration with the Palace and all its works. For their part, the Mahdist Ansar (as the followers of Sayed Abdulrahman called themselves) set up the Umma Party as their political arm, standing for independence.

The fact that the Sudan as a whole was unquestionably well-administered and content was to prove irrelevant. The ultimate ability of the vocal minority of political activists at the centre not only to outmanoeuvre its internal opponents but to upstage first one co-dominus and finally both was still unthinkable. And while it is possible to regard the last ten years of Britain's presence as dominated by the rivalry of the two great Sayeds, the administration's inability to reach any workable understanding with the emerging non-sectarian élite was assuredly the biggest obstacle to its continued control of the course of events.

In other respects government measures of this period to bring the Sudan forward in political terms were imaginative enough. The elaboration of local government through Province, District and Municipal Councils in place of Indirect Rule in the old sense, the establishment in 1944 of an Advisory Council for the Northern Sudan, the setting up in April 1946 of an Administration Conference under Sudanese chairmanship, and of a Sudanisation Committee to review the structure of government and the involvement of more Sudanese in its echelons, a progressive approach to labour legislation (begun at this time but unfortunately not completed until 1951) – all these measures, aimed at mobilizing political collaboration, were ahead of their time in

Major General Sir Hubert Huddleston, Governor General of the Sudan, 1940–1946.

'colonial' terms. It is true that the continued and deliberate isolation of the negroid and non-Muslim south was beginning to expose the government's approach to the future coherence of the Sudan to easy criticism.[7] But, in general terms, where history was to prove British policies in the Sudan at fault was not over the nature, but over the pace, of the measures taken to meet Sudanese aspirations. Lucky as the Sudan was in the personalities of those in Khartoum seeking to guide its destinies when the war ended – Governor General Huddleston, his Civil Secretary Newbold and Robertson, who succeeded the latter on his death in 1946, were men of outstanding quality – none of them then thought the Sudan had less than a good twenty years of British tutelage to come. Neither did the politicians in London, nor for that matter the politicians in Cairo or even those in Washington.[8] The educated Sudanese, on the other hand, viewed their emancipation in whatever direction as a much closer goal. The Mahdists amongst them saw advantage in collaborating with the government's initiatives: the anti-Mahdists maintained their boycott.

As the new Anglo-Egyptian negotiations approached, the complete re-shaping of Britain's concept of empire was already occupying the outsize mind of Ernest Bevin, though his zest was not shared by all members of Attlee's cabinet. Attlee himself, though his view of Britain's overseas responsibilities and of the art of the possible was narrower than Bevin's, admired his Foreign Secretary's unique potency and only rarely exercised restraint. If Bevin's imperial philosophy was revolutionary, this was not with any view to the disbandment of Britain's empire but simply to its restructure on the basis of equal partnership in a grand design. This latter was to involve on the one hand joint effort for the economic and social betterment of the empire's masses and, on the other, strategic collaboration in the face of threatened Soviet expansion into the free world.[9] In his thinking the two aspects were inseparable. What was new was his concept of partnership. And amongst his global preoccupations the Middle East occupied pride of place.

Accordingly he addressed himself robustly to the Egyptian negotiations with a purposeful optimism, seldom shared by the professional diplomats, let alone by the administrators in Khartoum. Along with his irrepressible sense of mission were paradoxically mixed both earthy realism and tactical skill. Together they may explain two controversial early decisions. One was to demonstrate to the Egyptian Government the open-handed sincerity of his own by agreeing at the outset to the rapid military evacuation of Egyptian territory once agreement on defence collaboration was assured.[10] The other was to refuse in advance of negotiations the pleas from Khartoum for a public statement of policy towards the Sudan,[11] which he rightly suspected would prejudice the reaching of any such agreement. The first of these decisions meant that no Egyptian politician, then or later, could accept less than rapid British evacuation and survive in the turbid waters of Egyptian politics. The second paved the way for the resentful suspicions entertained by the Palace in Khartoum of the manner in which Bevin and, in greater detail, his diplomats in Cairo pursued negotiations thereafter. Both the diplomats in Cairo and the administrators in the Sudan held a low opinion of the Egyptian ruling classes and their administrative integrity; where they disagreed was over the ordering of imperial priorities and procedures for pursuing them. To the diplomats the Sudan administrators seemed parochial dinosaurs incapable of appreciating that Britain's strategic necessities outweighed all other considerations. To the Sudan administrators the diplomats were 'gong-chasing' traitors to a noble cause – that of the Sudan's stable evolution to statehood, unencumbered by subordination to crooked Egyptians. Bevin's own sincere attempt to square the circle took the following form.

He first sought in March 1946 further to satisfy Egyptian sensitivities by removing, to Killearn's dismay, the old style Killearn from running things in Cairo[12] and by sending the notoriously un-imperialist Air Secretary Lord Stansgate to head the negotiating team in Cairo.[13] He then sought to allay Huddleston's apprehensions in Khartoum by publicly stating in Parliament on 26 March that 'no change should be made in the status of the Sudan as a result of treaty revision until the Sudanese have been consulted through constitutional channels', a life-jacket which the Sudan Political Service kept handy from then on. He also sought – though the Egyptians would have none of it – to separate the Canal Base issue from the Sudan question and deal with the former first. The impasse reached, primarily over the Sudan, in the Cairo negotiations in the ensuing months set in train Bevin's endeavour to draft a 'Protocol' on the Sudan which could remove the prime obstacle to a comprehensive understanding with the Egyptians.

Meanwhile the Sudanese activists took an unexpected step. Though excluded from the formal negotiations of the co-domini, they put together (Azhari again being the *animateur*) an all-party delegation to lobby in Cairo for a 'free democratic Sudan government in union with Egypt'. The Khartoum administration – caught, so the Foreign Office wryly suspected, 'on the hop' – could only declare the delegation an unrepresentative absurdity of no importance. Fortunately for them its cohesion was quickly fractured by disagreement over what was meant by union (*ittihad*),[14] and the pro-independence members withdrew. Thereafter, for the next six years, Sudanese lobbying in Cairo or elsewhere was strictly partisan.

The culmination of the laborious Sudan Protocol process – the prime example of Bevin's determination to square the circle – was reached in October 1946. Successive drafts had been confidentially discussed from August on with Huddleston and his Civil Secretary in London and an ostensibly final one received their reluctant approval on 9 October: 'if it was held to be necessary that we have a Treaty with Egypt and this was the only way of securing it'.[15] The problem of course was to find a form of words which combined a recognition of the King of Egypt's 'historic rights' over the Sudan – considered, as Huddleston said at the crucial meeting,[16] 'historic and obsolete' by the Sudanese but 'historic and continuing' by the Egyptians – with a cast-iron assurance to the Sudanese of their ultimate right to self-determination. Huddleston foresaw grave trouble in the Sudan over the sovereignty concession[17] and demanded the positioning of a second British battalion in the Sudan to keep order.

Bevin's plan was to present the draft to the Egyptian Prime Minister Sidki who, despairing of progress in Cairo, declared he was flying to London for private talks with Bevin to try to resolve the deadlock. Despite frantic representations from the acting Governor General (Legal Secretary Creed) that recognition of Egyptian sovereignty would indeed change the locally understood status of the Sudan and be regarded as a breach of Bevin's statement of 26 March, a view with which the head of the relevant Foreign Office department concurred, the die was cast. The talks went ahead amicably enough and, thanks partly to skilful footwork by the Egyptian ambassador in London, Abd al-Fattah Amr, an agreed document was indeed initialled on 25 October.[18] Its text, which was to remain secret until endorsed by both Cabinets, read as follows:

The policy which the High Contracting Parties undertake to follow in the Sudan *within the framework of the unity between the Sudan and Egypt under the common crown of Egypt* will have for its essential objectives to assure the well-being of the Sudanese, the development of their interests and their *active preparation for self-government and consequently the exercise of the right to choose the future status of the Sudan*. Until the High Contracting Parties can in full common agreement realize the latter objective after consultation with the Sudanese, the Agreement of 1899 and Article 11 of the Treaty of 1936 . . . will remain in force . . . [author's italics]

Despite Bevin's ingenuity, the circle was not to be squared. The text had in fact suffered revision right up to its final initialling and the extent to which Huddleston, still in London, continued to be consulted throughout is no longer ascertainable.[19] The substance, however, was unchanged and there is no evidence that Huddleston had given up believing that he would with luck be able to put the implications across on his return to the Sudan. What destroyed these hopes was not the revision of the texts but the one-sided and improper disclosures made, in circumstances which still remain obscure, on Sidki's return to Cairo on 26 October and given wide publicity there.[20] These enabled the Egyptians to proclaim jubilantly that Britain at last recognized Egypt's sovereignty over the Sudan and that their unity was assured. There was no mention of the balancing right of the Sudanese to choose their ultimate status.

26

Reactions in the Sudan were highly charged. Amongst the anti-Egyptian elements, which included Sayed Abdulrahman's Umma Party (and also, it has to be admitted, the British administration) *furore* ensued. There were alarming popular demonstrations and counter-demonstrations. On his arrival in Khartoum on 28 October after ten weeks in London, Huddleston was met by the threat of resignation from his three top advisers.[21] He telegraphed London that he was 'doing his best to hold the position, but [this is] difficult when I myself cannot come out into the open' – presumably because the full terms of the Protocol had still to be treated as confidential.[22] Meanwhile in London Attlee (Bevin being away in New York) sought in a statement to Parliament on 28 October to undo some of the damage caused by the one-sided leak in Cairo without at the same time prejudicing the chances of the whole draft Treaty. Bevin in New York set about seeking from Sidki an agreed and publishable interpretation of the Protocol as a precondition of submitting the draft Treaty to the British Cabinet and Parliament. This was beyond the powers, if not also the desires, of the ailing Sidki. The Wafdist majority leaders and other opponents were in any case in no mood to allow Sidki, who had no personal power base, his moment of triumph.[23]

In the Sudan uproar continued. Having failed to receive a disclosable letter of reassurance from the Foreign Secretary (its approval was in fact delayed by Bevin's absence in New York) and declaring the impossibility, in the after-math of the leaks, of putting the drift of the Protocol across, Huddleston insisted on flying back to London on 9 November to see the Prime Minister. He refused to return to Khartoum unless furnished with two letters from Attlee, one of which he could use to reassure the anti- Egyptian Sudanese and the other to pacify his British staff, both to the effect that the Sudan's right to choose its own future enjoyed a cast-iron British guarantee. Attlee secured Cabinet agreement and an undertaking to furnish these documents enabled Huddleston to set off on 21 November. But on his way through Cairo he was instructed by telegram not to use the approved letters after all, since Sidki was reportedly on the point of submitting the Treaty to the Egyptian parliament for approval and there was too much at stake.[24]

Huddleston dug in his formidable heels and refused to continue his journey. Finally on 3 December, in the absence of any sign of progress in Cairo with endorsement of the Treaty or of any response from Sidki to Bevin's insistence on an agreed interpretation of the Protocol, Huddleston was authorized to go ahead. The right of the Sudanese to opt, if they so chose when the time came, for secession from Egyptian sovereignty could be declared inviolable – despite further published statements by Sidki to the contrary. Huddleston returned to Khartoum on 6 December, acted on his instructions and drew predictably violent protest from Egypt. Two days later Sidki resigned and was succeeded by the uncompromising Noqrashi, whose first announcement was that his government would 'work to achieve unity of the Sudan under the Egyptian crown for ever'.[25] The Protocol, like the rest of the proposed Treaty, was dead. But though the bag was on the refuse-tip, the cat was out.

The high Wagnerian drama of the Sidki-Bevin episode is diminished by summary. Its especial relevance to this study is two-fold. Its importance lies, firstly, in what it reveals of the temper of Britain's concept of empire in the mid-forties. The anti-colonial views of a fair slice of the Labour movement were not shared by most of Attlee's Cabinet. Bevin, with Cabinet backing, was adamant that despite the exhaustion of the war Britain's imperial mission was undiminished: its pistons simply needed re-boring in accordance with a new formula. Herbert Morrison, who was to succeed Bevin in 1951, was even less anti-imperialist in his thinking. The Fabians faced both ways and got nowhere.[26] The Conservative Party for their part showed, as yet, barely any change from pre-war certainties. The second importance of the Sidki-Bevin encounter is that it set the tone for the next six years of further negotiation over the Sudan, the irreconcilabilities remaining unchanged.

The leading British administrators in the Sudan, of course, regarded the whole Sidki-Bevin exercise as an attempt to secure a defence arrangement with Egypt at the expense of the Sudan, to whose emergence into manhood – preferably independent manhood in close relations with Britain – they were professionally dedicated. The Foreign Office, though well aware that no Egyptian leader could reach a new understanding with Britain which did not incorporate recognition of formal sovereignty, however 'symbolic', over the Sudan, went along with Bevin's resolute belief that Sidki, if no one else, might see the need for compromise and secure Egyptian agreement to it. Farouk, in the Foreign Office assessment, for all his resentment at past British treatment, was thought too frightened of unprotected exposure to Soviet penetration to give Sidki's enemies their head.

Bevin himself was at no stage prepared to 'sell the Sudan for his treaty', in the anguished words of Robertson's diary entry of 8 October. From his initial Cabinet memorandum of 18 January 1946[27] to the end, the confidential records of the period are full of his refusals to consider any such thing. No doubt he found Huddleston's single-minded resolution – and in the forties a Governor General's ability to resist dictation from London was still barely questioned – difficult to accommodate within his own evolving vision of imperial policy and the tactics of compromise. But on only one occasion, following the *furore* over the Sidki leaks, do the records reveal him as momentarily losing patience with 'the attitude and set-up of the Sudan Government' and with their 'outmoded view of the role of empire'.[28] In any case – and this is the important point – Bevin stuck immutably to the principle, which indeed Sidki had orally accepted in the October talks, that the ultimate right of emergent peoples, including the Sudanese, to independence was universal.

This was also the message given to Sayed Abdulrahman when he flew to London in November, Attlee having yielded to repeated pleas from the Governor General to receive him. Sayed Abdulrahman caused something of a stir in the Foreign Office by demanding in a separate interview with the Minister of State, Hector McNeil, instant self-government and independence in ten years.

In Egypt, public *animus* on the sovereignty question may or may not have been stimulated by the politicians and the King for their own personal ends; public insistence that the Sudanese were in no sense a separate nation may also have been a bit contrived. But general resentment at Britain's military occupation, together with memories of political interference, were certainly genuine and served to reinforce and give substance to the others. These public resentments and the agility of political rivals to exploit them were something neither Sidki nor Farouk could control.

British exchanges with the new Prime Minister on the possibility of concluding the proposed Treaty struggled on for six weeks. In December Bevin sent him a message that 'if the Sudanese choose union with Egypt, the British Government will be perfectly content'. A new version of the Protocol was offered, in which reference to the Sudan's freedom of choice was omitted and replaced by a procedural formula; but this too was unacceptable to Noqrashi, as indeed it was, for the opposite reason, to Huddleston. On 26 January 1947 Noqrashi broke off negotiations and announced his decision to refer the issue to the United Nations (where it was to run into the sand). Only then did Bevin abandon his first attempt to reach a new deal with Egypt; and on 27 January he at last presented to the House of Commons a full account of the formulation and the fate of the Protocol. That he had, even thereafter, to defend himself against public suspicions of the kind recorded privately in Robertson's diary is evident from the wording of a statement he made in the House in May. 'In all the negotiations with Egypt,' he said, 'there has been and will be no attempt to appease the Egyptians at the expense of the Sudanese people. I offered a just settlement.'

His gamble had failed. Opinions differ as to whether he had been at fault in pursuing it in the manner described. Be that as it may, it will be suggested later that in the longer run the real loser by Egypt's insistence on continuing – indeed permanent – unity with the Sudan was Egypt herself.

Egypt's referral of the Sudan Question to the United Nations caused excitement in the Sudan; but since the Security Council debate led nowhere, nor did the excitement. Meanwhile Bevin took two decisions. Firstly, he informed his Permanent Under Secretary, Orme Sargent, of a change of approach to the problem: the necessary new atmosphere could no longer, he thought, be created by further negotiations but only by administrative measures to eradicate Egypt's obsession with the myth that Britain was out to separate the

Sudan from Egypt. The key was to associate Egyptians with the administration of the Sudan. (Orme Sargent resisted what he described as a 'policy of concessions', and drew a rebuke from Bevin.) Secondly, he replaced[29] the formidable Huddleston as Governor General with a Foreign Office official, Sir Robert Howe, who had been the Under-secretary handling the Sidki-Bevin episode. Both these changes were viewed with dismay in Khartoum. Howe was identified as the 'arch-appeaser', chosen by Bevin as an instrument in the pursuit of his suspect policies. Such misgivings, however, were soon disproved. Howe put on very quickly the mantle of his predecessor as a doughty defender of Sudanese rights. Within a few weeks, commenting on Bevin's new idea of seeking an accommodation with Egypt by unilaterally initiating a greater Egyptian share in the administration of the Sudan, he was writing to London: 'I am convinced that any such policy . . . is quite out of the question. Every Egyptian official in this country is a spearhead of anti-British propaganda and would get short shrift on his return to Egypt if he refused to play this role.' Shortly afterwards Robertson, in his private correspondence with the Sudan Agent in London, quoted the Private Secretary in the Palace[30] as saying of Howe, 'He out-Huddles Huddleston.'

Consequently, when the next phase of Anglo-Egyptian talks on the Sudan got under way in May 1947, between Ambassador Campbell and Foreign Minister Khashaba, Howe's response to further proposed concessions to Egypt was unenthusiastic. In his private correspondence Robertson must have enjoyed the irony of quoting Howe's observation that 'the FO never seem to learn the impossibility of under-the-counter negotiations with the Egyptians', whose practice was always to gobble up concessions offered as part of a deal which they rejected and to start again from there.

What became a major issue in the Campbell-Khashaba talks arose from a decision taken in Khartoum. The Sudan Administration Conference, chaired by Mekki Abbas (by no means a yes-man), had produced its recommendations for constitutional reform and accelerated Sudanization. These included the setting up of a country-wide Legislative Assembly (to replace the Advisory Council for the North) and of a partly Sudanese Executive Council (to replace the more restricted Governor General's Council). The recommendations were approved by the two Councils to be superseded; the Governor General was anxious to keep ahead of internal pressures and upstage Egyptian manoeuvres by pushing on with the necessary legislation, and both co-domini were informed.

Was their sanction – in practice Egypt's – essential? The British were in six minds on this legal issue. The Egyptians were not. In their eyes such constitutional proposals most certainly needed their sanction: indeed the Egyptian Government was entitled to make counter-proposals. Initial comments in those terms from Prime Minister Noqrashi compounded the British dilemma.

Regardless of legal niceties (not in fact clear cut) the prevailing Foreign Office view was that 'If the Egyptians attempt to hold up the policy of Sudanisation (to which they pay lip-service themselves), we shall have no option but to carry on without their consent, even if we break the letter of the Condominium arrangements by doing so'.[31] Bevin himself was much preoccupied at this time with the problem of finding an alternative to Egypt as a location for Britain's vital strategic base in the region. The Sudan was one possibility: if the proposed constitutional reforms would secure a Sudan favourable to Britain, they should, he told his staff, be pushed through on that count alone.

Noqrashi's next step was ingenious. For having held things up till December, he came out with constitutional counter-suggestions which went further and faster in the direction of Sudanizing the administration than did Khartoum's own – a ploy whose propaganda value even the ranks of Tuscany, in London, had privately to admire. Received three months later, in March 1948, the considered comments of the Egyptian Government on Khartoum's draft ordinance[32] went further still – indeed over the top. For they looked forward to the ending of a transitional period of three years (not the twenty to twenty-five years the Egyptians had earlier spoken of) when the Sudanese 'would take over the full responsibilities of administration under the common Crown and within the Unity of the Nile Valley' – the termination in fact of the Condominium. Khartoum's proposed legislation, they added, provided no suitable basis for 'joint discussion', a procedure which London had suggested as a possible way out.

Although the British were by now persuaded that Noqrashi's tactics were simply designed to block constitutional progress in the Sudan, Bevin's post-Sidki idea of associating Egypt more closely with the running of the Sudan was zealously adopted by Ambassador Campbell. He argued that concessions in this field – the appointment of Egyptians to the Executive Council, coupled with the formation of an Anglo-Egyptian Commission to supervise the Assembly elections and of a tripartite one to monitor progress towards self-government – might remove the blockage. The Governor General was just prepared to accept all this in exchange for Egyptian acceptance of the ordinance; but when Campbell declared that the acceptance, in addition, of an Egyptian Deputy Governor General would furnish the only hope of a breakthrough in Anglo-Egyptian relations, Howe dug his feet in. Fortunately for him, Noqrashi's refusal to consider joint discussion of the draft ordinance without prior agreement on Egypt's share in running the Sudan drove the Foreign Office to side more distinctly with Howe. The latter was now determined – and Sayed Abdulrahman was demanding – that the Self-Government Ordinance should be promulgated without further delay. Nonetheless the advice received by Bevin at this stage, March 1948, from the Attorney General was that promulgation without Egyptian sanction would emphatically conflict with the Condominium Agreement and could lead to an adverse judgement by the International Court.[33] This led Bevin to insist on the Governor General holding back on promulgation while further attempts were made to reach an understanding in Cairo. He was also anxious that the Sudan issue should not blow up in his face before 'stumps were drawn in Palestine' – as the Sudan Agent in London put it – on 15 May.

In the event, the prolonged endeavours of Khashaba and Campbell in their talks in Cairo to reach a draft agreement over the handling of the ordinance and associated 'concessions' were finally successful at the end of May. The process had exasperated the Palace in Khartoum by entailing repeated postponements of the deadline authorized by London for the promulgation of the ordinance in the absence of any such agreement. The diplomats in Cairo were equally exasperated by the pressures brought to bear on London by Khartoum. In a personal letter home in mid-May Campbell berated the Sudan Government for having set the country on a course towards 'premature' independence and identified as the root of the trouble the 'impertinent and forceful' personality of Sir James Robertson.[34] But approval of the Khashaba-Campbell agreement by the Egyptian Cabinet – despite further extensions of London's time-limit – was blocked by Noqrashi. King Farouk, however distasteful he found Noqrashi, was not prepared to risk dismissing him on this count; and on 14 June, despairing of progress in Cairo, Bevin authorized the Governor General to go ahead. 'At long last,' as Robertson put it, 'the battle was ended.'

But it meant that Bevin's second attempt to reach an understanding with Egypt on the political evolution of the Sudan (as a means to an agreement on the Canal Base) had failed like the first.

Why, one may wonder, did Noqrashi reject what was on offer and what was apparently acceptable to other leading Egyptians? The concessions tendered seemed to the Governor General alarmingly generous. Presumably they were considered by 'Old Nokkers' (as the Sudan administration called him) to be inadequate instruments to ensure the ultimate emergence of a Sudan permanently united with Egypt – an aim to which Noqrashi was wholly wedded. In his thinking, a more promising way of achieving it may well have been remorseless non-co-operation with the 'imperialists' in London and Khartoum, coupled with the continued deployment of inducements to secure the backing of a majority of educated Sudanese. Indeed such a policy, pursued with greater finesse, might perhaps have worked.

The Self-Government Ordinance was promulgated on 16 June to a chorus of protests from Egypt and her Sudanese supporters and of relief from those in the Sudan urgent for independence. Preparations for elections to the new Legislative Assembly went ahead. But polling, when it took place on 15 November, proved distinctly rowdy, since not only the radical pro-Egyptian groups but the anti-Mahdist Khatmiyya as well deployed a vociferous boycott. The resulting Assembly of seventy-five was therefore largely pro-independence and sympathetic to Sayed Abdulrahman, in whom indeed signs of a *folie de grandeur* were detected by the Palace.

Inadequately representative though the Assembly may have been, embryonic self-government was now in operation. The great hope in the Palace was that the ordinance might be gradually modified in such a way as to persuade the Khatmiyya to call off their boycott and detach themselves from the 'extremist' pro-Egyptians (whose strength the Palace certainly underestimated). Rumours of another impending bout of Anglo-Egyptian negotiations once the general elections in Egypt (due in January 1950) ended, were disquieting to the Palace since this would throw everything back into the melting pot. Moreover talk in Autumn 1949 of independence for Libya, Somalia and even Eritrea (none of them more 'advanced' than the Sudan) was whetting Umma Party appetites.

But once in office the expected new Wafdist Government in Cairo, despite a quick visit from Bevin, showed no signs of being any less resolute on the two old and still inseparable issues – British evacuation of Egypt and Egyptian unity with the Sudan – than Noqrashi had been. Stevenson, who had replaced Campbell in Cairo, sought like him to promote a deal on the former through an understanding on the latter; but he was told in August 1950 by Egypt's Foreign Minister, Salah ad-Din, that the only way forward in the Sudan was for Britain to clear out of it lock, stock and barrel and to leave the Egyptians and the Sudanese to work things out together.[35] Undismayed, he suggested to London the offer of further concessions to persuade the Egyptians to think again. Howe protested, arguing that 'all politically minded Sudanese wanted purely Sudanese government'; and he looked forward to the day when, after the next elections, the Sudan could mount a representative all-party delegation to discuss its future relations with Egypt. This was a forecast which, ironically, history was to fulfil two years later in an unexpected sense.

Bevin, now even more preoccupied with the fear of Soviet advances in the Middle East, saw no purpose in holding further fruitless negotiations and was inclined (as he put it to Howe in October 1950) to 'let the Egyptians stew in their own juice', while his search for an alternative British base in the area continued. Meanwhile he was content to see self-government further consolidated in the Sudan. In Khartoum Palace planning was not eased either by the 'obstinate' refusal of Sayed Ali al-Mirghani to allow his Khatmiyya followers (themselves, in Robertson's view, 'not disloyal') to collaborate or by Sayed Abdulrahman's Umma Party pressing at the end of 1950 for full self-government within a year.

Bevin, though not encouraged by Farouk's virtual denunciation of the 1936

Treaty in his Speech from the Throne of 18 November 1950, did hold a series of meetings with his counterpart Salah ad-Din in December. But there was, as preparatory minuting in the Foreign Office observed, 'no chance whatever of being able to justify to the Egyptians the fact that we have almost four times as many troops in the Canal Zone as the 1936 Treaty permits'.[36] The Chief of the Imperial General Staff was at the same time representing that 'the greatly increased threat of global war means that our allies would regard our evacuation of Egypt as almost treachery'. Salah ad-Din for his part reaffirmed the inseparability of the two old issues and made it plain that Egypt 'could accept no solution which did not recognize the union of Egypt and Sudan in word and in practice'. The old deadlock continued.

In that respect the departure of the ailing Bevin from the scene in March 1951 changed nothing. His constructive sense of purpose may have gone with him, but his successor certainly maintained in more simplistic form Bevin's determination to preserve Britain's dominant role in the Middle East. Confronted immediately with papers reviewing the Egyptian deadlock, Herbert Morrison simply wrote across them 'I am concerned at the tendency to get out of everywhere'.[37] Faced four months later with Egypt's unilateral abrogation of the 1936 Treaty, Morrison's comment in Parliament on 16 October was more in the Bevin tradition. 'HMG are not prepared to barter with Egypt the future freedom of the Sudanese to choose their own status in exchange for an agreement on defence.' Ten days later general elections returned the Conservatives to power and Eden to the Foreign Office.

The Egyptian Government, following their abrogation announcement and the uninhibited assumption by Farouk of the title of the King of the Sudan, broke off the deadlocked talks and referred the Sudan issue once again, but no more fruitfully than in 1947, to the United Nations. More pointedly they promulgated a constitution of their own for the Sudan, on the Egyptian model. Azhari, just re-elected President of the Graduates' Congress, declared the Ashiqqa's wholehearted support for Egypt's actions. The Legislative Assembly predictably took the opposite line, condemning the Constitution announcement as an attempt to impose Egyptian sovereignty on the Sudan without consulting the Sudanese people. Even the Khatmiyya, through their newspaper *Sawt as-Sudan*, declared the proposed constitution unsuitable. But though the gap between those who supported Egypt on principle and those who supported her for tactical reasons was visibly beginning to widen, Sayed Ali al-Mirghani would still not simplify the problems facing the Palace by prizing himself free of the Ashiqqa. A contemporary British gambit was to instruct Robertson to put privately to pro-independence leaders the idea of Dominion Status for the Sudan within the Commonwealth. They welcomed it, but Britain shied away from advancing the idea publicly on the grounds that the Egyptians would then say that this had of course been the British plan all along. Indeed something of the kind had long been nursed in many British heads.

Meanwhile the deliberations of the Sudan's own Constitutional Amendment Commission – set up six months before to recommend on the next step to full self-government and composed of Sudanese intellectuals (including Khatmiyya) under a British chairman – had been virtually completed. But the ostensible ending of the Condominium by Egypt's abrogation of it caused an awkward hitch, since it prompted twelve of the Commission's members to telegraph the UN Secretary General on 28 October 1951, requesting the appointment of a UN body to assume responsibility in the Sudan until the Sudanese were in a position to decide their future status. Britain's refusal to contemplate transferring control in such a way led the Commission to dissolve itself, leaving its chairman to formalize the outcome of its deliberations. His report, envisaging a country-wide two-chamber parliament, a half-Sudanese Executive Council and the beginnings of cabinet government, was laid before the Legislative Assembly with the advance blessing of Eden in January 1952. After minor amendment, the resulting draft Constitutional Ordinance was approved in May – only to become a new bone of contention with Egypt.

Other current developments further taxed the ingenuity of the Sudan Government. At Communist prompting, the Workers Trade Union Federation, which had never accepted the comprehensive labour legislation completed in 1951, staged some damaging strikes and amended its constitution to embrace total non-co-operation with the 'colonial regime'. At the other end of the political spectrum, the formation of a new and non-sectarian political party backed by conservative and rural leaders and calling itself (rather oddly) the Socialist Republican Party (SRP), seemed an encouraging sign since it favoured hastening towards statehood more slowly than the Umma and more independently than the Khatmiyya. But suspicions, however mythical, that it had British inspiration, coupled with its anti-sectarian flavour, alienated even Sayed Abdulrahman from the Palace. Altogether the extent of political disagreements within the Sudanese body-politic looked formidable. They were the context of Robertson's characteristic diary entry, 'They divide and we rule', quoted on p. 4.

Meanwhile public temper of an anti-British kind was developing in Egypt beyond the capacity, and perhaps the will, of its Government to control – a situation made all too manifest in the bloody Black Friday riots in Cairo on 27 January, which led to the dismissal of the Nahas Government by Farouk. The urgent need, under increasing American pressure, for a defence agreement with the new Government of Hilali was well understood by Eden; and the ploy adopted by him as a basis for re-starting negotiations with the new Egyptian Government was to tell them that Farouk's assumption of kingship over the

Sudan and Egypt's proposed new Constitution for it should be allowed to 'remain on the statute-book' pending the achievement of full self-government in the Sudan and the exercise thereafter of self-determination.[38]

Various formulas of this kind were discussed with the Americans, whose attitude to the Anglo-Egyptian dispute over the Sudan cannot be ignored here, any more than it could be at the time by the British Government. Attlee's guiding principle had always been that no other British foreign interests should be pursued in such a way as to jeopardize Anglo-American relations. The successor Conservative Government very much needed Washington's support in their handling of Britain's defence interests in Egypt – if only since America's influence in the Middle East was in process of overtaking that of Britain. But to carry the Americans with them, as this entailed, in their handling of the linked Sudan dispute was not easy. Caffery, the US Ambassador in Egypt, made no secret of his conviction that, in the interests of a defence agreement with Egypt, Britain should recognize Farouk's title to the Sudan regardless of repercussions there.[39] Secretary of State Acheson's reaction, when Eden sought his full backing in April for the presentation of a final formula to Hilali, was that the Sudanese should be consulted first, but, as he soon made plain, in such a way as to induce them to agree, since in the absence of progress the reasonably well-disposed Hilali would fall. Eden's reply in June that 'HMG really cannot keep the Egyptian Government alive by feeding the Sudanese to them'[40] provided the context for the startling remark by a senior US official (best left unidentified) that the British were holding up a vital Western defence requirement out of deference to 'ten million bloody niggers'. The conflict between two strands of American thinking is reflected in the contrasting reactions to it of the British in Cairo and Khartoum. Ambassador Stevenson, looking back at the end of 1953 on the whole period of Anglo-Egyptian negotiations in which he had been involved, sadly declared that 'the Americans were still conditioned by anti-colonialist obsessions to withhold full support for their NATO partners in negotiations with the Egyptians on the Canal'.[41] To the British in Khartoum, on the other hand, the Americans' fault lay in their unprincipled refusal to support the right of the emergent Sudan to self-determination. But this is to jump ahead of the narrative.

In the wake of Eden's 'final formula' ploy, Hilali responded to letters sent to him by Sayed Abdulrahman protesting at Egyptian propaganda and bribery by inviting him, as the main obstacle in Egypt's path, to send representatives to Cairo to discuss things. When the invitation was accepted in May, Sayed Ali al-Mirghani's reaction was revealing. He let it be known that if any agreement were reached between the Egyptians and his rival, he would announce his open alliance with the SRP. None was; but Sayed Abdulrahman was on the point of accepting a further invitation from the short-lived Hilali's even shorter-lived successor Sirri, when the most dramatic twentieth century development in Egyptian internal affairs knocked the whole chessboard into confusion. The revolution of 26 July 1952 signalled the permanent ouster of the King of Egypt, and of the Sudan, and the emergence of Muhammad Naguib as Egypt's new Head of State. All bids were momentarily off.

Naguib, having many connections with the Sudan, including a Sudanese upbringing and (by one account) a Sudanese mother, evoked widespread enthusiasm there – not least when he quickly made it plain that, unlike the old monarchy, the new Egyptian republic laid no claim to sovereignty over the Sudan. Since he also broke with the past by declaring himself ready to discuss the Sudan and the Canal as separate issues, the British Government moved as soon as possible to seek his agreement to Khartoum's outstanding constitutional proposals and to the holding of immediate elections on that basis.

But they were outmanoeuvred. For Naguib, having stalled until 21 October, now sprang his trap: his response must await discussions with the delegations from all Sudanese political parties already invited to Cairo.

One after another, to the dismay of the British, the delegations – from the Umma and the SRP no less than from the Unionist groups – trooped to Cairo and signed their agreement, with minor individual modifications, to Naguib's very different version of the constitutional way forward.[42] This not only accepted the Sudan's right of self-determination to be exercised within three years by a Constituent Assembly elected to choose between union with Egypt and independence (no other options being entertained); it further stipulated that before self-determination all expatriate officials whose presence might affect the Sudan's freedom of choice should be withdrawn, and that in the interim the powers of the Governor General should be restricted by subjecting him to the assistance of a five-man International Commission. The safeguards for the welfare of the South written into the original draft ordinance by giving specific responsibility in that respect to the Governor General were conspicuously absent from Naguib's agreement. With this in his pocket, he sent London a cavalier Note on 2 November 1952.[43]

The cards which before the revolution the Governor General still held were thus deftly removed by Naguib's sleight of hand. The parties' acceptance of Naguib's proposals made it impossible for Howe to plead effectively in London that they should be disregarded. Since talks with Egypt on Naguib's Note were deemed inescapable by London, elections in the Sudan on the basis agreed in Khartoum had to be deferred. This was to leave the Sudan with no 'representative' body to speak for it for fifteen months: Robertson later looked back on his failure to arrange the renewal of the old Assembly's life when its term expired in October 1952 as 'one of the greatest mistakes I made as Civil Secretary'.[44]

The performance in the ensuing drama of the flamboyant Salah Salem in the role of Egypt's Minister for Sudan Affairs was from this time determinant. He and his brother officer Zulfakar Sabri (also destined for prominence later in the story) had formed Naguib's entourage when receiving the Sudanese party delegations in Cairo. Salah's next mission was a lightning visit to the Sudan in January 1953 in the course of which he brought off two further political scoops. In the south he collected by various means enough signatures to enable Egypt to challenge the British argument that the southerners were alarmed by the absence of safeguards for their future under Naguib's proposed constitution. In the north he secured the signatures of the political parties to a document confirming the agreements already signed in Cairo and ending with the triumphant words 'These parties have unanimously agreed to boycott elections held under any other statute.' Even Robertson, in his diary, showed signs of despair.

London too recognized that they had been outmanoeuvred. If the Sudan dispute, agreed by Naguib to be treatable separately from the Canal, could not be laid to rest by some compromise over his constitutional proposals (which the Sudanese themselves evidently accepted), what hope was there of moving on to an understanding with him on the Canal? Such an understanding was now more acutely needed than ever, as the Americans and the Egyptian mob in their different ways were both emphasizing. Within a month the apparently inevitable was accepted and a final Anglo-Egyptian Agreement on the Sudan, broadly on Naguib's terms as already accepted by the Sudanese party delegations in October, was concluded on 12 February 1953. Its main provisions were the following: self-determination in the form of a choice between a link with Egypt and complete independence would be exercised within three years by a Constituent Assembly elected under a law to be drafted by the Sudanese Parliament; and three Commissions would be appointed forthwith, one to advise the Governor General during the transitional three years, one to monitor the imminent general elections and one to supervise the Sudanisation of the Administration, Police and Defence Force before self-determination. No specific reference was admitted to any special responsibility for the South to rest with the Governor General. Indeed the terms left the Governor General and the Political Service with little or no constitutional power to influence the course of events.[45]

The curtain seemed now poised to drop on the long drama of the dispute, though this particular denouement had never been expected. Naguib's *coup de théâtre* was a bitter blow to the Political Service. As they saw it, half a century's dedicated work to prepare the Sudan for independent statehood, preferably with a continuing British link, was now to end ingloriously. If their friends as well as their enemies amongst the politically active Sudanese had now cast in their lot with Naguib's Egypt, the probability was that they would 'self-determine' in the direction favoured by Cairo. Even the Southerners and waverers in the North would see, when the choice had to be made, that the paternalist British had effectively abandoned them. The Governor General's resulting *cri de coeur* to London over the weakness of the position in which the Agreement left him was judged defeatist in London. Selwyn Lloyd, the Minister of State, was despatched to Khartoum in an attempt to put heart in him. Howe's refusal to counter Egyptian propaganda, on the very proper grounds that he and the Political Service, if the real battle was to be won, had to be seen as impartial by the Sudanese public in the run up to the elections, was also decried by London as supine. Robertson was equally dispirited. In a private letter to the Sudan Agent in London the day after the Agreement was signed, he wrote: 'We have been defeated by Egypt, by our own Foreign Service and Embassy, and by America – helped by the folly and short-sightedness of the Sudanese leaders. Unless a miracle happens, the Sudan will be swallowed up by Egypt: of course that might have happened anyhow, but it is more certain now.'[46] Robertson's monthly confidential letters to Province Governors and others had been known for some years as 'Uncle Jimmy's soothing syrups'; but even if he had not been on the point of retirement, Uncle Jimmy could hardly be expected to bring them much comfort now.

His gloomy interpretation of Naguib's strategy was made without benefit of the subsequent disclosures by the latter's henchman, Zulfakar Sabri, published nine years later. Although public assurances had been given (and been written into the Anglo-Egyptian Agreement) to guarantee a 'free and neutral atmosphere for self-determination', Zulfakar makes no bones about declaring that the key operator, Salah Salem, 'considered the apparent waiver of Egypt's age-long claim to sovereignty was a tactical move that would allay the suspicions of the pro-independence groups while allowing him to make surreptitious use of the transitional period to bring off, by hook or by crook, a Sudanese vote in favour of some link with Egypt'.[47] Only when the British had been dislodged, so Zulfakar records his own thinking, could Egypt 'propose suitable links with the Sudan'. Indeed Salah Salem himself barely troubled to conceal this strategy at the time. On his January visit to the Sudan he had told the British Head of the Political Secretariat that 'he paid lip-service to the principle of self-determination but only as a step towards the unity of the Sudan with Egypt'.[48] Eden, for his part, publicly insisted more than once in the days following the Agreement that, if the Sudanese opted for independence, this would not exclude their then seeking a link with Britain or the Commonwealth – an interpretation rejected by Naguib. 'The difference between Naguib's interpretation of independence and ours', Robertson observed, 'recalls the Sidki/Bevin business.'

A month after the signature of the Agreement and the holding by the Governor General of a commendably dignified public ceremony to mark it, the new Self-Government Statute was duly promulgated and preparations went ahead, under the scrutiny of the agreed Electoral Commission, for elections to the critical new parliament. Whatever machinery might be used when the day came to decide between Unity with Egypt and Independence, the dominant grouping in the interim legislative body would surely be well placed to influence the outcome.

The next two months were a testing period for the unhappy Governor General. Already criticized by Downing Street for defeatism over the effect of the Anglo-Egyptian Agreement and for his 'supine' attitude towards Egypt's mounting campaign of propaganda and personal vilification, his decision to postpone the Sudan elections from May until after the imminent rainy season, thus giving a five-month space for Egyptian propaganda to exploit, aroused further Churchillian disapprobation. The deferment was in fact no fault of Howe's, since the Indian chairman of the newly appointed Commission to supervise the elections insisted on satisfying himself about electoral procedures throughout the country and could not complete his examination before the onset of the rains. At this stage Howe, unwisely perhaps, signalled his intention of going off in May for his long annual summer leave. Churchill's temper exploded and he drafted a telegram so critical of Howe's whole behaviour that his accompanying minute to Selwyn Lloyd looked forward to Howe's resignation on receiving it and recommended the withholding of his pension rights. The telegram was fortunately watered down before despatch, and Howe modified his leave plans. But Churchill, who had just taken over control of foreign affairs from the ailing Eden, was by now so provoked by Egyptian interventions in the Sudan and by difficulties in the current Suez negotiations that he was seized with the idea of denouncing the Sudan Agreement and proceeding unilaterally there.[49] When the Suez negotiations finally broke down on 12 May, Howe instantly and without consulting London issued a proclamation in Khartoum reassuring the Sudanese that the Sudan agreement was not affected and would be fully implemented. Churchill was not pleased. Nor was he easily deflected from his inclination to denounce the agreement, despite Howe's proclamation, and he ordered troops in Suez to stand by for despatch to Khartoum.[50] Fortunately wiser counsels prevailed and the whole idea was dropped. Salisbury was appointed Acting Foreign Secretary in June and Churchillian interventionism temporarily subsided.

In the Sudan the rains and the extended preparations for the elections took their course. Sayed Abdulrahman and the Umma remained singularly confident – despite the evident rapprochement of Sayed Ali al-Mirghani's Khatmiyya with the Ashiqqa, campaigning together (as Naguib had advised) under the banner of the National Unionist Party (NUP) and under Azhari's leadership. The middle-of-the-road SRP, as sectarian allegiances reasserted themselves, went progressively into eclipse. The Southerners scarcely knew which way to look.

What seems in retrospect more surprising than the rhetorical forecasts of the parties in the long run-up to the elections was the miscalculation in the Palace of their probable outcome. Robertson had gone (in mid-April); but Luce, who took over part of his functions as Adviser on Constitutional and External Affairs, recorded up to the last minute in his private letters to the Sudan Agent in London a steady confidence in the emergence of a pro-independence majority – undeterred by the evidence, of which there was plenty, of Egyptian inducements, financial and other, in the opposite direction.[51] He, like the authorities in London, was doubtless encouraged by Sayed Abdulrahman's final decision (in August) to break with Egypt and release himself from the old agreement with Naguib of October 1952 on the grounds that Naguib was blatantly breaching it himself. Moreover, Sayed Abdulrahman took the shrewd step later in August of declaring in favour of a republican régime, when independence came, thus covering his electoral flank.

When the elections finally took place in November, the outcome was a shock to the British. The NUP won a clear overall majority, gaining 51 of the 97 seats in the Lower House and 23 of the 30 elected seats in the Senate, the Umma share being no more than 23 and 3 respectively. A NUP Government under Azhari, on which Ashiqqa, Khatmiyya and Southerners were represented, took office accordingly. There was elation in Egypt.

But surprises were still to come before the curtain finally descended on the Condominium. Nobody, Ambassador Stevenson had said to the Egyptian Foreign Minister back in 1950, could separate the two countries (Egypt and the Sudan) living on the same river, unless the Egyptians did so by antagonizing the Sudanese.[52] It was a prophetic observation.

The first attempt to open the new Parliament on 1 March 1954, in the presence of Naguib and Selwyn Lloyd (Britain's Minister of State) was thwarted by 30,000 disgruntled followers of Sayed Abdulrahman running amok outside the Palace, where Naguib was ensconced, and killing the British Police Commandant, amongst others who tried to disperse them.[53] The postponed opening took place peacefully and without Naguib's presence ten days later. The State of Emergency declared by the Governor General following the 1 March riot was terminated.

Meanwhile Selwyn Lloyd, who remained in Khartoum for a week after the riots, had formed the opinion that Howe's handling of the situation again needed toughening up. Prospects of further Mahdist violence, already lively thanks to the probable prosecution of Sayed Abdulrahman's son, Siddiq, for complicity in the 1 March disorder, were reinforced by indications that Azhari, under Egyptian pressure, intended tabling in parliament a motion to replace the Umma member of the Governor General's Commission with a second pro-Egyptian member. This would dangerously unbalance the Commission and enrage the Mahdists. Selwyn Lloyd urged Howe to declare a new, anticipatory, State of Emergency, which would involve suspending the constitution. Churchill weighed in, proposing once more the despatch of British troops and the evacuation of British women and children. The wavering Howe was persuaded by his staff to resist these proposals, and his representations that such measures would only inflame the situation were backed by the Chief of Staff in London. Instructions from Downing Street in reply were that, if no compromise was reached with Azhari over maintaining a workable balance in the Sudanese membership of the Commission, Howe should declare the British Government's intention of giving the Sudan its independence on British terms and without reference to Egypt – a possible, and characteristically Churchillian, course of action which Selwyn Lloyd had rashly mentioned to Sayed Abdulrahman during his visit to Khartoum. The Palace staff, who believed the best hope of bringing the Sudan to independence now lay in scrupulous observance of the treaty and the self-government statute, relying on Egypt overplaying her hand, were aghast. Fortunately, under pressure from Foreign Office officials, Lloyd advised Cabinet that it should be left to he Governor General to decide whether and when a Constitutional Emergency should be declared. In the event the replacement of the Umma Member of the Commission by a relatively harmless Southerner was approved by the Legislative Assembly on 21 April. Sayed Abdulrahman and his party kept the peace, removing the need for declaring an Emergency. Churchill relaxed. The episode illustrates a striking reversal of attitudes as between London and Khartoum; for whereas the latter had originally deplored the home government's capitulation to Naguib's terms for an agreement on the Sudan, it was now Churchill's government which was minded to denounce the agreement while Khartoum was adamant about carrying it out. There can be little doubt that on this occasion Khartoum was right.[54]

It was not, however, a recrudescence of anti-Egyptian Mahdism that was to distance the Sudan from the new rulers of Egypt. The gradual estrangement of the bulk of the professedly unionist NUP – so far as their professions had not all along been simply assumed to hasten the ouster of the British – must be laid at Egypt's door. Some of course remained genuinely committed to unity, the most vociferous being Muhammad Nur ad-Din, Azhari's rival for leadership of the Party and its Vice President; but an indication of Azhari's own thinking was privately given by him to Luce as early as mid February 1954. 'Having escaped from domination by Britain, the Sudanese [he told him] had no intention of putting themselves under Egypt.'[55] Luce himself may have misjudged the temper of the electorate in 1953 but from then on he established himself as the most unruffled and clearsighted of Robertson's successors and the major influence behind Howe, hitherto an inconspicuous Governor General, in his astute handling of the political scene. Few of his colleagues in the despondent Political Service would have subscribed to the view Luce privately recorded on the morrow of the electoral triumph of the Party publicly committed to Unity with Egypt – 'I still firmly believe that the Sudan will get its independence in the end.'[56]

The handling in 1954 by Egypt's Revolutionary Council of its interests in the Sudan was a main factor in disabusing the Sudanese of the enthusiasm Naguib and his fellow revolutionaries had initially generated amongst them. The progressive demotion and final removal in November of Naguib from the Egyptian leadership was a prime cause of their disenchantment. The over-playing of his hand by Salah Salem in particular, both in Cairo and in the Sudan, antagonized many – in particular Sayed Ali al-Mirghani and senior Khatmiyya politicians, with whom he held talks in Cairo on the nature of future linkage between the two countries. So angry was he with their reserved attitude that he broke off the discussions and roundly described them on Cairo Radio as 'traitors'. The other member of the Revolutionary Council with special responsibility for Sudan affairs, Zulfakar Sabri, who was appointed as the Egyptian member of the Governor General's Commission, similarly over-did things. His visible interventions in the 'free and neutral atmosphere' of the transitional period enraged, amongst others, the Commission's genuinely neutral Pakistani Chairman as well as its original pro-Egyptian Sudanese member.

Even without Egyptian provocation the increasing fragility of Ashiqqa-Khatmiyya cohesion in the NUP tested Azhari's astuteness. Though by no means all his early manoeuvring was visibly designed to widen the growing breach with Egypt, the Egyptian Government's treatment of him and its support for his rival Nur ad-Din must, as events proceeded, have streng-thened his latent preference for the Sudan's ultimate independence.

In marked contrast to Egypt's maladroitness, the Governor General's hand-ling of the rapidly evolving political scene was beyond reproach. His scrupulous observance of his altered constitutional role and his avoidance of any clash with his Advisory Commission increasingly enabled him to win even Azhari's confidence. If Azhari had initially assumed the need to continue playing the Egyptian card to trump British machinations, he soon found the old tactic less compelling. There was no sign of any intention in the Palace to delay the advance to self-determination or to reimpose control by cultivating Mahdist and other opposition elements. Luce's heterodox but shrewd convic-tion that 'the best way we can help the Sudanese to save themselves from Egyptian domination is to remove ourselves as quickly as possible'[57] was not of course made public. But Palace co-operation with the planning of the Sudanisation Committee to effect without restraint the withdrawal, in advance of self-determination, of all but a handful of British officials must have helped to disarm suspicion.[58]

To confirm Britain's goodwill, an invitation to Azhari to pay an official visit in November to London (where he was well received[59]) was engineered by Luce. London's own apparent loss of interest over recent months in promoting a 'satisfactory' outcome to the approaching exercise of self-determination could be ascribed to preoccupation with negotiating an end to the other quarrel with Egypt (the evacuation of the Canal Base); but it evoked much protest from Luce. He was also much exercised by the Governor General's desire, expressed in July, to retire in March 1955. Egyptian agreement to the appointment of a British successor could hardly be taken for granted. Even if Howe remained the titular holder, his prolonged absences from Khartoum, largely for health reasons, would leave the Palace without a central figure, known and respected by the Sudanese, to ensure both stability during the final stages and goodwill towards Britain thereafter. To Luce's dismay Eden assured Howe in October that he could continue acting as Governor General from the UK if necessary. In a personal appeal to Howe, Luce went as far as threatening the resignation of himself and others if a British Governor General were not present for at least eight months of the year.[60] In the event, Howe did return for some months before Knox Helm, whose appointment was approved without argument by the Egyptian Government, replaced him in March 1955.

Meanwhile, proposals by the Embassy in Cairo (following the dismissal of Naguib in November) for a new and more sympathetic look at Egyptian aspirations in the Sudan occasioned further irritation amongst the few British left in Khartoum and marked, so Luce privately recorded, 'the lowest point yet reached by the Embassy for stupidity, gullibility, cynicism and disregard for Sudanese interests'. What lay behind this outburst was that, as he had written to Bromley at the Foreign Office shortly before, he did 'not for a moment believe that the Egyptians had wavered in their determination ultimately to get control of the Sudan'. To his relief, the Foreign Office, though in more diplomatic terms, also rejected the Ambassador's proposals.[61]

Luce's endeavours, however, to extract from the British Government a public assurance of its readiness to afford moral, material and financial assistance to the Sudan after self-determination were fruitless. Even when advanced by the Governor General designate to Eden personally in mid-February 1955, the plea was rebuffed on the grounds that His Majesty's Government had to avoid accusations of seeking to influence the constitutional outcome. A senior Foreign Office official let it be known to the Sudan Agent that the Government was now more concerned to promote good relations between the Sudan and Egypt than with the Sudan's own future. The Government's apparent lack of concern over the outcome of self-determination may have been reinforced unwittingly by the statement in Howe's last despatch from Khartoum to Winston Churchill on 8 March: 'We are going out on an immense tide of goodwill and friendship.'[62]

Be that as it may, the estrangement from Egypt of the NUP and of Azhari in particular was certainly gathering strength. On 16 March Azhari gave public utterance for the first time to his party's desire for independence.[63] On 1 April the NUP Parliamentary Group in a redefinition of Party policy avoided any commitment to future linkage of the Sudan with Egypt. Cold-shouldered later that month by Nasser at the Bandung Non-aligned Conference and mobbed in Cairo on his way home, frequently criticized by the Egyptian press and irritated by the behaviour of Salah Salem (not least by the niggardly attitude he adopted in talks on a revised division of Nile waters), Azhari was now more clearly set on personally leading his country to independent statehood.

August 1955 was a critical month. In the South widespread discontent over the handling of its interests by Northern politicians and newly installed administrators erupted into bloody disorders and a mutiny of Southern troops. Knox Helm, being their Commander-in-Chief, flew back from leave and insisted on the surrender of the mutineers – not, as the latter pleaded, to British troops, nor, as the Egyptians urged, to forces from both co-domini, but to units of the Sudan's own Defence Force. Though the leader of the mutineers finally agreed on surrender, it was only partially effected.[64] In any case the Southerners' ancient hostility to the North remained close to the surface. In Azhari's view, the Government's problems in the South had been aggravated by Egyptian machinations there, most conspicuously by Salah Salem's assiduous canvassing for pro-Egyptian support. Salah's dismissal from the Ministry for Sudan Affairs by Nasser at the end of August, though he was kept on as an adviser, suggests a tardy recognition that his handling of the Egyptian case in the Sudan had been a major miscalculation throughout.

During the same month the Sudanisation Committee reported the completion of its task. The 'free and neutral atmosphere for the exercise of self-determination' had in that sense been achieved well ahead of the three-year dateline originally prescribed. Azhari, in whom by now the Egyptians had lost all confidence, proceeded to take the remaining fences at a gallop.

Having dismissed from office without mishap his pro-Egyptian rival Nur ad-Din, whom the indefatigable Zulfakar had been publicly lionizing, he promoted a formal request by Parliament to the Governor General on 16 August to put the self-determination procedure into motion forthwith. (The prior withdrawal of all British and Egyptian troops was amongst the requirements.) Later in August he secured a resolution in parliament, which had both Sayed Ali al-Mirghani's and Sayed Abdulrahman's support, in favour of a plebiscite as a means of establishing the country's choice between Unity and Independence, in place of electing a Constituent Assembly for that purpose. Though eventually dropped as impractical, a plebiscite was initially seen as offering less scope for Egyptian manipulation than would new elections. As the climax approached disagreements between Egypt and Britain over constitutional procedures and over the composition of the International

Military Parade to mark evacuation of British and Egyptian troops from the Sudan, November 1955. At the saluting base Sir Knox Helm with British, Sudanese and Egyptian GOCs.

Commission to supervise self-determination dragged on, but became in the upshot irrelevant.

Azhari played his hand internally with consummate skill. He outflanked both mounting Party and Parliamentary opposition as well as an unprecedented joint statement on 3 December by the two Sayeds – anxious to secure for themselves and their rival sects the maximum credit for the final step into statehood – in favour of the immediate formation of a National Government. Sayed Ali al-Mirghani was increasingly irritated by Azhari's non-sectarian attitudes and saw advantage in supporting the opposition's pressure for a coalition government as a means of dislodging him from the premiership. The idea of short-circuiting the path to self-determination was clearly in the wind, and was encouraged by the Palace. Azhari's precise tactics were not yet disclosed.

Knox Helm's departure on 15 December, on leave though known to be final, was the signal for Azhari's next move. Having taken soundings in various quarters – though Mahjub, the leader of the parliamentary opposition, was to claim in his memoirs that he had privily fixed things on his own with Azhari[65] – he contrived to bypass any further interventions by the Co-domini or by the Sayeds by promoting a private motion in Parliament, unanimously

46

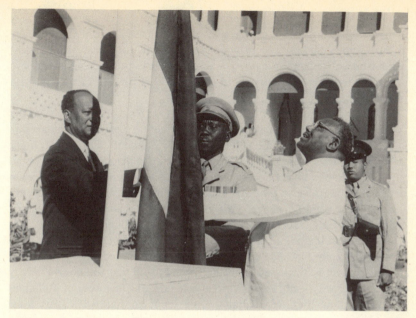

Isma'il Azhari raising the Sudan flag on Independence Day, 1 January 1956. Facing him, Opposition Leader Mahjub.

adopted on 19 December, in favour of an instant self-determining declaration of independence by that body itself. Resolutions were simultaneously passed both for the interim appointment of a four-man Council of State to replace the vanished Governor General as Head of State and also, as a palliative to Southern disaffection, for consideration (though not much was ever given) of the recent demand of the Southerners for federal status under the new constitution.

Britain with relief and Egypt with reluctance accepted the Sudan's own chosen technique for the formal winding-up of the Condominium. Azhari's crowning achievement was thus to ensure that the striking of the Co-domini's flags for the last time on 1 January 1956 took place with himself at the flag-pole.

Self-determination was thus complete. No further mention was made, then or later, by the new independent republic of a formal link with either of the Co-domini, though a sensible desire for close informal relations with Egypt was declarable now that the threat of absorption had been finally dispelled. Whether the old call for 'Unity of the Nile Valley' had ever been more in the Sudan than an anti-British and anti-Mahdist rallying cry is debatable. What is less open to question is the maladroitness of Egypt's response to it. Repeated claims in monarchist days to perpetual sovereignty over the whole valley showed a misjudgement of an emergent people's natural sensitivities; equally so did Egypt's undisguised manoeuvring thereafter to secure a dominant position once the other Co-dominus was ousted. The outcome might well have been more favourable to Egypt, had she played her hand from 1946 on with greater skill.

As for the relinquishment of British power (and British power is what the Condominium had been all about), this had of course been visibly under way since the promulgation of the Self-Government Statute in March 1953, if not earlier. Elsewhere, too, much had been happening to Britain's standing as the centre of an empire since Bevin's endeavour to reshape its philosophy a decade earlier. But the Sudan was the first dependency in Africa to cross the finishing line under the wind of change. This in itself may explain much of the head-shaking amongst members of the Political Service outside the Palace at what seemed to them the premature relinquishment of British control. Their reactions to the course of events described have not figured in this narrative account but will be discussed in chapters 5 and 6. All that will be said here is that the paternalist embrace which they extended, as members of a lifetime service, to those they were administering set them somewhat apart from colonial practitioners, posted from country to country, elsewhere. A similarly unique quiddity distinguishes the Sudanese people from other Arab and African subjects of empire. Together these peculiarities contributed to the amicable, almost jocular, atmosphere in which the transmission of power was effected in the Sudan and to the degree of personal goodwill which survived it.

3 The South West Arabian episode

There are no problems as complex as those of constitutional reform. Attack on innovations is inspired by partisan fanaticism: the defence of them wilts in the doubt of their efficacy.

Machiavelli

And in the case of sedition men do not effect what they wish unless they maintain some kind of peace with their fellow conspirators.

Saint Augustine

The British Empire's acquisition in 1839 of a toehold in South West Arabia, expanding over the century into a stockade with distant guard-posts and finally shrinking into the dimensions of a grave, is not an episode in British history which attracts much moral acclaim. When Captain Haines occupied Aden as a port of call in the name of the East India Company, morality of course was not an issue. In those days the criterion of imperial expansion was simply that of national interest, the potential advantage or disadvantage to the natives of the area being a matter of little or no concern. By that criterion the establishment of a port of call midway between the fabulous East and the feverish West – and Aden is the finest natural harbour along the whole sea-lane – should have received the unquestioning applause of the British authorities at both ends of that prized trade-route, particularly as it marked the upstaging of other ambitious European powers. The relative lack of interest shown by those responsible in Bombay in the achievements of Captain Haines and the treatment finally accorded to that courageous, imaginative but obstinate man after fifteen years (without leave) in command of his unenviable outpost are therefore all the more remarkable. Had he been a Frenchman pioneering France's imperial interests he would have ended his days in an honoured niche of the Pantheon in Paris instead of a debtor's cell in the prisons of Bombay. He has received, 120 years after his death, one scholarly tribute; other investigators have been less generous in their assessments.[1]

But Haines' prime relevance here is that he recognized, long before the powers in Bombay and London, that a coaling and trading station on this wild coast could only be maintained by pushing into the hinterland and keeping its turbulent denizens at bay by a combination of military prestige and diplomatic ingenuity. His premise was correct but the inescapable conclusions were never effectively drawn by the nineteenth century imperial policy-makers. The fateful expansion into the interior did indeed take place over the years but in so reluctant and half-hearted a fashion, compounded by the differing attitudes of London and Bombay, that the ultimate failure of the enterprise was, we may

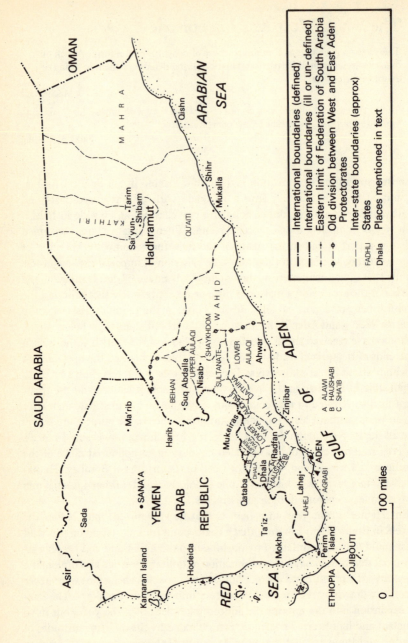

South West Arabia on the eve of independence.

OMAN

ARABIAN SEA

MAHRA

Qishn

Shihr

KATHIRI

Tarim
Sai'yun· ·Shibam

Mukalla

Hadhramut

QU'AITI

W A H I D I

SULTANATE

SHAYKHDOM

LOWER AULAQI

Ahwar

ADEN

SAUDI ARABIA

Ma'rib

BEHAN

Suq Abdalla
UPPER AULAQI

Nisab·

Harib

Zinjibar

OF

Mukeiras
AUDHALI
DATHINA
UPPER YAFA
LOWER YAFA
FADHLI

A ALAWI
B HAUSHABI
C SHA'IB

YEMEN

ARAB

REPUBLIC

SANA'A

DHALA
Dhala
Al
HAUSHABI

Radfan

GULF

Sada

Qataba

AGRABI
ADEN

Ta'iz·

LAHEJ
Lahej·

Asir

Kamaran Island

Hodeida

Mokha
Perim
Island

DJIBOUTI

RED SEA

ETHIOPIA

International boundaries (defined)
International boundaries (ill or un-defined)
Eastern limit of Federation of South Arabia
Old division between West and East Aden
Protectorates
Inter-state boundaries (approx)
FADHLI   States
Dhala   Places mentioned in text

0   100 miles

50

think, guaranteed from the start. To hindsight there were only two valid alternatives: either the whole hinterland should have been subjected to outright occupation and imperial disciplines, or Aden should have been isolated from it but rendered impregnable, leaving the interior to its own (or Ottoman or Yemeni) devices. Neither alternative was adopted.

Aden, it should be explained, had not in earlier days been the squalid collection of hovels and 800 villagers encountered by Haines. Indeed as early as 100 AD the name Eudaimon [Lucky] Arabia was specifically given to it by the anonymous author of the *Periplus of the Red Sea*. (By the time Eudaimon was Latinized to Felix, the term applied to the whole area.) Thereafter, long before Europe entered the scene, it had been a hugely prosperous port, enjoying both its landward role as the Eye of the Yemen (when Arabia *was* Felix) and its seaward role as the link, with the monsoon to back it, between India and the Levant.

The centuries passed. In the fifteenth the Portuguese altered the course of history by rounding the Cape. Thereby they restructured European trade-lanes to the East, destroying in the process Aden's ancient centrality, challenging Ottoman control of the frontiers of Islam and replacing the understood pattern of piracy along the coasts of Arabia with a new and unnatural one. Which of these developments was the main cause of Aden's decay scarcely concerns us here.

The substitution first of Dutch and then of British dominance of the Indian Ocean and the expulsion of the Ottomans from the Yemen by local uprisings continued the process of decline. In the seventeenth century the surge in world demand for the new luxury of coffee (a Yemeni invention) offered some reprieve; but Mokha, on the Yemen's Red Sea coast and nearer the centres of production, took pride of place. Moreover, by the mid-eighteenth century coffee plantations in the East and West Indies under European control were eating into the Yemen's profitable monopoly.

But trade advantages in Arabia were not what led Britain, through the agency of the East India Company, to plant her flag on its southern coast. Two more weighty matters successively exercised her policy-makers. Firstly they were facing European rivalry for predominance in and beyond the Indian Ocean. French privateers, using Mauritius as their base, had been challenging the East India Company's shipping for some years. But it was Napoleon's occupation of Egypt in 1798 that stirred Britain into taking more positive steps to protect her Indian possessions and the sea-lanes leading to them. Napoleon's eastward ambitions were successfully scotched by the defeat and expulsion from Egypt of his troops; and the situation looked comfortable enough for a time. It was not long, however, before Britain's ascendancy East of Suez was threatened by a different power in Egypt in the person of its viceroy, Muhammad Ali. As part of his plans to break free of his Ottoman suzerain and acquire an empire of his own he turned his attention, with French encouragement, to Arabia and the establishment of wider boundaries to his influence right across the Peninsula. In 1832 he occupied Mokha and other Yemeni coastal villages and was revealed to be bent on the conquest of inland Yemen and thereafter the rest of the Peninsula.[2] Palmerston's sharp eye for imperial advantage saw the need to block Muhammad Ali's ambitions.

Since steam navigation was now overtaking sail, the need for safe bunkering on the route to India had already been under study at both ends of that route. Haines, after carrying out detailed surveys of the coast of Southern Arabia, had reported on the advantages of acquiring Aden as a coaling station; and in 1837 he was authorized by Bombay to strike a cash deal for its purchase with the Sultan of Lahej, who owned it. The deal, though struck, went sour. The Sultan reneged on his bond, and Haines withdrew to Bombay. The conflicting views of the authorities in India and London on the best response are of interest here as foreshadowing the divided control that was to dog British policy in South West Arabia for a century.

Palmerston, distrustful of Muhammad Ali's activities in Yemen and by now further east,[3] was all for the Government of India re-occupying Aden with adequate British forces at its disposal.[4] The East India Company's Court of Directors in London, preferring the safety of sail and the Cape route, were against it; but its Secret Committee, the device used by the governmental Board of Control to side-step or overrule the court as a whole, was headed at this moment by an aspirant for Palmerston's favour. The Court's views on this particular issue were accordingly ignored.[5] In India too the authorities were not of one mind. Following the dismissal by Palmerston of a suggestion that the biddable Imam of Muscat should be encouraged to relieve India by doing the job himself,[6] the Governor in Bombay, with whom immediate responsibility lay, favoured military action: the Governor General in Calcutta, preoccupied at the time with the more important problem of countering Persian and Russian intrusions in Afghanistan, wanted no additional military enterprises in his domains. The slowness of communications compounded the confusion.

In the event Haines was finally provided by Bombay (without Calcutta's advance section) with two ships and a few men to secure, peacefully if possible, the re-occupation of the village ostensibly ceded under the Sultan of Lahej's bond two years before. As it transpired, the armed resistance of the Abdali tribesmen and their local allies was only overcome by an assault involving heroism of the astonishing kind almost taken for granted in the nineteenth century.[7] The British flag was hoisted once more over Aden on 19 January 1839 and was to remain there, for better or worse, for 128 years.

Meanwhile Muhammad Ali, who had made plaintive enquiries on hearing rumours of the original purchase of Aden, was brusquely told on Palmerston's instructions to keep his troops away from what was now a British possession.[8] He was further warned that Britain could not 'view with indifference any attempt to invade or conquer the country lying at and beyond the mouth of the Red Sea',[9] and would welcome signs of his withdrawing from the Yemen and concentrating on 'improving the administration of the provinces confided to him'. (The fact that he had already manifested his independence of the Porte was ignored.) In 1840 Palmerston, with the support of friendly European powers and of course the Ottoman Sultan, finally insisted on Muhammad Ali's withdrawal from Arabia and Syria.

A detailed account of the tribulations of Haines – or of his successors over the next hundred years – would be out of place here. One purpose of drawing attention to the start of the story and, in the following paragraphs, to certain features of what followed, is to illustrate a detectable pattern which repeated itself in one form or another from the start to the finish of British involvement in South West Arabia. Divided and sometimes discordant control between the policy makers at home and abroad is of course a familiar aspect of Britain's colonial history. In the case of Aden it was particularly acute,[10] and remained a continuing incubus to those on the spot, not only while the East India Company was responsible for India (until 1858) but equally thereafter, right up to the Raj's final surrender of its South West Arabian responsibilities to the Colonial Office in 1937. Even then the differing approaches of the various ministries in London with their conflicting priorities continued the problem in a different form.

Two things immediately became apparent to Haines. One was the extravagantly fractious nature of the tribal structures in the hinterland and their capacity for intrigue. The other was that the Aden station – whether its purposes were to be limited to a port of call and bunkering, whether it was conceived as the nucleus of a profitable commercial entrepôt, or whether its prime function was strategic – was not tenable without the contriving of accommodations with the inland tribes, or at least with those in the immediate vicinity. A port of call without a garrison would soon be overrun; and a garrison immured within its walls and forbidden to venture out of them would soon be locally regarded with derision, would denude the administrator in charge of any influence on the tribal scene and, in terms of morale, would quickly run to seed. From time to time the validity of these propositions was to be recognized by the authorities at one or other end of the imperial chain of command – Palmerston himself was quick to recommend to Bombay in 1839 the signature of Treaties of Friendship with the shaykhs in the vicinity of Aden threatened by Muhammad Ali. But no far-reaching policy conclusions were ever drawn or, if drawn, ever consistently or constructively acted upon. It is of course possible that, had there been an effectively paramount Arab (or Ottoman) authority controlling the interior, or had the promotion of such a

thing accorded with the wider perspectives of imperial policy, the maintenance by Britain of a purely civil and commercial settlement on the coast
could have been represented to such an authority as harmless, indeed bene-
ficial. In such circumstances its security might have been guaranteed. But
imperial policies over the years kept equally at bay Ottoman pretensions to
sovereignty, renewed soon after Muhammad Ali's withdrawal, and the claims
to lordship over the area of the Zaidi Imam of the Yemen. In the area itself
tribal particularism was, and remained until the end of the British presence (if
not longer), so extreme that the emergence of a paramount tribal head able to
speak for anyone else was never on the cards. Indeed the paradoxical feature of
tribal structure in South West Arabia was that in no ordinary sense was it
either tribal or structured – an oddity to which we shall return. Britain did
from time to time seek to build up the pre-eminence of the Sultan of Lahej in
the West, but this was never accepted by other ruling shaykhs. In the East, the
pre-eminence of the Qu'aiti Sultan of Mukalla was never in doubt; but the
Kathiris in their enclave resented it, and the Mahra and Wahidi were outside
his control.

Two other awkward aspects of the scene were to contribute their share to
the complexities of the problem with which Britain had landed herself.
Firstly, as the town and port of Aden evolved towards prosperity, the huge
influex of Yemeni labourers in search of a livelihood radically altered the
composition of its mixed community. The influx was needed to meet the
demand for labour; it was unstoppable for that and other reasons, and was
ultimately fatal. Secondly, the commercial enrichment of Aden, which became
part and parcel of British policy, and Britain's contrasting unconcern for the
development of the interior destroyed whatever community of interest could
otherwise have been nurtured between them and placed the one increasingly
out of sympathy with the other. The contrast between the two grew in inten-
sity over the decades and was certainly, if unwittingly, reinforced by British
policy. In Aden, as its wealth expanded, its expatriate merchants and
entrepreneurs – many of them, like its humbler bureaucrats, being Indian –
were simply there to make money and were only concerned with the hinterland as a source of labour or, to the modest extent relevant, of produce from
which a trading profit could be drawn. Since the Aden authorities were not
authorized to subject the interior to administrative control, the merchants
were naturally disinclined to challenge the gauntlet of tribal levies and
plunderings through which trade goods, such as they were, had to pass. The
commodities and contracting opportunities on which the settlement's prosperity depended, especially after its establishment as a Free Port in 1850, were
effectively independent of the tribal life-style and political disorganization
inland. The interior for its part continued to live by rules, primaeval but
cherished, of its own; and these were to prove distinctly more complicated

than anything of the kind experienced by the representatives of empire elsewhere in the Arab world.

Indeed, when the structure of the hinterland was finally studied, it proved to be hardly tribally organized at all: though the situation varied from area to area, it was not in general broken up into tribal patrimonies under patriarchal control of a familiar kind. Instead, whatever family, group or individual – autochthonous or immigrant – had been able to establish ascendancy in a particular locality became (though the term may have been a late accretion) the local *dawla* (government). The influence of a *dawla* – whether under-pinned by religious standing, peace-making reputation, diplomatic ingenuity or simply fighting prowess – sometimes extended quite widely, sometimes barely went beyond the gates of a hill-top fort. Sometimes a state consisted of a confederation of small tribes which scarcely recognized the primacy of a central family at all. The tribal and 'non-tribal' fractions which a *dawla* was able to regard as its subjects accepted or rejected the *dawla*'s suzerainty as the spirit moved them or as passing interests dictated. Often enough both the class of *qadi*s who dispensed customary justice and the dominant shaykhs within the domains of a *dawla* were tribally distinct from the latter; and the landowning tribesmen had little in common, socially or even ethnically, with the *dawla*'s other subjects, the landless and therefore inferior *ra'ya*.[11] What gave a *dawla* permanence and power was its ability to fuse the whole amalgam, by traditional rewards and penalties, into some kind of cohesion in pursuit of common interests against its neighbours or against outside interference.

The system – for it was a system, even if it was a System of Anarchy[12] – worked well enough on its own primaeval terms and to the satisfaction of those living by it until the 1880s, when the influx of precision rifles, largely contraband from Djibouti, set in train the disintegration of that system, making every rifle owner increasingly his own master.[13] Whereas in the past the relative prosperity of a *dawla* and its subjects had been a function of the former's ability to muster the latter for recognized common purposes, groups armed with accurate rifles were now able to pursue separate interests on their own. Altogether a weak *dawla* became as likely to be ignored or challenged by his subjects as to be obeyed. Almost more damaging to tranquillity was the effect of the new weapons on the practice of blood feuds – a feature of life in South West Arabia so widespread, so absorbing and so constant as to stultify almost all centripetal instincts.

Before, and even more after, this disruptive development, British attempts to reduce the shifting congeries of 'independent' rulers to orderly classification were consequently hazardous. From the outset of British penetration of the hinterland it became customary to speak of the 'Nine Tribes' as composing what was ultimately called the Western Aden Protectorate, but this was recognized as a gross oversimplification. When it became British policy in the

1880s to sign treaties (Protective or Exclusive) with independent *dawla*s, sultans, rulers, shaykhs or whatever, the number of such treaties signed by the Resident in Aden is not easy to establish, though in 1902 thirty were officially reported.[14] Later still when Advisory Treaties (signed only with the more important) replaced the earlier model for reasons to be mentioned, the precise total of these, too, figures differently in different sources.

These points are relevant for two reasons. Firstly, they illustrate the fragmented and centrifugal nature of the inland communities. Secondly, and by the same token, the *dawla*s were always hard-pressed to retain the allegiance of their adherents and prevent the dissatisfied from transferring it elsewhere or simply breaking away on their own. In one respect only were rulers and their subjects of one mind. This was that they all subscribed to the antipathy that marked, throughout a century of British domination, relations between the rich, structured and largely foreign township of Aden and the poverty-stricken, unstructured and largely xenophobic hinterland.

Decades were to pass before British, or British Indian, policy makers reconciled themselves to any serious need, in Aden's interest if no other, to introduce up-country even the rudiments of imperial control. To those governing India in the nineteenth century South West Arabia was a matter of concern only in the sense that other powers had to be kept out. When the Turks reoccupied the Yemen in the 1870s and posed a threat, Viceroy Tenterden took the plunge of proposing that South West Arabia should be taken into formal protection; but Gladstone was then in office and he had 'every conceivable objection' to such expansionist ideas, which might expose Britain to argument with other European powers.[15] The imposition of individual Protective Treaties was all the successor Tory Government thought appropriate; and the Government of India's 1886 plea that 'a small sum of money be spent on establishing once and for all an effective Protectorate from Shaykh Said [in the extreme west] to the borders of Oman' was again rejected.[16] Similarly in 1903, when Viceroy Curzon, in the context of boundary delimitations between Ottoman and British controlled areas, planned to step up intervention in the disputed frontier zone coupled with displays of strength in the area, the Secretary of State resisted the idea and closed the debate by warning Curzon that he 'would view with misgiving any tendency to extend the range of our interference with the tribes'.[17] The return of the Liberals to power in 1906 reduced still further the likelihood of any such expansionism. The 'old groove of masterly inactivity in Arabian politics' was the watchword recommended in that year by the India Office.[18] In any case the practical effect of Protective Treaties on the tribesman's way of life was negligible.

In Aden itself the impact of the British presence was very different. The opening of the Suez Canal in 1869 gave a tremendous fillip to Aden's importance, both strategically and commercially. Little Aden – the other peninsula enclosing the port area – had just been purchased from the *dawla* concerned to pre-empt renewed French aspirations in the area. (Disraeli's notorious acquisition six years later of the Khedive's shares in the Suez Canal was a similar shrewd stroke in the game against France.) The purchase of the coastal strip joining the two Aden peninsulas followed shortly; and steam having now finally replaced sail for oceanic shipping, Aden, already a main entrepôt in the region, was all set for prosperity. Not that commercial prosperity was synonymous with social progress. At the turn of the century the 'stagnation' of Aden, described as 'this uncared-for portion of the British Empire', was deplored in a *Times of India* editorial on 2 December 1902.

Even if funds were made available to develop Aden, its freedom to develop without interference from outside was seen to entail the clearer definition and the closer control of the inland *cordon sanitaire*. This in turn required an understanding with the Ottomans over the limits of their sovereignty to the north: hence the partially successful frontier delimitation exercise between 1902 and 1905. Three years later the Young Turks' revolution produced a new cause for concern, for the understanding reached between the Young Turks and the Yemeni Imam encouraged the latter to demonstrate by force of arms his ancient claims to suzerainty in and beyond the frontier zone.

At this point a brief account of these claims is needed. Before the British arrived on the scene, and despite the rise and fall of rival dynasties in successive power centres in the area over the preceding millenia, no strict geographical distinction had been made between north and south. The whole area – from Asir in the far north to Aden in the south, from the Red Sea in the west to the Empty Quarter in the east (and including perhaps the Hadhramut below it) – was loosely known as the Yemen. Having been Islamized early on, it was naturally regarded as part of the Islamic community and therefore subject to the attention of the rulers of Islam. In political terms this was especially the case when the Ottoman Empire sought to establish control over the whole *umma* (the community of Islam). The Yemen of course was included within that term, and by the sixteenth century Ottoman authority was installed in Sanaʿa. The extent to which it was recognized varied from area to area. Amongst those who resisted it, the Zaidi Imams, non-conformist Shiʿa, whose dynasty had established itself in the tenth century in the northern highlands, stood out prominently. They became powerful enough to oblige the Ottomans to withdraw in 1636 and to extend their own supremacy throughout much of the old loosely defined Yemen, claiming it in the rest.

At no stage, however, did the Ottoman Sultan renounce ultimate overlordship, and in 1849, after the withdrawal of the upstart Muhammad Ali, control was forcibly reasserted. By now the British had occupied Aden and had tentatively pushed their influence some way inland. Most of the hinterland chiefs in this area had long since established their independence of the Zaidi

Imam;[19] and never was Britain to admit either Zaidi or Ottoman sovereignty in the neighbourhood of Aden or indeed further inland and along the coast into the Hadhramut, whose sea-port capital, Mukalla, had also attracted imperial interest. In the successive bouts of confrontation which ensued, the Ottoman Sultan, to whom the Yemen was always a secondary concern, could more easily be warned off than could the Imam, whether the latter admitted formal subordination to Istanbul or not. While, therefore, the Sultan accepted in 1902 the delimitation of a boundary with the British zone, and although the resulting agreement was endorsed by the Anglo-Turkish Convention of 1910, the Imam's own claims remained unabated. Nor was he any the more inclined to renounce them when World War I brought the final collapse of the Ottoman Empire. Indeed Britain's poor performance in the Aden area during the war had been closely observed in Sana'a; for though Turkish troops advanced in 1915 to the very outskirts of Aden ('the Turks are on the golf-course', as a cable from the British military commander dramatically reported), no attempt was made to push them more than a few miles back before the Armistice. This apparent sign of British weakness, coupled with Britain's wartime moves to promote rebellion in the north by a rival aspirant for local power,[20] stimulated the Imam into demanding in 1917 that the whole of South West Arabia, Aden itself excluded, should be recognized as his. There was therefore no love lost between British and the Imam when the Armistice left the Imam on his own.

Nonetheless, the adoption of a coherent policy either towards the Imam or within the area under British 'protection' was complicated both at this stage and for the next twenty years by repeated changes in the division of imperial responsibilities in the area. Hitherto South West Arabia had been the Bombay Governor's responsibility under the supervision of the Viceroy at one end and the India Office at the other. Wartime needs and their financial implications had compelled in 1917 some redistribution as between India, the War Office and the Foreign Office. After the war, wrangling continued between the three of them; and very soon the fray was joined by the Colonial Office. Even within the latter opinions differed. In 1922 its influential Middle East Committee recommended the abandonment of all South West Arabia, save Aden and the adjoining Sultanate of Lahej – a proposal strongly resisted by the Resident and dropped. Four years later a rather similar proposal – to abandon to the Imam those inland shaykhdoms which he then occupied or claimed – was put forward by the Foreign Office in the interest of better relations with the Imam; but on this occasion the Colonial Office joined the Resident in resisting it.[21] Meanwhile the debate between India and the India Office, re-engaged in 1921, on the reallocation of responsibilities for South West Arabia and the financial implications of this[22] was only settled by Cabinet intervention in 1926. A bizarre situation then prevailed in which political responsibility for the hinterland lay with the Colonial Office, to which the Foreign Office had surrendered it (having earlier captured it from Bombay), while Bombay held on to administrative control of Aden town. Security responsibility lay with neither Bombay nor the Colonial Office but with the Royal Air Force on behalf of the War Office. By 1932 Bombay yielded its residual powers in Aden to the Central Government of India, though this scarcely answered pleas for simplification from the Resident.[23] Finally in 1937, largely because South West Arabia could scarcely be accommodated in India's new federal structure, the Viceroy, despite (native) Indian protest, gave Aden up. Accordingly political and administrative responsibility for both Aden and the interior was now for the first time in Colonial Office possession. During those kaleidoscopic twenty years the interests of the area itself had tended to be lost in the maze, a situation no less damaging to the cause of orderly evolution than the previous century of indifference from Bombay. The long-suffering man on the spot, by now a Governor rather than a Resident, at least knew what bit of what government to address.

Recognition that South West Arabia was emphatically part of the Arab rather than the Indian world was now complete, though in the absence of any other Arab responsibilities the Colonial Office simply added Aden to those of its Central African Department. But the elaboration of a 'forward policy' in the Protectorate was still subordinated to considerations of what would suffice to make Aden itself secure. This primarily depended on keeping the Imam at bay. Various attempts had been made during the twenties to reach an understanding with him. The mission mounted in 1925 by Sir Gilbert Clayton, whose diplomatic skills in negotiating with Arabs were formidable, came nearest to success. He himself believed that the Imam personally would have yielded on the key issue of withdrawal from areas occupied by him on the wrong side of the frontier, in exchange for deferment of the sovereignty issue, but that pressure from his xenophobe entourage frightened him into refusal.[24] Be that as it may, the incompatibility of British and Imamate objectives extended well beyond the disputed frontier zone in the west.

However, by the time the next initiative was taken *vis-à-vis* the Imam in 1934, the Imam himself needed a respite in the south since his northern territories were receiving unwelcome attentions from Ibn Saʿud. Reilly, the experienced Governor, set out to negotiate an understanding with him in Sanaʿa with some optimism. His enthusiasm was not universally shared in Whitehall. As usual, government departments were not of one mind over the treatment of South West Arabia. 'It will be eminently satisfactory', so a senior Colonial Office official minuted, 'if, despite the scepticism and lukewarmness (to put it mildly) of the FO and IO, then their coldness and finally the FO attempts to wreck the whole thing, Col. Reilly (whom the CO have backed throughout) brings this off.'[25] But bring it off he did. Or so it was thought. The Treaty of Sanaʿa,[26] signed in February 1934, included in its terms perpetual peace and friendship in exchange for Britain's recognition of the Imam as King of the Yemen and agreement to defer the settlement of the frontier pending the conclusion of definitive negotiations before the Treaty's forty-year term ended. It was over what could and could not be done in the area in the meantime that the wording gave scope for different interpretations. To the British it was crystal clear from the undertaking by both parties to 'prevent interference by their subjects or from their side of the frontier with the people inhabiting the other side' that the Imam at last recognized (if tacitly) the validity of the 1910 Anglo-Turkish Convention on the frontier. But what was meant by 'frontier'? Reilly himself reported (a trifle ambiguously) that 'a political and not a geographical boundary was intended'.[27] In the Arabic text, which it was agreed should prevail, the plural term *hudud* could indicate something distinctly less linear than the singular 'frontier' of the English text; and to the Imam the crucial provision in Arabic for the maintenance of the *status quo* prohibited any political or administrative changes in the British area generally.[28]

This was not how the British interpreted it. To them the Treaty placed a formal seal on their right to promote change and progress on their side of the frontier as delimited with the Turks – something which by the mid-thirties they had at last begun to recognize as a moral obligation. But the right to promote change was not admitted by the Zaidi Imam, apprehensive as he was of the effect upon his own Shafeʿi subjects of improvements in the condition of their fellow Sunnis in the adjoining British zone. His continuous meddling thereafter in the latter would be justified in his reasoning as a response to impermissible British alterations in the administrative *status quo*.

Not that London entertained any great enthusiasm for development of the interior, much less any thoughts of imposing direct rule as a means to that end. An astonishing symptom of this reluctance is that it was not until 1933 that the Governor obtained a single Political Officer to operate outside Aden in the vast western hinterland and another (following his own first visit to the interior of the Hadhramut) for the even vaster eastern area. Both those appointed – Hamilton in the west and Ingrams in the east – were men of remarkable calibre, but their intervention in the freedom of the *dawla*s' administrations (such as they were) was deliberately minimal. In the west Tribal Guards had earlier been established in the hope of enabling the *dawla*s to protect the trade routes passing through their territories: now, Government Guards had to be instituted to protect the passing through them of the Political Officer. In the east, for all the wealth it had long derived from Hadhrami commercial and indeed political influence in south-east Asia,[29] security up-country was even less prevalent, the ruling Sultans being disinclined, as well as unable, to enforce it. Ingrams made it his first task to achieve peace (and it was a remarkable achievement) between the '1400 separate governments'[30] regarded as subject to the Quʿaiti Sultan of Mukalla and the

Kathiri Sultan of Sai'yun (in whose names Ingrams acted) and to create a Hadhrami Legion to preserve this peace.

But now there was to be a major change in Britain's relations with the whole area following the surrender in 1937 of British India's residual interest, as already mentioned, and the concentration of political responsibility throughout in the hands of the Colonial Office. The change was heralded by the issue of the Aden Protectorate Order-in-Council of March 1937, which in effect extended formal British protection even to bits of the hinterland where no individual treaties had ever been signed, right up to the borders of Muscat and Oman.[31] One outcome was the gradual replacement of the old and barely meaningful Protective Treaties by Advisory Treaties signed with the rulers that mattered, beginning with the two important eastern ones of Qu'aiti and Kathiri. To be the recipient of an Advisory Treaty was a distinction of importance, since, like the much earlier treaties signed with rulers in the Gulf, the award conferred a kind of legitimacy and shield against internal challenge. On the other hand, the new model, of which thirteen were to be signed between 1937 and 1954, required recipients in the Western Protectorate (WAP), as we may now call it,[32] to accept the Governor's advice 'in all matters connected with the welfare and development of their states' and, in the case of the Eastern Protectorate (EAP), 'in all matters except those concerning the Mohammedan religion and custom'. If this sounds singularly like the principle of Indirect Rule fashionable earlier in Britain's African colonies, the practice was rather different. The Resident Agent and his Political Officers, in the WAP particularly, made as much use as they could of their new advisory status to insist on administrative improvements. There were, however, many ways in which the implementation of 'advice' could be avoided without ponderously invoking, as the Treaties allowed, appeal to the Colonial Secretary. And even where administrative progress was acceptable to a ruler, his subjects could make objections felt. Even such basic needs as the opening of roads was unwelcome to tribesmen whom the insecurity of trade routes provided with a life-style and a livelihood. The opening of schools and the recruitment of pupils was often resentfully identified with the ancient local practice of taking hostages for good behaviour. In 1940 Governor Reilly, though emphatic that 'we cannot now exercise suzerainty without improving conditions', referred sadly to the 'apathy and even open opposition of many of the chiefs and the innate conservatism of the tribes and their distrust of any measures that might disturb their old ways'.[33]

Less expectedly, the development of the interior and the extension of British intervention inseparable from it was unwelcome even to some British officials on the spot, who regarded as the ultimate unwisdom the Colonial Office policy of promoting British methods of administration and Western institutions of any kind in this peculiar Arab environment, where freedom from outside authorities was prized above all else. Ingrams himself was to become the most articulate critic of the 'colonial' approach; and he quotes a warning given to him in 1935 by none other than Lake, the Chief Secretary in Aden throughout the mid thirties, who was himself convinced of the folly of his own home department's missionary zeal. 'The nature of the Colonial Office,' he told Ingrams sorrowfully, 'is such that it cannot stop. It has to go on and on. It won't work.'[34] Nor did it work, for all the dedication of many good men going stolidly 'on and on' – not at least in the timescale which history was to allow. Though declared a 'forward policy', it was a policy of half-measures, neither hands-off nor hands-on.

The policy had outside critics too. Apart from the expected protests of the Imam, Fascist Italy, which had its own designs on Arabia following its seizure of Abyssinia, voiced strong objections. Halliday, who sees no virtue of any kind in Britain's record in the area, declares British fear of Italian influence to have been the major reason for 'Ingrams' Peace' and for the subsequent introduction of Advisory Treaties.[35] A Foreign Office memorandum of September 1937 does admittedly say that 'steps taken in the last year or two to tighten control over outlying positions in the Protectorate have been partly due to a desire to forestall Italian claims and intrigues'.[36] But keeping Fascist intervention out of the area (and there was much evidence of it) was assuredly not the principal motive. Rightly or wrongly, it was 'the nature of the Colonial Office . . . to go on and on'.

Another symptom of the sharpening imperial conscience was the passing in 1940 of the Colonial Development and Welfare Act and the wider application of the old 1929 Colonial Development Fund. Though a praiseworthy initiative to have been taken during the dark days of World War, the benefits received by Aden and the Protectorates were on too modest a scale, now and subsequently, to make a serious impact on the course of history there. Throughout the war the policy in the Protectorates pursued by the Governor (Hathorn Hall for most of it) and endorsed in detailed Colonial Office memoranda remained resolutely unchanged, based on 'the maintenance of treaty obligations and the furtherance and development of local Arab autonomy'. The promotion of administrative improvement was criticized by Ingrams in the East for interfering too much and by Seager, his opposite number in the West, for interfering too little. Governor Hall, though recognizing that 'a fundamental issue was at stake in dealing with petty chiefs guilty of hopeless misrule', was swayed by neither. 'Progress by persuasion', he argued, should be the watchword; and the Colonial Secretary agreed.[37] But to what longterm end? Hall saw 'such tutelage eventually leading to some form of federalism', amongst the endlessly feuding shaykhdoms; but there is no sign that anyone in authority was much concerned with serious planning for the future or even saw need for it. The pace of post-war history was not foreseen.

Nor was the fact that Britain's right to remain the dominant power in the Middle East after the war (if the Allies won it) would carry with it obligations to produce on a greater scale than before the means to advance its social and economic well-being. To many in the region, South West Arabia included, Britain's unrivalled standing in the Middle East had been revealed during the war to be precarious. In its aftermath the emptiness of the imperial coffers was scarcely understood there. Achilles had been shown to be pregnable: he was now considered niggardly as well.

Before proceeding with an account of Britain's hesitations in grasping the South West Arabian nettle during the decade following World War II, it will be as well to take a wide-angle look at her external preoccupations as they affected the Middle East, in one corner of which this nettle was growing. The decade concerned was to end with the Suez cataclysm of October 1956. Before that page was turned, five years of Labour government were followed by five of Conservative; but the preoccupations of both lay within the same pre-Suez frame of reference.

The imperial policies of the Labour period bore, as already described in the two previous chapters, the powerful imprint of Ernest Bevin. Two doctrines relevant to the present chapter were upheld by him. One was the vital strategic importance he attached to the Middle-East – an article of faith on which he was able to overrule Attlee's agnosticism with the help of the Service chiefs who even made its acceptance a condition of their soldiering on.[38] The second was Bevin's dedication to the principle of political collaboration, in place of old-style domination, in dealings with the empire's territories. On the first of these two counts South West Arabia, or at least a secure base at Aden, could only gain in importance, Indian independence notwithstanding. But how could South West Arabia fit into Bevin's scheme of imperial co-operation? Though Aden itself had prospered and might be ready to advance, the Protectorates had barely emerged from a century of disregard and political stagnation. By no visible means could Britain, particularly in an impoverished state, raise the Protectorates urgently to a level at which collaboration as between equals would be meaningful.

Measures were certainly taken to move things forward a bit in both. In the Crown Colony, for example, an embryonic Legislative Council to operate alongside the ten-year-old Executive Council was inaugurated in January 1947, a Labour and Welfare Department shortly after. A more pregnant development for Aden was the decision taken during the Abadan crisis in Iran in 1951 to site a major British Petroleum refinery there, its implications in the labour field passing unnoticed. Not far inland the important Abyan cotton scheme took off in 1947, and a few new schools and new medical provisions struggled into existence.[39] But in general the contrast between Colony and Protectorates became even more glaring; and the substitution of Ahmad as

63

King of the Yemen for the murdered Yahia in 1948 did not turn out to increase the prospect of Imamate acquiescence in any radical advances in the area under British protection. Indeed one of Ahmad's first acts was to seek Arab League endorsement for his stand on 'territorial rights' in the south. The *modus vivendi* Agreement[40] which he was nonetheless persuaded to sign in January 1951 after an Anglo-Yemeni Conference in London seemed momentarily promising but still left the *status quo* ill-defined and effectively unaltered. Yemeni incursions became progressively more marked and were to lead to a clash of opinions in Britain's Cabinet between the Colonial and Foreign Secretaries over the advisability of air reprisals on Yemeni territory.[41]

Nor did the Conservative take-over in England in October 1951 promise a change of tempo in the orchestration of development in South West Arabia. Two relevant but conflicting convictions in the politico-strategic domain were currently upheld. On the one hand, the dogma that Britain still retained paramount great-power responsibility in the whole area from Africa to Hong Kong was upheld with even greater confidence, and belief in the efficacy of a chain of bases from which to fulfil this role continued to hold sway. On the other hand, perspectives were dominated by the conviction that global war was once more the presiding threat to peace and that nuclear armament was the inescapable and only possible response to it. The incompatibility of these two convictions received little scrutiny. The fear of armed Soviet intervention in southern Asia notwithstanding, the more immediate threats to peace and British predominance there were of a local or regional nature – challenges to which the nuclear weapon and global strategy were irrelevant. To the extent that such challenges were foreseen, the belief that they could be dealt with militarily on the cheap – without expensive re-equipment, let alone additional Service manpower in the area – was equally unscrutinized by the political policy-makers. It is true that each of the three Armed Services, which had a genuine concern for the maintenance of Britain's world standing as well as for their individual effectiveness (and career structure), steadily protested at the economies to which its own re-equipment was subjected; but such inter-service competition for bigger shares of the limited defence budget only underlined the defects in overall planning and co-ordination. The whole problem was compounded by the differences in their approach to it of the defence departments on the one hand and, on the other, of the political departments concerned (Foreign, Colonial and Commonwealth Relations Offices). The former have in the nature of things to plan well ahead: the latter were inclined, and only equipped, to deal with problems as they arose. So far as there was at this time a strategy for military intervention in the outposts of empire, this was based on the twin concepts – and they were little more than concepts – of a strategic reserve in the UK and of air-lift capabilities. It has also to be remembered that in the aftermath of war the British electorate entertained no enthusiasm for expensive peace-keeping overseas.[42]

How did all this effect our area? The importance of Aden as one of Britain's chain of bases was taken as read. But as a strategic base it was hardly better equipped or manned than it had been in the previous century; and as for the forcible imposition of discipline in the fractious hinterland and its protection from Yemeni (or other) incursions, the only British instrument at hand consisted of a few RAF aircraft. Until 1956 the Aden-based Protectorate Levies remained the only ground troops at the Governor's disposal. Moreover, the loss in 1954 of Britain's base in Egypt led, after much heart-searching, to the transfer of Middle East Command Headquarters to Cyprus (and of some elements to Libya) – indifferently sited to supervise the security of southern Arabia.

Meanwhile on the political front in the area itself, and in the face of growing criticism from outside, measures were adopted to re-vamp British influence and acceptability, though the two were by no means synonymous. In the Colony the Municipal Council was given in 1953 an elected majority, Aden College was opened, a Broadcasting Service was inaugurated to counter external ones. In the hinterland, Sultan Fadhl of Lahej having been dismissed as mentally unstable, further Advisory Treaties were signed with his replacement and with two more Western rulers. In January 1954 Governor Hickinbotham assembled the treaty shaykhs of the Western Protectorate at Lahej to canvas to them the concept of federal union (and instructed the Resident Adviser in Mukalla to act similarly in the Eastern Protectorate – a project which sank without trace). A much earlier Resident, Stewart Symes, who was subsequently to show himself a progressive Governor General of the Sudan, had actually taken a similar initiative, also at Lahej, in 1928; but the assembled shaykhs had shown themselves extremely wary of any collective measure that might lead to the removal of their individual treaties of protection, and even the annual meetings to which they did then agree, as a means of settling disputes and discussing problems such as common defence against the Yemen, were abandoned by Symes' successor, Hathorn Hall. The latter's argument was that the Lahej Pact, as it was called, 'did not achieve results commensurate with its elaborate and expensive facade', the chiefs showing themselves 'to be still in too primitive a social and political state to bear the application of a centripetal force that was not of their own choice'.[43] Now, two decades later, Hickinbotham tried again.[44] But his proposals, at least in the form sanctioned by the Colonial Office,[45] aroused no more enthusiasm than those of Symes – not only because of the rulers' congenital particularism but also since they could be represented or misrepresented, and immediately were so by eager critics in Cairo and elsewhere, as a trick designed to consolidate colonialist control. The opportunity was seized by Egypt and the Yemen to promote tribal dissidence both by the media over the air and, on the ground, by the distribution of rifles smuggled in from the north. Ominous desertions in the Protectorate Levies were one response.[46]

A concurrent and more important omen in Aden itself was the proliferation of trades unions. Trade unionism had initially been promoted by Hickinbotham who had witnessed, as Manager of the Port Trust before his appointment as Governor in 1951, the Colony's 'disgraceful' labour conditions.[47] Indeed he remained to the end critical of the attitude of Aden employers, most of them expatriate, to their workers. What he did not foresee was the longer term consequence of encouraging the largely Yemeni labour force to organize itself. For in the year of the Suez débâcle the number of unions leapt in a few months from eight to twenty-four, when they engaged in a wave of strikes and formed a Confederation (ATUC), the politicization of which was to prove the biggest single problem confronting the authorities.[48]

Yet another ominous development in 1956 was the signature in April by Egypt, Saudi Arabia and the Yemen of the Jedda Military Pact. For what was happening in South West Arabia could by this time no longer be isolated from the wider Arab world. If the future of the Sudan had been treated largely as a function of Britain's relations with Egypt, the future of South West Arabia was now subject to much wider Arab and international pressures under the rising and (from Britain's point of view) baleful star of Gemal Abdulnasser. Openly committed as he was to ridding the Middle East of Western domination, everything seemed to be going his way. The Bandung Conference of 1955 had confirmed his stature amongst the non-aligned. Britain's base in Egypt had already been successfully negotiated away. King Saʿud, partly owing to his irritation with Britain over the Buraimi dispute, was happy at this stage to contribute to the removal of British influence from Arabia. In March 1956 General Glubb was dismissed from his key position in Jordan. And now, in April, the Jedda Pact gave Nasser his entrée into the previously closed world of the Yemen, close to another British nerve centre.[49]

Britain's problem in that nerve centre was how to satisfy nationalist stirrings in Aden Colony without jeopardizing sovereign control, how to rationalize the chaotic separatism of the Protectorate *dawla*s, and how to do both without the two processes getting awkwardly out of step. A massive exercise in August–September 1955 by the Colonial Office to establish an agreed 'Long Range Policy' for the area was marked by the vigorous disagreement of Governor Hickinbotham with the policy, as finally approved, of treating the future of the Protectorate in isolation from that of the Colony.[50] In May 1956 the tone of the Conservative Government's attitude was set by authorizing Lord Lloyd, a junior Minister for the Colonies, to make the following announcement in Aden during a visit to the area:

I should like you to understand that for the foreseeable future it would not be reason-able or sensible or in the interests of the Colony's inhabitants for them to aspire to any aim beyond that of a considerable degree of internal self-government . . . Her Majesty's Government wish to make it clear that the importance of Aden both strategically and economically within the Commonwealth is such that they cannot foresee the possibility of any fundamental relaxation of their responsibilities for the Colony.[51]

As for the Protectorates, though Hickinbotham, on the basis of the Long Range Policy paper, had just urged the Western rulers once more to consider some form of closer association, Lord Lloyd said nothing to encourage reviv-ing the idea of federation as a step towards nationhood, let alone towards independence. To do him justice the many rulers he called on during his tour showed no inclination to discuss the federal proposal, each of them simply taking the opportunity to demand greater protection against Yemeni-Saudi subversion and more explicit assurances that Britain intended to stay.[52] But if his message invited no acceleration in the hinterland, it applied a positive brake to expectancy in the Colony. Elsewhere in the changing Middle East Britain's policy was at least in movement (witness the Baghdad Pact, later re-edited as CENTO, Eden's 'NATO for the Middle East'). Her only concern in South West Arabia seemed to be the maintenance, against whatever odds, of her sovereign rights in Aden.

Two months later Nasser nationalized the Suez Canal Company. The war which followed marked not only the end of the decade we have been consider-ing. The history of the Middle East and Britain's standing in it would never be the same again. If Britain's determination to hold fast indefinitely to her base in Aden was undiminished, indeed enhanced, the odds against her doing so lengthened.

As the dust of Suez settled, no fundamental change was visible in Britain's attitude to her East of Suez role. Sandys' 1957 Defence White Paper, though recognizing the inadequacy of Britain's strategic reserve, still considered the nuclear deterrent to be the symbol of her continuing greatness and the prime requirement of national defence. Conventional forces had to suffer, and improved air-lift provisions together with the formation of various specialized military units were the only conspicuous advance in their ability to meet the risks of non-nuclear 'limited war', such as South West Arabia (amongst other areas) might present.[53] How then did the situation there look on the ground at this stage of early 1957?

Aden, whose ranking as one of the four biggest bunkering ports in the world was suffering severely from the closure of the Suez Canal, was now a city of 137,000, over a third of the total being immigrant Yemeni workers. Within the local community, party politics of a structured kind were still, as the next Governor was to observe, sadly undeveloped; but all three parties which did exist demanded change.[54] Even the old and toothless Aden Association stood for internal self-government within the Commonwealth. The South Arabian League (SAL), which had roots outside the Colony in Lahej as well as within it, had earlier called for union of the Colony with the Protectorates and more recently (a source of internal dissension) for union with the Yemen too. The aims of the Aden-based United National Front (UNF), formed in 1954 and now consisting of the more ardent nationalists together with a break-away leftwing of SAL and a number of 'Free Yemeni' exiles from the north,[55] were for union of Aden, the Protectorates, a 'reformed' Yemen and even Oman as a single independent state. (The point left unstated by both SAL and UNF was how the envisaged state would be run and by whom.) Of a more covert nature, outposts of the Arab Nationalist Movement and of the Syrian Ba'th were quietly at work under outside guidance. On none of these political activists were the implications of Suez lost – even without constant reminders from Cairo and Sana'a, whose broadcasters had just introduced the emotive term 'Occupied South Yemen'. As yet, but not for long, ATUC and its member unions were broadly ready to listen to advice from sympathetic representatives of the British TUC and were ostensibly more concerned with improving conditions of work than with invading the corridors of power. The Aden housing situation, already gravely inadequate, had been worsened by the stationing there since October 1956 of a second British battalion. It was shortly to be made graver still by the transfer to Aden of Britain's Middle East Command – an embarrassment which Governor Luce privately deprecated.

As for the hinterland, despite modest trappings of development, most of the cavalier rulers still preferred to prance jealously round their separate paddocks than to harness themselves together and enter the arena as a body. Immediately after Hickinbotham had made his March 1956 appeal to them, the young and ambitious Sultan Ali of Lahej had sought to set up a committee under his own chairmanship to explore the modalities of federating. But this had been discouraged by the Governor as suspect and self-seeking.[56] Moreover the Sultan's involvement in the activities of the South Arabian League – now canvassing independence for a union of Protectorate and Colony – was growing increasingly undisguised. Security in the Western Protectorate was helped neither by the constant interventions of the Imam (who was on the point of receiving six shiploads of Czech arms[57]) nor by the murder in August 1956 in Dhala of the Protectorate's leading peace-maker Muhammad Darwish.

Meanwhile the Eastern Protectorate, of which we have said little, was absorbed by the prospects, fanciful though they then proved, of oil being discovered in one or other of its sultanates. The separatist inclinations of the four Hadhrami sultans, from each other as well as from the Western Protectorate, were thereby accentuated. More disturbingly, they were now beset by mounting rebellious agitation. The decline in Hadhrami career-making in south-east Asia had sent many young men elsewhere, not least to Arab countries where they readily adopted the 'socialist' revolutionary cause. Its doctrines spread through their agency to their homeland.[58] Moreover, the sultans' ability to dominate their scattered subjects had always been dependent on the more immediate local influence of such proxy elements as the wealthy and respected but sometimes critical al-Kaff family in Tarim. Since sultanic rule (under advice) was seen by Britain as the only option, powers behind thrones had to be accommodated and opposition groups forcibly suppressed. The two central Sultans, Qu'aiti and Kathiri, were ready enough to accept British help in reinforcing their own grip but were even less disposed than their more backward counterparts in the WAP to submit to closer imperial disciplines or to face, by visibly doing so, growing anti-imperialist criticism from elsewhere. The most remote of the four – the widely dispersed and largely non-Arabic speaking Sultanate of Qishn and Socotra – was barely administered at all.

Into this unpromising scene, on the eve of the Suez War, Luce, fresh from the Sudan, had arrived to replace Hickinbotham as Governor. Trevaskis, the WAP Resident and progenitor of the federal concept, had long experience of struggling against the odds to galvanize the *dawla*s. The new Resident in the EAP was Boustead, a lovable eccentric: not one to rock boats but certainly one to entertain the crew – including Luce, who found the fustiness of imperial Aden 'as depressing as stale tobacco smoke'. If disproportionate space is given here to Luce's governorship, this is largely because, to hindsight, it was in *his* four years that the die was cast. He was by general consent the 'most states-manlike Governor Aden ever had', setting on the scene, rendered jittery by the Suez fiasco, a 'tone of quiet confidence'.[59] Had his more radical recommendations, been accepted in London, it is just possible that the writing on the wall might have been erased and a more orderly rubric substituted. But they were not accepted; and though his successors continued for some time to express optimism, the critical years were Luce's.

Bound as he was, on first arrival, by his Government's insistence that there could be no fundamental relaxation in British sovereign control of Aden 'for the foreseeable future', his immediate conclusion[60] was that the old idea of federalizing the hinterland should not be actively pushed. For if a federation were established, this would clearly lead to a demand for independence; and an independent hinterland could not be squared with a dependent Aden. What he saw as vital in the interior was two-fold: firstly, evidence that the treaty promises of protection meant what they said and, secondly, a wholly new dimension of development funding. Only by these means could the tribesmen see merit in the British connection. The extension of British administrative intervention over the past twenty years had meant increasing interference in the freedom of traditional life-styles with few material advantages to offset that loss. Tribal disaffection was also an easy target for Yemeni trouble-making. The only effective answer was a manifest heave-ho on development, which was in any case a moral obligation. The response from London was not encouraging.

At the expense of jumping ahead, a summary of the subsequent evolution in Luce's thinking,[61] is worth injecting at this point to illustrate both the readiness of a latter-day imperial proconsul to meet changing circumstances with a changing policy and the reluctance of a latter-day imperial government to give him the means to pursue it. Within a year Luce was arguing that the pull of Arab nationalist fervour made it idle to imagine that the position in Aden could be held for more than a few years by foot-dragging constitutional concessions. In the WAP four rulers had just spontaneously resurrected the federal project; and early federation with the prospect of independence to follow now seemed to him the best way of securing for all of them a more respectable posture in the Arab World. Though not contemplating an early withdrawal by Britain, which would mean abrogating treaties and breaking faith with friends, he now favoured a commitment to gradual disengagement over a period of ten years during which a successor state, covering both Aden and the hinterland, could be built up with a fair chance of determining its own destinies in treaty relationship with Britain. A year later, though federation – of the Western Protectorate, the Eastern remaining disparate and aloof – had been accomplished in March 1959, Luce recognized that time was running out. However, the possibility of a merger between Colony and Federation was now at least in the air; and continuing use of the Aden base would, he argued, be better secured by negotiating treaty rights with an independent entity than by insisting on the indefinite retention of sovereignty. Even if such an approach was unsuccessful, it would be, as the Forces Commander in Aden shrewdly observed, a 'less expensive way of losing a base'. The merger idea hung fire, for neither party was yet ready for it; but by September 1960 and with his own departure imminent Luce was recommending to London, for discussion with his designated successor, the surrender of British sovereignty within two years, the conversion of Aden Colony into a Protectorate and the simultaneous encouragement of its merger with the protected Federation. At every stage his views were too radical for his masters in London. We must now return to 1957 and examine the fraught background against which they evolved during those critical four years.

Galvanized by Suez, Arab zealotry, so far as it impinged on South West Arabia, was already actively hostile to the British presence there. Apart from anti-imperialist propaganda on the air, this hostility manifested itself on the ground through the ready agency of the Imam. The idea of substituting subordination to the Imam for subordination to Queen Elizabeth held, it is true, little or no attraction for the Protectorates, let alone for the more politically conscious Adenis to whom the Imam's Zaidi despotism was repellent. But both were ready in their different ways, as a means of extracting conces-

sions from Britain, to exploit the Imam's claim to overlordship, his pinprick-
ing breaches of the *status quo* across the frontier and the impact on outside
opinion of his depiction of Britain as the aggressor. Much more dangerous in
London's eyes were the wider objectives behind Nasser's patronage of the
Imam and the readiness of the Saudi policy-makers of the time to support
them.[62] If Eden's obsession with 'toppling Nasser' collapsed with Eden, the
problem of dealing with Nasser's potent brand of anti-imperialism remained
unsolved; and the belief that a solution was essential as part of the West's
defences against Soviet penetration occupied Luce's thoughts as well as those
of Westminster. The extent of the Soviet threat to the Middle East may have
been exaggerated, but it was a prime concern of all Western establishments of
the time.

The conundrum which Britain never solved was how to harness Arab
opinion against the perceived Soviet threat to the Arabs while simultaneously
defusing the Arab threat to herself. In the context of South West Arabia it was
judged impolitic to lash out at the Imam and thus strengthen the hostility of
the other Arabs at the very time when some kind of accommodation with Arab
aspirations was recognized as essential in measuring up to the greater Soviet
challenge. The awkwardness of steering a consistent course in these circumstances can be illustrated by two conflicting aspects of current British policy
towards the Imam. On the one hand, by treating the Imam's incursions into
South West Arabia with a certain delicacy, Britain sought to avoid Arab
castigation: on the other, the Foreign Secretary failed to push for a positive
understanding with the Imam's Crown Prince, Badr, when he visited London
for discussions in November 1957 on his way (significantly) to Moscow.[63]

The promotion in the Middle East of the kind of anti-Soviet consensus
Britain hoped for was made no easier by such local developments in mid-1957
as the revolt of the Imam of Oman against the Sultan of Muscat or the
attempted dethronement of King Husayn of Jordan – both these unwelcome
initiatives having the support, covert or open, of such outside Arab governments as were caught up in the anti-imperialist fervour generated from Cairo.
By early 1958 Nasser created further problems for Britain by establishing the
union of Egypt with Syria and securing the improbable adherence to this
'socialist' union of the conspicuously non-socialist Kingdom of Yemen.

Amongst the nationalist groups in the Aden area to be fired by this Nasserite
coup de théâtre was the increasingly anti-British South Arabian League, which
declared in favour of South West Arabia also joining the United Arab States
(as the tripartite union was called). So did Sultan Ali of Lahej, who was
thereupon dismissed from office in July 1958 on the grounds that by communicating with the governments of Egypt and the Yemen he had breached
his treaty with Britain.[64] Most of the Lahej soldiers defected to the Yemen,
taking the State funds with them. Disturbances in the Colony were such that

71

the Governor declared a state of emergency, which was not lifted for twelve months.

It was at this stage, and partly as a response to the goings-on in Lahej, that six Western rulers flew to London, and on 14 July 1958, after discussions with the Colonial Secretary, Lennox Boyd, announced their decision to federate:[65] a promising step in the British view but somewhat overshadowed as a news item by the bloody overthrow on the very same day of the broadly pro-British monarchy in Iraq. The concomitant troubles in Jordan and the Lebanon were further evidence of the potency of the Nasserite spell.

In Aden itself the April 1957 reopening of the Suez Canal had restored prosperity, but not peace. Violent disturbances in October 1958 following the imprisonment of two journalists for sedition led to a major attempt by the Governor to control the trouble-making Yemeni workforce by forcibly repatriating 240 of its members. The following month, with plans gestating in London for the granting of independence to nearby Somaliland, the decision was announced of a less far-reaching constitutional concession in Aden Colony. The Legislative Council, which had been wholly nominated on its foundation in 1947 and given an elected minority in 1955, would now have an elected majority. The Aden Municipal Council[66] already had one; and since at least half of those elected to it were ardent nationalists, it was felt that any substantial widening of the franchise in the elections for the much more important Legislative Council was unacceptably hazardous. The elections in January 1959 were consequently boycotted by 63 per cent of the restricted electorate of 21,500. The boycott was contrived by the UNF and ATUC (now virtually indistinguishable) and their political mentors in Cairo, who declared the setting up of a legislative body on so limited a franchise to be another colonialist trick. The franchise issue was indeed a thorny one: the best the Governor could do about it was to set up a committee with the unhappy task of defining who was an Adeni as liberally as possible.[67] To Luce himself even a 27 per cent poll was not too discouraging; and at least a Legislative Council with an elected and moderate majority would now be there for three years.

The Federation of the Arab Emirates of the South, as it was first called, was formally inaugurated the following month. In the related treaty document defining the Federation's relations with Britain and guaranteeing British protection, the most important clause, as Luce saw it, was that which enshrined the promise of ultimate independence.[68] This did not escape notice in the Colony; and at a press conference questions were asked of Lennox Boyd who was in Aden for the inauguration. He parried them by declaring it premature either to fix a date for the Federation's independence or to talk about the Colony eventually joining it.

This latter possibility was of course under British scrutiny, and Luce apparently secured agreement in London to the preparation of a statement envisaging such a merger. Authority to release it, however, was steadily with-held. For if the 'Long Term Policy' of August 1955, with its explicit prefer-ence for keeping Colony and Protectorate apart, had by now been tidied away, there were still voices in the Conservative Government, notably that of Julian Amery, Minister of State for the Colonies, resistant to any constitutional step which might jeopardize British control of the Aden base. Its maintenance, as *The Times* expressed it on 12 February, was now essential to secure the flow of oil from the Persian Gulf – a new strategic imperative. By this stage Luce's own view, shared by Heath (later Air Marshal Sir Maurice),[69] the Commander of British Forces in the Arabian Peninsula, was that the preservation of British rights to use the base would be better sought by means of a treaty, negotiated while goodwill still existed, than by the forcible maintenance of sovereignty. The key date by which they considered a merger of the Colony and the Federation essential was, understandably enough, the end of 1962 when the tenure of the Colony's newly established and reasonably moderate Legislative Council would expire.

The aspirations of 'progressive' Adenis for incorporation in a wider Arab entity, that is, the United Arab States (of Egypt, Syria and the Yemen), were at this stage held in check by the fear of finding themselves administered by the Imam. If, however, a republican revolution occurred in the Yemen – and there were constant rumours that one was imminent – Luce himself reckoned that the position in South West Arabia might become untenable.

Already the handling of the increasingly politicized trades unions with their largely Yemeni membership was a major problem. Strikes proliferated, reach-ing eighty-four in 1959. Attempts were made, with British TUC assistance, to improve labour relations; but political abuse (as the British saw it) of the strike weapon resulted in the production of new industrial legislation.[70] Based on the advice of British ex-TUC officials and promulgated in August 1960, this made strikes illegal without prior reference to arbitration by an Industrial Court. Despite outside criticism of the ordinance from the ILO and elsewhere, it did achieve at one level a measure of success; but ATUC itself was by this time less interested in industrial relations than in opposing colonialism and in political confrontation with Britain's evolving constitutional plans for the Colony.[71] Indeed, under the leadership of Abdullah al-Asnaj, ATUC largely replaced the United National Front as the main focus of political activity there.

There were of course political dissidents in the hinterland too, attracted by the increasingly anti-British posture of the South Arabian League. But to the British these were, or seemed to be, a nuisance of an old and manageable kind. Moreover, by the time Luce left in September 1960, the Federation embraced the whole Western Protectorate (save one small area) and one Eastern state, the adjoining though somewhat isolated Wahidi, which had little in common with the rest of the EAP. No observer was surprised that the machinery of togetherness worked, so far, indifferently well: the wonder was that it worked at all, particularly with so little material, or even moral, backing from the Government in London. What seemed to worry the federal ministers most, however, was the speed of democratization in the Colony and the powers given to 'jumped-up nobodies' there, coupled with rumours of its approaching autonomy and even independence. At a final meeting which the federal leaders requested of Luce to voice their fears, the Sharif of Beihan, a robustly Tudor figure, wittily observed that if the British Government ever decided to leave the Colony, they should hand it back to its original owner, the Sultan of Lahej – his own longstanding enemy. Luce could only tell them that his successor would be considering what should happen to Aden after December 1962 (that key date) and agreed that the future of Colony and Federation should not be considered in isolation.

Whatever satisfaction the federal ministers may have drawn from this can hardly have been strengthened by the motion put to the Aden Legislative Council a few days later, on 12 August, indicating the popular wish for full independence within two years – even though a less far-reaching motion was in fact adopted. The Federalis, as we had better henceforth call them, were also uncomfortably aware that ATUC and the extreme nationalists were loudly calling for the withdrawal of Britain from the Colony and for the union of Aden, the Protectorates and a 'reformed' Yemen in a single republican state, linked with the UAR. Luce's own final recommendations to London were, as already noted, that before the end of 1962 Aden should be released from British sovereignty and converted into a Protectorate, covered by the treaty with the Federation but retaining its individuality within it like the other member states.[72] The moderates in Aden, on whose goodwill Britain depended, would see merit in joining forces with the Federation: if left on their own by Britain's relinquishment of direct colonial control, they would be quickly overrun by the Nasserist caravan. The Federation meanwhile needed much greater financial and material support to give it teeth and substance.

Sir Charles Johnston, who now replaced Luce, was a fine scholar and distinguished diplomat but lacked colonial administrative experience to guide him. He found no instant backing in London for Luce's radical proposals. Moreover, he was faced on arrival in Aden with directly opposite advice on the merger idea from his staff in the Colony and his staff in the interior, each advancing the cause of its respective parishioners. For if merger was to come, the Adenis wanted to take over the interior: the interior wanted to take over Aden. His own immediate impressions were that Colony and Protectorate were 'absolutely complementary' and their merger obviously desirable.[73] In view of the misgivings about a merger evident in both and reflecting the age-old dissension between them, his recommendation was for tripartite discussions between the British Government and them, aimed at securing acceptance

Aden in the dark.

of principle, deferring the problems of detail to which the merger would in practice give rise. Meanwhile the next stage in constitutional advance in the Colony should be visibly elaborated. What may seem in retrospect to be missing was a sense of the extreme urgency of material measures to give plausibility and conviction to the Federation, or an awareness that Arab revolutionary fervour could not be kept at bay by diplomatic gradualism. Tripartite discussions did take place in London with the hardpressed Colonial Secretary, Iain Macleod, but not until June 1961. In preparation for them the options were twice discussed by the Cabinet during May. 'The real problem', so Prime Minister Macmillan uninhibitedly recorded in his diary was 'how to use the influence and power of the Sultans to help us keep the Colony and its essential defence facilities'; and the plan approved at the second discussion was 'to merge the Colony with the Federation of Rulers and give as much power as we can to the Sultans who are on our side'.[74] When Macleod presented the proposals to the tripartite conference, surprisingly everyone agreed in principle that merger, preceded by constitutional reform in Aden, would be an admirable thing:[75] it was only when they returned home that the practical difficulties re-surfaced.

The biggest of them, though not then rated so highly, was the intense

75

opposition within ATUC to any kind of merger sponsored by Britain. Since the tripartite talks were ministerial, there was no question of inviting non-governmental leaders such as al-Asnaj of ATUC to participate. It was from about this time that al-Asnaj began to receive the favourable attentions of the British Labour Party, a development which marked the widening of an ominous crack in the hitherto broadly bi-partisan approach to the South West Arabian problem of Conservative and Labour Parties or at least of their leaders. The Labour Party's apparent adoption of al-Asnaj as the best bet was followed by their despatch to Aden a few months later of a fact-finding mission led by George Thomson. He was, as one observer put it, 'given the treatment' by ATUC and was even privily spirited into the Yemen to meet tribal dissidents who had defected there.[76] The Federal leaders, whose intelligence sources always kept them abreast of what took place in Aden, were understandably aghast at these indications of the partiality of Her Majesty's Opposition for their declared enemies.

As 1961 advanced, however, two developments must have encouraged the ruling party in London to believe that Britain's position in the Arab world was mending. In August the Kuwait crisis, involving an apparent threat from Iraq to the shaykhdom's newly independent integrity, enabled Britain to demonstrate its military ability to protect an Arab friend. The operation – based on Aden – also served to vindicate the Services policy of reshaping their potential to meet the needs of 'limited war' overseas. Secondly, in October Syria broke off the union with Egypt; and the collapse of the United Arab States carried with it the ostensible separation of the Yemen from Nasser's embrace. But if this was welcomed in Britain as meaning an end to Egypt's ability in physical terms to cause trouble in the area, it was to prove a notable miscalculation. A development further afield brought more damage to stability in the Eastern Protectorate: the pattern of revolutionary change in south-east Asia impoverished the Hadhramut, whose relative affluence had always come from there.

The Colonial Office had during these years a trayful of problems. South West Arabia was not at the top of the pile; and repeated changes of Colonial Secretary – four in the space of three years – were not calculated to secure urgent attention to problems near the bottom. Sandys, who took over in mid-1962, certainly addressed all problems with impressive impatience, though that is not the same as a sense of urgency. Thus when he convened another conference[77] of Adeni and Federal ministers in July 1962 to solve remaining difficulties over the next step towards a merger, his method of securing their agreement was to prolong discussion throughout the night until everyone present was too exhausted to offer further resistance. On paper his achievement was considerable, bearing in mind that the 1962 Defence White Paper had, with strong US encouragement,[78] upgraded the importance of

Colonial Secretary Duncan Sandys with ministers from Aden Colony and the Federation at constitutional talks in London, August 1962

maintaining and reinforcing Britain's strategic bases east of Suez. The agreement sketched out appeared to solve the basic problem that, whereas the Adenis wanted constitutional advance (i.e. the complete Adenization of both Executive and Legislative Councils) before a vote on the merger, the Federalis wanted Aden's acceptance of the merger before this was jeopardized by constitutional advance. The ingenious formula now devised sought to side-step the problem. The merger proposal would be put to the existing Adeni Legislative Council for approval but would envisage constitutional advance in Aden coinciding with 'accession day'. Adeni misgivings over absorption into a federation recognized as backward were to be allayed by a clause giving Aden the right to opt out after six-year trial. Britain's own purposes would be served by excluding the sovereign base itself from control by the new federation.[79] Altogether the ingenuities were signal; but they reckoned without the growing determination of ATUC and its new political manifestation, the People's Socialist Party (PSP), animated if not controlled by Cairo, to disrupt them.[80]

Sandys pursued the ministers home with a letter formally setting out the agreed proposals, to take effect from 1 January 1963, and confirming that it was Britain's intention to lead the people of South West Arabia 'as soon as practicable to sovereign independence'. The proposals were put to the unreformed Aden Legislative Council on 26 September 1962. Despite, or perhaps because of, violent PSP demonstrations and the arrest of al-Asnaj, they just scraped through.[81]

The following day the Imamate of Yemen (Crown Prince Badr having succeeded his redoubtable father on the latter's death a week earlier) was overthrown by revolutionary republicans nurtured by Egypt and led by her nominee, Colonel Sallal.[82] Had the order of these two events – the vote in Aden and the coup in Sana'a – been reversed, there is little doubt, as Governor Johnston himself records,[83] that the merger would not have been approved, let alone the retention by Britain within the intended new State of sovereignty over the Aden base. Indeed, for those who liked the idea the case for union with Yemen had received a splendid boost. Four members of the PSP flew to Sana'a and were rewarded by Sallal with ministries. The air was now filled with forecasts that colonialism in South Yemen was doomed.

Merger with the Federation (re-named the Federation of South Arabia) was now on the Adeni statute book, the shot-gun wedding formally registered. But what chance had it of surviving? It was not difficult for Opposition spokesmen in the House of Commons, when the subject was debated there in November, to protest that Aden's accession had been forced through without adequately consulting the Colony's inhabitants.[84] By this they meant that the issue should have been referred to a new Legislative Council elected on a revised and widely acceptable franchise. They must, however, have known that for the

British Government to have shelved the merger until the Adenis could eventually settle their thorny franchise issue (on unpredictable terms) would have meant missing the last train to the desired destination. Everyone knew that the policy adopted was a gamble. Events in the Yemen had simply lengthened the odds.

Whether 'everyone was reassured', as Johnston loyally records, by Sandys in the course of his tour of the area in December is open to question. Certainly the revolution in the Yemen had given the Federal rulers a special need for reassurance. The Yemeni royalists whom they – in contrast to the activists in Aden – obviously favoured as the lesser of two evils were in fact fighting back with Saudi backing. But the backing given to the Republicans in Egypt was of a different order and was clearly a threat to the Federation. The agreement announced, thanks to American pressure, at the end of December by the Egyptians and Saudis for reciprocal withdrawal of their forces from the Yemen consequently gave instant, if premature, comfort to the Federalis – premature since Egypt, instead of removing her troops as promised, sent more.

In Aden itself the prospects of getting away with the 'ingenious formula' (and the retention of the base) were not enhanced by the progressive emancipation of Britain's territories in Africa – a policy tacitly adopted by the Cabinet well before Macmillan's famous 'wind of change' speech to the South African parliament[85] in February 1960 but by now taking visible effect. Moreover, the plausibility of the new Federation as a leap forward was not helped by the heavy-handed control, however well-intentioned, of civil servants in Government House and in London, few of whom had experience of managing an Arab operation as delicate as this one. Of more immediate local concern was the death in office of the moderate Adeni leader Hassan al-Bayoomi, whose robust influence had been largely responsible for getting the merger approved. The aim of his successor as President of the Supreme Council, Zein Baharoon, was to conciliate an opposition no longer open to conciliation. Johnston himself, though intellectually aware of the strength of the current Arab passion for unity (and therefore for release from residual British domination) remained confident that independence could be successfully conferred on South West Arabia later in the decade, 'always provided we can retain effective use of the Aden base for as long as we may require it'. He never questioned the primacy of that requirement. Global considerations, oil strategy and 'the protection of Arab and other allies' imposed it; and the Malaysia Agreement of 1963 added a new reason for maintaining a stepping-stone to South East Asia.[86]

In his thinking Johnston reveals little difficulty in falling in with the policies of the government of the day in London. He was less at ease with officers of the Colonial Service in the territory, who, he says, never understood their

Governor's problem in getting material support from London for development on the scale they saw as essential and who were often critical of the imperial policy-makers.[87] Haines would have sympathized.

It was one such Colonial Officer, the indefatigable federalist Trevaskis, who now succeeded Johnston as Governor in July 1963. A plea had been advanced at his prompting from the Governor's office six months earlier for a crash programme of development in the Federation, but Colonial Office disillusion over the Federation's viability was already far advanced. Officialdom in London at this stage favoured a 'Singapore solution' for Aden itself, whose relations with the hinterland would be of the same kind as those of Singapore with the new Federation of Malaysia. Sandys himself, however, in the course of discussions with Trevaskis and Colonial Office officials in August, came down unexpectedly in favour of the principle of ceding sovereignty in Aden (and presumably its temporary conversion, as in Luce's old idea, from colony to protectorate) in exchange for the acceptance by an independent South West Arabia of satisfactory arrangements for the security of the British base. A further constitutional conference to pursue these plans with representatives of the Federal and Aden Governments was scheduled for December in London. The breaking of this news was followed by strikes and violent demonstrations in Aden, which Trevaskis interrupted by deporting those Yemenis regarded as their ringleaders. Upon his arrival at Aden airport on 10 December on his way to the conference, an assassination attempt was made with a hand grenade. In shielding him from the explosion (for which he was awarded a second George Medal) George Henderson, one of his ablest lieutenants, lost his life and fifty people were injured. The bomb missed Trevaskis but it killed the conference; an emergency was declared in both Aden and the Federation; the idea of surrendering sovereignty in Aden sank for the time being beneath the surface.

The day after the assassination attempt, the UN General Assembly passed a resolution which quickly became a rallying-cry for those seeking to hasten the end of the British presence in Aden. The resolution arose from the activities of the Special Committee on Colonialism (the 'Committee of 24'), which had been fruitfully lobbied by PSP representatives. In May the Committee had resolved to send a mission to Aden to 'make recommendations for the grant of early independence'. The mission was refused entry in Aden, a rebuff which did not improve the tone of its report or of the Committee of 24's recommendations to the General Assembly. The resolution adopted by the latter on 11 December 1963 called for the abrogation of the constitution in South West Arabia and for elections throughout the area on the basis of universal suffrage as a step to immediate self-determination and independence.[88] Under threats from the PSP such elected members of the Aden Legislative Council as had voted for the new constitution mostly caved in. In London support within the Labour Party for the ascendant al-Asnaj became more marked; and the prospect of the Labour Party coming to power in the forthcoming British elections was not lost on the Federalis.

A proposal by the Governor to transfer to the Federal Supreme Council responsibility for internal security in Aden aroused no enthusiasm amongst its members. The writing on the wall grew increasingly lurid. A minor rebellion of a familiar kind in the unadministered wilds of Radfan was promoted (in nationalist publicity terms) into a major liberation war by Britain's decision to mount a full-scale military operation by British and Federal land forces to suppress it, instead of relying on the old, controversial but relatively painless technique of air action.[89] And the decision to bomb the Yemeni frontier town of Harib in reprisal for Egyptian-Yemeni bombing of areas in Beihan within the Federation secured an exceptionally bad press in the outside world. Sandys flew out in May 1964 and agreed to hold a further constitutional conference to name a date for the independence of the Federation.

But by now a new anti-British organization in the shape of the National Liberation Front,[90] less disposed to negotiate than even Asnaj and the PSP, had broken cover. Its leader was Qahtan ash-Sha'abi, previously a supporter of the South Arabian League until the latter had lost favour in Cairo and had turned for support to Saudi Arabia. It was later alleged that the Radfan revolt had been stage-managed by the NLF, which also set about infiltrating the Federal Army (the erstwhile Protectorate Levies, recently handed over to Federal control). The target of these new revolutionaries, as we shall see, was not limited to the British or the Federalis.

In the Colony meanwhile the Legislative Council, whose life had been further extended by Order-in-Council for another six months for this purpose, was struggling with the thorny franchise problem. A draft bill – which strengthened the Arab complexion of the electorate but still inevitably excluded the vast Yemeni work force – was finally approved in March 1964. Work on the preparation of electoral law and electoral lists could at last begin.

Sandys' new Constitutional Conference 'to discuss the constitutional progress of the Federation towards independence and other matters' assembled in London in June 1964. Its participants were limited to representatives of the Federal and Adeni governments – a criterion which again excluded al-Asnaj and his PSP[91] but did not thereby save the occasion from angry confrontations. Unexpectedly, after four weeks of discussion, an ostensibly promising agreement (Cmnd. 2414) was hammered out. Once elections had been held for a new Legislative Council in Aden based on the revised franchise, a meeting would take place between its representatives and those of the inland states to agree arrangements for the transfer of sovereignty to the united Federation, now comprising Aden, sixteen Western Protectorate states and one Eastern. What was to be done with the other three Eastern states, if they could not be persuaded to join it, was obscure. Another conference would be convened by

Britain to agree on a date for the Federation's independence (not later than 1968) and to conclude a defence agreement under which Britain would retain her military base in Aden. An understanding was also reached on giving the Federation a constitutional face-lift. One casualty was the defection to Cairo of the current President of the Federal Supreme Council, the Fadhli Sultan, in circumstances that baffled analysis and seemed to do him little credit.[92]

The crucial Adeni elections took place in October. This time the PSP boycott was only declared as a formality and 76 per cent of the 8,019 registered electors voted. In the outcome Baharoon, whose main opponent was the suspected and currently imprisoned perpetrator of the attempted airport assassination of the Governor, just scraped enough support to form the new government of Aden State. In theory there was some hope that the London agreements might therefore go ahead.

But two days before the Adenis voted Baharoon in again, the British electors voted the Conservatives out. Trevaskis, called home for discussions with the new Colonial Secretary, was unable to convince an idealist of Greenwood's stamp that the alternatives were a strong Federation under British protection or anarchy under anti-British auspices. A clash was inevitable. Trevaskis was removed.

Greenwood, undeterred by the new Government's renewal of the Tory pledge to grant the Federation independence by 1968 but to maintain the British base,[93] was convinced that the key lay in co-operation with al-Asnaj. On a visit to Aden in December he was encouraged by a surprise joint declaration of Adeni and Federal ministers in favour of a unitary state, in which the powers of the individual state rulers would clearly be diminished. Whether many of the Federal leaders understood what they were voting for is doubtful, though it was one of them, the redoubtable Sharif Husayn of Beihan, who apparently engineered it as a means of baulking any British idea of withdrawing Aden from the Federation after the agreed six years' trial.[94] Despite this windfall Greenwood, as he reported to Parliament on his return, 'took the opportunity to reaffirm that the Government [was] determined to carry out to the full its treaty obligations in the area'.[95]

In the hope of furthering the unitary project Greenwood announced plans for yet another Constitutional Conference (al-Asnaj this time to be included) in March 1965. The plan, however, had to be abandoned, partly owing to the reluctance of the three (unfederated) Eastern rulers to participate and of the Western ones to sit down with the likes of al-Asnaj, and partly no doubt owing to threats published by the NLF to kill anyone who attended. In the ensuing recriminations between the Adeni politicians and the Federalis the new Governor, Sir Richard Turnbull (who had brought with him the credit of stage-managing the transfer of power in Tanzania but had no experience of negotiating with the Arab mind[96]) unwisely or naively took Baharoon's proffered

Prime Minister Harold Wilson facing uncertainties in South West Arabia, October, 1965.

resignation as President of the Aden Council at face value and accepted it. The man chosen to replace him was Abd al-Qawi Meccawi, who had been picked out some years earlier by Luce as the most promising of the young nationalists. What he promised now was confrontation, and one of his first acts was to join with the PSP in demanding immediate implementation of the radical UN Resolution of December 1963. He further withdrew the twenty-four Adeni representatives from the Federal Council.

Prime Minister Wilson's position was certainly awkward. In June 1964, shortly before taking power, he had stated in the Commons, 'We do need Aden as an essential centre for peace-keeping operations in a wide area round it and as an essential staging post in our communications with the East'; and now in December, after admonitory pressures from the US President Johnson, he had assured Parliament that Her Majesty's Government 'cannot afford to relinquish our East of Suez role', though he was careful to add that 'a base held against the wishes of the local government and local population is a wasting asset'.[97] A few weeks later his Defence Secretary, Denis Healey, introduced the 1965 Defence White Paper, which declared that it would be 'politically irresponsible and economically wasteful to abandon Aden'.[98] The modalities of *retaining* Aden were left obscure.

Certainly Cairo was out to scotch any such intention. Plans had been gestating there for a merger of the nationalist groups in 'Occupied South Yemen'. Back in July 1964 at a meeting of their representatives in Cairo Nasser had persuaded the PSP and SAL to merge into an Organization for the Liberation of the Occupied South (OLOS). The NLF, apparently indifferent to Egyptian patronage and critical of the 'milk-and-water' tactics of the PSP, stayed out. Nasser made two further attempts in early 1965 to draw them in but they continued to deride the PSP leaders as 'drawing-room diplomats', a description which would have caused surprise in the drawing-room of Government House. It was not in fact until the middle of 1966 that Nasser finally obliged the three most prominent leaders of the NLF to sign the 'Alexandria Agreement', accepting fusion with the Front for the Liberation of Occupied South Yemen, or FLOSY, as OLOS had meanwhile been re-styled. Even then the rank-and-file of the NLF – the 'secondary cadres' in ideological terms – reacted by expelling two of the old-guard signatories, Qahtan ash-Shaʿabi and his cousin Faisal. Finally at a full party conference in the Yemen in November 1966 all ties with FLOSY were formally broken and the two Shaʿabis were readmitted to a united NLF.[99] Though this is to look ahead, the real nature of the battle under way for control of South West Arabia was thus revealed. It had little to do, save in a symbolic sense, with the ousting of British imperialism.

In May 1965, while these developments were in train, Greenwood, in the hope of some accommodation with Meccawi, proposed the appointment of a two-man commission to design a constitutional structure for a future sovereign independent state of South Arabia. Meccawi's immediate response was to oppose the suggestion on the convenient grounds that the UN Resolution made it superfluous. One member, the admirable Sudanese judge Abu Rannat, withdrew under Arab pressure and Meccawi administered the *coup de grâce* by banning the entry into Aden of the other, Sir Ralph Hone, as an 'illegal immigrant'.[100] The Constitutional Commission idea was in fact revived a year later when, at the formal request of the Federal Government but in even less propitious circumstances, Hone and Sir Gawain Bell, previously Governor of Northern Nigeria, were sent to set about this unenviable and ultimately academic task.[101]

Still trying, Greenwood reverted to his proposal for a conference in London of all interested parties, and on a further visit to Aden in July secured agreement to the formation under his chairmanship of a preliminary working party representing all groups except the NLF (outlawed by Turnbull the previous month). The working party assembled in August but broke up on the refusal of Meccawi and al-Asnaj to discuss anything except the implementation of the UN Resolution. Violence in Aden was now reaching new heights. More senior British figures (and many others) were murdered; and when Meccawi declined to condemn the assassination in September of the much respected Speaker of the Legislative Council, Sir Arthur Charles, Turnbull dismissed him and his Government and with London's approval reimposed direct British rule over Aden state. The timing of this drastic measure was unfortunate, since Britain's Minister of State for Foreign Affairs, George Thomson, was at that moment in Cairo seeking audience of the Egyptian President in the hope of developing an improved understanding.[102] Nasser declined to see him.

The dismissal of Meccawi may have given the Federalis new hope – as perhaps did the retirement of Greenwood shortly after and his replacement as Colonial Secretary by Lord Longford. Moreover, in November, following continuous pressure from Washington and Commonwealth capitals for the maintenance of Britain's military role East of Suez,[103] Lord Beswick, a junior Minister for the Colonies, was despatched to Aden with a message of reassurance to the Federal leaders. Three months later, however – and despite a public declaration by Minister of Defence Healey on a visit to Australia in January that Britain had 'no intention of ratting on her commitments in the Middle East' – Beswick was despatched again with a very different message. There were more reasons than the critical state of sterling for the policy switch reflected in the new Defence White Paper (Cmnd. 2901) which had just been presented. One, no doubt, was the view already encapsulated by one critical observer that 'Aden base consumed more security than it can ever produce'.[104] But whatever the precise motive, Beswick's message this time was that Britain now intended to abandon Aden (transferring such base facilities as the region required to Bahrain), leaving South West Arabia independent by the promised date of 1968; and there would be no defence agreement. The Federal Rulers angrily told him Britain's behaviour was dishonourable. Senior British staff in the Federal Army were equally outraged.[105] Nasser triumphantly announced that the liberation of Occupied South Yemen was now finally assured and that he would keep his troops in North Yemen until the assurance was implemented in 1968. Not, as he made clear, that the ouster of Britain from South West Arabia alone was enough. Nor could the declaration of her intended withdrawal from Aden be an occasion for a new understanding with him, as Britain hoped: it must be followed by her withdrawal from the rest of Arabia, including the oil-bearing Gulf States.

The expansion of Britain's military facilities in Bahrain and Sharjah, however, went ahead and the Prime Minister continued to insist that Britain had a duty to assert her influence East of Suez and that the Government would not default.[106] There was less bravado in the Labour Party as a whole; and in October the Party Conference, with scant regard for official Cabinet policy, approved a plan for total military withdrawal from everywhere East of Suez[107] – 'not a plan', observed Foreign Secretary George Brown testily, 'but a scuttle'.

In Aden, if it was clear enough that revolutionary nationalism was winning, it was by no means clear which revolutionary nationalists would prove the winners – FLOSY or the NLF. Nor was the basis of their mutual hostility yet altogether apparent. One related source of uncertainty, which by this time hampered Government House, was the lack of reliable intelligence in Aden, the Special Branch having been virtually annihilated. Faced by the militant NLF's announcement that they had severed all ties with FLOSY, the latter hastily set up with Egyptian backing its own military instrument in the shape of the Popular Organization of Revolutionary Forces (PORF).[108] The fact that al-Asnaj had hitherto held out against violence as a means to his ends may be counted as creditable, but this and his neglect of the hinterland had an intimate effect on the outcome. Whether or not the British would continue to be a target of violence, the process of withdrawal was clearly not going to be peaceful. Accordingly and despite her previous opposition to interference from that quarter, Britain fell back in December on an appeal to the UN for its good offices – a proposal which Meccawi himself chose to condemn in the absence of any recognition of FLOSY as sole representative of the South Arabian people.[109] Before the UN put together a mission in response, the Federal leaders renewed their pleas for continued British protection after withdrawal. For that matter they announced their acceptance of the Hone-Bell Report and its constitutional proposals for a unitary state. The report was published as a Green Paper by the Federal Government in February. If the Federal authorities had been slow to take notice of it, the

British authorities, who had promoted its commissioning, never took notice of it at all.

The Federal leaders, whatever inadequacies their record had made manifest, had some justification for feeling betrayed. If Britain was not going to protect them when independence came, at least until some kind of accommodation might be reached with the revolutionary nationalists, where else could they look for protection in a hostile world? The offer which George Thomson took out to them in March, of six-months air cover in exchange for advancing the date of independence to the approaching November, had understandably little attraction. Nor was it likely that the UN mission which finally arrived in Aden on 2 April would offer them any relief. Composed as it was of representatives of Mali, Afghanistan and Venezuela, its sympathies were not with those tainted with collaboration with colonialism. Indeed they refused to have any dealings at all with the Federal Government; and when the latter therefore declined to allow them use of its broadcasting station, they left the territory in high dudgeon and somewhat farcical circumstances.[110]

Another British emissary, Lord Shackleton (Minister without Portfolio), was now sent out in a final attempt to produce order out of the growing chaos. Turnbull seems to have fallen foul of him, perhaps because he was by now too disillusioned with the chaos to accept that any new plan *could* bring order out of it – an argument which had recently drawn fire from the Foreign Secretary, George Brown, during discussions with him in London. At all events the general disarray was by now such that – as the next and final High Commissioner was to put it – 'the British Government did what governments often do in such circumstances. They unceremoniously changed the man at the top, as they had changed his predecessor'. Accordingly on 20 May Sir Humphrey Trevelyan replaced him.[111]

His task ('poor man', said Harold Macmillan on hearing of his appointment) was to contrive British evacuation and 'if possible, to leave behind an independent government which could ensure peace and stability in South West Arabia'. The possibility was indeed remote. Trevelyan, though he took pains on his arrival to consult assembled members of his staff, who were by no means of one mind, had few illusions that the government he would leave behind would be the Federal one. He has made it clear that, in his view, 'the policy of developing and modernizing the States through the rule of the Sultans [had been] bound to fail'; and although the Hone-Bell unitary constitution had been publicly accepted by the Federalis, Trevelyan 'refused to take the trouble of reading it'. By now, indeed, the Federal leaders were sorely demoralized. Whether their inability to impose themselves and give life to the Federation (before as well as after the merger with Aden) was inherently predictable, or whether the charge lies more properly with the tergiversations of successive British governments, is open to controversy. Both, it must surely be admitted, contributed to the *dégringolade*. Neither, at all events, was any longer in a position to halt it.

On the very day of Trevelyan's despatch to Aden, King Faysal personally appealed to Harold Wilson for the maintenance of British defence responsibilities in Aden in the face of Nasser's revolutionary threat to Arabia generally. Any embarrassment this may have caused the Prime Minister was removed two days later when Nasser closed the Straits of Tiran to Israeli shipping; and, with an Arab-Israeli war imminent, King Faysal felt obliged to turn about and 'support an Arab brother in peril'.[112]

For Trevelyan himself the most elusive of his tasks was to find someone in the growing turmoil with whom to negotiate the modalities of Britain's withdrawal and to whom power, in the formal sense remaining, could be transmitted. This could only be one or other (or in theory both) of the anti-British nationalist movements, the old collaborative class in Aden itself being by this time as powerless as the Federal leaders.

What was now the relative strength of the rival revolutionary groups, preoccupied as they were with violent attempts to exterminate each other? FLOSY had hitherto been Nasser's chosen instrument, and the Arab League had dutifully announced its backing for FLOSY in March. The NLF's main revolutionary cadres had spurned Nasser's final endeavours to fuse the two movements. Nasser's only resource thereafter seemed to be the public crediting to FLOSY of all newsworthy revolutionary manifestations in the territory, most of them in fact the work of the NLF. The latter indeed already regarded Nasser as deviating from the right path, and their view of his diminishing relevance was reinforced by his humiliation in the June Six-day War. The strength of the NLF had in the past lain in the immediate hinterland of Aden: they now began progressively to undermine what was left of the *dawla*s further afield and to challenge FLOSY's dominance in Aden itself and in that movement's ATUC stronghold. In the Hadhramut too NLF sympathizers had been actively exploiting economic discontent, stirring up local hostility to Sultanic rule, and penetrating the Hadhrami Legion. These developments in the east added to the popularity of the main NLF in the west.

George Brown's announcement to Parliament, in the immediate aftermath of the June War, of £10,000,000 in military aid for the Federation coupled with air and naval protection after independence (still planned for January 1968) won applause from the Conservative Opposition, but from nowhere else. It had indeed little meaning for, as Crossmann recorded in his diaries, 'George is passionately determined to get out of Aden at all costs and the package is solely designed as a cover for this operation'.[113]

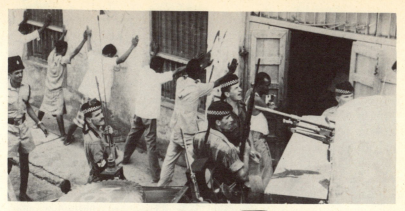

The Argyll and Sutherland Highlanders reoccupying Crater, June 1967.

The prospects of 'getting out' decently were not improved the day following George Brown's statement by a mutiny in the Federal Army on 20 June. Its amalgamation, expedient but ill-prepared, with the more tribally-based Federal National Guard was the source of the trouble. But though inspired by personal and tribal rivalries for position amongst their respective officer groups rather than by political or ideological promptings, the effect was the same[114] and the inability of the Federal authorities to reimpose order diminished what little credibility they still retained. In all the circumstances, the inclination within the armed forces to look to one or other of the nationalist movements seeking to dominate the scene was perhaps understandable. During the same bloodstained month the NLF, in their determination to outbid FLOSY for the limelight in Aden, succeeded in occupying its Crater quarter and holding it for a fortnight, until Colonel Mitchell and his Argylls retook it under the critical scrutiny of the world media.

The Federal leaders were in despair. They had sought at unpublicized meetings in Eritrea the previous year to reach an accord with FLOSY – clearly the lesser of the two evils confronting them – and been finally rebuffed.[115] They now received further humiliation from Trevelyan. For the High Commissioner, having secured UN agreement to send a mission to Geneva to discuss future arrangements with South West Arabian representatives, brushed aside the proclamation by the Federal Supreme Council of the new unitary constitution and simply advised its members to go to Geneva and get whatever terms they could. Some went, others preferred to decamp for safety to Saudi Arabia. Whichever course they chose, the NLF overran their states, eastern[116] as well as western, in their absence. In August the residue of the Supreme Council invited the Federal Army to take over control. The latter was in no state to oblige.

FLOSY too was losing ground. In September it made a bid to restore its position with an invasion by its military wing, PORF, from the Yemeni frontier. This nearly succeeded, if in nothing else, in restoring unity in the NLF's divided leadership. In point of fact the Federal Army (or South Arabian Army, as it was now styled) for all its lack of cohesion still held the key; and when the PORF forces went on to attack those of the NLF at Shaykh Othman on the outskirts of Aden in early November, the Army made a critical decision. It declared in favour of the NLF, and the latter's ultimate victory was virtually assured.

Before this internal bloodletting reached its own climax, Trevelyan's search for an *interlocuteur valable* had continued. He had hitherto been reluctant to regard the NLF in that light; and the latter's warning that anyone venturing to negotiate with the imperialists would be liquidated was a lively discouragement to other possible volunteers. According to Trevaskis' account, Trevelyan had by June (the month in which he lifted the year-old order outlawing them) transferred his 'preference' from FLOSY to the NLF; and FLOSY was later to attribute the victory of its rivals to British collusion with them. Be that as it may, Trevelyan, announcing on 4 September, after a quick visit to London, Britain's recognition of the nationalist forces as representative of the people, offered talks with any of them, without discrimination. The NLF's response was to demand exclusive recognition of themselves as a condition of agreeing to talk (as indeed al-Asnaj had done on FLOSY's behalf two month's earlier on Taʿiz radio),[117] and this was not forthcoming. The NLF thereupon shelled Government House and the British military headquarters, three-inch mortar shells at the former, two-inch at the latter – protocol, as Trevelyan records, being thereby observed.

Chaos mounted in Aden. Details have been too fully described elsewhere to warrant repetition here. The withdrawal of Egyptian troops from the Yemen in October, following Nasser's reconciliation with the Saudis in the aftermath of the June War, effectively removed FLOSY's last hopes. It also enabled George Brown (indulging in something of a *non-sequitur*) to declare in the House of Commons on 2 November that British protection of South West Arabia would no longer be needed after independence and that withdrawal would be completed before the end of the month. The South Arabian Army having confirmed its allegiance to the NLF four days later, the Foreign Secretary announced on 7 November the British Government's willingness to meet NLF leaders in Geneva. Shackleton was despatched there for this unenviable meeting at which he declared on 21 November Britain's readiness to hand over the keys of office to the NLF. The last British troops and the High Commissioner left Aden on 29 November; and Qahtan ash-Shaʿabi, temporarily reintegrated into the NLF leadership, returned home in triumph. South West Arabian independence was now complete, though the circumstances of its achievement left many question marks hanging in the turbulent currents of air. Only in geological terms was the Aden volcano extinct.

Some of the political lava fell on the other side of the Arabian peninsula, in the Persian Gulf, which is the subject of the next chapter. Before closing this one, a number of issues which so brief a chronological account has left unexamined may be worth picking up. There is no need to give further emphasis to the belief running through the whole of this chapter that, regardless of whether the practice of empire itself was good or bad, this particular manifestation of it was mismanaged from the start. If, when it eventually came to be formulated, the declared objective of every imperial venture, so far as this related to the receiving end, was to administer, educate and develop a dependent people to a point at which it could move from tutelage to independence without disruption or alienation, this objective clearly was not achieved in South West Arabia. But could it have been, had British policy there been more imaginative or more determined? Obviously, throughout the first century of British involvement the area as a whole attracted no 'constructive' consideration in India or in London. So far as the hinterland was concerned, the principle was constantly reaffirmed of non-interference in the internal and domestic affairs of the tribes. As for Aden itself, though its development as a commercial and bunkering station was of course pursued, such attention as the Bombay authorities gave to the welfare of its inhabitants was largely due to the number of Indians settled there.[118] Could the Colonial Office, when they finally assumed responsibility in 1937, have made a success of it? Could they not straight away have recognized the need, and found a means, for fusing the interests of Colony and Protectorates, despite the history of mutual antipathy? Could the established policy of leaving local power in the hands of separatist *dawla*s – whether one regards that policy as a form of imperial liberalism or simply as the cheapest means of retaining imperial control – have been so refashioned as to bring the whole hinterland forward in unison with the Colony? Clearly this would have entailed, quite apart from a different dimension of development financing, a degree of administrative dictation and of military intervention that would have aroused violent resentment. (In purist terms it would also have meant a breach of the Protective or Advisory Treaties, though that might have been easier to justify than the final 'betrayal'.) The alternative extreme of eschewing direct intervention altogether – the Ingrams preference for allowing Arab tribalism to work out its own destinies, while offering nothing more than friendly advice – was clearly unconstructive in Colonial Office terms. Whether either of these two stools would have provided a secure imperial posture is debatable: what is beyond debate is that, by falling between them, Britain's policy was a recipe for discomfort. Lake's lament in the mid-thirties that the Colonial Office 'do go on and on' and that it wouldn't work in South West Arabia may well deserve respect. But it was never effectively put to the test. As it turned out – perhaps owing to the World War and Britain's resulting impoverishment – the Colonial Office in this instance, so far from going on and on, stopped short.

One possible alternative approach to the problem, which had its supporters over the years, would have involved admitting the Imam's dubious claim to sovereignty over the whole 'historical' Yemen and doing a deal with him. All that Britain was fundamentally concerned about until very late in the day (in interests which we can admit to have been wider than imperial prestige) was the security of her own sovereign rights in Aden itself. This was from time to time on offer from Sanaʿa. Two things, however, ensured its rejection: one was that it would have meant disavowing treaty obligations towards Protector-ate rulers who had supported Britain's long-standing resistance to the Imam's pretensions and had constituted the *cordon sanitaire* round Aden; the other was a moral scruple about delivering anyone, particularly a Shafeʿi community, to mediaeval Zaidi despotism. Even so it is arguable that a deal of this kind with the Imam would, as things turned out, have proved a lesser evil – both for Britain and for the rulers and their subjects. The Imamate of course was recognizably obsolescent; but when it was finally overthrown in 1962, it is just possible that a deal of the same kind could still have been struck, if not with the immediate revolutionaries in the Yemen, then (after the reconciliation of the monarchists) with their successors. The 'Free Yemenis', Aden-based as many of them were before Sallal's *coup de main*, must at least have seen the merits of a reasonably liberal, reasonably stable and unquestionably pros-perous Aden. The unsurmountable obstacle no doubt lay in Cairo; but by the time that the Six-Day War of 1967 had reduced the height of that obstacle, history in South West Arabia had moved irretrievably on.

The belief that the ultimate débâcle might have been avoided if the suc-cession of proposals put forward by Luce during his governorate had been taken up by London has already been advanced (p. 69). It will not be apparent till the relevant papers are released why in particular the final recommendation from a man whose views were certainly respected in Westminster was rejected. Had sovereignty over Aden been surrendered by 1962, as both he and the Commander of British Forces in Aden both urged, the course of history over the following five years would at least have been forced out of its otherwise inescapable groove.

The next question worth exploring relates to al-Asnaj. Had the inclinations of the British Labour Party in opposition been given consideration by the Conservative Government or been constructively pursued by the Labour Party on coming to power in 1964, could al-Asnaj have delivered a solution before the NLF upstaged him? Whatever else less favourable may be said of him, al-Asnaj did during those critical years command a dominating position amongst the nationalists and trades unions in Aden; and until the NLF altered the

ground rules, he remained wedded, in public anyway, to the tactics of negotiation rather than to brute force. Al-Asnaj had of course three weaknesses:
unlike his ultimate rivals, he had no constituency in the hinterland; he reviled,
and was heartily detested by, the Federalis; and to the British Conservatives
he bore with increasing definition the mark of the Nasserite beast. So this
conceivable alternative too, if it was one, was never seriously pursued.
Nonetheless there are those who maintain that the policy he stood for,
however distasteful to the Conservatives, was not all that different from that of
the Labour Government when they finally opted for total withdrawal, and that
a peaceful deal might have been struck between them, had it been done in
time.[119] There are others who regard al-Asnaj's handling of the Labour Party
from the start as a confidence trick, his ability to deliver a solution being in
fact non-existent throughout. His support came mainly from the voteless
Yemeni workforce: Adenis with votes would never have elected him to
power.[120]

What then is to be said of the policy that London did adopt while options
were still open – that of federating the protected states, initially without, and
ultimately with, formal linkage to Aden? The idea, as has been shown, had a
longer history than has often been recognized. A positive though short-lived
initiative in that direction was taken by Symes as early as 1928. Indeed even
before that, as well as continuously after it, the archives show that something
of the kind was always recognized in London, however vaguely, as the objective. But even when it was actively revived, it never received from London the
kind of determined backing that might conceivably have got it off the ground
in 1954 and have gradually given it the muscle its British devotees on the spot
believed possible. Hickinbotham in a despatch of June 1956, having deplored
the tendency of the British media to declare that the rulers had been subjected
in 1954 to strong British pressure to federate, added: 'More is the pity that no
pressure *was* brought to bear, for if it had been the whole affair would have
been concluded successfully within a few weeks'.[121] The Colonial Office
response to this sally was to have his despatch printed for circulation in
Whitehall with the quoted passage cut out.

It is also arguable that, had Britain seen fit, once federation was adopted,
publicly to release its federal child from paternalist control straight away,[122]
the Federation might by that token have qualified for outside Arab toleration –
as the Gulf States were able to do on receiving full independence in 1971. The
absence of democracy could scarcely have been a bar to acceptability in Arab
eyes: certainly it did not prove to be so anywhere else, even in the case of the
Marxist régime that replaced the Federation as the first independent government of South West Arabia.

It is true that federalism, as a sort of testamentary bequest from a dying
empire, was by this time losing, or had already lost, credibility all over the

place, wherever it was bequeathed. It proved wholly ineffective in the West Indies, where it was inaugurated in 1958 after a decade of preparation and abandoned four years later. The federating thereafter of the eight small residual Caribbean units hardly got beyond agreement of principle at an initial conference. It failed to hold as a linkage between Singapore and the rest of the Malaysian Federation, which lasted only from 1963 to 1965. In East Africa, the Federation of Tanganyika (as it was), Kenya and Uganda, for all the initial enthusiasm of Nyerere when it was planned in 1961, never got off the ground. The Central African Federation of what were then Northern and Southern Rhodesia and Nyasaland was imposed by British fiat in 1953, was recognized as unworkable by 1960 and was finally interred in 1963. For that matter France's ideas in the 1960s for federating her colonial territories in Africa were abandoned as impractical before being put to the test. Only in Nigeria can the federal approach, by surviving, be said to have caught on.

In point of fact, in none of Britain's dispiriting experiments with federation were the circumstances remotely similar to those obtaining in South West Arabia. Moreover, when federation was formally embarked upon in South West Arabia in 1959, it had not already failed anywhere else. On both these counts, therefore, it cannot justly be said that the South West Arabian experiment ignored from the start the lessons of precedent. It failed for reasons of its own. Whether it was bound to fail, had it been pursued in different and more determined ways, is not perhaps self-evident – though the general proposition that the concept of federation involves a pooling of interests unnatural to a people as supremely individualist as the Arabs is difficult to gainsay.

One aspect of the federal conception in South West Arabia to which this chapter has paid little attention relates to the Eastern protectorate. At no stage did the rulers in the EAP (apart from the Wahidi) show any inclination to merge with their western neighbours in a federal project, with or without Adeni participation. The boundary between the WAP and the EAP, though defined mainly as an administrative convenience, symbolized in EAP eyes a genuine separateness. Their two principal sultans had always regarded the western states as too contemptibly backward to merit their co-operation; and Aden itself in a different way was no less distinct and remote. Neither before nor after the withdrawal decision was formally taken is it clear what future, in such circumstances, the British authorities envisaged for them. According to British officials who worked up to the end in the EAP, their absorption by Saudi Arabia may well have been in Britain's mind. Whether such a future would have appealed to its inhabitants is at least questionable. As things worked out, the NLF gave them no option.

When the federal endeavour finally crumbled in South West Arabia the mutual slaughter between the NLF and FLOSY, however horrific, was something in which Britain was strictly not concerned. Why then, once the date of withdrawal was publicly known, did the British in Aden continue to be a target of terrorism for both contenders for the succession? Richard Crossman recorded, rather oddly, in his Diaries on 27 October that Britain had been 'miraculously lucky ... getting out without a British soldier being killed'.[123] British military casualties 'from December 1963 until shortly before withdrawal', according to the Defence White Paper of February 1968, were 135 killed and over 900 wounded;[124] and casualties certainly continued after Crossman's diary entry. Nor was it a matter of getting caught accidentally in the crossfire. There is evidence enough from eye-witnesses of much deliberate killing long after withdrawal was assured and given a date. Admittedly any nationalist with a gun may have found a mindless satisfaction in levelling it at those who represented the departing imperial power. Moreover, as long as Nasser was distantly in control, his general strategy required that the British should be harried and humiliated even after this treatment ceased to serve any strictly South West Arabian purpose. There seems, however, to have been more to it than this in the case of the NLF. According to one analyst, the practice of violence for its own sake was in NLF philosophy a vital mental preparation for independence and the expected exercise of power.[125] Those who wish South West Arabia well and who have observed the course of history since the establishment of the People's Democratic Republic must hope that the practice of violence as an end in itself – or even as a means of retaining power – has finally been abandoned.

On 21 May 1990, as this book went to print, the governments of the YAR and the PDRY jointly declared the union of the two countries on a comprehensive basis implying the abandonment of its extremist policies by the government of the latter as the junior partner. The announcement was greeted instantly and almost universally with enthusiasm in both countries. Wellwishers will hope that this time the project will succeed.

4 The Gulf episode

We do not wish it for ourselves any more than any rational man with an estate in the north of England and a residence in the south would have wished to possess the inns on the north road. All he could want would have been that the inn should be well-kept, always accessible, and furnishing him, when he came, with mutton-chops and post-horses.

Lord Palmerston[1]

Some of the political lava from the Aden volcano, we said in the last chapter, fell into the Persian Gulf. Indeed there were observers of the Gulf scene who, judging the circumstances in the British-protected shaykhdoms there to be very similar to those prevailing in South West Arabia, foresaw a similar cataclysmic *dénouement* in the Gulf. How similar were the circumstances? The question cannot be answered without historical retrospect. What were the origins and objectives of Britain's curious position in the Gulf until 1971? What was the relationship, formal and informal, between Britain and the Gulf shaykhdoms?[2] What was the nature of society and of traditional government there? What in short would Britain be withdrawing from? And how do the answers to these questions compare with the corresponding data concerning South West Arabia?

The English East India Company, incorporated in 1600, aimed to secure for Britain against all comers the lion's share of the lucrative Asian trade with points west. Apart from the oceanic voyage round the Cape, there were two main routes between the Mediterranean and India. Of these, the sea-lane from Suez along the southern coasts of Arabia was the geographical focus in chapter 3; the other, starting through Syria like so many land routes to the Orient, branched south in Mesopotamia and became sea-borne at the top of the Persian Gulf. The East India Company established a 'factory' (agency) at Basra in 1723, having opened one at the other end of the gulf, at Gombroon, a hundred years earlier. Control of this Gulf route was periodically regarded by the British as even more important than control of the South Arabian sea-lane. Maritime pride of place within the Gulf, as in the Indian Ocean, meant in the first place upstaging successive European rivals – Portuguese, Dutch, and finally the persistent French; a process not completed until the nineteenth century. Use of the Gulf trade-route also meant securing the acquiescence of the Ottoman authorities in Mesopotamia as well as the grant of preferential treatment from the Persian Court. Both these pre-requisites were broadly achieved, though the going was not always easy. In even more local terms a dominant maritime role in the Gulf meant mastering the complex rivalries of

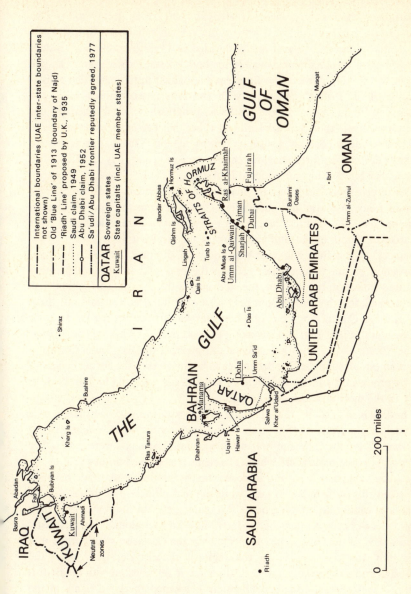

The Gulf States since 1971.

Sources for boundary proposals: Buraimi, Memorials 1955 (Archive Edition, 1987; J. B. Kelly, Eastern Arabian Frontiers (London, 1964) and Arabia, the Gulf and the West (London, 1980).

the indigenous Arab sea-faring communities, collaborating with them or suppressing them as suited British interests. Since Persia was a power of regional importance, whereas the coastal Arab shaykhs had no rich hinterland to give them geographical substance, it was on the Persian side of the Gulf that the East India Company, when it finally decided in 1778 to establish a resident representative specifically responsible for both coasts, located him. The site chosen was Bushire, where the Residency remained until 1946. The vicissitudes marking Britain's relations with the Persian authorities while her supremacy in the waters of the Gulf was progressively established do not concern us here – though it is worth observing that Persia's traditional weakness as a maritime power was always a British benefit. What do concern us are Britain's dealings with the shaykhdoms on the Arab coast, out of which arose the peculiar relationship surrendered in 1971.

The received wisdom is that the maintenance by the East India Company's navy of peace at sea in and outside the Gulf was from the first continually challenged by the piratical practices of Arab tribes living along the coast towards the mouth of the Gulf and known collectively, if inaccurately, as the 'Joasmees' (Qawasim), and that the safety of shipping required the total destruction of the Joasmee fleet. Hence the final and full-scale expedition mounted from Bombay in 1819, the storming of the then Qasimi capital, Ras al-Khaimah, and the burning not only of several hundred Qasimi craft there and in other Qasimi ports but of a considerable number in the harbours of independent nearby shaykhdoms along the 200 miles of what was designated as the 'Pirate Coast'. This holocaust accomplished, the East India Company set about establishing the Pax Britannica in Gulf waters to the lasting benefit of all – a process on which the Viceroy Lord Curzon was able to look back in 1903 as 'the most unselfish page in history'.[3]

This received wisdom, though endorsed by extensive and painstaking case records in the India Office archives,[4] has recently come under critical scrutiny.[5] Were the Qawasim in truth congenital pirates? Or were they rather established maritime traders whose merchant fleets posed an obstacle to the East India Company in its aim of cornering the profitable sea-trade between India and the Gulf? Who, in fact, were the real pirates? The arguments on both sides cannot be explored here. Two amongst them, however, are worth quoting as early illustrations of the inter-shaykhdom jealousies characteristic (even today) of the Gulf scene. Apologists for the Qawasim would argue that their only traditional rivals in the regional sea-carrying trade were the Muscatis; and that the latter, whose collaborative relationship with the British was already well established, deliberately blackened the good name of the Qawasim in Britain's eyes. On the other hand some authorities declare that Muscat's main rivals in the carrying trade to India were not the Qawasim but the 'Utub of Bahrain and Kuwait;[6] and the British never quite treated *them* as

Viceroy Lord Curzon addressing the 'Chiefs of the Arab Coast' on HMS *Argonaut* at Sharjah, 1903.

congenital pirates.[7] Piracy in any case is a relative term; and if we end this diversion by recalling Alexander the Great's conversation with a captured pirate two thousand years earlier, we do so more for its charm than for its questionable relevance. 'How dare you molest the sea?' demanded Alexander. 'How dare you molest the whole world?' replied the pirate. 'Because I do it with a little ship only, I am called a thief. You, doing it with a great navy, are called an emperor.'[8]

One other feature of Britain's clash with the Qawasim is interesting in the light of much later history. The period during which Qasimi piracy (in the British version) was especially tiresome was when the Qawasim in the early nineteenth century were under the potent influence of the Wahhabi zealots inland, in what is now Saudi Arabia. In Aitchison's words, 'It was by instigating the Qawasim tribe to acts of piracy in the Persian Gulf that the Wahhabis first attracted the attention of the British Government.'[9] But the British in India saw no attraction in becoming embroiled with these desert fundamentalists who were even further from Bombay than the Gulf shaykhdoms. Certainly they watched with interest the attempts of the Ottoman Governor in Baghdad to deal with the Wahhabi problem. But by an irony of history it was the then dictator of Egypt who, though no friend of the British, saved the day for Britain. For by twice campaigning in Arabia (1816–1818 and again twenty years later) to suppress the Wahhabis, Muhammad Ali relieved Britain of any immediate need to confront Wahhabi expansionism herself. Had Egyptian expeditionary forces not served these warnings to the Wahhabis just when the latter were on the crest of an expansionist tide, there is little doubt that the Gulf shaykhdoms would today be part of the Saudi kingdom. Even in the interval between the two Egyptian invasions, the Wahhabis succeeded in re-establishing themselves so effectively that by the early 1830s (the shaykh of Sharjah's appeal in 1825 for British protection against them having fallen on deaf ears) many of the Gulf shaykhs found it expedient to embrace for a while the doctrines of the Wahhabis, if not also their political hegemony.[10]

When the second Egyptian invasion of Wahhabi Najd took place, Muhammad Ali's own aspirations in the Gulf worried the British much more than did those of the Wahhabis. For in 1839 – the year, significantly, of Britain's occupation of Aden – the Egyptian general, Khurshid Pasha, having again reduced the Wahhabis, pushed on across the peninsula with the conquest of Bahrain and even further afield on his agenda. In the face of this challenge to their predominance in the Gulf, the Government of India, on Palmerston's instructions, took action to warn him off.[11] Even the expediency of turning Bahrain into 'a regular protectorate' was for a short time seriously considered. But Muhammad Ali's more sensational victories in Syria at this time against the Ottoman Sultan (from whom he had openly thrown off allegiance in 1831) had disturbed other European powers as well as Britain; and Palmerston had little difficulty in promoting a joint demand that Muhammad Ali should abandon his imperial ambition and withdraw his forces from both Syria and Arabia.[12] Egyptian aspirations in the Gulf did not again disturb the British until 120 years later. But all this is to jump ahead and we must revert to 1819 and to British policy towards the Gulf shaykhdoms.

If the British were then disinclined to embroil themselves with the Arabian hinterland and the forces, Saudi or Egyptian, competing for position there, they were fully determined to make their own influence supreme in the sea-lanes through the Gulf to India. Having captured Ras al-Khaimah[13] and destroyed the 'Joasmee' fleet, the commander of the expeditionary force from Bombay set in train the first of a series of treaties with the coastal shaykhs, by which over the next 100 years the relationship between the shaykhdoms and Britain was progressively, if casually, elaborated. Under this 1820 Treaty,[14] the shaykhs along the Pirate Coast – of Ras al-Khaimah itself, of Sharjah (also Qasimi and normally the more influential), of Umm al-Qaiwain, Ajman, Dubai and Abu Dhabi – bound themselves to 'the cessation of plunder and piracy by land and sea for ever' and to the establishment of a 'lasting peace between the British Government and the Arab tribes'. The shaykh of Bahrain was 'admitted' to the Treaty the following month.[15] Qatar was at this stage regarded as a dependency of Bahrain, Kuwait as an Ottoman fiefdom. Muscat

(Oman) was – even then – handled differently, as an independent soveriegn state.

British shipping was thereafter treated with circumspection in Gulf waters; and the next round of agreements engineered by Bombay – the Maritime Truce of 1843 between the 'pacificated' Arabs, made 'perpetual' in 1853 – was designed to keep the Gulf free of declared inter-tribal warfare at sea (which the 1820 Treaty had not outlawed with piracy) and by doing so to prevent the forcible disruption of the pearling industry which gave the shaykhdoms their main livelihood. But however altruistic in its immediate purposes, the truce entrusted the British Government with the supervision of its enforcement, thus giving Britain a referee's rights of calling the players to order. Amongst the remaining nineteenth-century treaties the most important to our theme are those known as the 'Exclusive Agreements' of 1892.[16] These, signed as before with the 'Trucial' shaykhs and with Bahrain, explicitly prohibited them from having dealings of any sort with, or ceding territory to, outside powers other than Britain. Though the main stimulus behind these Exclusive Agreements when they were signed was renewed Ottoman interest in the area, the object was to keep everyone else out as well, notably the French and the Russians; and it was these agreements which constituted the basis of the special relationship between Britain and the Gulf States until 1971. Much the same exclusive arrangement was accepted by the Shaykh of Kuwait in 1899[17] and finally in 1916 by the Shaykh of Qatar,[18] his independence of Bahrain being by this time accepted. Ottoman aspirations as well as the threat of German penetration-by-railway-construction[19] having collapsed with World War I, and rumoured Russian designs on the warm waters of the Gulf having for the time being been laid to rest, Britain was able by the end of the War to regard the Gulf as *mare nostrum* and so present it to the outside world. Curzon's old vice-regal pleas for a positive policy of unquestioned supremacy in the Gulf had thus finally borne fruit.

But where, juridically and constitutionally, did all these signatures leave the Gulf shaykhdoms? Certainly their status was uniquely curious, even by imperial Britain's standards of curiosity. Two aspects, one external and one internal, deserve attention because of their implications once the Gulf had ceased to be a forgotten backwater and was emerging into international limelight.

Firstly, did these documents place the states emphatically under British protection? They were not 'protectorates', so far as that term can be said to have enjoyed precise definition in the nineteenth century. On several occasions the British authorities in India and London debated the possible advantages of conferring protectorate status here and there, and a number of requests to be taken under formal protection were received between 1825 and 1903; but the decision was always against it.[20] Even protection in a less formal sense was not explicitly conferred by treaty on any of the states, except the late-comer Qatar[21] – and in her case the agreement was drawn up in 1916 when Britain and Turkey were at war. Nonetheless, in communications with the Ottomans Britain described Bahrain in 1892 and Kuwait in 1914 as being 'under British protection'. As a general rule, however, the preferred description for all of them was simply 'states in special treaty relations with Britain'.[22] It was not until 1949 that they were first publicly accorded the title of 'British Protected States'.[23]

In jurists' terms the difference between a Protectorate and a Protected State was that, while both (unlike Colonies) remained foreign territory, in a Protectorate the Crown reserved the power to make laws for its 'peace, order and good government', whereas in a Protected State the sovereignty of the ruler was recognized and such rights as the Crown exercised had to be acquired by treaty.[24] In the case of the Gulf states the obligation to protect them against aggression, by land as well as by sea, may be said to have flowed by implication from the Exclusive Agreements; for these, by depriving the rulers of the right to deal with the outside world, implicitly imposed on Britain the obligation of defending them from it. But it has to be admitted that attempts by jurists to define the nature of a British Protected State have a somewhat *ex post facto* look. Indeed the indeterminate status of the Gulf shaykhdoms wears in retrospect all the marks of that scrupulous imprecision characteristic of so many of Britain's imperial contrivances. Britain may be said to have made up the rules of the game as she went along, with the result that no one really knew what they were. Perhaps for that reason Britain's right or obligation of protecting them was never seriously questioned, any more than was her right or obligation of representing their interests in the outside world.

The second and more controversial question that arose from the treaties concerns the extent to which they left the internal affairs of the shaykhdoms free from British interference. There can be no doubt at all that in the early years, when the safety of the sealink with India was all that mattered, the British were not concerned in regulating what went on inside the shaykhdoms.[25] The principle, if not always the practice, of non-interference was steadily upheld. One reason for the Government of India's refusal to interfere may have been financial. Since half the cost would fall on them under a longstanding agreement with the home authorities, they were always opposed to suggested initiatives in the Gulf involving, as a landward role would have done, expenditure. The trouble of course was that internal affairs and external affairs could not long be kept separate. Although there are various early instances of the overlap causing technical breaches of the principle of non-interference, the prime examples come later; and we shall cite them in due course. But in general the right of all recognized rulers to run their own internal affairs remained explicit. There was no doubt an unconcealed expectation on the British side that the Political Resident's advice would be listened to; and the boundary between offering advice and enforcing it may have been as narrow as a vocal inflection. But the British were well aware, even in the early days, that if maximum advantage was to be drawn from them, 'special relations' had to be good relations and that good relations were most conveniently fostered by upholding the principle that in internal affairs the local rulers were their own masters.

The fact that some of the shaykhs whose local sovereignty was recognized by the treaties ruled as few as a thousand subjects[26] may be thought to have given the whole treaty arrangement an air of farcical imbalance. Certainly it can be argued that by signing treaties with whatever tribal leaders seemed to be in charge in the coastal villages along the sea route to India in 1820, Britain's policy had the effect of legitimizing, perpetuating and indeed fossilizing a fragmented political system that just happened to prevail there at the time. This fragmentation, it can then be represented, would not otherwise have survived the rationalizing pressures of history; for without British patronage these tiny mini-states would long since have been absorbed by, or merged into, larger ones of sensible size. On this reading Britain was at fault not for interfering too much but for interfering too little. Had the British seen advantage to themselves in bringing these small shaykhdoms under the sovereign control of one of their sizeable neighbours – Saudi, Persian, Omani – or alternatively of colonizing the area themselves, it is unlikely that by nineteenth-century criteria they would have regarded the treaties as an unsurmountable obstacle. But neither the East India Company nor the Government of India (which took over responsibility in 1858) nor the Imperial Government of the time wanted more than the peace at sea under British supervision that the treaties gave them. Accordingly, until well into the twentieth century nothing was done to release the shaykhdoms from the fragmented isolation in which, as in aspic, the treaties preserved them. And by the time new considerations presented themselves and something more than peace at sea was at stake, the possibility of quietly engineering a more coherent structure was scarcely an option. Criticism of Britain's policy for failing to impose more unified arrangements in the days when she could have got away with it is at least nearer the mark than the more familiar but naive charge of deliberately keeping the area fragmented in order to divide and rule. The British authorities saw no advantage in applying themselves in either direction, reckoning that their wider interests were best served by leaving the local situation loosely defined.

Without, for the moment, pursuing twentieth-century developments further, enough has already been said to provide a preliminary answer to the first two questions posed in the opening paragraph of this chapter. These concerned the origins and objectives of Britain's curious position in the Gulf and the nature of the relationship improvised between the British Government and the shaykhdoms.

The dominant status Britain arrogated to herself arose initially, we can see, from the determination of the East India Company to ensure in its own trading interests the safety of the Gulf sea-lanes to India. As the nineteenth century advanced, however, communications with the Raj entailed more than just security for shipping in the Gulf. Palmerston himself had regarded British supremacy in the area as a strategic necessity in a much wider context. Political, and if need be, military resistance to the perceived ambitions of other powers – France, Russia, Germany and of course Turkey – constrained the British to devise a means of keeping those powers (and any other aspirants) out. The means ultimately adopted was the Exclusive Agreements of the nineties. Their terse and somewhat throwaway appearance was deceptive. As the twentieth century took its course, other considerations would present themselves, calling for reinterpretations of the rubric. The upshot so far, however, was that the Gulf States remained bound to Britain in the special but immobile relationship engineered in the nineteenth century for nineteenth-century purposes. No 'forward policy' – the fine old term we kept bumping into in South West Arabia – was envisaged.

It will be convenient to offer at this point a somewhat preliminary answer to the third of our opening questions as well by examining the internal features of the shaykhdoms as distinct from their relations with the imperial outsider. What then was the nature of society and of traditional government in them?

Of the small groups of immigrants from the Arab heartland pushing in this direction over the centuries, some had settled along the coastline and turned to the sea for a livelihood, others had remained inland and nomadic. Relations between the two categories were never painless (and still are not), but with one conspicuous exception history and economics in the Gulf area favoured the coastal ones; and it is with the coastal communities, or rather the dominant families within them, that we are concerned. The functions of leadership in them were, in Western terms, both civil and military. A shaykh provided in his person the government and administration of his subjects; he protected the tribal unit from its neighbours (subordinating any of these that he could); and, in a way that distinguished coastal society from its inland equivalent, he supervised the exploitation of the sea in its three manifestations – fishing, pearling and coastal trade – to the maximum benefit of his shaykhdom. For these purposes, tough, fast, sailing ships with armed men on them were needed. The activities of these rudimentary navies were legitimate war, protection of the shaykhdom's trading vessels, or piracy, depending on the point of view of the recipient of their attentions.

If found wanting in any of these fields, a shaykh's family might dethrone him. He could equally be replaced, and frequently was, by more summary means by a jealous family aspirant for power. He therefore needed the qualities of leadership to stay on top – not always easy in a tribal society based on the 'democracy' of the *majlis*. Sitting in his *majlis* a shaykh was by tradition open to the pleas, protests and proposals of all his subjects; and if his judgements in his *majlis* or his behaviour outside it were unacceptable or ineffective, his tenure of office would be at risk. In broad terms this 'shaykhly system', as we call it, survives to this day. And while it is true that the signature of treaties with imperial Britain in the nineteenth century and the implied protection that went with them conferred on this tribal particularism a kind of enduring legitimacy, the system would hardly have survived without popular consent. In societies or states as small as these personal autocracy was and, in a modified form perhaps still is, an understood and acceptable mode of governance. Indeed, though this is not the place for presumptuous generalizations, in the Arab world as a whole statecraft and the ordering of society were always, and have remained, 'personalized' to a degree no longer easily understood in the West.

We can now proceed with a summary account of the evolution of Britain's relations with the Gulf states in the twentieth century with the aim of establishing, firstly, how the resulting situation compared with that prevailing, as relinquishment approached, in South West Arabia and, secondly, what it was that Britain relinquished.

No further treaties or agreements of a comprehensive kind were found necessary by the imperial power to define, modify or update the overall relationships.[27] As long as the course of history did not throw up new *desiderata*, the British authorities – the Government in India and the India Office in London – were content to leave things in the juridical sense indeterminate. Even as late as the thirties, when a growing measure of outside interest in the area was predictable and the Foreign Office was growing restive at the 'hand to mouth' approach of those responsible, the India Office maintained the view that 'HMG should accept as little responsibility as possible for the Arab states round the Persian Gulf, and if there were any doubt about their independent status, the India Office would not wish that doubt to be resolved but to keep the situation as fluid as possible'.[28] This was scarcely a tenable attitude for the Foreign Office to endorse while at the receiving end of claims continually being lodged by Persia, Iraq and Saudi Arabia to sovereignty here and there – the Persians claiming the whole of Bahrain, the Iraqis the whole of Kuwait, and all three sundry islands or other chunks of territory belonging to one shaykhdom or another. Questioned on one of many occasions by the Persians, the Foreign Office could only declare that 'the Gulf States were a special preserve of HMG whose policy towards them rested on a kind of Monroe Doctrine';[29] and an India Office minister in reply to a parliamentary question on the extent of Britain's protective responsibilities limited himself to the vague generality that 'the States are in treaty relationship with HMG under which they enjoy in varying degrees His Majesty's protection'.[30]

Indeed, in respect of both the internal and the external affairs of the Gulf states the British Indian authorities (Curzon excluded) continued right up to the end of the Raj to treat this fringe area of their geographical responsibilities with rigorous detachment – an attitude which, though calculated, astonished the British Legation in Tehran in 1937[31] as much as it dismayed the Foreign Office. The latter was no longer concerned only in theory: not only was it responsible for diplomatic relations with the Gulf states' bigger neighbours but by 1937 the Foreign Office was already expecting to fall heir to departmental responsibility for controlling the Gulf. The Political Resident's supervision of Arab states from Persian soil by virtue of treaties which the Persians did not recognize was increasingly resented in Tehran; and the Residency was due to be transferred to Bahrain in autumn 1939. The transfer fell victim to the outbreak of war and only took place in 1946 on the eve of Indian independence. Until then and despite growing imperial needs the Government of India was content to leave the execution of policy on the Arab side of the Gulf to a single Indian Service colonel in Bushire (who was simultaneously a consul general in Persia responsible to the Foreign Office through the Legation in Tehran). Throughout this time the only subordinate staff he had in dealing with the Arab states were a Political Agent in Kuwait appointed in 1904, a Political Agent in Bahrain, also appointed in 1904 and responsible for the other eight shaykhdoms as well, a cold-weather-only Political Officer in Sharjah from 1937 and an indigenous Residency Agent in Sharjah since 1823. If only because of the distances involved and the difficulties of communication, the Senior Naval Officer in the Gulf frequently served – with great effect – as bearer of the Political Resident's advice to the remoter rulers. Gunboat diplomacy had not yet, at least in this area, come under critical scrutiny; and the number of recorded occasions on which bombardment, actual or threatened, of the palaces of recalcitrant trucial shaykhs, for reasons varying from indulgence in forbidden slave traffic to unacceptable discourtesy, may raise in retrospect an eyebrow.[32] The human machinery for supervision was indeed minimal. As the Resident in Bushire demurely observed in 1939, 'we achieve our object with astonishing economy'; and he attributed this to the goodwill accruing through 'non-interference, square deals and genuine protection'.[33]

But what *was* Britain's 'object'? And how, in terms of administrative pragma, was it achieved? Examples chosen to illustrate the technique will start with three from the period when responsibility still lay with the Government of India.[34]

First, as the presence of British subjects gradually increased, the securing of capitulatory rights for their protection was judged essential. Jurisdiction over them and over other expatriates (in some cases only non-Muslim ones) was successively ceded without visible reluctance by rulers, and corresponding Orders-in-Council were issued, in respect of Bahrain (1913), Kuwait (1935) and Qatar (1939). In the Trucial States – always a case apart – steps were not judged necessary until 1946. Jurisdiction had not been sought there before since the seven rulers concerned, so the Political Resident blandly put it, were 'under the wholesome impression' that non-natives in their territories had been under British jurisdiction for years.[35] It was nonetheless decided that the proprieties should now be observed. Cession was sought from each of the seven and, a little unexpectedly, granted. As will be seen in connection with the setting up of the Trucial Oman Levies, the acquired rights of jurisdiction were interpreted as justifying rather more intervention in internal affairs than simply the extension of British court process to the categories covered.

A second British object, touching the rulers' interests and the principle of non-interference more nearly, arose from the scent of oil. No doubt the British could have controlled the allocation of oil-prospecting concessions, as and when they might be sought, by reliance on the old Exclusive Agreements. But as a reinsurance against undesirable foreign intervention in the area, they secured – between 1913 and 1922 – undertakings from all the rulers not to grant any oil concession except to a person approved by the British Government. Such a requirement, the Exclusive Agreements notwithstanding, might certainly be said to impinge on a ruler's right to manage his internal affairs; and to the extent that the British initially sought to exclude non-British applicants, they had (and maybe deserved) difficulties here and there. The object of extracting these undertakings from rulers was of course to keep out undesirables, a category into which it was never politically possible to classify the Americans;[36] but even to the end, the letter of the old Agreements was enforced to the extent that a prospective oil concessionary had to obtain a 'political agreement' from the British side by side with the ruler's concession agreement. It should be added that oil prospecting, once it got under way, drew Foreign Office attention to the inevitability of interference in several other respects, notably over the delimitation of state boundaries (subject everywhere to dispute) and over the physical security of prospecting oil men in areas of tribal lawlessness. The authorities in India showed, however, no eagerness to interfere in such faraway problems.

A third area in which it was found necessary, during the period of Indian Government responsibility, to override the principle of non-intervention arose from the development of air links with India and beyond. The freedom of the seas was still as important as ever to indigenous and foreign shipping and trading, and naval predominance in Gulf waters remained strategically vital to the imperial power; but when in the early thirties the need arose for secure air routes to the East, the Gulf acquired a new importance.[37] The route originally followed kept to the Persian side; but when the right to use it lapsed in 1932, the development of staging-points and airports on the Arab side became essential. The right to exploit a ruler's territory for this purpose could only be secured by agreement. Bahrain and Sharjah were the first locations chosen. The Ruler of Bahrain raised no objection but his counterpart in Sharjah resisted in the belief that a British airport on his territory would threaten his independence. His resistance was overcome; and as the economic benefits of housing a British airport became apparent, he had to fight off the attempts of his jealous neighbour in Dubai to obtain its transfer there. No difficulties, incidentally, were encountered elsewhere in the Gulf when air traffic expanded after World War II and further sites and facilities were negotiated.

Until the transfer of the Political Residency to Bahrain in 1946 and the final take-over of responsibility for it by the Foreign Office the following year, it is clear that imperial involvement in Gulf affairs was as limited as the Government of India could contrive, and that even where interference was judged necessary the letter of the treaties was broadly observed. In the mid-thirties there was much inconclusive debate between the various British authorities affected as to what constituted 'interference' and how much of it the promotion of British interests required.[38] After the war the tempo quickened. The need to secure improvements in the management of the Gulf's internal affairs, by one kind of pressure or another, was perceived as increasingly acute. The stimuli were multiple. The Gulf's oil being seen as vital in future, if not already, to Britain and her allies, a strategy to ensure its availability was essential. Surplus revenues accruing to Gulf states, Kuwait in particular, were seen as jeopardizing the stability of sterling unless channelled in the right directions. The stirrings of moral responsibility for progress in the broad sense in her Protected States were now awakening. And international interest in an area claimed by Britain as her exclusive preserve was becoming such that tolerance of her special relationship would soon be at risk if order was not brought into the 'chaos' of internal administration. But given the circumstances of the treaties and the declared independence of the states, how was pressure to be applied without losing the goodwill of their governments?

By the early fifties the strengthening of British representation in the Gulf was under way, and in 1952 a major review of requirements was conducted by a top Foreign Office official, Sir Roger Makins.[39] His report confirmed the need for enlarging the staff at the Political Resident's disposal throughout the area. Economic and military advisers on the spot, the upscaling of existing Political Agencies, the posting of subordinate Political Officers where none existed and their ultimate conversion into separate Political Agencies in Qatar and the Trucial States (at first in the latter as a whole, then in Dubai and Abu Dhabi separately) – all this was gradually put in train, though not completed until 1961. But a more promising technique for promoting progress in the internal administration of the States was seen in London to lie in persuading their rulers to employ British advisers – political at the top, technical below – who, while properly distancing themselves from British official control, could be relied upon to advance British interests as well as those of the governments employing them. The trail had already been blazed in Bahrain since 1926 when, its Ruler having asked for a British Adviser, a young Colonial Officer, Charles Belgrave, was recruited for him.[40] The influence which Belgrave acquired over the years with the Ruler's backing may before his retirement in 1957 have aroused resentment amongst the Ruler's more restive subjects (and even in the Political Residency), but the progress in administrative disciplines which he succeeded in accomplishing was such that it was regarded by some as unparalleled in the Arab World.[41] Attempts to reproduce the Belgrave pattern elsewhere were not conspicuously successful, being made perhaps too late for the pattern to be reproducible.

The chance had indeed been missed in 1938 in Kuwait, whose Ruler's spontaneous request for a 'Belgrave' had been turned down. The attempts made from 1946 on to persuade the same Ruler and his successor to engage a Political Adviser make an ironic story, for they were then steadily resisted. Even the urgings of Winston Churchill in person in 1953 were unsuccessful: indeed the only response from the Ruler, and he was by no means ill-disposed to the British connection, was a threat to abdicate.[42] He had been furnished since 1950 with a British Financial Adviser and other technical ones, but the prize of placing in his employ an eminent administrator (and a whole string of them were identified as suitable) eluded Britain's grasp. The Ruler's reluctance to control the interventions of his power-seeking and avaricious relations left the management of Kuwaiti administration, as the Foreign Office saw it, in a state of chaos. The Ruler of Qatar, by 1950 enjoying a £6 million income from oil, accepted in that year a Financial Adviser, but it was not a position, nor a place, to attract the eminent at the time. In all three of the states already producing oil the number of British advisers in specialized fields – agriculture, education, policing, etc. – expanded in the fifties; but the absence of a British hand at the political tiller in Kuwait continued gravely to exercise the Foreign Secretary and his staff. As for the Trucial States, still without oil and administratively primitive, the placing of British advisers in the employ of individual rulers would have served little purpose. The technique adopted over the years had simply been to extract from new rulers, as a condition of recognizing them on their accession, a vague undertaking to accept the Political Resident's advice; and only in one case, that of the ill-fated Saqr bin Sultan of Sharjah in 1951, was the condition fully explicit.

But in these Trucial States, where inter-shaykhdom fighting was still common, where control by the rulers of petty tribes inland was uncertain or non-existent, and where the collapse of the pearling industry had left the rulers without the financial means to promote security, let alone development, a more relevant kind of intervention than the provision of British advisers was gestating in London. This was a project, first discussed there in 1949, to set up on Trucial territory a security force under direct British control – a striking departure, one might think, from the declared policy of leaving the rulers to manage their own internal affairs. When first envisaged in London, the recorded object was simply to prevent the traffic in slaves[43] – a practice which all Gulf shaykhs had undertaken in successive stages between 1820 and 1847 to suppress, but which still continued with the active connivance of some of the Trucial ones. If, however, the home government initially viewed the project in this restricted light, the Political Resident for his part saw the prime function of the proposed force as the establishment of law and order in these fractious shaykhdoms.

In the final upshot it was agreed in London that the objectives of the Trucial Oman Levies, as they were to be called, should be publicized as three-fold: the protection of British Political Officers, help in the preservation of law and order and 'assistance to the rulers in fulfilling their obligations in regard to the slave trade'. The question now arose, almost incidentally it seems, as to whether the establishment of such a force required the advance consent of the rulers in whose territories it would be operating. By 1950 the Foreign Office and its legal advisers had satisfied themselves, perhaps a little oddly, that such consent was unnecessary under the terms of the Trucial States Order in Council of 1946 (the jurisdictional document which they themselves, of course, had had a hand in drafting).[44] It was deemed advisable, however, once the formation of the force's nucleus was privately under way in Jordan, to notify the rulers. This was duly done. The fact that the notification was greeted with positive enthusiasm[45] may perhaps suggest that direct British involvement on land was no longer suspect or at least that value could be extracted from it. Nonetheless, as a departure from the principle of non-interference, the formation of the Trucial Oman Levies must rank high. The force, tiny at first (seventy men) but ultimately of well over brigade strength, was placed under the Political Resident's command – the only recorded instance, as a later Political Resident (Luce) used happily to observe, of a British diplomat commanding a private army.

There was of course no question of the Political Resident controlling such internal security forces as existed in the other states. A small number of British officers, army or police, were made available to the rulers there, but that was different: they were the Ruler's servants. In the case of the Trucial Oman Levies the only misgiving about their establishment under British control that exercised the Foreign Office was over the reactions of Ibn Saʿud. For Ibn Saʿud still regarded the Gulf states as his subordinate satellites over which he had been expecting to recover his 'ancestral suzerainty' when Britain's position there disintegrated (as he was reported to foresee) in twenty years' time.[46] Though not as unwelcome to him as the delimitation of inter-state boundaries – a matter to which Britain shortly turned her attention – the formation of the Levies was seen by Ibn Saʿud as a sign of Britain's new policy of 'hemming him in'.

What concerns us here, however, is the further evolution in Britain's interpretation of her responsibilities, under the treaties, for the good government of the states. The doctrine propounded in the early fifties with increasing confidence in London is best illustrated by quotation from Foreign Office briefs and reports.

It has always been accepted that in the last resort the Political Resident should intervene to prevent maladministration

The international responsibility of Her Majesty's Government involves indirect responsibility for their internal stability, and the British jurisdiction over foreign nationals . . . involves a direct responsibility for internal security and impartial justice. Since Her Majesty's Government will be blamed for any shortcomings, they must find means to ensure that the administrations are above reproach.

An especially Delphic sentence in the directive given to the new Political Resident (Burrows) on 24 July 1953 reads:

Her Majesty's Government can no longer afford to confine themselves to the role authorized by the treaties. It is essential that Her Majesty's Government exert sufficient influence in the shaykhdoms to ensure that there is no conflict between the policies of the Rulers and those of Her Majesty's Government.[47]

It is a far cry from the distant but formally correct attitude of the Government of India. The motives for the revised doctrine were not wholly imperial self-interest. For one thing, Britain as protecting power, responsible for the external relations of the states, was quite often required to accept on their behalf international obligations under world conventions. Compliance could hardly be guaranteed without internal intervention. Another motive was a quite genuine desire to promote a better life for the people, primarily through improved administration. Foreign Secretary Eden, on receiving in 1953 a report on progress achieved, or lack of it, minuted severely: 'All this is very disturbing . . . In many spheres we seem to be failing to discharge our responsibility adequately.'[48] Seen from London, the business of persuading the states to do things for their own obvious good should not have been all that difficult. The view from Jufair (in Bahrain) where the Political Resident sat was not quite the same. Persuading independent rulers to accept advice, particularly since progress meant change and the old ways were cherished, was never plain sailing.

Moreover, the entrance of a new theme was already audible. As early as 1951 the Political Resident – the last of those from the Indian Service – was himself observing that full independence was perhaps no more than two decades away and consequently the gradual relinquishment of anything detracting from independence (capitulatory jurisdiction, the management of postal services, quarantines, etc.) must soon be taken in hand. The Foreign Office agreed that '[we] could not impose our wishes and reduce local responsibility in states whose ultimate independence we envisage'.[49] How the two themes – increased intervention and its progressive relinquishment – were to be harmonized is left obscure. But the Resident, Hay, fully agreed that improved administration was the first requirement.

Hay was also turning his attention to future political structure in the Gulf as a whole. The rumour, baseless at this time, that Britain was planning a federal union of the Gulf states had already been causing concern in Tehran and Baghdad.[50] Hay considered that the gap between the more advanced states in the north and the more primitive ones in the south ruled out any present idea of federating them all in any real sense, as distinct from possibly encouraging a joint council on common services; but he favoured a union of the Trucial States, and as a first step he went ahead in 1952 with bringing their rulers together to form a Trucial States Council.

Within the states themselves the British were at this stage less enthusiastic about pushing the rulers in the direction of democracy, not just because this would jeopardize their relations with the rulers but because political opposition to the 'shaykhly system', like opposition movements in other Arab monarchies under British patronage, was likely to rub off on themselves. Rub off it did, and quite painfully, when a 'nationalist' opposition movement developed in the fifties in Bahrain. In 1954 the movement's Higher Executive Committee, the title rather grandly chosen for its eight-man directorate, demanded a range of political and administrative reforms – Labour Law and trades unions, a legal code, rent control, greater elective participation in government and so on. Most of these were in fact already under study at Belgrave's prompting but the Ruler was hesitant. The Committee also demanded the dismissal of Belgrave, a demand pursued with renewed zest when General Glubb was dismissed by King Husayn from his comparably powerful and long-held role in Jordan in March 1956.[51] Rioting and violence on several occasions were only just contained, and Britain's Foreign Secretary, Selwyn Lloyd, visiting Bahrain the day after Glubb's dismissal, was a target for some of it. The movement received encouragement from Nasser, and the Suez invasion that autumn might have been expected to give it a further boost. In fact it evidently distracted local attention from internal reform to higher things. Suez at all events can hardly have reinforced the belief popular in Bahrain (so Belgrave insists) that the nationalists had the backing of the British authorities – a belief which might well have been revived when the movement's three leaders, sentenced by a Bahrain court to imprisonment in

December 1956 and accommodated by the protecting power in St Helena, were released five years later to the ruler's dismay on appeal to the Privy Council. But by that time the vigour of the reformists had waned.[52]

There were also stirrings of reformism in Kuwait. Indeed they had begun in 1938, partly as a response to the maladministration of the ageing ruler, Shaykh Ahmad bin Jabar, and partly in the context of the Palestine *imbroglio*. In the mid-fifties, following the accession of Shaykh Abdullah as-Salem, a more liberal ruler than his predecessor, pressure for reform was again in the air. But this was differently angled from the movement in Bahrain and its impact was less dramatic.[53] Kuwait too had for a time a High Executive Committee, but this was a very different thing from the 'Higher' one in Bahrain, for it reflected little more than pressure from members of the ruling family for the delegation of some of the Ruler's personal administrative control – something which in principle the British favoured. But the Committee got nowhere quickly and the Ruler replaced it with an equally ineffective Advisory Council. The embryonic popular demand for a representative assembly had to wait till 1962.

Mention has already been made of British intervention of a more positive kind in the internal affairs of the Gulf as a result of oil discoveries in the three northern states and the expectation of them in the rest. Britain's early measures to discourage the allocation of oil concessions by rulers to non-British companies may be open to criticism. This is scarcely the case with the steps she later took, however interventionist, to delimit rulers' boundaries. Such delimitation was inescapable, for oil concessionaries of whatever nationality had to know the geographical limits of their concessions. With the exception of Kuwait (whose territorial dispute with Saudi Arabia had been settled in 1922 by the creation of a neutral zone, and whose boundary problem with Iraq was of a different order), no Gulf state was without boundary disputes of the usual tribal kind with its neighbour or neighbours. Even in the case of quarrels of this kind between one protected state and another, Britain's acceptance of responsibility for settling them was by no means automatic – a fact which suggests that her right under the treaties to demarcate boundaries was questionable, even if barely questioned.

The British handling of the time-honoured dispute between Bahrain and Qatar over ownership of Zubara (a village on the Qatar peninsula) and the Hawar Islands illustrates one approach. For whereas in the past Political Residents had repeatedly sought to promote or impose a settlement – most recently in 1937 and 1939 – the attempt had by the forties been abandoned, the attitudes of the two parties being visibly irreconcilable. As prospects of oil in either area decreased, resolution of the dispute was doubtless less essential.[54] On the other hand, in the case of Qatar and Abu Dhabi, between whom a dispute flared up in the fifties both over their land boundary and over a string of offshore islands (all these areas being suspected of bearing oil), Britain resolved the former by simply announcing her own views in 1955 and the latter by appointing an outside commission of enquiry in 1961 and informing the two rulers of its conclusions.[55] Within the Trucial States anything as mappable as linear frontiers was virtually non-existent; and if maps were to be produced for potential oil concessionaries, direct intervention was unavoidable. At considerable expense of effort, a workable delimitation in most areas was achieved in 1956. The point of interest for us is that before the process was embarked upon all seven rulers were required to accept the Political Agent's decisions, the implication being that Britain's right to fix boundaries by *fiat* was indeed open to question.

No such simple solution, of course, presented itself where the dispute lay with an independent outside country – Saudi Arabia in the case of Qatar and Abu Dhabi, Iran in the case of sundry small disputed islands, quite apart from the Iranian claim to Bahrain itself. In such cases Britain's responsibility for the conduct of the state's external affairs obliged her to seek solutions by negotiation or arbitration. Though generally upholding the claims of her Gulf protégés, Britain had long been reluctant to force matters to a head at the cost of good relations with countries of the importance of Saudi Arabia and Iran.

Unfortunately the area disputed between Saudi Arabia and Abu Dhabi was of such prime importance to the opposing oil concessionaries, American and British, let alone to the opposing governments, that there was no escape from seeking a settlement. The long drama of the Buraimi Dispute, as it came to be called though much more territory was involved than that strategic group of oases, cannot be examined in detail here. There had never been any likelihood of Ibn Saʿud treating with respect the old 'Blue Line' laid down by the Anglo-Ottoman Convention of 1913 as the eastern boundary of Najd. It lay far to the west of any frontier remotely acceptable to the king of the resurgent Wahhabi state, even before oil added a new dimension to the issue. Attempts by Britain in the 1930s to negotiate a settlement (affecting Muscat as well as Abu Dhabi) had been fruitless; and the boundary claimed by the Saudis steadily advanced eastwards, reaching in 1949 grotesque proportions (see map 4). An agreement to go to arbitration had eventually been reached in 1954, but the proceedings collapsed in 1955 when the British delegate withdrew in protest at the improprieties of the Saudi delegation. This led to the use of the Trucial Oman Scouts to help the Sultan of Muscat (whose own rights to certain of the Buraimi oases Britain supported) to evict a small Saudi occupying force from Buraimi[56] – not the kind of function envisaged in the purposes of the Political Resident's private army as originally defined. The eight-year severance of diplomatic relations with Saudi Arabia which ensued (though the formal context of the breach was the Suez war) and which effectively marked the end of Britain's once paramount influence with Ibn Saʿud, serves as a lurid demonstration that the conduct of the Gulf states' external affairs was not, for

Britain, all cakes and coffee. Saudi boundary claims against Abu Dhabi were again to become a lively issue for the British fifteen years later, as we shall see. Agreement on the delimitation of the Saudi-Abu Dhabi frontier was not in fact reached until after Britain's withdrawal from the Gulf. It is arguable that Britain's withdrawal was what made agreement possible.

The adjoining Saudi claim against Qatar relating to the supposedly oil-bearing base of the Qatar peninsula, if not to the whole of it, had also dragged on since the twenties. In the thirties, interestingly enough, it was the India Office and the Viceroy himself who stood by Qatar's rights while the Foreign Office would have favoured buying Ibn Sa'ud's goodwill at the expense of Qatar. World War II interrupted the argument until 1944 when the Americans pressed for a settlement. On this occasion too the India Office stood by Qatar. The dispute was not laid to rest for another twenty years. By that time Saudi Arabia was sufficiently awash with oil elsewhere for the King to relax and reach agreement with the Ruler of Qatar over an area now regarded as unpromising. What is of interest to our theme is that whereas in the twenties the British had reprimanded both parties for communicating on the subject direct, and whereas in the forties they still regarded negotiation on Qatar's behalf as a British responsibility, by 1965 they seem to have raised no objection to the King and the Ruler settling matters without British intervention.[57]

As for Iran's claims, by far the most conspicuous was her enduring insistence on sovereignty over Bahrain, regarded on paper as a province of that metropolitan country. At no stage did Britain admit the validity of the Iranian claim; but the importance of maintaining the goodwill of the Shah, particularly after the Musaddeq interlude (1951–1953), was fundamental to Britain's Middle East policies as a whole. On the other hand, while Britain was more than reluctant to engage in a collision with the Shah on any issue, even less could she put at risk her whole position in the Gulf by failing to protect Bahrain from the Shah's grasping fingers. No escape from this dilemma presented itself until the eve of withdrawal. Long before that time the paucity of oil in Bahrain's territory was apparent. What was by then at stake was the Shah's pride. Hoist as he was on a petard of his own manufacture, he must have been relieved when a technique to render it harmless was, as we shall see, invented in 1970. Amongst the other Iranian claims to smaller islands up and down the Gulf, the only ones that were to cause trouble were those concerning two small islands near the mouth of the Gulf, coveted by the Shah for strategic rather than oil reasons. The quite remarkable trouble they were to cause will be examined later.

As the fifties progressed, the dramatic expansion of the Gulf's known and suspected oil wealth had a double effect on Britain's exclusive position there. It gave the Gulf states a new and legitimate sense of their own importance and it aroused mounting scrutiny in the outside world of what was going on in an area hitherto closed to it by Britain. Both these trends must have cast doubt on the practicability of the interventionist policy confidently adopted only a year or two earlier. It was in fact already apparent that the Gulf states could no longer be fenced off from the rest of the world, that they were set on the path towards self-assertion and ultimate release from British tutelage and that diplomacy rather than dictation must be used in guiding them along it. Ironically the high point in Britain's conviction of the necessity, and therefore the propriety, of intervention in the internal affairs of the states was reached just when it was becoming impracticable. As in the Sudan and South West Arabia, what Britain miscalculated was not the direction, but the pace, of history. And this miscalculation was reinforced by the unwillingness of the rulers, self-assertive or not, to discharge Britain from her responsibility of protecting them from outside aggression, whether the threat came in domineering terms from Iran, in Arab socialist/nationalist terms from Nasser's Egypt, in territorial terms (and after the 1958 revolution there, in ideological terms) from Iraq, or in communist terms from Moscow.

At this stage (mid-1950s) all the states were still, in Britain's view, lamentably ill-prepared to approach the future unaided or, with the possible exception of Kuwait, as separate entities. The problem was how to secure the modernization of their administration without resorting to modes of interference which would now arouse sharper external criticism as well as more sensitive resistance from rulers. Whereas the latter needed a new public image to present to the world, Britain needed their goodwill now more than ever as the oil stakes mounted. Thus while assistance in the development of internal security arrangements was welcome, political pressure to decentralize and respond to, or pre-empt, public demand for participation in the running of the state was not. In Bahrain, the one state in which the Ruler had gone some way towards decentralization and elective procedures, the experiment had evidently whetted rather than quietened popular aspirations: an object lesson, so other rulers may have felt, in the dangers of democracy. As for material development, the states enjoying oil revenues in the fifties scarcely needed financial help; but in those without oil and therefore totally undeveloped the British Government were no more generous in the provision of subsidies than they were in South West Arabia. Small sums had been made available to the Trucial States in 1952 and in subsequent years for the development of water resources, the promotion of agriculture and other modest purposes; but help in the virgin field of education was largely left to Kuwaiti generosity. In the absence of any major teacher-training initiative anywhere in the Gulf, the rising generation in all states were largely taught by Egyptian recruits, bearing, it was feared, a political message from Cairo. The British shook their heads but did little else.

It will now be as well to pause before we enter the decisive sixties and consider how the situation as it had evolved by this time in the Gulf compared with that prevailing in South West Arabia, where Britain's relinquishment of power was already in prospect.

The Gulf of course contained nothing remotely similar to Aden Colony or the British strategic base there. Even when the latter was wound up in 1967 and Britain's military headquarters in Arabia were transferred to Bahrain, nothing comparable with the Aden base was attempted. What we are here concerned with is the supposed resemblance between the Aden Protectorates and the Protected States of the Gulf. They both consisted of formally independent mini-states in treaty relationship with Britain. In exchange for protection against aggression from outside (more explicit in the Protectorates than in the Gulf), the rulers in both had surrendered to Britain the conduct of their external affairs, and the exclusive nature of the relevant agreements was not dissimilar. But in all other respects the resemblances taper away. Rulers in the Aden Protectorates were formally obliged by their treaties to accept British advice on internal affairs (save in certain specified fields) but because of the curious structure of tribal society were not always able to implement it even if they wished to. Rulers of the Gulf states were explicitly absolved under their treaties from a comparable obligation, but were in general more disposed to listen to advice offered and much better able, in terms of the structure of society, to put it into effect by *fiat*. The Gulf states were centred on coastal townships with a correspondingly urban life-style, and the dominance of their ruling families was unchallenged. In the Aden Protectorates the situation in the states was (with the exception of Quʿaiti Mukalla and perhaps Lahej) in all these respects the reverse, a system of anarchy being endemic and cherished. Moreover, rulers in the Protectorates were in some instances selected and imposed by the British, instead of acquiring their position by traditional tribal process, and their authority was therefore more likely to be questioned than was the case in the Gulf. Poverty in the Protectorates was of a different order from poverty in the Gulf even before the discovery of oil in the latter and of course totally so after it. The political disaffection towards Britain radiating from Aden had no parallel in the Gulf (the Suez disaster of 1956 notwithstanding), which at this stage moreover still lay in Nasser's pending tray. The Gulf states may have felt from the King of Saudi Arabia something of the threat the Protectorate states felt from the King of the Yemen, but they were too discreet to give public expression to their misgivings. Nor was there any parallel in the Gulf to the dragooning of the Protectorate states into federation – least of all into a federation like that of South West Arabia subject to direct British tutelage. While therefore relations of both groups of mini-states with Britain had a similar origin in imperial history, while both had suffered from similiar disregard from the Government of India for a century, and while both may have been saved by British protection from absorption by a more powerful

Arab neighbour, circumstances in the Gulf when the sixties opened were conspicuously dissimilar to those in the Aden Protectorates.

Britain's own standing in the Arab World generally had of course plunged dramatically downwards in the second half of the 1950s. The evacuation of her strategic base in Egypt, relatively dignified and orderly though it finally was, symbolized everywhere her declining power. The Suez episode in November 1956 illustrated that decline in infinitely more humiliating terms. Even in the well-disposed Kingdom of Jordan, the dismissal a few months earlier of General Glubb had been a sign of the times. The union of Egypt and Syria in February 1958 seemed to indicate that Nasser's Arab nationalism was carrying all before it. The bloody overthrow of the monarchy in Iraq that July dislodged a further British *point d'appui*. Britain's interventions in Muscat since 1957 on the Sultan's behalf against the Oman rebels were the object of orchestrated Arab protests. British Aden was visibly under threat. Palestine provided more than ever the theme for a genuine anti-British rallying-cry. And behind it all Soviet influence was clearly spreading[58] as British influence receded.

In such circumstances it may seem surprising that in 1960 Britain's position in the Gulf was still effectively unopposed. The most obvious explanation is that the Gulf rulers had no other acceptable protection to turn to – the US, as protector of Israel, being ruled out. The obverse of the same coin was that what remained of British paramountcy in the Gulf was unquestionably linked to the survival of shaykhly rule. For both parties the oil stakes were higher than ever. Altogether it was in the interests of both that their mutual dependence should not be called in question – particularly when the Soviet Union was visibly advancing towards the area on one front and Nasserite Arab socialism on the other. These summary observations, however, should not be taken as ignoring either the growth amongst Gulf commoners of anti-British resentments or the awareness within the British establishment that the shaykhly system could only survive in the longer term by some degree of accommodation with its internal critics.

At the same time the antiquated nineteenth-century treaties had become for both parties something of an embarrassment, if more for their form than their effect. One Gulf state, predictably Kuwait, was already anxious to slough off hers, without in the process repudiating British protection. Unlike the others, Kuwait was recognized as just large enough and more than wealthy enough to face the world on her own. For Britain the replacement of an outmoded relationship by an internationally irreproachable Treaty of Friendship would be intrinsically virtuous. Moreover, it would not prejudice the maintenance of Britain's hegemony in the Gulf as a whole: no military withdrawal was involved, since there was no (operational) British military establishment in Kuwait to withdraw. Kuwait, either on her own or on Britain's initiative, was already a member of sundry international bodies; and in sponsoring Kuwait's application for membership in UNESCO in May 1960, Britain had informed its Director General that she 'regarded Kuwait as responsible for the conduct of her international relations'.[59] Thus her release from formal subordination to Britain needed no more than a confirmatory document; and in June 1961 the relevant exchange of notes was signed by the Ruler and the Political Resident, terminating the old treaty and recognizing Kuwait's sovereign independence. 'Nothing', as the signatories nonetheless recorded, 'shall affect the readiness of Her Majesty's Government to assist the Government of Kuwait, if the latter request such assistance'. The undertaking was invoked within a matter of days. Iraq, having instantly and with Soviet backing rejected the concept of Kuwaiti sovereignty and having ostensibly threatened invasion, the Ruler requested military assistance from Britain. This was quickly provided and the threat evaporated.

The reality of that threat was subsequently questioned, but it was clearly real enough to the Ruler at the time. This is not the place to examine its reality.[60] The point for us is that, though British protection was successfully invoked under the new treaty, the episode unquestionably reinforced the inclinations of rulers elsewhere, threatened or potentially threatened from other quarters, to keep a hold of nurse. No requests for the termination of the old treaties were then, or indeed ever (until 1971), received from any of them. Kuwait's admission to the Arab League a month after the flare-up can have given the other rulers little reassurance, for though the League felt constrained to replace in September the British force in Kuwait with one of its own, the military measures actually taken were unimpressive.

Nonetheless, Kuwait had blazed a trail, and the release of the nine remaining states from tutelage was recognized as inevitable in due course, whether they wanted it or not. So how did Britain now envisage preparing them for independence? Luce, having just arrived as Political Resident with his experiences in South West Arabia fresh in his mind, saw no hope of any of the nine surviving as separate entities if British protection were withdrawn.[61] But under the letter of the treaties Britain had no power to enforce the kind of political, social and economic advances that might transform the nine into a single viable entity and thereby make possible at some point in the future the smooth and orderly relinquishment of Britain's protecting role. The mutual jealousies between the states seemed to Luce such that only some traumatic revelation, such as a direct threat of Soviet penetration, could stimulate them into sinking their differences. He was of course in no position in 1961 to foresee the traumatic revelation administered by his own Government seven years later. The overthrow of the monarchy in the Yemen in 1962 might have been expected to concentrate the minds of the Gulf rulers. But the Imam was not a monarch they admired; and the only aspect of his overthrow which worried them was the evidence it gave of the continuing involvement in Arabian peninsula affairs of President Nasser, with his propagation of republican socialism.

As far as the British were concerned, what was clear was the need for a closer understanding with the Americans over the maintenance of stability (under British auspices) in the Gulf and the abandonment by the Saudis (under American auspices) of their bid for aggrandizement and enrichment at the expense of states under British protection. The vast quantities of oil awaiting exploitation in Abu Dhabi and Qatar were by now apparent. As for the actual exercise of protection in the Gulf, the continued availability of the Aden base was judged essential. The 1961 operation in Kuwait, which might prove a prototype, would scarcely have been possible without it.

There was one aspect of Gulf government over which Britain did see means of pressurizing the rulers. This was their administration of justice. Attempts had indeed been made since 1948 to modernize their court system by urging the adoption of a British-drafted corpus of law and the employment of professional Arab judges. Little progress had been achieved. But capitulatory jurisdiction had been surrendered in Kuwait without disaster;[62] and the policy now adopted to stimulate the other rulers into modernizing their courts was to offer them similar retrocession, progressively and on condition of specific improvements. In other fields of administration progress throughout the states[63] was desperately unhurried, save in Bahrain where by 1964 the new Ruler, in the hope of disarming political criticism from his increasingly well-educated citizenry, had authorized a series of social and economic innovations.[64]

As the British (explicitly) and the Rulers (privately) saw it in the mid-sixties, the prime threat to the survival of the shaykhly system came not from within nor from its bigger neighbours but from Cairo. To Luce the best answer seemed to be in promoting, from behind the scenes, a much closer intimacy between the small Gulf states and Saudi Arabia, based on their fundamentally shared interests and their rulers' common fear of Nasserism. The fact that at this stage Saudi Arabia was demanding the surrender of three quarters of Abu Dhabi's oil-bearing territory was awkward. Nonetheless Luce pleaded with London, and continued to plead throughout his six years as Political Resident, that the pursuit of Peninsula Solidarity, as he called it, would offer the best prospect of preserving stability when the time came for Britain to terminate her treaties. (The promotion of an understanding between King Faysal and the Shah on ways to maintain by joint effort the future stability of the Gulf – the other prong of Luce's policy urgings – was certainly adopted in London. The Shah's visit to King Faysal in November 1968 was not the only contact between the two in the ensuing period.) Already by 1964 – and this was before Abu Dhabi soared up the league table – 31 per cent of non-communist oil production came from the Gulf area, and over half of this went to Britain and her allies. In such circumstances, and quite apart from the virtues of stability as an end in itself, it was clearly imperative that Britain should by one means or another ensure the continuance of stable conditions for the production and export of oil.

Whether or not Peninsula Solidarity was to be adopted as the objective, solidarity between the Gulf states themselves was obviously desirable; and the prospects of their agreeing to unification of some kind were once again examined in London. But the prospects looked dim, even without reflecting on Britain's dispiriting experiences elsewhere in her vanishing empire of feder-ation as a cure for fragmentation.[65] Even within the seven tiny Trucial States, where the Council of Rulers (now equipped with a Development Office) had been encouraged for over a decade to promote cohesion, separatism still prevailed. The only cement Britain might have furnished was financial – and this was not forthcoming.

What *was* by contrast forthcoming[66] was an offer of £5 million from an Arab League (effectively an Egyptian) mission visiting the Trucial States in late 1964, its aim being less to encourage their attachment to each other than their detachment from imperialist Britain. By March 1965 the five smallest states, with the Qasimi rulers (mindful perhaps of 1819) in the lead, had accepted the League's offer, Shaykh Saqr of Sharjah telling a protesting British Minister of State (George Thomson) that he would do as he thought fit, whatever his treaty obligations to Britain. A month later his family, with British encourage-ment, deposed him. Thereupon the Qasimi ruler of Ras al-Khaimah assem-bled his men at arms and informed the Political Resident that he would have no further truck with Her Majesty's Government until his cousin was restored. A plane-load of Arab League technicians having been refused permission to land, Luce visited Ras al-Khaimah and persuaded the Ruler to think again. On his advice the seven rulers then cabled the Secretary General of the League that any contribution to their development plans would be welcome provided it was channelled through the Trucial States Council. None proved forthcoming on these terms. This first move by Cairo to wean the Trucial rulers away from their treaty obligations to Britain was thus frustrated. By way of consolation to the rulers, Her Majesty's Government scraped together £1 million for their development budget. Trucial States cohesion, however, continued to elude the British. Since Shaykh Shakhbut of Abu Dhabi was now a member of the oil-producers' club, and by that token even more averse to merger with his six impoverished neighbours, Luce turned privately to the idea of federating the six under the leadership of Dubai with financial subsidy from the oil states further up the Gulf. But the idea, when mooted, of terminating Abu Dhabi's membership of the Trucial States Council was greeted with such dismay by the oil-less rulers that it had to be dropped.

On the other hand, the hope that all nine Gulf states might after all see merit in uniting was given a new lease of life in July 1965, when their rulers unexpectedly assembled together, for the first time in history, in Dubai. What galvanized them into this unprecedented gesture of togetherness was not just British pressure. Certainly they were closely watching developments in South West Arabia in the wake of the British promise of independence for the Federation by 1968. This may not have stimulated enthusiasm for federation as such, but must at least have drawn their attention to the dangers of disunity and the opportunities it offered for revolutionary Arab nationalism to exploit. They may also have seen the recent Arab League venture in the Trucial States as an Egyptian warning shot across their bows. Altogether, the time for reconciliation was at hand; and if nothing concrete emerged from the Dubai meeting, it had at least set a precedent.

But even if it came about, Gulf solidarity would not provide much future protection, in Luce's view, without Saudi collaboration and leadership; and King Faysal's goodwill at this stage depended on the settlement of his boundary dispute with Abu Dhabi. Shaykh Shakhbut was as resolutely opposed to a compromise over his frontiers as he was to using the new wealth of his shaykhdom to transform it into a replica of Kuwait.[67] Shakhbut seemed indeed the main obstacle to progress in any direction. Luce would have welcomed his disappearance, and it is ironic that the appeal by his family for British help in persuading Shakhbut to abdicate was only forthcoming after Luce himself retired in July 1966.[68] Shaykh Zayed's resulting accession had little immediate effect on the solubility of the boundary dispute with the Saudis. He went at once to pay his respects to King Faysal and was given short shrift. He was to fare no better on a second visit in May 1970. Britain's own attempts to promote a more accommodating posture from the King were fruitless.

By this time the prospect for continued stability under British auspices in the Gulf faced other obstacles. The decision of Her Majesty's Government in February 1966 to withdraw lock stock and barrel from Aden by 1968 meant the disappearance of the base on which Britain's military dominance in the Gulf had hitherto depended. The announcement had also led within hours to President Nasser repudiating his August 1965 agreement with King Faysal on mutual military withdrawal from the Yemen and declaring that he would keep his troops indefinitely in the peninsula, or at least until Britain's withdrawal from Aden was implemented.[69] The mounting Dhofar rebellion against the Sultan of Muscat, led by the Popular Front for the Liberation of Oman (PFLO) with Soviet and outside Arab support, was another current and

Shaykh Shakhbut, Ruler of Abu Dhabi (1928–1966) outside his palace.

geographically close source of concern to the Gulf rulers. On the local scene, the death of Shaykh Abdullah as-Salem, the Ruler of Kuwait, had removed a powerful believer in the value of the defence commitment in his Treaty of Friendship with Britain.

Luce's final plea was two-fold: firstly that his Peninsula Solidarity idea should be accepted and resolutely pursued; secondly, that if withdrawal from the Gulf was regarded as inevitable in a decade or so, Britain should not repeat the mistake made in Aden of declaring in advance a fixed date for it but should, by retaining flexibility in its timing, ensure that preparations were first completed for a smooth and orderly disengagement. As had been the case when he left Aden, Luce's final recommendations were not pursued.

There was indeed little sign of any constructive policy emerging in London for the long-term security of the Gulf. What did emerge, as the abandonment of Aden drew nearer, were repeated statements by responsible ministers that they had no intention of abandoning the Gulf.[70] Indeed on the very eve of Britain's final withdrawal from Aden in November 1967, Minister of State Goronwy Roberts was sent out to reassure the anxious rulers that Britain was fully determined to continue fulfilling her treaty obligations towards them.

But the rulers' relief was shortlived. Two months later, in January 1968, the luckless Goronwy Roberts was sent again with a very different message. (The parallel with the two successive missions to Aden of Lord Beswick in November 1965 and February 1966 (see p. 85) is, to say the least, striking – though Lord Beswick was received on his second mission with much less courtesy than was Goronwy Roberts on his.) The message now was that, so far from remaining indefinitely, Her Majesty's Government would be removing their military establishments from the Gulf by the end of 1971 as part of a general withdrawal from commitments East of Suez. This clearly implied, though no formal notification was given till April, the relinquishment of the special relationship which had preserved the Gulf states for 150 years. The Rulers, apart perhaps from the independent-minded Shaykh Saqr of Ras al-Khaimah, were dumbfounded by this abrupt reversal of the assurances given only a few weeks before.[71] Britain's representatives on the spot, who had naturally been repeating those assurances as a counter to the bad news from Aden, were shamefaced as well as dismayed. The Political Resident, Crawford,[72] telegraphed personally to the Head of the Foreign Office, vainly urging reconsideration. A certain consternation was apparent amongst Britain's allies as well, from Washington to Singapore – though the Shah, to whom the Western powers paid such court as an asset in the context of East–West confrontation, was openly delighted. So of course were critics of Britain's remaining imperial pretensions elsewhere in the world. The reactions of those in the Gulf itself who were keen to see the last of the British were more subdued than might have been expected. The Popular Front for the Liberation of the Arabian Gulf (PFLOAG) – the new title recently adopted by the PFLO to mark the expansion of its aims beyond the frontiers of Oman – might scarcely have existed.

The ostensible reason for the Government's change of policy was Britain's financial straits, luridly symbolized by the devaluation of sterling on 18 November. Treasury pressure, however, was not the only, perhaps not even the primary, stimulus involved.[73] Labour party leaders, whether or not they wholly shared it,[74] were increasingly exposed to the hostility of party ideologists to the practice of empire. Twenty years after Ernest Bevin's death, these two pressures taken together were evidently irresistible. The British public, taking its petrol pumps for granted, was not greatly concerned. Kuwait's independence was now seven years old and nothing untoward had happened

Shaykh Eissa bin Salman, Ruler of Bahrain since 1961, with Sir William Luce, Political Resident, 1961–1966.

there in the last six: indeed the Ruler had felt secure enough to allow the establishment of an elected parliament in 1962, and this was interpreted in London as a sign not just of democratic virtue but of stability. Moreover oil production in the Gulf states had by 1968 risen to new heights; Abu Dhabi was awash, Dubai and Muscat had both struck oil; and whatever might happen politically in the Gulf states, they could not, in Nasser's words, 'drink the stuff'. The temporary embargo on Arab oil supplies to specific Western countries in the context of the Arab-Israeli war of June 1967 had given the British public no sleepless nights, though it may have indirectly contributed to the Government's decision to devalue sterling that November. The Conservative Party, it is true, was loud in its protests when the decision to fold these last imperial tents in the Arab World before the end of 1971 was made public by the Prime Minister in Parliament on 16 January.[75] Then and at intervals over the next two years the party's leaders declared that Labour's 'shameful and criminal'[76] decision would be reversed if the elections due in 1970 returned the Conservatives to power – a possibility on which some of the rulers pinned their hopes.

Meanwhile the Foreign Office and the Ministry of Defence, in their respective fields, addressed themselves to the problems presented by the withdrawal announcement. On the military side, one significant step was the appointment of a Defence Adviser to the nine states in the impressive shape of Major General Sir John Willoughby.[77] In the political field there were of course plenty of fairly minor concerns – planning, for instance, the retrocession of Britain's residual responsibilities, judicial and administrative; a process involving the sort of punctilio at which the British were by now rather good. They also addressed with renewed zeal the thorny issue of inter-state sea-bed boundaries. The promotion of a common currency to replace the Indian rupee, a fairly obvious *desideratum*, ran up against the ancient particularisms.[78] This did not matter much, but there were three major problems which did.

The biggest – and the other two were directly related to it – concerned the future inter-relationships, political and structural, between the nine tiny states from Bahrain to Fujairah. The premise, of course, was that if they did not hang together, some outside executioner would string them up separately. What Britain regarded as essential was that some kind of union, able to stand on its own feet and qualify for international recognition and UN membership, should replace, before protection was withdrawn, a string of shaykhdoms which could not individually fulfil these requirements. The rulers themselves were uncomfortably aware that their best hope of survival was to pool differences and join forces. The differences, it is true, were more formidable than the forces. But it is one of the significant ironies of the time that whereas in South West Arabia Britain's announcement of a fixed date for withdrawal caused an even greater upsurge of internal hostilities, the corresponding announcement in the Gulf had the opposite effect. In this respect, at any rate, Luce's old objections to the declaration of a terminal date in the Gulf were misplaced. Without much need for further encouragement, the nine rulers set themselves to pursue in earnest the idea of federation, to which they had given half-hearted attention in recent years.[79] The advantages of presenting a united image to the outside world when confronted with it in three years time were obvious. But there were obstacles, those of outside fabrication appearing at the outset even more formidable than those of the rulers' own making.

In the first place, the Shah condemned the project on the grounds that the biggest of the shaykhdoms, Bahrain, was a province of Iran. In the second place, King Faysal refused to sanction it unless his claims to most of Abu Dhabi's territory were met.[80] Since Britain was still the protecting power, the circumventing of these external obstacles was formally her responsibility. Moreover, and quite apart from the moral obligations of defending the rights of her protégés and of leaving a stable political structure behind her on withdrawal, Britain had in the case of Abu Dhabi's territory potent financial reasons for not allowing British oil company estates to slip into Saudi/American possession. On the other hand Saudi goodwill, like Iranian goodwill, was regarded by Britain as a vital policy requirement, and not only in a Gulf context. While the British took stock (such stock as they had), the rulers were encouraged to go ahead with their federal discussions.

The Bahrain problem proved much the easier to solve. Whether the Shah's longstanding claim to sovereignty over Bahrain was a genuine obsession or whether by the continual discharge of verbal missiles he had simply hoisted himself on his own petard, there was one matter on which he now certainly felt strongly. This was the danger that, following the possible return of the Conservatives to power in Britain, he would not after all be left to dominate the Gulf himself. It would therefore suit his book to deprive the Conservatives of one justification for cancelling or deferring Britain's withdrawal. In January 1969 in an ostensibly throwaway remark in New Delhi he had declared that 'If Bahrain does not want to join our country, we shall never resort to force to oblige them to do so';[81] and now, in late 1969, he accepted a suggestion that the Secretary General of the UN should be invited to settle the status of Bahrain by an 'ascertainment' of its people's wishes. His acceptance had a properly statesmanlike look, and when the Bahrainis made it plain the following April to the appointed Italian investigator, as the Shah must have known they would, that their preference was for independent Arab statehood, he gracefully relinquished his claim.[82]

But if the UN adjudication removed a potential obstacle to the setting up of a Gulf federation which included Bahrain, Bahrain itself was now distinctly less enthusiastic at the prospect of merger with the less developed small fry down the Gulf. Thus the removal of one obstacle to a union of the nine led to the erection of another. Moreover, the Shah soon made it plain that another condition must be fulfilled before he would recognize, or indeed permit, a Gulf federation. This was that Iranian rights to certain small islands near the mouth of the Gulf – Abu Musa and the Tunbs, of which the Qawasim of Sharjah and Ras al-Khaimah respectively had long been in possession – must first be satisfied. This further demand, as we shall see, was to cause complications of a grotesquely disproportionate size.

As for the Saudi-Abu Dhabi dispute, little or no progress was detectable. When Shaykh Zayed paid a further visit (for other purposes) to Riadh in May 1970, King Faysal took the opportunity to present him with yet another version of his boundary claim, less extreme than his astonishing 1949 demands but still requiring the surrender of a stretch of the coast between Abu Dhabi and Qatar, a huge slab of oil-bearing desert inland and a whole group of oases at Buraimi, where Zayed himself was born and raised. Much as he wanted to be on good terms with his powerful neighbour, Zayed could clearly not accept this dismemberment of his patrimony. As for his British protectors, for all their efforts in the past to promote an agreement, they saw no merit – nor any ultimate advantage to Zayed – in seeking to impose a settlement now, one which would be overturned in any case as soon as they had gone. Nor could they see any prospect of persuading King Faysal by diplomatic means to accept one before their protective responsibilities (as things stood) lapsed. In these circumstances all they found it appropriate to do was to urge the hard-pressed Zayed to avoid provoking the King and to advise the Abu Dhabi oil concessionaries (not all of them by this time British) to steer clear for the present of the disputed areas. But the King's unwillingness, unless he received satisfaction over his boundary claim, to sanction a Gulf federation with Abu Dhabi in it was a serious concern.[83]

In June 1970 the Conservatives were, a little unexpectedly, returned to power by the British electorate. The implications of their election manifesto and of the opening policy statement in the Commons by the new Foreign Secretary, Douglas Home, were that the previous government's policy of precipitate withdrawal from the Gulf would be reconsidered in consultation with leaders in the Gulf.[84] Within a few days they were faced with declarations not only by the Government of Iran but, less predictably, by those of Saudi Arabia and Kuwait, all deprecating any idea of Britain retaining a military presence in the Gulf area (of which their own countries were of course a part) after 1971. The fact that the rulers of the protected states actually wanted British forces to stay was evidently of no concern to the rulers of other Arab monarchies. But would the new British Government prolong that military presence and the old protective role? Judging by the Conservatives' pre-election bravado of 1968 and 1969 they were virtually committed to doing so, but more recently and on assuming power such commitments had been hedged a bit. It was of course recognized that, in the event of a federation materializing, as was hoped, the maintenance of Britain's special position could not then be based on the old treaties with individual shaykhs. Although the elaboration of a new treaty with such a federation would certainly arouse protest in an anti-imperialist age, it was unlikely to provoke forcible Arab opposition of the kind encountered in South West Arabia. By now, as one observer has acutely put it, the golden years of Anglophobia in the Middle East had passed.[85]

The British Government held its hand. Perhaps to the Foreign Secretary's surprise, his representatives in Arab capitals, when asked for their views on the desirability of prolonging the British presence in the Gulf beyond 1971, were uniformly unenthusiastic. The Political Resident in Bahrain himself now judged it impractical to reverse the process which the previous Government's decision had set in train. Douglas Home, whose personal inclinations were known to favour staying on in the Gulf, called Sir William Luce out of retirement and sent him off in August, as his special representative, on the first of what proved to be many trips to consult rulers and governments concerned and to report his findings on the most appropriate policy to adopt. Judging by the opinions he had expressed since his retirement in 1966 (but before the Labour Government's announcement of January 1969), Luce's views were likely to be robust.[86] The gospel he had been preaching during those two years was that, should Britain withdraw without making proper provision for the stability of the area thereafter, a dangerous power vacuum would be created in the Gulf, which would assuredly be exploited by forces hostile to Western interests. For this reason, foreseeing as he long had that Britain could hardly maintain her special position beyond the seventies, his plea had been that the timing of its termination be kept undeclared and flexible and that the interval should be used constructively. This would involve promoting a close understanding between the two major pro-Western powers in the area (Saudi Arabia and Iran) and pursuing at the same time his own long-held concept of Peninsula Solidarity under Saudi leadership amongst the states within the peninsula, including Oman and perhaps North Yemen. Both these arrangements would be aimed at maximizing local resistance to both Soviet and (in the Nasserist or Ba'thist sense) Arab nationalist penetration or subversion.

On the other hand, Luce's initial reaction[87] to the withdrawal announcement (and Douglas Home can hardly have been unaware of it) had been that the announcement set so many consequences in motion that it was probably irreversible. Well before he was able to submit to Home in December a report on his first round of investigations, he had been left in little doubt that his initial reaction was correct; and his discussions in capitals outside the Protected States – in Cairo and Baghdad as well as in Tehran, Riadh and Kuwait – clearly reinforced it. He found the Gulf rulers themselves less worried over the relinquishment of Britain's political position than over the withdrawal of physical protection. Amongst the dangers they saw ahead, internal subversion may well have bulked largest; but this had never been Britain's direct concern and would obviously be even less so when constitutional independence was complete.[88] Britain's treaty responsibilities related to external aggression. Potential external aggressors in the military sense could only be Iran or, in the context of Abu Dhabi, Saudi Arabia; and no British Government, least of all a Conservative one, would welcome a clash of arms with either. A much greater danger to stability in the Gulf after withdrawal might of course come from Soviet communism or Nasserite Arab nationalism. But that danger could scarcely be envisaged as taking the form of armed invasion; nor would a British military presence be any protection against other forms of penetration. Moreover, it was increasingly clear that the world as a whole – and particularly its Arab components outside the Gulf – would deprecate a reversal of the decision to put an end to the last relic of British imperial policing in the Middle East. Even in Washington, where Britain's previous and existing contribution to the security of America's own interests in the Gulf was by this time widely acknowledged, majority opinion seemed now to favour letting the withdrawal decision stand. Something of course, Luce reckoned, might be done to reassure the nervous rulers that Britain would not lose interest in the security of their states, but in strictly military terms this could hardly be of more than token scale if widespread condemnation was to be avoided.

The British Government's outline intentions, unquestionably reflecting Luce's first report, were not made public until March 1971, and the Foreign Secretary's presentation of them to the House of Commons was conspicuously low-key.[89] The existing treaty relationships, he said, would indeed be terminated at the end of 1971 and he gave a brief account of what Her Majesty's Government were prepared to offer a Union of Gulf Emirates in the way of continuing links and assistance, on the assumption that such a union emerged from the discussions proceeding amongst the rulers. The vital thing, as Home said, was to ensure that before withdrawal took place a viable political structure was in place, enabling the nine small states to project a joint *persona* on the international screen.

Healey, from the Labour benches, must have enjoyed teasing Home over his 'belated conversion'. Home's response to this sally was not ineffective, but when questioned closely about the possible stationing of British troops in the Gulf after independence – particularly if no union had by then established itself – his reply was a trifle equivocal. Conservative back bench opinion clearly needed soothing, but the imminence of a debate on the annual Defence Estimates provided Home with an alibi of sorts. In point of fact the Chiefs of Staff had already concluded that the progressive squeeze on their total resources virtually ruled out the continued stationing in the Gulf of British armed forces in any operational capacity, whatever the rulers might wish; and the Defence Estimates when presented to the Commons on 28 October contained no identifiable provision for commitments in the Gulf after 1971.[90]

The next step therefore was to bring pressure to bear on the nine rulers to press ahead with their plans for unification. The enthusiasm of Bahrain having visibly diminished, now that the Shah had relinquished his claim to sovereignty, and a meeting of Deputy Rulers in October having got nowhere, the federal initiative was in fact in low gear; but it was hoped that the public reaffirmation of Britain's approaching withdrawal would compel acceleration, whether or not Bahrain opted out.

But even if the rulers themselves could be stimulated afresh into sinking their old differences, two of the three external obstacles remained. King Faysal, though he joined with Kuwait in twice sending a mission round the

Gulf states in January 1971 to urge the rulers on, was still understood to require satisfaction over his territorial claims on Abu Dhabi as a precondition of giving his sanction – recognized as a *sine qua non* – to a union with Abu Dhabi in it. And the Shah's insistence on the 'restoration' to his sovereignty of the three disputed islands, whose Arab ownership Britain had continuously upheld,[91] had become increasingly categorical. Failing their surrrender, he would see to it that the federation initiative collapsed – and his influence with one or two of the rulers was known to be such as to make the threat alarmingly real.

To the urgent resolution of these problems Luce was meanwhile addressing himself. He had indeed submitted a further report to Home just before the latter's March statement in the House. King Faysal, despite the Abu Dhabi frontier stalemate,[92] had evidently come round to recognizing the value of a union but his final approval was now reported to depend on all nine states joining it. The Ruler of Bahrain consequently dared not make public his desire to opt out, thereby obstructing consideration of a union of the remaining eight or, should Qatar as was likely follow suit, of the remaining seven. It was not until 14 August that Bahrain felt confident enough of escaping the King's displeasure to declare itself a separate sovereign entity, terminating its old treaties with Britain and applying for membership in the UN. Qatar, diminutive for independent statehood though it was in population terms, was not to be upstaged by its old rival and quickly did the same. The eagerness for separate status manifested by Bahrain and Qatar reflected their consciousness of being 'superior' to the seven smaller shaykhdoms; and mini-states were no longer a rarity in the world as a whole. Both signed the new Treaties of Friendship proffered by Britain.[93] These contained a provision for 'consultation in case of need' similar in form to the 'consultative' clause in the 1961 Treaty of Friendship with Kuwait, which the latter had invoked to secure military protection from Iraq.[94] The British preferred to omit from the published treaty documents other mutual assistance provisions of the kind Home had envisaged in his March statement to Parliament. These, covering military training facilities, naval visits, overflying and staging rights, development assistance, intelligence advice and the like, were in some cases more obviously advantageous to Britain and for that reason were left for provision in documents of a less public kind. The UN, as well as the Arab League, gave both these new mini-states a welcome, such international recognition furnishing a measure of territorial inviolability.[95]

The problem of providing for Gulf stability (so far as this was possible) thus narrowed to the contriving of an equally viable future for the remaining seven shaykhdoms. But the point to which the problem had narrowed was disturbingly sharp. Of the seven states, whose total population was then hardly more than that of Qatar and a good deal less than that of Bahrain, five were penniless and none was viable on its own. This meant, since Britain could not responsibly withdraw without leaving a plausible authority in control, that their unification was essential. In July, just before Bahrain had broken away but knowing what was afoot, six of the seven rulers had in fact met to discuss a provisional federal constitution. Ras al-Khaimah had stood aloof,[96] but the sharpness of the problem lay elsewhere. For the Shah was unremittingly adamant that no such union would be permitted unless and until his demands for Abu Musa and the Tunb islands were satisfied.[97]

Neither of the two rulers concerned could accept the 'compromise' solutions, as he called them, offered by the Shah, since they would lead after an interval to the surrender of Arab sovereignty over the islands. For Britain the problem had wider ramifications. If on the rulers' behalf she resolutely opposed the Shah's pretensions, the damage he could, and promised to, inflict on British and CENTO interests, quite apart from the interests of the rulers, was formidable. Moreover a definitive clash with the Shah would obstruct the promotion of the collaborative understanding between Iran and Saudi Arabia which Luce and his government still regarded as the best way of filling the post-withdrawal power vacuum in the Gulf. But if, on the other hand, Britain withdrew support for the two Qasimi rulers and 'colluded' with the Shah, not only would she be pilloried by the Arab World, which was closely watching her behaviour, but her influence in the seven states would vanish, and with it her ability to promote the union initiative. Indeed the old Trucial States and their oil resources would, as Luce saw it, be up for grabs. The problem had all the marks of insolubility. Yet on its solution, for all the demographic insignificance by world standards of the area concerned, much wider interests than the mere upholding of Britain's honour visibly depended. And the weeks were slipping by.

Some aspects of Britain's frantic manoeuvring to square the circle remain conjectural. But one thing is clear. To the Cabinet's credit a solution by duplicity – by secretly conniving with the Shah at the advance seizure of the islands, holding back the formation of the Union until the Shah, his object achieved, condescended not to destroy it, and leaving enough time before withdrawal to make the same sort of friendly terminal arrangements as had been agreed with Bahrain and Qatar – was at no stage acceptable, even assuming it were practicable.

The dilemma was acute. Luce continued to shuttle to and fro, seeking a more saleable compromise from the Shah and a less total *non possumus* from the two rulers. There was no response. Since it was clear enough that the Shah would seize the islands at some point whether or not Britain was still formally responsible for protecting the Arab states, the only honourable course for Britain was to tell the rulers frankly that she was not in a position to stop the Shah by force of arms and to warn him that the international condemnation which his action would arouse would have Britain's public support. Even more disagreeably, it was clear that in the absence of any agreed solution the only sequence of events which might secure the establishment of the Union in time to conclude with it the essential testamentary agreement would indeed presuppose the Shah's seizure of the islands taking place before Britain's protective relationship with the Union's prospective members was terminated. The value of British protection would be thereby shown up as illusory. However humiliating all this would be, the scenario indicated must have seemed a lesser evil in the interests of the Gulf's future stability than withdrawing with the islands problem unresolved and with no union established. But in the hope that the lesser as well as the greater evil might be avoided, the search for an agreed solution continued as the summer sweated on into autumn. The Shah at least went as far as conceding that the rulers were free to discuss federation provided they did not actually federate.

With only a month to go before withdrawal was due, Luce was rewarded with a minor breakthrough. In terms of a median line between the two coasts of the Gulf, Abu Musa lay unarguably on the Arab side, and the Tunbs on the Iranian side. The possibility of treating the two differently had been examined. It would have meant Britain standing up to the Shah on Abu Musa and establishing a British military presence on it, while letting him have his way over the Tunbs and offering Ras al-Khaimah financial compensation for their loss. Possibly because the Shah himself recognized some force in the median line argument, in October a slight modification had been detectable in his posture. The amended formula he advanced still implied the surrender of Arab sovereignty after an interval, and was therefore unacceptable to either ruler;[98] but it did offer an element of sharing, and the change enabled the ruler of Sharjah to put up counter proposals. A tolerable solution at least to the Abu Musa problem hove hesitantly in sight. Under it Iranian soldiery would occupy unopposed a defined half of the island leaving the other half to Sharjah's administration, neither party would be required to give up its claim to sovereignty, revenues from oil (if found) would be shared and the Shah would give Sharjah substantial monetary aid. In the nick of time – 23 November – agreement on this basis was reached.

Shaykh Saqr of Ras al-Khaimah, however, maintained his adamant rejection of a similar arrangement over the Tunbs. Particularist as ever, he also continued to hold out against participation in the proposed Union of Seven, though this had not discouraged the remaining six, led by Abu Dhabi and Dubai, from pressing ahead with plans for its formation. Advised by Luce that Britain had done her best but could not contemplate forcibly opposing the seizure of the Tunbs which might take place any day now, Shaykh Saqr privately resigned himself to losing them. He refused, however, to take any action indicating foreknowledge of Iranian intentions. He would not, for example, give any warning to his posse of police on the larger Tunb, much less withdraw them and avoid the risk of casualties. He, like the British, no doubt recognized that in the Shah's eyes the strategic value of the tiny Tunbs (distinctly more plausible than Abu Musa's) was such that sooner or later the Shah would almost certainly impose total Iranian control of them, whatever 'sharing' agreement were reached. They were perhaps too small to share.

The Shah being confident by now of securing the substance of his demands, there was no serious danger of his sabotaging a union of the states, whether or not Ras al-Khaimah continued to exclude itself. The rulers of the other six, having been seized of the situation, were able to announce on 25 November amid general jubilation that agreement had been reached on the establishment of the Union, the simultaneous termination of the old individual treaties with Britain and the expected signature in their place of a joint Treaty of Friendship. The Union of Arab Emirates was admitted to the Arab League on 6 December. As in the case of Bahrain and Qatar, the only dissenting voice was that of South Yemen, though Iraqi recognition of the new state was declared to be conditional on the annulment of the Abu Musa agreement and though the Saudi delegate evidently expressed reservations in deference to the King's unresolved frontier claim.[99] The Union's admission to the UN followed on 9 December.

The Shah landed his forces on the Tunbs, as well as on Abu Musa, on 30 November. Why he should have chosen to do this twenty-four hours before the formal ending of British protection is uncertain: possibly he wanted as much of the resulting Arab odium as possible to fall on Britain's head. It is also uncertain whether the British knew in advance of the Shah's chosen timing. The fact that the Ruler of Sharjah announced his Abu Musa Agreement on 29 November and had a welcoming party ready on the island when the Iranian troops landed the following day, implies that he had been forewarned of the timing of the Abu Musa landing. If, as seems likely, the British were aware that the Shah would occupy the Tunbs the same day, they may have calculated that the timing would now make little difference: even if the Shah considerately waited until Britain's defence obligations had been terminated, critics in the outside world would in any case hold Britain up to execration and doubtless to charges of duplicity.[100] What Britain may not have foreseen was the violence of the reactions of two of the Arab countries, Iraq and Libya. The former – and Iraq had visibly been courting Ras al-Khaimah for months – instantly announced the severance of relations with Britain. On 7 December Libya summarily nationalized Britain's oil interests in its territory.

But at least Britain's basic objective in the Gulf had been achieved. Even though a union of all nine states cohesive enough to stand on its own had proved impracticable, the emergence of three separate, internationally recognized entities had at least made possible the signature with each of them of new agreements, mutually satisfactory and externally irreproachable, along with the peaceful relinquishment of Britain's outmoded hegemony. No local endeavours to jettison the shaykhly system along with its British life-belt had complicated the process. The Trucial Oman Scouts were handed over to the Union (which Ras al-Khaimah shortly joined) as the nucleus of a federal defence force.[101] The Treaties of Friendship with all three entities included provision for consultation in case of need. Continuing British help in developmental and defence training fields was welcomed. Overflying and staging rights for the RAF were extended, as were training facilities for British troops. As for the relinquishment of Britain's judicial and administrative responsibilities, the necessary steps had been progressively taken up and down the Gulf. Some of them obviously entailed legislative provision by the governments of the three new states; but the procedures were painlessly accomplished, and the Political Residency passed out of history on 26 March 1972.

It was not a heroic end but neither was it, as in Aden, a horrendous one. The prime difference between the Gulf and South West Arabia was that the relationship between rulers and people was that much stabler in the Gulf, and internal opposition that much less pronounced. The trail blazed by Kuwait in 1961 could be followed without demographic difficulty: there was no irreconcilability in the Gulf between centre and periphery of the Aden/hinterland kind. Unlike South West Arabia the Gulf as a whole was rich and growing richer. The Nasserist Arab nationalism which had played so traumatic a role in South West Arabia, was by 1971 well past its zenith. The Gulf advance towards statehood had enjoyed the backing of all its Arab neighbours and of the UN, whereas the South West Arabian Federation had been held up to execration by both. As regards the British presence, such troops as she had in the Gulf were never, as had been the case in Aden, damagingly conspicuous; nor had their housing requirements generated the kind of inflationary shortages and social resentments created in Aden. As for political relations with the populace generally, such anti-British animus as manifested itself in the Gulf bore no comparison with South West Arabian experience. There were occasions, notably in Bahrain, when popular opposition to Britain's Middle East policies, actual or imagined, took active form, as for instance on the outbreak of the Arab–Israeli war of June 1967.[102] But British interference in the internal affairs of the Gulf had aroused over the years singularly little active opposition; and this very fact had made interference less necessary. There was nothing in the Gulf hinterland to compare with the tribal resentment at imported disciplines endemic in South West Arabia; and no measures were ever taken by Britain in Gulf townships of the kind which the colonial administration of Aden was obliged to take and which opposition groups there were so ready to condemn. If the old reluctance of the Government of India to intervene constructively in South West Arabia had proved a recipe for ultimate disaster there, the tradition established by that government of non-intervention in the Gulf[103] may, by contrast, have contributed to the painlessness of ultimate disengagement.

5 Comparisons without odium

Comparison is the expedient of those who cannot reach the heart of the things compared.

Santayana

As the foregoing chapters have demonstrated, Britain's relinquishment of power in the three territories concerned followed no uniform pattern either in its motivation or its manner. The compulsions in each case were conspicuously different. So too was the nature of Britain's constitutional role in the three territories, though this affected the style of relinquishment less than might have been expected. At the beginning of this study the contrasting background to the successive exercises in disengagement was summarized in three sentences. 'Withdrawal from the Sudan was dictated largely by the private requirements of British policy towards Egypt. Withdrawal from South West Arabia was forced upon Britain by a crescendo of much more public pressures. Withdrawal from the Gulf was determined less by external political hustling than by Treasury calculations and the fading of imperial will.' That was shorthand and needs elaboration. In this chapter an attempt will be made to elaborate by surveying the three episodes in wider focus and from different angles.

Obviously the quarter century concerned witnessed an evolution in Britain's attitudes to her overseas role at the political party level, at the official level and at the public level. In each sector perceptions and priorities were changing, in the same general direction certainly but not at the same pace. External pressures, friendly and unfriendly, hortatory and hostile, impinged; and the response to them in Britain was seldom uniform across the board. In the Arab World itself, of which our three territories are part, the pervading influence of Gemal Abdulnasser, whose comet was in full blaze until the final stages of the last of our three episodes, bore directly and balefully on Britain's behaviour; but its very potency did of course stimulate reactions here and there in Arabia which were useful to Britain. All these and other phenomena which helped to determine the course of Britain's disengagement from the area will be touched upon; but though that process can now be recognized as a single evolutionary sequence, it is the contrasting features of our three episodes in that sequence that concern us here. What we shall therefore be considering in this chapter is the manner in which these various contributory pressures and influences reinforced the contrasts.

We shall also investigate the extent to which relations between those making policy in London and those executing it in the field conflicted in each of the three episodes and why. We shall then turn to a comparison of the attitudes of the inhabitants of the three territories to the prospect of independence and the influence they had on British policy and procedures. Finally we shall take a look at the constitutional aftermath in each of the territories concerned, since the different political directions in which their respective communities faced or turned on independence adds a further dimension to the contrast between the successive episodes.

At the beginning of our period until well into the fifties, Labour/Tory bipartisanship in foreign policy was still broadly intact. The tacit agreement not to differ, at least in public, had no doubt been strengthened by wartime experience of coalition government; and the maintenance of a common posture towards the outside world, in particular towards those parts where Britain exercised a dominant role, was perhaps reinforced by the general uncertainty in the immediate aftermath of war about the direction in which world history would move and the role Britain would or should or could play in it. This is not to say that there were not dissidents, as there always had been, in the wings of both major parties; but cabinets could still broadly count in foreign affairs on the public support of shadow cabinets. This happy arrangement was not to last long. The explanation does not lie in the attitudes of one party stagnating and of the other moving on. During the period concerned dominant attitudes at both ends of the political spectrum evolved, if not *pari passu* with the evolution in Britain's international standing, then at any rate a pace or two behind.

To illustrate, in 1946 even a Labour government was imperialist; by 1970 even a Tory one recognized that the game was up. The illustration oversimplifies, and might seem to ignore the rift between the two parties in their approach to overseas responsibilities that broke open in the mid fifties. But two points are worth re-emphasizing in this context. Firstly, governmental handling of the Sudan issue and consequently the task of those implementing government policy in the field were barely affected by the stark divergence in party attitudes which in the next decade or so disrupted attempts in the field to apply a consistent policy in South West Arabia and which later were to cause at least temporary confusion in the Gulf. The second point – which might seem to conflict with the first – is that the party which set in train much of Britain's decolonization, or at least actively accelerated it, was Tory – under the supple leadership of Macmillan from 1957. Not only did he see it as a means of rejuvenating his party's image at home, but his success in restoring the special relationship with the US (disrupted by the Suez affair) through his close friendship with Kennedy played a major part in his re-shaping of Britain's overseas role. Moreover, the prosperity engendered in continental

Europe by the Treaty of Rome (1957) obliged him to see the salvation of Britain's economy lying in its progressive un-coupling from the colonial caravan and its attachment to the European high speed train.[1] The second aspiration was of course not achieved until de Gaulle finally gave it his blessing. Macmillan's thinking and that of his intimates in the party, Macleod in particular, lay this way long before his wind-of-change speech hit the headlines in 1960.[2] Indeed two years before he took over as Prime Minister in 1957 he was subjected, as Chancellor of the Exchequer, to Treasury pressures to rid the economy of the expense of maintaining colonies and subsidizing their development; and one of his first acts as Prime Minister was to set up a cost-benefit review of the colonial position.[3] This is not of course to suggest that by this time anti-colonialism was not distinctly further advanced on the Labour benches. The Labour version, though philosophically of a different order, was certainly more explicit and insistent; but the electorate had kept them out of power since 1951 and continued to do so until 1964. It is also clear that in Macmillan's mind the shedding of non-essential territorial responsibilities in the African colonies was one thing; relinquishing control of essential strategic foci East of Suez would have been quite different.

The main point is that basic attitudes to the practice of empire were evolving during these twenty-five years on both sides of the political divide. This too can be illustrated symbolically. Thus while there was nothing totally bizarre in Wilson's appointment in 1964 of Greenwood – an established anti-colonialist and pacifist – as Colonial Secretary, such an appointment would have been unthinkable under Attlee in 1946, for all Attlee's own misgivings about the maintenance of empire. On the Tory side, quite apart from the departure from the centre of affairs of the towering traditionalist Churchill in 1955, such representative imperialist figures in the earlier period as Sandys and Amery found themselves well to the right of prevailing Conservative thought by 1971. A corresponding evolution in the proconsular view of imperial responsibilities, the attitude of the man on the spot, was as we shall see equally evident.

The bi-partisan approach to Britain's overseas role held, so we have suggested, till the mid fifties. The handling of the Sudan problem was therefore not significantly affected, so far as initiatives taken by Britain were concerned,[4] by the change from a Labour to a Conservative government in October 1951. When we come to our two later episodes, the rift had developed and the rules had changed. While it is demonstrable that the Suez affair split the country, at the popular level, in a manner not reflecting party affiliations, the Conservative Government in its handling of the mounting problem of South West Arabia faced not just the hostility of the Arab World (and much of the rest of the world as well) but also increasing criticism from the Labour opposition. Tory insistence on the indefinite maintenance for strategic reasons of sovereignty in Aden[5] and therefore of British control over the hinterland protectorates was not at first directly challenged from the opposition front-benches, though the criticism of government policy by ideologues behind them steadily mounted.

The strands of which official Tory policy East of Suez was woven were in fact already multiple and complex by 1957, though they were not perhaps consciously separable at the time. At party grass roots a nostalgia for imperial stature of the old kind was certainly potent, but higher up in the hierarchy the changed circumstances were recognized. At that level dominion over palm and pine was no longer an end in itself. Once sovereignty over the Indian raj was surrendered, the importance of Aden was obviously in one sense diminished. But there were new compulsions for retaining this and other strategic assets, not directly associated with colonialism in the traditional sense. A conviction that Britain was still responsible for the security of Western interests (oil of course in particular) East of Suez was the main compulsion. The resulting concern over strategic bases, as a means to that end, was reinforced both at the time of the 1957 Defence Review and thereafter by powerful pressures from the Services in their own as well as in what they saw as the national interest. The Foreign Office was also institutionally anxious that its ability to influence affairs in Arabia and Asia should continue to have military presences behind it. Perhaps even more important to the political policy-makers was the US government's new-found desire that Britain should continue its policeman's role in the whole area. That role certainly differed in its purpose from a colonial role; but even if residual anti-colonial instincts in the US enabled Washington to expect that the former could be exercized without the latter, the distinction was less apparent in London. In the Arab World the distinction was not recognized at all: a foreign presence in any shape or form seeking to call tunes there was by definition colonialist. Below, we shall examine separately the influence of these divers pressures on Britain's policy-making, Labour and Conservative, over the whole period. It should be borne in mind that in all three episodes the timing and effect of British general elections resulted in control passing in mid-stream from one party to the other: from Labour to Conservative (1951) in the case of the Sudan, from Conservative to Labour (1964) in the case of South West Arabia and from Labour to Conservative (1970) in that of the Gulf.

Enough has been said in chapter 2 of the robust, if re-shaped, imperialism espoused by Bevin as Foreign Secretary from 1946 to 1951. A good trades unionist's enthusiasm for instant nationalization in the industrial sense at home did not for him entail instant nationalization in the political sense in territories where Britain's predominance, in his view fundamentally bene-volent, was long established. Progress towards independence by mutual con-sent was assuredly desirable, but for him the defence of the West and its Third

World friends and dependencies took precedence over all other benchmarks. Britain's military supremacy in the crucial Near East had to be maintained; his approach to the problem of the Sudan could not therefore be separated, despite the pleadings of its Governor General, from his search for an understanding with monarchist Egypt over the future of the Suez base, since monarchist Egypt would not allow the issue to be treated separately. In his handling of the Sudan, the Conservative front bench could go along with him, despite the activities of the 'Sudan lobby', encouraged by members and ex-members of the Sudan Political Service, amongst Tory members of Parliament. Had Labour still been in power, even without Bevin, when the revolution took place in Egypt in 1952, it is possible that an even more determined attempt to reach an understanding with the republican revolutionaries would have been mounted, but unlikely that the outcome, as described in chapter 2, would have been greatly different. Eden's obsessive anathema towards Nasser was a later development. It is also possible but again unlikely that, had Naguib not been ousted by Nasser in 1954, Egyptian aspirations in the Sudan, where Naguib was widely popular and admired, would have been more fruitfully pursued. As things worked out, both co-domini were finally upstaged by the Sudanese themselves.

By the time the Sudan was struck off the British Government's list of overseas problems, South West Arabia was firmly on it; but prospects of a bipartisan approach to it were receding. In Aden Colony nationalist stirrings and workers' agitation were already coming together as a focus of opposition to the massive and slow-moving British presence. Both these anti-imperialist rumblings, like others elsewhere, were urged on by Cairo (where political opposition was given much shorter shrift and trades-unionism was unknown). In the Protectorate the Governor's most recent (1954) attempts to stimulate a joint move forward from the archaic separatism of the protected states, as their best defence against outside Arab hostility (Yemeni, Egyptian and at this stage Saudi), had roused little response. The Conservative government was still, as the fateful year of 1956 began, wedded to a policy of treating the future of the Colony in isolation from that of the Protectorate despite the contrary pleadings of Governor Hickinbotham. The home government's current doctrine, carried to Aden by Lord Lloyd in May, fell, as Trevaskis puts it,[6] 'tragically short of what was required', making no concession to self-government fervour in the Colony, instilling no urgency amongst Protectorate rulers, and holding out no hopes of future independence to either. The fact that members of the Labour opposition were already undisguisedly sympathetic to aspiring left-wing nationalists and trades unionists in Aden and unsympathetic to archaic autocrats in the hinterland was lost on neither. But Tory policy in South West Arabia was still not openly condemned by Labour leaders. The impetus given to anti-British animus and to Arab nationalism by the Suez disaster later that year made even more essential the adoption of more enterprising policies in both Colony and Protectorate. Some progress was indeed made under the Conservative government, as described in chapter 3. But so far as the Colony was concerned, constitutional advance was too slow to satisfy even moderate opinion, and in the Protectorate the backing given to the federal project was too cautious, and to infrastructural development too slight, to give the whole set-up prospects of plausibility.

Whether the Labour Party, had it been in power in the years when the South West Arabian problem was still perhaps soluble, would have handled the growing crisis differently is doubtful. In opposition, though their sympathies were clearly at variance with those of the Conservatives, they gave no hint of a thought-out alternative policy. When the merger between Aden and the Federation was debated in the Commons in November 1962, Healey attacked 'the tying of Aden Colony . . ., by far the most politically advanced territory in Arabia, to the reactionary shaykhdoms'[7] but made no positive suggestions for a better solution. The decision of June 1964 to grant the merged Federation independence not later than 1968 was a Conservative one; and though the agreement reached with its ministerial representatives included the sovereign retention by Britain of the Aden base, this was not repudiated by Labour's leaders at the time or on taking power after the October 1964 elections. Indeed the aspect of Sandys' ingenious solution which aroused most criticism from them, when he secured parliamentary approval of it, was the non-representative nature of the Aden Legislative Assembly through which the package had been bulldozed. But the problem of widening the franchise without surrendering electoral control to the immigrant Yemeni workforce was not one to which Labour leaders seemed to have paid any detailed attention.[8] On assuming power both Wilson and Healey, his Defence Secretary, publicly endorsed not only their predecessor's date of 1968 for South West Arabia's independence but also – and despite mounting anti-imperialist pressure from the body of the party – the maintenance of Britain's East of Suez role and the retention of the Aden base (with a hedging clause or two about local acceptance of it). Assurances too were continually given to the Federalis right up to the dramatic switch in policy associated with Healey's Defence Review of February 1966, that Britain would continue to fulfil her treaty obligations to them. By that time the situation in Aden was already so out of control that a Tory Government might well have reached the same conclusion over the impracticability of retaining the base, though they would certainly have promised something more substantial in the way of a defence commitment to the prospective new state. Whether such a commitment would have prevented the merged Federation, or the new concept of a unitary sovereign state in friendly relations with Britain, from disintegrating seems highly improbable. The chance of contriving a satisfactory outcome had been long since lost. In the writer's view this is dateable to the pigeon-holing by London of Luce's final recommendations of September 1960, if not indeed to the policy of minimum interference adopted by the Government of India from 1837 onward. As the 1960s proceeded, despite the gulf that by this time separated the two parties in their treatment of Britain's role overseas, it probably mattered little which of them was in power in Britain. The outcome in Aden could not by then be designed in London.

As for the Gulf, Britain's last outpost of empire in the Arab World, the question already at issue by the beginning of the 1960s was not whether, but when and how, withdrawal should be stage-managed. On neither side of the party divide was the expediency of surrendering or at least re-shaping Britain's visibly outmoded relationship denied. And however unsympathetic the grass roots view in the Labour party of the shaykhly system, its leaders never disputed the principle that the future political complexion of the shaykhdoms was their own concern. What mattered to both parties in London was the emergence of a formal structure, internationally recognizable, to which full sovereignty could properly be surrendered. They differed marginally over the timing of the change, much more over the manner of its announcement. Though it is not easy, even in retrospect, to justify the abruptness with which the Labour Government repudiated in January 1968 the assurances of continued protection renewed only two months before and their failure to prepare the ground by the courtesy of prior consultation, the decision itself can now be seen as unexceptionable. Britain's innings in the Gulf (though cricket was not an imperial legacy that ever caught on there) had to be declared closed. The Tories certainly would have wanted a few more runs to be on the board before declaring. Though the metaphor risks getting out of hand, the best the Tories could do, on taking over the captaincy, was to see that the shaykhly players, unaccustomed to the game, were helped into their pads. The deftness with which Luce, the groundsman, adjusted them, with help from some of their visiting supporters, won applause from all but a section of the bystanders; and when stumps were finally drawn, there was no unseemly invasion of the pitch.

We can now proceed (with relief from metaphor) to examine the divers influences which bore on Britain's relinquishing of power in the three successive episodes.

During the Sudan episode the prime concern of the authorities in London was the maintenance, in the face of Egyptian resentments and Soviet aims, of Britain's dominant strategic capacity in the Middle East. Over this basic objective, and over the cardinal importance of the Middle East and of Arab co-operation with Britain, there was no disagreement between Bevin and the defence and political departments. Though the Chiefs of Staff were distinctly less optimistic than Bevin that a satisfactory alternative base to Suez was obtainable[9] (misgivings which were in the event justified), their main worry was the pressure exercised by Bevin and even more by Attlee for a major reduction in service manpower in the Middle East to conform with Britain's post-war financial exhaustion.[10] They went along with Bevin's concept of pursuing a joint ('confederal') defence organization in which all Middle Eastern countries could play their part as political equals; but Britain's inability to reach any understanding with Egypt in Bevin's time was enough to block whatever prospects of success in that direction there might otherwise have been. So far as concerned the Sudan and the danger which so preoccupied Khartoum of its falling a casualty in the pursuit of an accommodation with Egypt, the Sudan itself was seldom regarded by the Chiefs of Staff as having a major strategic value; and they naturally shared the Egyptian priorities of the Foreign Office and its diplomats in Cairo. Khartoum's anguished resentment at the subordination of the Sudan's interest will be examined further. In the final clash with Egypt as the end approached in the Sudan, Service chiefs and Foreign Office officials were, however, distinctly helpful to the Palace in Khartoum in resisting Churchill's cavalier inclinations.

When South West Arabia became a major issue, the Service Departments were still influential enough to secure political attention – though they were scarcely as powerful as they had been in 1947 when Montgomery and his fellow service chiefs were able, by threatening resignation, to compel Attlee to accept their strategic assessment of the centrality of the Middle East in Britain's politico-military priorities. Their loss of influence under the subsequent Conservative Government may be attributed to two causes. Firstly, the priority given by the Government to nuclear armament weakened the previous focus on conventional defences, which formed the Services' stock-in-trade. Secondly, financial pressures on the defence budget aroused increasing rivalry between the three Services, each anxious to maximize its own share of the total allocation. They no longer spoke with one potent voice. Sandys' 1957 Defence White Paper, quite apart from imposing further severe curbs in the Services' manpower, was a determined governmental attempt to establish single overall control within their structure;[11] but in the financial constraints prevailing inter-service competition was not easily overcome. Moreover, as a result of Sandys' nuclear strategy, the Navy found itself with a diminished role and the Army suffered especially unwelcome reductions.

The concept of a chain of bases as a means of preserving Britain's strategic dominance East of Suez, though accepted without challenge until the sixties, was scarcely subjected to scrutiny as to their precise role until it was recognized that the nuclear umbrella was irrelevant to the maintenance of peace in restive areas of the Third World. Hitherto the role of overseas bases was conceived primarily in Air Force terms. In the case of Aden, not till 1956 was a requirement for a British army presence there considered necessary. The Suez affair, the closure of the Canal and the erection thereafter of an air barrier by Arab states from Syria to the Sudan strengthened the argument of the Services that Britain's peacekeeping responsibilities entailed the deployment of army troops and of naval units the other side of the barrier. Between 1957 and 1959 developments in Oman, the Yemen, Jordan and further afield, all requiring British military attention, endorsed the recognition, shared by Healey, that overseas military commitments were likely to increase rather than the reverse while empire in the old sense shrank. For such purposes the old Sandys reliance on UK-based air mobility was no substitute for troops on the ground. Thus the role of the selected bases expanded in Service terms.

But world strategy was not available in an economy size, and the cost of this expansion created grave financial problems. In Aden, which became an independent unified command in 1958, the British military presence had quadrupled by 1960, causing desperate overcrowding and occasioning the biggest military accommodation programme ever launched. The argument prevailed that the provision of cheaper accommodation of an obviously temporary kind would play into the enemy's hand; and, ludicrous though it may seem, the programme was still proceeding when withdrawal overtook it. Throughout this period of increased overseas deployment the individual Service Departments could advance demands which combined self-interest with a genuine sense of responsibility for peace and stability in overseas territories grappling with independence or struggling towards it; but in planning ahead for expensive re-equipment to meet the requirements of 'limited war' – a concept which gained further favour when Watkinson replaced the still nuclear-minded Sandys as Minister of Defence in 1959 – the Services did not always see eye to eye with political departments nursing their own financial priorities. The ending of conscription in 1960 increased their problems. Indeed, the continued division of overseas responsibilities within the government machine was no doubt one reason for the failure of policymakers at the top for two decades after the war to conduct a thorough-going central reappraisal of Britain's changed and changing overseas role.[12] The Foreign Office itself had then no serious kind of forward planning unit: the tiny low-level section set up by Bevin in 1947, partly as a defence against pressures from the Chiefs of Staff, having little more than seminal significance.[13]

By the time South West Arabian independence was in the offing under Conservative auspices and even more, of course, when the intention to withdraw without a defence commitment was declared by the Labour Government, the influence of Service Departments in the making of policy there was visibly waning. The transfer of residual base facilities to the Gulf brought them little relief; and when withdrawal from East of Suez was finally decreed, their role was simply to carry out Cabinet orders. By then governmental priorities lay in the context of Europe; and when the Conservatives were re-examining in 1971 Labour's decision to end Britain's military protection in the

Gulf, it was clear to the Chiefs of Staff that the already planned redeployment of Britain's overstretched services would by itself prohibit the continued stationing of operational troops in the Gulf.

We turn now to the one conspicuous irony which Britain's later imperial history suffered (or enjoyed) throughout the period of our three episodes. This was the postwar discovery by the United States that Britain's 'colonial' dominance from Egypt to the Far East, however ideologically reprehensible, now served America's own purposes. Anti-colonial traditions were not of course suppressed overnight. They were still active and able to complicate matters for Britain throughout her confrontation with Egypt which so radically affected the Sudan episode. The Foreign Office brief given to Churchill for his talks in Washington in January 1953[14] made it plain that, failing wholehearted American backing in Cairo, the attempt to reach agreement with Egypt would fail. This degree of backing was not forthcoming. The recorded judgement of Stevenson, Britain's ambassador in Cairo, looking back that year over the period of his tenure, was that 'the Americans were still conditioned by anti-colonialist obsessions to withhold full support of their NATO partners in negotiations with the Egyptians on the canal'.[15] It is certainly the case that their impatience with Britain's inability to reach an understanding with Egypt over strategic requirements undercut the sympathy they should have shown, ideologically speaking, for Britain's insistence on the Sudan's right to self-determination.

As early as 1945 Bevin had wanted the Americans as partners in the Middle East in general terms. He remained, however, resolutely opposed to the stationing of US forces in the area. There was also a strong tendency in the Foreign Office and other departments to resent their intrusion as commercial rivals. At that stage Washington was not prepared to accept any part in propping up an outmoded imperial position.[16] But things were gradually changing, thanks partly to the advocacy of Loy Henderson, America's roving commissioner in the Middle East. At the Pentagon talks of October 1947 the British objective, as defined in the joint Foreign Office/Chiefs of Staff brief,[17] was 'to get the USA to realize the importance of Britain's role in the Middle East to them as well as to us'; and a certain American willingness was displayed to do so. Both sides agreed that the British role was to maintain the necessary bases in exchange for American economic and political backing. Nonetheless in the years that immediately followed the Middle East policies of London and Washington – as their respective attitudes to Palestine and to Musaddeq's Iran, let alone to Egypt, illustrated – were by no means in harmony. At no stage, however, did any British interest outrank in Attlee's time the importance of American goodwill; and it was not until the Suez War of 1956 that a British (Conservative) government took the risk of flouting it.

After Suez Macmillan's success in restoring an Anglo-American understanding was greatly assisted by US recognition that defence of the West and of world order in the Cold War obliged her to take, however reluctantly, the role of global policeman. She had, however, neither the resources of military manpower nor, in the Middle East and the Indian Ocean, either the system of local alliances or the command structure to be able to dispense with the contribution made by Britain's traditional control, 'colonialist' or not, in that whole area.[18] American encouragement for the maintenance of Britain's bases in the region was for this reason increasingly assured. The Vietnam War was of course a manifestation of America's own 'neo-imperialist' compulsions at this period. To the Conservatives under Macmillan and Home this US attitude was wholly welcome. To the Labour government from 1964 on, already looking forward to the day when defence responsibilities overseas could be relinquished and when Britain's diminished resources could be diverted elsewhere, American exhortation to continue policing this troublesome zone were something of an embarrassment. But Wilson, no more than Attlee or the Tories, could dispense with American goodwill; and his early pronouncements in 1964–66 on the necessity of maintaining Britain's East of Suez role – reaching, as one commentator has described it, 'a pitch quaintly reminiscent of backwoods Toryism'[19] – were the consequence. Inheriting, as they did, their predecessor's commitment to the federation of the Aden Protectorate, the Labour leaders certainly found it embarrassing to be seen collaborating with what they regarded as a ramshackle bunch of feudal autocrats against the wishes of Aden's progressive activists; but since the security of the Aden base evidently demanded it, and since the maintenance of that base was an American requirement, they went along with the federation policy, giving full support to such related exercises as the Radfan operation bravely enough. The abandonment of Aden, whatever Washington's views, became inexorable for reasons of its own. When the focus of Britain's residual strategic role in the area switched to the Gulf, Washington had no hesitation in endorsing it, despite the clash with British interests in that area surviving from the still unresolved Buraimi episode. Wilson's final decision to withdraw from the Gulf aroused some initial dismay in Washington, but its irreversibility was soon recognized there, as it was in Tory Westminster.

Another source of pressure for the continuance of Britain's East of Suez role, to which all British governments had to respond throughout this period, came from the Commonwealth. The centrality of Aden as a vital strategic link was not radically effected by the ending of the Raj, if only since India, and for a time Pakistan, joined the expanding Commonwealth. But quite apart from Britain's continuing strategic obligations towards the sub-continent, Australia and New Zealand emphatically looked to her for continued leadership in preserving security in the Indian Ocean and beyond. Britain's activities, political and military, in Malaysia from the end of the war until the independence of the Federation of Malaya was finally contrived in 1957, and thereafter in Malaya's confrontation with Indonesia from 1963 to 1966, were also highly relevant. The reassurances given by Wilson and Healey on the Labour Party's assumption of power in 1964 that Britain was determined to fulfil her East of Suez obligations were for all these reasons conspicuously welcome in the Commonwealth countries affected. The subsequent decisions to withdraw first from Aden and then from the Gulf were not; and the process clearly damaged, especially in Australasia, Britain's standing as the focus of Commonwealth cohesion.

But if American and Commonwealth pressures worked a little awkwardly for the Labour leaders in one direction, Arab pressures worked much more awkwardly in the opposite one. Despite the volume of literature which pours out on the subject, it is already difficult for those who did not live through the period of Britain's expulsion from the Middle East to appreciate the phenomenal impact on the scene of Nasser and his anti-imperialist revolution. Today the Arabs may view his personality, his behaviour and his achievements with less devotion, but from 1952 till his death in 1970 he simply bestrode the Arab World, and other by no means petty men could only peep out, like Cassius, from under. Amongst expatriates working in the area at the time the extent of his transmogrification of the ordinary Arabs' self-image and of their attitude to foreign tutelage was only gradually recognized. His top political priority was to rid the Arab world of the relics of British domination and his voice carried, literally and metaphorically, to the furthest peasant hut and bedouin tent. He had of course his Arab enemies within and outside Egypt but they proved almost powerless against the spell he cast far and wide.

What concerns us here is Nasser's contribution to the process of Britain's withdrawal. This differed in each of our three episodes. In the case of the Sudan his confrontation with Britain was localized. His star had only just risen and Britain was still the dominant power in the Middle East. He won his battle for the removal of Britain's military occupation of his own country but failed, in circumstances already described, to secure the formal coupling of the Sudan to Egypt when the British yoke was removed from it. When South West Arabia became the case at issue, his star was at its zenith and his ability to generate anti-British enthusiasm displayed a potency to which Britain had no answer. Such room for manoeuvre as Britain possessed against his destabilizing tactics was further restricted by a certain ambivalence in America's attitude to him. In the Sudan episode and in Britain's concurrent wrestling with Egypt over the canal base, before and after the overthrow of the Egyptian monarchy in 1952, at least part of the American establishment had been, more covertly or less, sympathetic to the ouster of British hegemony, still seen in such quarters as colonialist.[20] Now, in the aftermath of Suez, Nasser attracted a good deal of American admiration; and Washington's practical interests were seen to lie in weaning Egypt away from the Soviet embrace. Consequently and despite the value increasingly placed by Washington, in its wider perspectives, on the maintenance of the Aden base, Britain's endeavours to square the constitutional circle in South West Arabia and to head off Egyptian penetration through the Yemen seemed to attract little American enthusiasm. The instant US recognition of the regime established under Nasser's patronage by the Yemeni revolutionaries in 1962, to cite one illustration, was seen by Britain as unhelpful. But regardless of American cold-war preoccupations, Nasser's ability to cause Britain the maximum discomfiture in South West Arabia (and of course elsewhere) was a determinant factor in shaping the manner, if not also the timing, of Britain's expulsion. The fact that Nasser himself backed the wrong horse in the final race for the prize of power in South West Arabia is, so far as the hustling and humiliation of Britain was concerned, irrelevant.

As for the Gulf episode, Nasser's contribution in the fifties and later to popular effervescence in Kuwait and Bahrain against the shaykhly system, and by that token as well as by larger ones against Britain's supervisory presence, was by no means negligible. Indeed in every town in the Gulf Nasser's portrait hung for years on almost every commoner's wall, side by side – whether for reasons of loyalty or of discretion – with that of the local ruler. By the time that the oil explosion had radically transformed the importance of the Gulf and of its rulers, Egypt was more concerned with hastening the departure of the British from the Gulf states than in upsetting internal political stability in them. The Arab League's abortive attempt under Nasser's prompting in the mid sixties to wean the Trucial States away from dependence on Britain was made with the collaboration, so far as it was obtainable, of most of the rulers themselves. Nasser's own humiliation in the 1967 war with Israel provoked anti-British demonstrations in much of the Gulf, despite Britain's innocence of the charge of connivance with Israel; but it set in train the dissolution of his power to influence the course of history everywhere in the Arab world. Moreover, by this time Saudi determination to play a dominant Arab role in the Gulf was meeting with more success. In this the Saudis had the backing of the Americans, now less agitated over Egyptian-Soviet relations and less reluctant to accept a supervisory role in the defence of Western interests in the Middle East as Britain's successor in this complex and unenviable task. Britain's own relations with the Saudi monarchy were also recovering from the Buraimi confrontation; and whereas King Saʿud had in the mid fifties inclined to collaborate with Nasser in the ouster of British influence from the Arabian peninsula, by May 1967 his successor, King Faysal, was sufficiently alarmed by Nasserite penetration to appeal personally to Prime Minister Wilson for the reconsideration of his decision to dismantle the Aden base. Once the Arab trauma of the Six-Day War had been sufficiently overcome for Faysal to turn his attention again to the Gulf, his concern was quietly to prevent revolutionary Arab nationalism of Nasser's or any other kind making further inroads there; and his mild opposition to the prolongation of Britain's special position had as its premise an aspiration to restore his own family's traditional dominance (as he saw it) over the shaykhdoms. Nasser's revolutionary spell had never, to be sure, held any attraction for the shaykhly families there, whatever the views of their subjects. By the time Britain's withdrawal from the Gulf was in sight, Nasser's star had waned; and when the wealthy successor states there emerged in 1971 into independent sovereignty, Egypt formally welcomed them, regardless of their political complexion, into the comity of Arab nations – as indeed Nasser had done ten years earlier with Kuwait.

Nasser's inspirational pan-Arab philosophy on the one hand and his equally fervid pursuit of Egypt's own national regeneration on the other did not always exert an equal appeal in the wider Arab world. But the personal fascination he exercised everywhere, even after his 1967 setback and indeed until his death in 1970, was scarcely affected by the ups and downs of Egypt's posture and achievements, caused at least in part by the double nature of Nasser's vision.

His contribution at all events to the three episodes we are considering clearly differed in each. Britain's aim of course in each case was to stage-manage her withdrawal in dignity and good order, leaving a well-disposed independent regime behind her. Nasser, whose spell was especially potent during the second episode, was easily able to prevent that happening in South West Arabia. He did not manage it in the first and last of the three uncouplings. Indeed it is one of the ironies of Nasser's phenomenal impact on Middle Eastern history and of his hustling of British influence out of it that he failed not only in the Sudan and in the Gulf but even in South West Arabia to contrive that the regime which replaced the British was one wholly to his liking. Azhari in the Sudan had turned out to be neither revolutionary in the Nasserite sense nor in favour of subordination to Egyptian control once the British had been successfully eased out with Egyptian help. In South West Arabia the victor in the final race for the succession was not FLOSY, on whom Nasser had lavished his patronage throughout, but the Marxist NLF who regarded him as a deviationist from the true Arab revolutionary path. In the Gulf the shaykhly system, for which Nasser had no sympathy, emerged unscathed from Britain's departure: most of the rulers indeed were reluctant to see Britain go.

As for other external pressures affecting the manner of Britain's exit from the three territories, the Soviet Union (with reservations in the case of South West Arabia) was broadly able to leave the relevant course of history to the Arabs themselves. Even allowing for the ambivalence of Arab attitudes, revolutionary or not, to Soviet power or patronage, the removal of British imperial supervision – particularly since its replacement in different form by US supervision was not what the Arabs as a whole could welcome – could only be seen in Moscow as helpful to Soviet aspirations.

The contribution of Arab powers (apart from Egypt) to the course of history, as earlier chapters will have shown, differed in each episode. No other Arabs played a significant role in the first. The complex involvement of the Yemen in South West Arabia gives that episode a unique character. But however tiresome Yemeni intervention, monarchist and republican, may have been to British policy-makers, it was never in itself determinant. The determinant factor, so far as the manner of Britain's departure is concerned, was Nasser and his inspirational maleficence. It was he that set Aden ablaze. The evolution in Saudi attitudes to the British presence in South West Arabia and the Gulf – a function of the Saudi regime's changing relationship with Nasser – has been summarized above. In the Gulf episode, the aspirations (well before the end) of Iraq, monarchist as well as revolutionary, to dominate the Gulf ran counter to Egyptian objectives at the time, as the Kuwaiti drama of 1961 made plain. Even thereafter Ba'thist Iraq's ostensibly ideological threat to the survival of the shaykhly system played in a sense into Britain's hands in the stage-managing of her departure. In that process, however, the regional power with which Britain and the Gulf States had primarily to contend was not Arab but Iranian.

Apart from the influence on the scene of individual outside powers, the contribution of the United Nations cannot be ignored, particularly since its bearing on the course of events differed markedly in each of our three episodes. During the period of the Sudanese struggle for independence the General Assembly had not yet become a platform for the Third World to anything like the degree it reached later, and the great powers were still broadly able to supervise its deliberations. Thus when Egypt's claim to sovereignty in the Sudan and to the right of terminating British domination there was referred to the UN in the forties and again in the early fifties, the world body, largely under British pressure, proved unable or unwilling to pass judgement. Had the debate concerned taken place ten years later, there can be little doubt that Britain would have found it distinctly more embarrassing, regardless of the rights and wrongs of the Egyptian case. As the British were to find in the South West Arabian episode, the enlarged General Assembly, under the promptings of its recently established Special Committee on Colonialism (the Committee of 24), was able to cause Britain a good deal of embarrassment, however tendentious and unbalanced she regarded the relevant anti-colonial resolutions and initiatives devised in New York and however little attention she and her protégés in South West Arabia initially paid to them in practice. The fact that, as the end approached, the British Labour government actually sought UN mediation was as much a symptom of the UN's growing influence as it was of Britain's desperation in South West Arabia. By contrast, when withdrawal from the Gulf became an issue, Britain was no longer a serious imperial power, anti-colonial hostility towards her was ebbing and the UN was no longer under strong Third World pressure to intervene. Nor was there any vociferous clamour from the Gulf citizenry for the removal of the imperial yoke. Such pressures might perhaps have grown more demanding had the Labour government not pre-empted matters by its 1968 announcement on withdrawal East of Suez. So far then as the UN contribution is material to the story, this was comparatively marginal and remote in the Sudan episode, clamourously hostile to Britain in South West Arabia, but content to observe the final contortions of British imperialism in the Gulf without actively intervening.

Thus far in this chapter we have been comparing our three episodes of 'decolonization' in terms of the evolution of rival party approaches to the process in London, of the differing attitudes to each episode of the US and the Soviet Union, of the contributions to the process of Arab powers outside the territories concerned, foremost amongst them by a long way Nasser's Egypt, and finally of the parabola of UN intervention. We turn now to a quite other aspect of the whole story, namely the extent to which the conceptions of those making policy in London and those executing it in the field were and were not in harmony in each of the three episodes.

Two introductory generalizations may be ventured before engaging in particulars. The first is that anyone who ever represented Britain (and the British were assuredly not unique in this respect) in a dependent foreign country tended to take on, wittingly or unwittingly, a kind of protective colouring by osmosis, unless he was totally out of sympathy with that country and its aspirations. This always constrained him to see most issues in a rather different light from the home-based politician or bureaucrat. In the case of the three dependent countries or territories we are concerned with here, this generalization needs refinement, illustrative of the dangers of using the term colonialism as a catch-all. Those who represented Britain in the Sudan, though the Sudan fell within the Foreign Secretary's brief, were by no means Foreign Service officials. Ostensibly, from the occupants of the Khartoum palace downwards, they served the co-domini: in practice they served the Sudan Government headed by the British Governor General, and their immediate loyalties were to the people whom he and they were there to govern. Those who represented Britain in South West Arabia were Colonial Service officers. If the Governor himself was not from the same stable, relations could be strained. One Colonial officer, purporting to represent the feelings of those who served under a professional diplomat (Johnston), put it this way: 'A Colonial Service officer, like a parish priest, was prepared to fight his superiors in the interests of his people, while a Foreign Service officer, like a Jesuit, was so loyal to his master's greater interests that he was prepared to be callous about individual cases.'[21]

Be that as it may, those who governed or administered South West Arabia were subject to much closer control and scrutiny by the home government, in their case the Colonial Office, than were their approximate equivalents in the Sudan. The latter enjoyed, until the end approached, a species of autonomy from 'interference' by their home government unprecedented in the history of British colonialism proper. Finally, those who represented Britain in the Gulf, with the exception of two Political Residents (Hay, a survivor from the Indian raj, and Luce), were professional diplomats. Some, admittedly, were only so by adoption: a considerable number were in fact erstwhile members of the Sudan Political Service – indeed there was a period in Luce's time as Political Resident when all four Political Agents, and for good measure the Consul General in Muscat as well, came like Luce himself from that pedigree stable. But their function now was not to administer. They were sent there by the Foreign Office, which they had meanwhile joined, largely because they spoke Arabic; and in their acquired guise as diplomats they had perhaps already accustomed themselves (as of course had their diplomatic colleagues from the start of their professional lives) to the vagaries of London policy-making and to the subordination of local *desiderata* to the wider interests of their home government. By that token, and since administration was not their task, Britain's representatives in the Gulf differed from those administering the Sudan or partially administering South West Arabia. All the three categories, however, the Political Service in the Sudan, the Colonial Service in South West Arabia and the Diplomatic Service in the Gulf were subject to the generalized rule ventured at the beginning of the preceding paragraph, namely that as a result of immersion in the local scene they tended to acquire a protective colouration and a pronounced sympathy for the people in whose destinies they were in one way or another involved. Not perhaps to the same degree: the deepseated attachment to their parishioners of lifelong members of the Political Service was doubtless stronger than that of most Colonial Officers in Aden, who came and went; and the paternalist involvement of those Aden Colonial Officers endowed them in turn with a more marked local tincture than that acquired by the diplomats supervising Britain's special relations with the Gulf. But even there the syndrome operated.

The second preliminary generalization affecting the evolving relations between London and the man in the field relates to the revolution in communications, still by no means complete when post-war decolonization began. In much earlier days, when communications across the world were as yet undeveloped, the man on the spot did what he thought proper and got, if he was lucky, approval from London afterwards, by boat. Today, with facilities for instant communication, the man on the spot is often regarded as little more than an articulate postman: indeed important messages are frequently delivered by orbiting politicians. This profound procedural change in the management of overseas affairs was nearing completion by the time our second episode began. At the time of the Sudan episode, however, it had not advanced all that far, or at least not far enough to prevent the man on the spot from continuing to enjoy a residual measure of autonomy. This was particularly the case, at least in Huddleston's day, with the Sudan's Governor General, whose functions were in any case traditionally different from those of a colonial governor. In the ten years leading to the relinquishment of power there only one senior British politician ever visited Khartoum. The man on the spot was still referred to as the recognized expert and was given rather more opportunity to hammer away on London's policy-making anvil. Huddleston certainly expected his representations as the recognized expert to receive attention, and they generally did so. Subsequent Governors General, and even more the men on the spot in our two later episodes, were given shorter and shorter lengths of discretionary rope.

A second and related consequence of the revolution in communications was that foreign policy problems could less than ever be treated in separate compartments. No longer was there any prospect of things being done in one corner of the globe without instant repercussions elsewhere. If the man on the spot, especially the remoter spot, remained by the nature of his preoccupations unlikely to have a complete grasp of the global implications of every local policy decision, the compulsions to which the home government was now subjected became alarmingly multiple. Whereas the former was fully involved in keeping perhaps two or three balls in the air, the latter had now to juggle so many that some were almost bound to drop.

Of our two preliminary generalizations, then, the former suggested that, while men in the field were all likely to see things in a rather different light from those at home, the degree of difference varied in our three episodes, by virtue of the different professional compulsions of those representing Britain in each territory. The second generalization drew attention to the diminishing scope for independent action by those in the field as the revolution in communications proceeded. We will now review in rather more detail the tensions generated in each episode between the home government in London and those representing Britain on the spot.

The task is easier, and sometimes more entertaining, in the case of the Sudan. The release of state papers, though some have been judiciously withheld, provides one source. Published personal accounts, though there too discretion or prejudice may prevail, are another. The most illuminating, however, at least in respect of the attitudes of the Sudan Political Service, lies in the private records and correspondence of some of those at the head of it, now either open to inspection[22] or made available privately to the present writer. One continuous source of documentary evidence covering the whole decade leading up to the declaration of the Sudan's independence consists of the weekly 'Top Secret' exchange of correspondence between the Civil Secretary in Khartoum (or his effective successor when the post was abolished) and the Sudan Agent in London, described in chapter 2 as the Governor General's 'personal ambassador' there, able to lobby the Foreign Office and other agencies under the counter, as it were.

Huddleston was both the last and the most formidable Governor General of what may be called the old school, raised in the full imperial tradition and with long military experience in the Sudan behind him. His standing there and his unparalleled knowledge of the whole country were nowhere questioned, and he was justified by the practices of his time in expecting full weight to be given to his representations in London. However, when their opinions differed, he was pitted against an even more formidable figure in the person of Foreign Secretary Bevin. The resolution with which Huddleston resisted dictation from London, and of course from his formal superior Lampson, and even from Lampson's ambassadorial successors in Cairo, has been discussed in chapter 2. But Huddleston was also a supremely loyal servant of the Crown, not given to airing his resentments in public, nor even recording them in private papers for the benefit of future researchers. Even his final and apparently unexpected dismissal by Bevin – for that would seem to be the cause of his retirement[23] – was not something he allowed himself to speak resentfully about, save in private to his immediate family. Fortunately for those interested in the tensions between London and Khartoum between 1946 and the Sudan's independence, his immediate subordinates were less inhibited, at least in what they wrote confidentially to each other or recorded privately in diaries and the like. The belief, however misplaced, that Bevin and his diplomats in London and Cairo were prepared to sell the Sudan down the river Nile for a mess of Egyptian potage (of one recipe or another) was held and privately expressed by all those in positions of authority in the Palace at Khartoum throughout Bevin's tenure of office and, *mutatis mutandis*, thereafter. Huddleston's successor Howe, himself a career diplomat, felt on many issues almost equally strongly – the first of our two preliminary generalizations applying in full. Huddleston indeed, writing to the Civil Secretary of Howe's appointment in one of his rare post-retirement indulgences in committing his thoughts to paper, observed that he 'defied anyone to sit in the Governor General's chair for three weeks without becoming anti-Egyptian' and thereby, though he did not say so, critical of the contrivings of the Foreign Office. But Howe would not, for instance, have written to the Minister of State, as Huddleston did at one stage, accusing him, and in effect the whole Cabinet, of 'wishful thinking and, like all wishful thinking, at base dishonesty'.[24]

For detailed documentation of the reactions of Governors General and their top lieutenants to London's handling of the Sudan issue we must look to what the senior members of the Sudan Political Service privately recorded. Suspicions and irritations were not, to be sure, all one-sided. State papers reveal at least something of Bevin's occasional testiness with the 'outmoded' attitudes in Khartoum, of the impatience of Britain's diplomatic negotiators in Cairo with Khartoum's obstinate refusal to simplify their impossible task of seeking an understanding with Egypt, and of the difficulties (sometimes a good deal less marked) at official levels in London in seeing eye to eye with the urgings of the Sudan Government. In the final stages a curious reversal of these roles in one respect is visible, with Conservative leaders in London and the diplomats in Cairo criticizing – with a curious lack of understanding for the march of time – refusals from the Palace in Khartoum to exercise 'imperial' control over the local scene and the speed with which the Palace was positively accelerating for tactical reasons the Sudan's last steps to self-determination. The personal clashes between Prime Minister Churchill, no less imperious than imperialist, with Governor General Howe in 1953 and 1954 were described in chapter 2. What finally enraged Luce and the last Governor General (returning to the other side of the coin) was the apparent disinterest shown by Her Majesty's Government in influencing the ultimate constitutional outcome in the Sudan and in contributing materially to that country's future prosperity and goodwill towards Britain. All these continuing elements of tension between the central government and the men on the spot can be illustrated without difficulty from documentary sources;[25] a few have already been cited in chapter 2. It will be simplest to examine the Khartoum side of the coin first.

The sense of 'betrayal' which exercised the Palace, particularly but not only in the period before the Egyptian revolution and before Naguib's dramatic reshuffling of the pieces on the chessboard, will already be apparent from chapter 2. So too will the resistance displayed by Huddleston and Howe to London's, and even more to Cairo's, handling of the Sudan issue. The words distrust, appeasement, even treachery fall continually from the pens of the Civil Secretary and of the Sudan Agent (Mayall first and Davies thereafter) in London. 'Bevin is selling the Sudan to get his treaty' (October 1946). The Foreign Office 'were suffering from a fit of pique because the Sudan Government wouldn't say the sort of things the Foreign Office wanted them to say' (January 1947). Bowker (Minister in the Cairo Embassy) was 'trying to screw concessions to Egypt out of the Sudan Government' (February 1947). Howe, the Middle East Undersecretary, was 'the worst appointment [to succeed Huddleston] they could possibly have made . . . one of the principal supporters of the treachery'. Foreign Office people all lived in a world of unreality, 'off the contents of diplomatic bags' (March 1947). 'I distrust the FO and Service chaps who want a treaty with Egypt, not realizing that to concede anything to Egypt means no settlement but only an immediate demand for something more' (April 1947) – a distrust rather curiously reinforced by Creech-Jones, the Secretary of State for the Colonies, who privately warned them to treat the Foreign Office and its diplomats with suspicion. (He was of course at odds with Bevin on the Zionist issue.) The Sudan Agent, Mayall, was particularly incensed by the behaviour of quite senior Foreign Office officials: 'I hate being treated as a baby by whippersnappers' (July 1948). One head of its Information Department was described by him as 'the Flatulent Fish with his swarm of sprats' (January 1948). Robertson wrote that Howe's own comment, on hearing of Bevin's dealings with Egypt's ambassador, Amr, was that 'the FO never seem to learn the folly of under-the-counter negotiations with Egyptians' (April 1948). 'I think the present [Cairo] Embassy staff is probably the weakest and most appeasing of any we have ever had in Egypt. Their efforts are really sickening' (February 1949). Of Haselden, the Sudan Agent in Cairo, Mayall wrote that he was 'the one man from the Sudan who does not seem to get contaminated by the intrigues of the Embassy' (May 1949).

By June 1949, with news of impending new negotiations with Egypt reaching him from Mayall, Robertson's resentments were mounting.

Just when we seemed to have got the Sudan on a fairly even keel politically . . . we are once more to be plunged into a fight to resist Egyptian infiltration, assisted by the British FO. I am a bit tired of struggling to prevent them undoing all our work in the Sudan . . . *We* have to administer this country . . . and have no information about what the FO are trying to do regarding Egypt, except what you have told me.

Of Bowker's successor in the Cairo Embassy, a particular *bête noire* in the correspondence, Robertson's deputy wrote to Robertson on leave in August 1949 that the man was 'making a laughing-stock of himself, running around right in the Egyptians' pockets, his perceptions completely blunted by his frenzied gong-chasing'.

And so it goes on, though it should be stated that every now and then over these years tributes were also paid to individual cases of helpfulness and good sense in the Foreign Office. By February 1951 the new British Ambassador in Cairo is described by Mayall as 'almost as big a menace' as his deputy, ridiculed above. Two months later the new Foreign Office formula for negotiations over the Sudan was 'almost as meaningless as Sidki/Bevin . . . perhaps intentionally' – though Mayall's successor as the Sudan Agent changed this tune into 'the FO have done us very well' in their brief for those negotiations. This reversal of opinion was endorsed six months later by Robertson, though the Ambassador conducting them, Stevenson, was still a target for criticism. As the negotiations wore on Robertson unhappily reports the local belief, based on accounts given to him by prominent Sudanese of telephone messages from Naguib, that 'it's all nearly settled, since the Americans are obliging the

British to come to heel' (February 1953). And when a few days later the watershed Anglo-Egyptian Agreement was indeed signed, Robertson, now on the eve of retirement, writes a final *cri-de-coeur*: 'I feel to have been defeated and to have let down the Sudanese people and my own Service . . . We have been defeated by Egypt, our own Foreign Office and Embassy, and by America, helped by the folly and shortsightedness of the Sudanese leaders.'

Luce now replaced Robertson at the Sudan end of the correspondence. Davies at the other end renewed the attack on Foreign Office 'appeasement' of Egypt, whose present government 'was bad but the next one [would be] worse', and he quotes the current Middle East Undersecretary at the Foreign Office as saying that 'Sudan independence was never more than a dream' (April 1953). We now reach the period during which, as already described, Churchill was for a time directly in control of foreign affairs and was all for denouncing the Anglo-Egyptian Agreement. Luce, who strongly favoured attempting to make it work, wrote in May 1953 'Churchill is more of a headache than the Egyptians'. But he did urge the Foreign Office, unsuccessfully, to present the Egyptians with a Grand Remonstrance over their improper interventions in the Sudan in the approach to the critical elections there, now imminent. Following the shock NUP electoral victory that November, Davies learnt that the Government, in order to reinforce British influence in the Sudan, were thinking of posting Chapman Andrews (the *bête noire* of Khartoum Palace) as Trade Commissioner there, a post established earlier as an embryo embassy. Davies rose verbally to the occasion. 'I regard Chapman Andrews as the sort of thing one might see through the bottom of a bathyscope', though one would have to get 'a good deal lower than Professor Picard to have much chance of success'. He added that 'no-one in Cairo ever seems to learn anything, and the FO appear equally gullible' (November 1953). Two of his March 1954 letters to Luce are well up to standard. Invited by the relevant African Department of the Foreign Office to see twenty or thirty telegrams which they 'had failed to show him before', he describes its new Head, who showed 'not the faintest interest in the Sudan', as the 'most dough-like' he had ever known. (The man concerned left, as it happened, a month later, 'unlamented' and wearing 'the puzzled air of a man who cannot remember whether to change his underwear on Tuesday or Thursday'.)

As for the politicians, a few of them, after the bloodshed outside the Palace in Khartoum and the killing of the British Police Commandant, 'took' [says Mayall] 'their swords out of the umbrella-stand', but after a few flourishes quickly put them back again. Luce, though he clearly enjoyed the correspondence, writes soberly in July 1954, 'I am not one of those who think the FO made a nonsense of it from start to finish . . . We can make the transitional period work by not interfering'; and he gave a shrewd note to Howe to take for his discussions in London, in which he argued that the NUP, the likely winners in the next elections, would themselves almost certainly choose independence (serving Britain's own aims better than would independence secured by a victorious Umma Party) '*provided* HMG's mistaken attentions to Sayed Abdulrahman', who was being somewhat lionized in London, 'do not drive them closer to Cairo'. Luce in fact reserved his private spleen at this time for the Governor General himself, whose 'selfish irresponsibility' in proposing to absent himself from Khartoum for the most critical five months of all drove him to threaten resignation. But by November Luce's private anger was redirected at the Embassy in Cairo, whose recommendations to London for a new look at Egyptian aspirations in the Sudan, 'marked [he writes] the lowest point yet reached by the Embassy for stupidity, gullibility, cynicism and disregard for Sudanese interests'. Fortunately, but in more diplomatic terms, the Foreign Office rejected the Embassy's ideas; but Luce was unable to convince London that the Government's policy towards the Sudan 'must be made *public*' (January 1955). We must know, he writes, whether HMG 'are prepared to follow through their policy of the last 55 years' and help the Sudan to independence and thereafter. 'If not, let them stop leading the Sudanese up the garden path.'

By this time Knox Helm had been nominated to succeed Howe, and was briefed by Luce to pursue the matter in February 1955. But Helm – as the Sudan Agent, and later Helm himself reported – was given the brush-off successively by Eden, his Minister of State Nutting, and the Permanent Undersecretary. No financial aid to the Sudan was envisaged, partly owing to Treasury pressures and partly since 'HMG had to avoid accusations of seeking to influence the constitutional outcome'. Helm felt that 'the FO had simply lost interest' (March 1955). Howe, on the point of retirement, appealed to Churchill himself, signing a powerful draft of Luce's, saying that the new 'spirit of independence . . . was the best hope of achieving a united Sudan, friendly to Britain . . . It would be tragic if HMG did not follow up their policy of assuring the Sudanese free self-determination by repeated public condemnation of Egyptian intervention and breaches of the Agreement. HMG must consider *now* what assistance they can give to an independent Sudan and not throw away 60 years of effort'. Moreover, 'by encouraging the Sudanese to withstand Egyptian intrigue and threats and to choose their future freely, we shall strengthen the cause of independence and thus best serve the interests of the Sudan and Britain and, inspite of herself, of Egypt also'. (The fact that over the remaining months the Sudanese, under Azhari's deft guidance, would take matters into their own hands and insist on complete independence was not, of course, at that stage forseeable.) There was no more response in London to Howe's last pleading than to Helm's first.

The above quotations covering the whole dramatic decade certainly illustrate the passionate attachment of the Sudan Political Service to what they regarded as the interests of the Sudanese. They also suggest an almost parochial disregard for the compulsions under which negotiators in Cairo were obliged to pursue what they regarded as higher policy; and Khartoum's resentments over 'higher policy' were not always expressed in private. Counter-attacks on Khartoum by Cairo Embassy were not infrequent, though seldom approaching the virulence of Campbell's comments on the head of the Sudan Political Service, Robertson, quoted on p. 32. It is a tribute to Bevin that he resolutely pursued until the end of his epoch the faint possibility of reaching an understanding with successive governments in Cairo without being put off either by his own irritation with Khartoum's 'outmoded' view of empire or by what his Minister of State reported to him at one point as Huddleston's 'Messianic frame of mind',[26] and without ever modifying his own insistence that the Sudanese must be allowed to choose their own future. The historian Holland's attribution to Bevin, in his handling of the Middle East, of the trades unionist's negotiating mentality – 'Never give anything away for nothing'[27] – is a bit unjust. After Bevin's (and Morrison's) departure, Tory and Foreign Office circles – though there too 'higher policy' imposed conflicting demands – gave distinctly greater support for the concept of an independent Sudan than Khartoum, in such private exchanges as those quoted, was disposed to recognize. Moreover, in some of that correspondence – and particularly in the Sudan Agent's more colourful passages – one can detect the soldierly habit of whistling in the trenches and the tendency to lay the blame for disasters at the front on the errors of the Command Staff, comfortably ensconced behind the lines.

For those in the field in South West Arabia in the next decade of imperial decline the problems were certainly accentuated by the change of government at home in October 1964 from Tory to Labour, the two parties having by then different perceptions of 'higher policy' in the area. Not all state papers of the final period (or indeed all those of the earlier) have yet been released and we cannot at present know the full extent to which the men on the spot argued the toss with either party in power. Nor is there available anything to compare with the 'top secret' correspondence between the Sudan Government and its Agent in London. It is nonetheless clear from such evidence as is available that disagreement between London and those in the field was fairly continuous. Four of the six Governors of Aden during the crucial period 1951 to 1967 – Hickinbotham, Johnston, Trevaskis and Trevelyan – published accounts of their stewardship. The other two, Turnbull and Luce, have left no similar testaments, though Luce's personal papers and his correspondence with his son are often revealing. All published memoirs by those in authority tend, of course, to be suspected by readers as self-defensive *apologiae*; and allowance must certainly be made for that instinct, particularly when the writers were involved in an inglorious period of their country's history. An earlier Governor, Reilly, was employed after retirement by the Foreign Office as adviser on South West Arabian affairs: his advice, as it figures in state papers, was uniformly balanced and impressive. He too published in 1969 an account of the episode to date, characteristically eschewing criticism or mentions of London-Aden disagreement over the years, including his own years as Governor.[28] There are in print contemporary accounts by professional journalists and others, who were present for some of the period and eye-witnesses to some of the events which they describe. And several Colonial Service officers who served in South West Arabia during the decade have contributed their first-hand impressions in books written in retrospect. So too have a number of Service Commanders who played a part in the story.[29] Interviews with authors and with other participants have helped to fill in the picture. Works by professional historians – some more objective than others – have of course been consulted too. In the published memoirs of politicians and senior officials involved at the London end, the affairs of South West Arabia feature in the nature of things only by chance or spasmodically – though in some cases, one may think, the chance to treat them spasmodically was readily seized.[30] Hansard is usually, though not always, a more illuminating source for the views held by politicians at the time.

Several examples of the tensions apparent between London and those in the field during this second episode have been cited in chapter 3. More will now be given. None, it may be added as a preliminary, affects the writer's hazardous belief, expressed in the Introduction, that people in authority do what they believe to be right. Though in some South West Arabian cases their route was circuitous and the effects were not foreseen, their sincerity is not in question. While it is true that in the Arab world, where so much is personalized, the actions of individual Arab leaders have often been dominant in the framing of history, circumstance (but not in the blind Tolstoyan sense), rather than the fumbling of individuals or policy clashes between personalities at the top, must take the blame or the credit for Britain's imperial evanescence post-war. In South West Arabia, one writer has said, 'the margin of error was often no wider than a minister's pending tray'.[31] But – though Johnston was one Governor who explicitly 'refused to accept a deterministic view of history'[32] – they were errors along a predestined course.

Before reviewing the evidence of tension between London and the field in the South West Arabian episode and comparing it with the tensions which had prevailed in the Sudan one, it will be as well to remind ourselves of certain differences apparent in the nature of the case. Firstly there was no-one in the Aden administration to compare with the Civil Secretary in Khartoum, promoting and symbolizing, as the latter did, a powerful sense of common purpose in the Service (an *esprit-de-corps*, if that term is still in use). It mattered little if Governors General in the Sudan – and most relevantly the last two – were sent in from outside: they were rapidly absorbed. In South West Arabia, where the Governor was more clearly the single policy-maker on the spot, all six Governors in the final period with the exception of Trevaskis were outsiders.[33] The confidence and loyalty of their Colonial Service subordinates had to be actively sought, and could not be 'mediated', as in the Sudan, by the Civil Secretary. Some, like Luce, secured it for reasons of personality more completely than others. Johnston, though generous in his tribute to his subordinates,[34] was always conscious of being regarded by them as a different breed. Moreover, and again in contrast with the Sudan, there were always differences of approach to their mission within the Aden and Protectorate staffs. Firstly, there were supporters of the minority Ingrams school. A Colonial officer supremely out of sympathy with Colonialism, Ingrams regarded the interventionist convictions of the majority as a fundamental error. The Advisory Treaties, the Federation ploy and all endeavours to subject the individualism of protectorate tribesmen (indeed Arabs anywhere) to British modes of social organization were misguided; and he quotes with something like horror the principle enunciated by Governor Johnston: 'As long as we British have formal responsibility for any part of Arabia, it is impossible for us to do anything but try to promote the institutions in which we ourselves believe – parliamentary government, tradesunions, etc.' For the Ingrams school this was a tragic failure of imagination. For the rival school of thought, represented by most of those in charge of the Western Protectorate, interventionism, instead of going too far, as Ingrams held, did not go far enough.

A second difficulty for Governors was that many British officials, as David Holden deduced from conversations with them in the Crescent bar in the midfifties, were 'afflicted with a familiar form of colonial myopia known as localitis' – involving in this case the die-hard assumption that South West Arabia's problems could be dealt with in isolation from the movement of Arab nationalism, that Nasser's propagandist appeal to rise up against the British was an ephemeral artifice, and that it could not anyway be allowed to deflect them from their own professional dedication to the genuine interests of South West Arabia.[35] Maybe Holden slightly overeggs the pudding.

A third problem for the man at the top in carrying protectorate officials along with him was the distaste some of them felt, in the fifties anyway, for the ostensibly blasé atmosphere conserved in Aden, the protocol in Government House, the racial separation, the social rat-race with its *memsahib* overtones, and all that diverted attention from the desperate need to develop the interior.[36] The penny-packages of financial help released by London, for all the efforts to enlarge them made by successive Governors, may have contributed to the detectable malaise in relations between Protectorate officers and the swelling bureaucracy in the Colony.

Successive Governors in Aden, then, could not always count on the single-minded support of their subordinates to the same extent as Governors General in the Sudan or indeed as Political Residents in the Gulf. This may have marginally affected their relations with the authorities in London. The authority to which they, unlike the other two categories, were directly answerable was of course (until very near the end) the Colonial Office, though the Foreign Office's responsibility for relations with all other Arab countries was often a cause of disagreement on policy towards, and in, South West Arabia.[37] The close concern of the Ministry of Defence was also on occasion a complicating factor.

Hickinbotham, whatever his personal defects as a Governor, can scarcely be criticized for his efforts to improve workers' conditions in the Colony, even if he did not foresee the consequences. On this issue, at any rate, he had London's backing. Where battle was engaged he stuck staunchly to three guns, though he may not have fired two of them with adequate priming. Firstly he met, like all Governors, resistance in London to his repeated pleas for financial backing and for greater recognition of the problems of controlling the hinterland. A Treasury paper stating 'we do not feel that there is any obligation on HMG for the provision of Social Services' in the territory shows what he was up against.[38] Secondly his initiatives to promote protectorate federation, conducted it would seem without much diplomacy or forethought, met not with positive opposition from London but with the more deadly weapon of half-hearted approval. The suppression by the Colonial Office of the passage on his federal initiative in Hickinbotham's despatch of June 1956, deploring the fact that 'no pressure had been brought to bear' (meaning allowed by London) on the hesitant rulers, has already been mentioned and illustrates the point just made. When, after his second fruitless initiative, discussion took place in the Colonial Office on whether, in the public statement Hickinbotham proposed to make, he should be allowed to include a reference to self-government as the future objective, the Secretary of State's decision ('after consultation with Cabinet colleagues') was to substitute 'maximum political and economic development'.[39] Similarly, when he proposed to set up a Committee under his own chairmanship to jockey the rulers along, he received a telegram stopping him.[40] Thirdly, he met with total disapproval in pressing the case for gradually bringing Colony and Protectorates together. He was particularly irritated by the bland insistence of the Government's 1951 Committee of Enquiry into Constitutional Development in the Smaller Colonial Territories that there was 'no organic connection between the Colony and the States'. In response he roundly declared: 'The policy I advocate and shall continue to advocate is the only one compatible with our obligations to the people over whom we exercise authority.'

All this was bound up with the production in 1955 of the Colonial Office paper on Long Range Policy in Aden Colony and Protectorate.[41] Hickinbotham's forthright comments (twenty-one pages of them) on the draft were described by the responsible Under Secretary as 'rather cantankerous'. The following summer, in June 1956, Prime Minister Eden figures in the continuing disagreement on policy between the Secretary of State, Lennox Boyd, and the Governor. Eden's characteristic minute, 'We must have a plan and work it through',[42] constituted a fine principle, but no 'plan' was ever decided. Eden fell back on accepting Lennox Boyd's minuted 'disapproval' of Hickinbotham's views and his conclusion, 'Let's await Hickinbotham's successor Luce in August.' It would however be unjust to Hickinbotham – or over-favourable, if that angle of vision is preferred – to see him as in permanent conflict with his political masters. He was certainly not; and if one telling illustration is in order, the notorious and controversial statement of policy by Lord Lloyd in Aden in May 1956, though sanctioned by London, proves on an examination of the Foreign Office files to have been jointly drafted on the spot by the visiting Minister and Hickinbotham.[43]

Luce duly replaced him in August. Despite his record in the Sudan as a formidable opponent of much home governmental thinking, he could at least be relied upon to eschew Hickinbotham's penchant for the 'cantankerous'. That was not his mode. As the personal letters he received on his appointment demonstrate, he was highly regarded in London. His representations, though forceful, were never confrontational. What is curious is that the progressively revised policies he urged from the time he had formed his own opinions were apparently given so little consideration. The evolution in his thinking has already been examined in chapter 3 and his resulting policy recommendations need not be re-stated here. The significant point is that in his search for solutions he was always a lap or two ahead of the policy-makers in London; and by the time it had taken them to cover the same ground, the problems had become virtually insoluble. Whether the immediate adoption of his final recommendation – for the surrender of sovereignty over Aden by the end of 1962 and the negotiation of continued military usage of the base with the independent government of a joint Aden/hinterland protectorate – would in the event have worked is of course questionable. What is with hindsight beyond question is that its pigeon-holing was fatal.

There is little sign of strain between Government House in Aden and the policy-makers in London during Johnston's tenure from 1960 to 1963, despite the rising political temperature in South West Arabia itself. Possibly Johnston's own membership of the Foreign Office (though the same syndrome did not operate with the last two Governors General in the Sudan) made serious disagreement with London improbable, whatever impatience he may have encountered amongst his subordinates. This emphatically ceased to be the case when his principle subordinate stepped into his shoes.

Trevaskis has written his own impressive *apologia*, *Shades of Amber*. His long service in the Western Protectorate had given him a uniquely comprehensive knowledge of Aden's hinterland states and a singular dedication to their interests. Nor was he either unfamiliar or wholly out of sympathy with Aden's politicians and their aspirations. His intellectual awareness, as disclosed in his book, of the potency of Arab nationalism and its Nasserite inspiration is equally beyond question, and his thinking was never static. Although in that respect he had originally been out of phase with the evolving perceptions of Luce, he quickly came, so his account tells us, to see the merits of the latter's final recommendations, including the surrender of sovereignty in Aden by 1962.[44] He was in fact no die-hard colonial, suffering in Holden's diagnostics from advanced 'localitis', though that may have been the impression, in hindsight and even at the time, of impatient outside observers. His disagreements with London policy-making were not confined to the period after the change of government in October 1964. He deplored the Lloyd declaration of May 1956, which he describes as 'getting the watchword precisely wrong', and he found little response in London at the official level during the Tory Government to many of his pleadings as Governor. As yet, of course, state papers of the period are not available to reveal the London end of the story he tells.[45]

If tension is too strong a word for his relations with the Conservative administration, that is not the case when Labour took over; and the tension evidently reached snapping point within a matter of months, when he was summarily replaced by Turnbull. By then of course, and indeed for some years before then,[46] Labour party sympathies were with al-Asnaj, whose undisguised hostility towards the hinterland rulers and to British protection of them set him violently at odds with the determination of Trevaskis in particular to protect them. Moreover, since Trevaskis had detected circumstantial indications that al-Asnaj was at least privy to his attempted assassination at the airport in December 1963, it would have been more than human for him to retain much residual sympathy for al-Asnaj and the movement he led. He had been the original begetter of the federal concept and remained wedded to it until the end. It is easy now, and may have been easy then, for observers of the failure everywhere else of federations as the key to decolonization, to conclude that Trevaskis was backing the wrong horse. It is much less easy to see what other runner under British colours could be entered in the race. The Tory Government itself was not disposed to venture more than a few shillings on the federal horse. Moreover (at the risk of flogging the metaphor to death), the federal horse on which the Tory gamblers did place their modest bet was not the one Trevaskis would have chosen to represent the imperial stud. In literal terms, he always considered the federal structure in the form sanctioned by London to smack too much of Westminster and of supervisory tutelage to strike root in the thin soil of Arabia; and in that at least he was unquestionably right. Moreover, the prospects of bringing the Hadhramut states either into a united federation with their Western equivalents (with whom they had never felt affinity) or later into a unitary state including Aden (with which they felt even less) were always minimal. With this latter problem Trevaskis' successor too was to grapple unsuccessfully. Trevaskis' mission as High Commissioner (the title of Governor having now lapsed) may be judged by the outcome a failure; the policies he stood for were overtaken by events and, finally, by the opposition of a government determined not to fall into the same evolutionary trap.

The task which faced Turnbull on his arrival in January 1965 would have daunted any man. The chaos out of which he was called to bring order was mounting daily. Having no previous experience of the subtleties of the Arab mind, he may not have been the ideal choice. His efforts to reconcile the rulers (Western or Eastern) with the Adeni politicians and to edge the whole federal contraption forward into a final agreement with the British Government were doomed to failure. Evidently he was unable to establish a close understanding with any of the conflicting federal groupings, much less with their radical and equally conflicting opponents. He rates high marks, higher indeed than those accorded to any of his recent predecessors, from one British official who was on the scene from 1960 until the end and who has published an eye-witness account of the closing stages.[47] Although by this account Turnbull was forgiven neither by Conservatives in opposition nor by Labour leaders in power, the evidence is not yet available for the stages by which he lost the confidence of the Wilson Government until the tension in his case too reached snapping point. At that point, following the arrival in Aden in April 1967 of Lord Shackleton, as the despairing Government's last emissary in search of a solution, he like his predecessor was summarily replaced.[48] As for the next and final High commissioner, his task was simply – though it was scarcely simple – to stage-manage Britain's ignominious withdrawal in as dignified a way as circumstances allowed. Trevelyan, though privately criticized by some as making a personal triumph out of a national disaster, carried out his task with great skill. The home authorities were only too ready to leave the modalities to him. He thus emerges as the only occupant of Government House in Aden – save perhaps Johnston – to have served his admittedly brief time without policy disagreement with the government in London.

As for the Gulf episode, an assessment of the degree of harmony or disharmony between London and those in the field from the time when withdrawal and independence were first explicitly accepted as the long term aim until they were actually implemented, that is from about 1951 to 1971, is hazardous. Very little has been published by any of those involved at either end; and for the critical period following the decision to withdraw from Aden, state papers are still closed. There has been trenchant criticism from outside of Britain's retreat from Arabia generally,[49] but as between the British Government and its representatives in the Gulf the published evidence of discord is slight. The point was made earlier, that once Sir Rupert Hay retired in 1953, having served as a bridge between the Government of India and the Foreign Office when responsibility changed hands, those representing Britain in the Gulf were, with the exception of Luce, members of the diplomatic service and by that token more accustomed than those administering the Sudan and South West Arabia to the subordination of local *desiderata* to the wider interests of their home government. For that matter there was no obvious occasion in the Gulf – until 1968 – for the kind of confrontations with London policy-makers that had been a feature in the Sudan and South West Arabia.

So far as disagreement existed at the begining of the twenty-year period concerned, this would appear to have been generated at the London end and at Foreign Secretary level. The records show that both Bevin (1949) and Eden (1953) expressed dissatisfaction with the slowness of progress in improving administration and developing social services in the shaykhdoms. This was the period when the necessity – in the interests of stability, world opinion and Britain's prestige as protecting power – of intervening in the internal affairs of the states more forcefully than the letter of the old treaties sanctioned had been gaining ground in London. Eden in particular had little patience with circumspect argument from officials, either in the Gulf or at home, that Britain was not in a position to enforce her wishes. He seized on the Makins Report of March 1952 as supporting evidence that intervention was essential to prevent maladministration; and minuted testily when officials from the Permanent Undersecretary down suggested that there were difficulties about implementing changes overnight.[50] Hay was not a man to challenge higher authority; but when he observed in his last despatch from Bahrain, 'The Foreign Office takes closer interest and is more concerned to ensure that the shaykhdoms are properly administered than the Government of India who were always most reluctant to interfere in their internal affairs,'[51] one suspects that his own inclinations lay with the Government of India. The Delphic instructions issued to his successor, Burrows – 'It is essential that HMG exert sufficient influence in the shaykhdoms to ensure that there is no conflict between the policies of the rulers and those of HMG' – indicate a recognition amongst the Foreign Office drafters that 'interference' might not be all that easy but that they must be able to defend their instructions against the impatience of the Foreign Secretary.

The next incumbent, Sir George Middleton, held office during a period of mounting opposition to the imperial presence from educated activists in

Bahrain and Kuwait – indeed it was a testing period in other ways as well for the man on the spot. But in the absence of any evidence of policy disaccord between him and London, we move on to the six years of Luce (1960–1966). As in Aden his incumbency was the critical one, if a positive policy for orderly withdrawal, when the time came, was to be adopted. During the four remaining years of Tory government, his prime concern was to persuade the London authorities to abandon Micawberism in favour of a more constructive approach to the future security of the Gulf in the face of the Nasserist threat to Western interests there; and he was exasperated at the absence of response on the part of both the Conservative administration and its Labour successor (from 1964) to his Peninsula Solidarity project. (Long after Britain's withdrawal the Gulf States themselves were to adopt something very similar in the shape of the Gulf Co-operation Council.) On one other, but related, issue he found Conservative hesitations distressing. This was their negative response to the Yemeni revolution of 1962.[52] The constructive response, as he saw it at the time and thereafter, would have been to come instantly to terms with the new regime in Sanaʿa and urge the monarchist countries in the area to do likewise – not out of any fellow-feeling for the Yemeni revolutionaries but as a means of terminating their dependence on Egyptian troops and the accompanying threat to the Arabian peninsula as a whole of invasion in the ideological sense by Nasserism. On this issue too his advice was not followed; and, as related in chapter 3, Nasser – however unsuccessfully in the long run – pursued the advantage offered. When the Labour Government took over, Luce found their ideas for re-structuring inter-state relationships in the Gulf – there was for instance an idea propounded from London for the absorption by Dubai of the other six Trucial States – unrealistic. But it was the Labour Government's 1966 decision to abandon the Aden base that more seriously disturbed him on the grounds that it removed the strategic pivot on which the defence of the Gulf had hitherto rested, as the protection from Iraq given to Kuwait in 1961 had demonstrated. Luce had of course left the Gulf before the 1968 decision to hammer the final nail into the coffin of Britain's Middle East empire.[53] Though he deplored at the time the crudeness of the Labour Government's carpentry, he played, as related in chapter 4, a major part in disabusing the subsequent Tory carpenters of any idea that life could be restored to the body in the coffin by drawing the last nail out again. His successor as Political Resident in the Gulf had reached the same conclusion; and from then on the functions of the Residency were simply to help ensure that the obsequies were decently managed and not disrupted by outsiders. There was no occasion for further dispute with London.

To summarize this survey of relations between those in the field and those in London in our three episodes, the disposition in the palace at Khartoum to argue the toss with London was more acute than was the case in Government

House in Aden or in the Residency in Bahrain – and this because the Governor General had historically enjoyed a greater degree of autonomy than had the other two proconsuls and was more single-mindedly concerned with the local interests of his parishioners than were the agents of the Colonial Office in Aden and of the Foreign Office in the Gulf. Such governors in Aden as Hickinbotham, Luce, Trevaskis and perhaps Turnbull saw various important issues, it is true, differently from the London policy-makers, but their more direct subordination to the home authorities and their clearer recognition of the obsolescence of British paramountcy in the Middle East ruled out of court the kind of positive resistance to London's dictates in which Khartoum frequently engaged. While there were certainly clashes of opinion between Aden and London, debate was generally conducted quietly on paper and with ostensible decorum. Nor, of course, was the Aden Government represented in London by an agent of the kind maintained there by the government in Khartoum, with whom privately to bandy resentments week by week for the benefit of historians. In the Gulf, policy alternatives on which disagreement might arise were in the nature of things more narrowly restricted. With certain exceptions, moreover, British relations with local authorities in the Gulf, the shaykhly governments, were reasonably harmonious and uniform. Accordingly, the task for Britain's representatives of translating to them the policy objectives emerging from London was less fraught than had been the corresponding experience in South West Arabia, where the reconciliation of rival local interests with each other – whatever policies the British Government adopted and however its representatives on the spot might seek their modification – grew progressively impossible. In the Gulf, therefore, though Luce as Resident continually recommended the adoption of a more constructive and forward-looking line in overall British policy in the area, the fruitlessness of his recommendations neither complicated Britain's relations with the rulers at the time nor affected, as may have been the case in Aden, the ultimate outcome. Later, the Labour government's summary change of policy East of Suez certainly aroused consternation amongst those on the spot. But this related to the manner and timing of the announcement: the basic principle of military withdrawal was challenged only by the rulers.

Amongst the inhabitants of our three areas the prospect of release from British control understandably aroused emotions of a different order than was the case amongst those exercising it. These emotions varied across the social spectrum, the resulting pattern of response repeating itself up to a point in each territory. The pattern took the following form. The educated but politically deprived, avid for a greater share in the exercise of power, were naturally the most enthusiastic to send the foreign imperialists packing. The traditional collaborators, rulers and shaykhs in particular, though not averse to the principle of independence, had from the start misgivings about their ability to preserve their own locally dominant role without some form of continued protection. Those in South West Arabia and the Gulf certainly hoped that the cession of political sovereignty by Britain, assuming that was on the way, would not mean the withdrawal of her armed presence; and though they received until very near the end assurances on that score, they hesitated to hasten even political disengagement. As for the masses, the emotions generated by the prospect of independent statehood depended on the extent of their tribal and other local loyalties, on the degree of intimacy and trust which the imperialist presence had succeeded over the years in establishing, and of course on the ability of nationalist agitators to attract popular support.

No doubt this three-fold pattern of response was a constant in broad terms in all episodes of decolonization everywhere. But its figuration in these three differed conspicuously from case to case. This can partly be attributed to marked differences in the national characteristics of the inhabitants of the three territories concerned, which were reflected in their response to the situations they successively found themselves in. In the make-up of the northern Sudanese (for these purposes we may disregard the politically deprived negroid southerners) there was and is a recognizable quiddity distinguishing them from the peoples of South West Arabia and the Gulf, as from other Arab communities. Perhaps this can be attributed to the merger in the northern Sudanese of two bloodstreams, Arab and African, and to a resulting combination of the quick wits and sharp minds of the Arab strain with the less sophisticated, less calculating and less volatile qualities of the African. Whatever the cause, the resulting characteristics engaged the instant sympathy of the British 'colonialist' on the spot; and this, coupled with the latter's life-long service in the Sudan, produced a kind of relationship at the personal level rarely manifest elsewhere. For one thing both parties, in cliché terms, laughed at the same jokes; and when relations in the political sense were under strain, personal relations even with those politically hostile were thereby able to survive. In our other two territories, though individual relations were often amicable and close, the intimate understanding right across the social spectrum so relished by the British in the Sudan was never experienced on the same scale. Even if this Anglo-Sudanese *rapport* can be represented as skin-deep or factitious, it certainly served to ease the process of Britain's disengagement or expulsion. For members of the Political Service the process was of course dispiriting enough at one level; at another level, thanks to the constant irruption of good humoured teasing on both sides, it never wholly lost a sense of fun.[54]

No comparable sense of 'fun' can be detected in the episodes of disengagement from South West Arabia and the Gulf. In the latter, it is true, and particularly in the case of Bahrain, that personal relations between Britain's representatives and members of the ruling family and other prominent personalities were often gratifyingly close, but at other levels of society intimacy was in the nature of things less marked and less widespread. In South West Arabia such close Arab-expatriate *rapport* was rarely achieved at any level: the rulers were as a whole too self-absorbed and too remote from daily contact, the tribes too naturally independent and wayward, the activists in Aden too deeply committed to hostility. Though there were assuredly exceptions, particularly in British relations with traditional 'collaborators', the divide which separated the indigenous community as a whole from, on the one hand, the large expatriate body in Aden and, on the other, the few Britons orbiting in the hinterland was never effectively bridged. Attempts to bridge it were certainly made by such British officials as spent long years in the territory but the short-term postings of the majority – something the old hands constantly deplored – handicapped their efforts.

The difference in the administrative responsibilities of Britain's representatives in each territory accounts of course for much of the variation in their understanding with the native populations. In the Sudan members of the Political Service were administrators in the full sense of the word, in close and daily contact with their parishioners, high and low. In the South West Arabian Protectorates the British political staff were, constitutionally, advisers to a set of formally independent rulers (not all of whom were deferential yes-men, chosen and imposed by Britain), and the extent of their administrative intervention and of their dealings with the rulers' subjects was by that token limited and random. Similarly, their enforcement in the states of local budgetary control and of such grass-roots developmental progress as budgets allowed, essential though such enforcement may have been, was strictly *ultra vires*. In the Gulf, day to day administration was even more emphatically the responsibility of the ruling shaykhs and their subordinates; and the representatives of the Foreign Office, though they certainly tendered plenty of advice, were not constitutionally advisers, much less administrators. Such familiarity as they enjoyed with the general populace was in a sense accidental;[55] and the effect of their departure on the lives of the indigenous communities was therefore less profound. It is true that, within and on the fringes of the rulers' administrations, Britons were active in sundry professional capacities. The fact that expatriates directly employed by the rulers were mostly British was of course a reflection of Britain's political dominance and certainly helped to give the scene an additional tinge of 'colonialism'; but such employees had little independence of action. Nor were they answerable to the British authorities. Only perhaps in internal security matters, and that only in the Trucial States, did official British intervention impinge directly on the lives of the citizenry. (Britain's responsibility for *external* defence impinged hardly at all.) And most such security interventions were conducted by request or consent of the rulers. The handling of internal security in South West Arabia and in the Sudan was wholly different.

Another aspect in which the approach to independence differed materially in each of our three territories was manifest in the field of organized labour. In the Sudan it took longer than was expedient, to the Civil Secretary's private regret, to elaborate a charter for the workforce in the public sector, in spite of the fact that this labour legislation was ahead of the field by the standards of the day. It is conceivable that some of the difficulties presented in the con-dominium's later stages by organized labour, notably in the railways, might have been mitigated had the authorities been quicker off the mark in codifying the relevant legislation. By the time this was completed, the workforce was already a field for manipulation by political activists. Nonetheless such challenges to British policy as organized labour presented in the Sudan were in no way comparable to those experienced in South West Arabia. There, though labour legislation was limited to Aden Colony, the politicization of the trades unions in the peculiar conditions described in chapter 3 created problems for the British unparalleled in colonial experience. The fact that, as an American observer put it in 1963,[56] 'free trades unions [were] only to be found either in democratic countries or in what is left of the British empire' may be a credit to Britain's imperial account; but in Aden at any rate it made the political book-keeping doubly complicated. In the Protectorates as distinct from the Colony, there was no direct British responsibility for labour legislation and too little industrial development to stimulate pressure on the rulers to take steps in that direction, whatever aspirations ATUC's activities in Aden may have generated amongst labourers in the hinterland. In the Gulf too there was little industrial development, outside the oil industry, to provide a base for trades union activity. In Bahrain, it is true, popular pressures resulted in the introduction by its rulers of a Labour Code in 1956, but the politicization of the workforce as such never created embarrassment for the British in the approach to with-drawal of the kind experienced in Aden and to a lesser extent in the Sudan.

In much the same way it was only in the Sudan and in Aden Colony, where Britain was administratively in the saddle, that the promotion of democratic principles played a significant part in the run-up to independence. When the Sudan episode in disengagement opened, Britain's own belief in the universal desirability of parliamentary government on the Westminster model and in its ultimate practicability was still potent. Teaching the nations how to live (as Milton phrased it in his *Areopagitica*, long before British imperialism was invented) was regarded, however naively, as Britain's mission. In pre-independence Sudan her standing and influence there were still such that her own type of elective democracy had been unquestioningly adopted as the proper objective, at least in principle, by the politically conscious, whether well-disposed to the British presence or hostile. The success of the anti-British parties in the 1953 general elections, however embarrassing, was not considered in Britain to affect the propriety of encouraging parliamentary practice on her own pattern; and this encouragement continued right up to withdrawal.

In the case of South West Arabia in the next decade British belief in universal suffrage as a specific for good government in the Third World was distinctly weakened when the principle was hijacked by her opponents in Aden and by the enemies of imperialism in the United Nations. The catch-word insistence of the latter's Committee of 24, endorsed by the General Assembly in its 1963 resolution, on the instant introduction of universal suffrage throughout the whole of South West Arabia was seen in Britain as a purely anti-imperialist gimmick, grotesquely impractical. Well before the end of empire there, popular hostility in Aden had reached a pitch which made the widening of the franchise in the Colony and the promotion of democracy outside it inconveniently dangerous to Britain's own perceived interests. Measures of a kind were nonetheless taken to implant the notions of democratic practice; but they were taken hesitatingly, and the seedlings never took root.

As for the Gulf, Britain never sought to undermine the shaykhly system of government by propagating her own. This was not because shaykhly autocracy was regarded with favour in itself but largely because it was seen as more accommodating to Britain's own interests than any alternative mode of government that might have been encouraged, or manipulated, into replacing it. Efforts were taken to improve and modernize the rulers' administrations, to encourage delegation from the centre and some degree of popular participation in bodies of an advisory kind; but though unsatisfactory rulers could and did run into trouble as individuals with their British mentors, no attempt was made to tamper with the fundamentals of rulership as such. It was perhaps a relief to Britain that no serious dallyings with democracy of a Western kind under pressure from below were sanctioned by shaykhly governments in the Gulf before withdrawal.

If therefore, in the words of Hartley Coleridge, freedom is a licence to be good and if, as the old imperialist was bred to maintain, to be good entails being democratic on the British pattern, then Britain's missionary endeavour to prepare these three territories for independence can hardly be judged a success. Nor in the aftermath have any of the three disclosed either aptitude or inclination to espouse the political principles which Britain cherishes and whose universal espousal the older imperialist took for granted as the right true end of empire. In the Gulf such modest experiments with parliamentary government as have been permitted (in Kuwait and Bahrain) have so far been reined back, leaving the shaykhly system still broadly intact. In South West

Arabia, political experimentation since independence has been of a kind conspicuously different from that once encouraged, however ambivalently, by Britain. The government of the PDRY may of course lay claim to 'centralized democracy' of the kind declared to be practised in the Soviet Union; but that is hardly what a century and a half of British tutelage hoped to leave in its wake. The fact that there are Western observers who consider the conditions prevailing in South Yemen to render more liberal models unworkable does little to make the outcome more creditable. Even in the Sudan, where the encouragement given by the British to the espousal of democratic principles was genuine, the aftermath has been a disappointment. The first attempt to put those principles into practice was short-lived, and such spasmodic endeavours as have been made subsequently to try again have met with little success. The best that can be said in this respect for Britain's political tutelage is that, as a constitutional model, democracy on the British pattern has never wholly lost its hold in the Sudan on the minds of the politically active.

Criteria other than the political aftermath by which the British record in these three territories can be judged, favourably or not, will be considered in the final chapter. The purpose of this one was to compare three episodes of disengagement. Its conclusion must be that, though they can all now be recognized as part of a single historical process – the mid-twentieth century imperative of decolonization – detailed compliance with that imperative in each case lay within conspicuously different parameters. In this exhumation for comparative study of three bodies from the same extinct family it is their contrasting features that give the autopsy its interest.

6 Epilogues and epitaphs

He must be more independent, must hear for himself what the feelings of the
Natives really are, and do what he thinks right and not be guided by the snobbish
and vulgar, over-bearing and offensive behaviour of our Civil and Political Agents,
if we are to go on peacefully and happily, and be liked and beloved by high and
low – as well as respected as we ought to be – and not trying to trample on the
people and continually reminding them and making them face that they are a
conquered people.

Victoria R.I.[1]

There are many striking aspects of the letter from which the above passage is
taken, written by Queen Victoria to her Prime Minister. That it should have
come from the pen of the ageing Empress is perhaps the most startling. It
might be thought almost equally remarkable that Lord Curzon, the Viceroy
designate of India, for whose instruction it was written and to whom Lord
Salisbury passed it on, expressed his whole-hearted agreement with the
Queen's 'wise injunctions', disclaiming any personal tarring with the 'insular
arrogance of the Englishman'. Modesty, if that is the converse of arrogance, is
scarcely the image Lord Curzon presents to the eyes of posterity.[2] Another
intriguing aspect of the letter is surely the question, what was Queen Victoria's
source for her description of the Indian Civil Servant – reputedly the cream of
the British upper-middle class – as 'snobbish and vulgar, overbearing and
offensive'? She had little opportunity herself to 'hear what the feelings of the
Natives really [were]'.

The present essay, however, is not concerned with the behaviour of
Britain's civil and political agents in India who have plenty of impressive
defenders,[3] but with that of their approximate equivalents in three much less
imposing outposts of empire. Whatever the basis for Queen Victoria's strictures on the ICS a century ago, would the occupant of the throne ever have felt
impelled to express similar concern about the Sudan Political Service, about
Colonial Officers in South West Arabia, or about those representing the
Crown in the Gulf?

Today the arrogance of imperialism, if not necessarily of its practitioners as
a body, is taken as read. With rare exceptions[4] the published 'feelings of the
Natives' who experienced it do little to improve the reading. Latterday
exponents of empire in our three territories, who have written their own
accounts, give understandably a more favourable impression of the behaviour
and achievement of their colleagues and of themselves. Where does the truth,
if ascertainable, lie? Whatever the ultimate verdict of history on the ethos of

empire – and it is still too recent a historical curiosity for an objective judgement – that ethos is already as undecypherable to the post-imperial generation
as cuneiform. The following paragraphs do not presume to decypher the code
but will only suggest a possible identification for a few of its wedge-shaped
incisions, as found in our three territories.

We are not primarily concerned in this chapter with what dominion over
palm and pine meant, post Kipling, to the imperial government in London.
The foregoing chapters have, it is hoped, presented a sufficient account of the
perceptions of policy-makers in Westminster and Whitehall as they evolved
over the years. In those quarters there may have been undertones of sentiment
– indeed overtones in the case of Churchill, for example – for or against the
practice of empire; but the maintenance of Britain's standing as a major
power, even when that role was recognized as diminishing, was regarded in
London strictly as matter of pragma. The criteria employed in defining policy
in any corner of empire were calculated in terms of the contribution which that
territory made or might make to the performance of Britain's world role. This
is not to deny that public opinion, a more sentimental organ, had some effect
on the shaping of policy. In the years preceding World War II public opinion
and government attitudes were broadly at one in treating the practice of
empire as something ordained by nature or by a perceptive providence. World
War II inevitably dented the smooth surface of this shared assumption. In the
aftermath of war, while governments in London were much occupied with the
maintenance of Britain's world stature despite her economic exhaustion,
public opinion was much more concerned with the recovery and fairer distribution at home of the good things whose provision the war had interrupted.
Not that the propriety of dominating large chunks of the benighted Third
World was actively called in question by the man in the street. The superiority
of the British way of life over all others was still taken for granted, as was the
assumption that the 'backward races' would naturally aspire to develop in the
same direction, with whatever British guidance they were lucky enough to
secure. But they would have to do more about it for themselves; and if they
failed to do so, that was their affair. This continuing grass-roots assumption of
British racial superiority was at least partially redeemed by a growing penchant, fostered by the popular cartoonists, for self-mockery – something not
practised with the same fervour elsewhere in the Western world, though
featuring as a fine art in Egypt.[5]

The widespread belief – active amongst policy-makers, passive amongst the
populace – in Britain's continuing imperial mission unquestionably survived
the battering of World War II. Even the end of the Raj in India in 1947,
however traumatic, affected it much less than might be supposed. Indeed in a
sense it provided practical confirmation of the declared aim of empire, which
was to train its subject peoples in the art of government and then release them

to exercise it for themselves, when they would be welcome to join the other self-governing members of the British Commonwealth with the Queen at its head. This stage had been duly reached in the sub-continent of India. The rest of the empire, or most of the rest, was simply 'not yet ready' to dispense with tutelage. There were therefore substantial areas of the globe where the imperial mission had to continue (though the White Man's Burden terminology had by now fortunately passed out of the currency).

What is remarkable in retrospect is that the attitude to empire, in Britain as a whole, was to swing from unquestioning acceptance to apologetic disavowal in less than a single generation. Today's penitence, like yesterday's pride, will doubtless be overtaken, both of them representing successive early drafts of a history to be written when perspectives have stabilized. Meanwhile, what is of interest here is the effect of this rapid transformation in the UK of attitudes to empire on its practitioners in the field during the course of that single generation. If their perceptions simply parallelled those of the policy-makers and the public at home, enough would already have been said. But though they too were changing, attitudes in the field were clearly different from those at home; and to an examination of them in each of our three episodes we now turn. If our attention is focused almost exclusively on Britain's political and administrative officials, this is not intended to deny the importance of the part played by members of other professions, military and civilian alike. It is simply one of the limitations imposed by so summary a study.

What manner of men, then, were those 'set under authority'[6] during the final stages of British imperialism in the Arab World? What view did they take of their obsolescent task? Whatever may be said of the privileges of exercising power, theirs was scarcely a comfortable profession; and since what the course of history required of the whole species was that it should do itself out of a job, one may wonder about the motives of those who went in for it. Were they driven by nothing more creditable than myopic nostalgia? Or by hay-making cynicism? Or by the absence of more gainful employment? Were they simply impelled by that antique English passion for 'trafficking with tribesmen on the roof of the world'?[7] Or by what? And as individuals, were they, in the words of the unappetizing stereotype once levelled at colonial administrators in Africa, 'first-class hearties with third-class minds'? Even worse, were they, to revert to the strictures of the Queen Empress, 'snobbish, vulgar, overbearing and offensive', as well as indifferent to the real feelings of the Natives? These are not questions easily answered with objectivity by one of the species, himself like the rest of mankind a prisoner of his own past.[8] The trouble is that they can hardly be answered at all by anyone else – by anyone, that is to say, without direct personal experience who has to rely on the accounts of others.

One approach which has been gaining favour amongst students of the ethos of empire, described as the 'sociology of imperialism', may be helpful. No

comprehensive sociological study of the Colonial Service as a whole has yet
been attempted. Profiles in this sense of those who served in a number of
individual colonies are in print, but the representatives of the imperial power
in South West Arabia have not been so scrutinized. Nor is such a study of the
social and educational antecedents of those who served after 1946 in the Gulf
to be expected: though classified as Diplomatic Service officers, their professional origins were perhaps too diverse to give the exercise much meaning.
But in the case of the Sudan, with its compact and unified Political Service, a
sociological analysis of its members was recently undertaken by an academic
specialist,[9] partly to test the validity of the once notorious 'Blacks-ruled-by-
Blues' syndrome.

When that Service was in process of establishment, its British recruits,
according to Cromer's design for it, were to be 'active young men endowed
with good health, high character and fair abilities'. Kirk-Greene's analysis
reveals that of the 393 graduate entrants over the half century of the Condominium, 93 were 'Blues' (i.e. had represented their university in a
recognized sport). This turns out to be the same number as those with Third
Class degrees; but any instant conclusion would be misplaced, for a majority
of those with 'Blues' were amongst the holders of First or Second Class
degrees (numbering in all 32 and 140 respectively). Athletic prowess was
judged, legitimately enough, as good evidence of the physical resilience that
service in the climate and conditions of the Sudan demanded.[10] But whether
having batted, kicked, rowed or shot for Oxbridge (the source of 90 per cent of
the entrants) necessarily produced good administrators is perhaps no more
self-evident than the supposition that a First Class degree must have done so.
It is certainly the case that some of those who left the greatest mark on the
Sudan were 'Blues' (like Robertson) or holders of First Class degrees or both
(like MacMichael[11]); but most of those whose personalities imprinted themselves on the scene possessed neither of these cachets. Luce and Henderson,
simply as examples, did not; nor did Douglas Newbold, generally regarded as
the most impressive and inspiring administrator the Service produced.[12]

The sociological profiling of its members does not, it would seem, do much
to explain the reputation as an élite corps of administrators which the Sudan
Service certainly acquired – and relished. Some of its members may have
relished it rather more openly than was seemly, but few of them would
seriously claim that as a whole they were more than 'active young men of fair
abilities', not noticeably distinguishable by that criterion from the ordinary
Oxbridge product of the time. What did perhaps distinguish them was a rare
degree of enthralment with the things they found themselves doing and with
the length of rope they were given to get on with doing them. An institution,
however, so highly regarded at the time, by itself as well as by others, was
bound to attract a measure of come-uppance from subsequent investigators.

The Sudan Political Service has not escaped this nemesis. In recent years this has come most readily from American scholars[13] Even at the time eulogy was not universal. The first British Trade Commissioner himself in his reports to the Foreign Office in 1953–54 expressed views critical enough to arouse surprise there.[14] His criticisms, however, were a good deal less barbed than the irony of a contemporary British officer in the Egyptian Administration, whose description of the Sudan Service as '100 per cent cock-angels and nothing else' quickly secured a place in the scriptures.[15] They were also sometimes charged with relapsing under the weight of their administrative burden into intellectual stagnation. Certainly the physical demands of 'trafficking with tribesmen on the roof of the world' – more accurately, either in one of its bigger deserts or, in the case of what were known as the Bog Barons, in one of its biggest swamps – gave them, or gives them in retrospect, an exaggeratedly macho air; and this too might have left their intellects as well as their wives[16] (an encumbrance which the young were until late on discouraged from importing) little opportunity to flower. But their collective contribution to *Sudan Notes and Records* (the best of all comparable journals) shows that they were by no means intellectually inert. Quite a number too managed to write valuable books on Sudan subjects – though their partiality for recording their current activities, and even their official Monthly Diaries, in rhyme (and subsequently publishing them) might lead those out for blood to damn them, like the unfortunate Cinna, for their 'bad verses'.[17]

In point of fact critical outsiders, on actually meeting specimens, are known to have been surprised at finding them more bearable and more interesting as individuals than their public image had prepared them to expect. And if the qualities sought in their standard recruitment process might have been expected to press them into a uniform mould, they at least prided themselves on the existence amongst their ranks of some notable eccentrics – though these were generally to be found amongst the minority recruited from other sources.[18]

Leaving superficialities on one side, however, other more serious criticisms are not easily rebutted. Certainly the Service never stirred itself till far too late to get to grips with the problem of the South.[19] Certainly it failed to prepare the Sudan as a whole, politically and in economic terms, for independence in the manner and at the pace that history was to demand. Indeed a number of recent writers find little difficulty in demonstrating that, throughout the Condominium, Sudan Government policies were unprogressive, not to say philistine.[20] The validity of such strictures, to the extent that they are adopted from the standpoint of half a century later, may be open to question. By the standards of the day, so the defence may argue, progress was as balanced, as imaginative and as fast as was judged wise. A failure to foresee the inevitable would be easier to condone than would the related charge of failing to adapt psychologically to the inevitable when it manifested itself. In that too there may be at least partial truth. The fact that most of the Service, to general surprise, went about their usual administrative duties, as if nothing unusual was afoot, until they were given their farewell tea-parties by the Sudanese, might be regarded as corroboration. A more generous interpretation would also be possible.

What meanwhile did the Sudanese themselves think of them? In view of the country's past history, of course, to find themselves administered at all may perhaps have blinded the masses to the defects of British rule in the early days. At the very least the new administration must have been seen as a signal improvement on anything in the collective folk-memory. The charge of arrogant despotism levied later on, in the Sudan as elsewhere, against the practice of empire as an institution by those eager to be free of it would seem to have been seldom encountered here in personal terms. Indeed there is evidence that the hot-tempered martinet with the soft heart (a stock figure in fiction but by no means fictitious) was viewed by the Sudanese with more affection than was the opposite British prototype whose emotions were kept calmly under control. Of one such martinet, the redoubtable Major Bramble, two relevant things are recorded of his time as District Commissioner in Omdurman. One is the memorable rubric he gave a newly arrived graduate assistant for the proper administration of the Sudan – 'Severity tempered by Justice'. The other is that when in 1935 his retirement in his mid-sixties was at last decreed, the citizens of Omdurman petitioned *en masse* for his retention.[21] But the Sudanese were singularly tolerant of the less eccentric too; and if the Sudan Service's reputation as successful administrators was justified, the secret may lie as much as anything in the qualities of the people they were administering. 'The Sudanese', declared one of their first province governors on independence, 'are so confident that they are the best people in the world that it is impossible for them to think there is somebody who looks down on them. As a result, the Sudanese worked with the English as equals in a way which did not exist in other parts of the Empire'.[22] If that explanation of Anglo-Sudanese harmony would not be universally endorsed, it may at least be as good as any other. Finally, if the Sudan administrators' dedication was almost uncomfortably intense,[23] it was at least redeemed by a shared enjoyment of the absurd. Historians of empire, should the urge to analyse its oddities continue, may well conclude that those who governed the Sudan were not, after all, paragons but that, if no more definitive generalization can be made about them, they were at least a happy breed of men.

Whether that last generalization can also serve as epitaph on those who sought to govern South West Arabia is less evident. As compared with the Sudan, physical conditions were even less agreeable for those toiling round the Protectorate hinterland and were scarcely more inviting for those chairbound in the Aden hot-house. The likelihood of assassination was everywhere real enough. As for being merely taken hostage or beseiged on a hill top, that hardly counted. Despite the risks and the raging sun, there were certainly some – a higher proportion perhaps in the years before 1946 than afterwards – who found the life enjoyable and, in the case of those in the Protectorates, stimulating, precisely because the experience was shared by so few. Of the latter, Hamilton and Ingrams, different as they were, are supreme examples. They were explorers as well as political functionaries; and in all professions the breaking of new ground is enthralling. Neither of the two, however, were amongst those Englishmen romantically smitten between the two World Wars by the 'spell of Arabia' – a sickness of the imagination, as Hamilton himself expressly describes it. 'Such oafish spirits', he wrote at the time, 'gravitate to the Arabian Peninsula like dung-flies to a camel track and do us much harm in Arab eyes'.[24] The fascination for such as Hamilton and Ingrams lay rather in the private challenge and drama of the job: the enjoyment, in Hamilton's case at least, was experienced in retrospect. The peoples he sought to pacify in the Western Protectorate were grotesquely separatist and quarrelsome, reconcilable only in resistance to the Imam in Sanaʿa: indeed Ingram's experiment in peacemaking between the tribes in the Eastern Protectorate was itself repugnant to those in the West. The government in Aden in the thirties was far too starved of manpower and equipment to enforce any general pacification, without which the orderly administration and development of the interior was impossible. The only forces in the WAP at the disposal of Governor Reilly in those days (apart from a Royal Air Force squadron[25] and a Political Secretary in Government House) consisted amazingly of one Political Officer, raised gradually after the war to the power of twelve. The EAP was no less sparsely equipped.

In all this the circumstances in South West Arabia bore little resemblance to those prevailing at the same period in the Sudan. Nor did the resemblance ever grow much closer. 'Officials', writes Bidwell, 'who had served a regular apprenticeship in India or Africa often gave up in despair at the problems they encountered.'[26] Bidwell himself, posted to the WAP as a Political Officer in 1955, was generally out of sympathy with the policies prescribed from London but clearly found the job itself intriguing, sometimes hilariously so, until he relinquished it after four years in favour of more intellectual pursuits. Another young Colonial officer[27] sent to the same area in 1961 quickly reached the conclusion that the whole set-up was an 'insufferable mess' and sought escape from it after three years by transfer to the Diplomatic Service. Ironically the Foreign Office accepted him and posted him straight back to the WAP to continue the same role (on less favourable rates of pay) for another three years. The mess remained insufferable, though he served with distinction in it, sharing with others in the vast hinterland an unfavourable view of the bureaucrats in Aden who wrote copiously about it to London without venturing, save rarely and by aeroplane, beyond the perimeter of the city. Even Governor Johnston's one and only visit to the area where this officer worked was to say goodbye, a circumstance which evidently mystified its inhabitants.

Indeed, the historic lack of sympathy between the denizens of the interior and those of Aden city found a distinct echo amongst the two separate groups of expatriates governing them. In part this was due to their contrasting lifestyles, in part to the unlikelihood of those in outstations finding themselves transferred to the central bureaucracy.[28] The stuffy protocol and metropolitan manners of the expatriate community in Aden (which Luce, as mentioned in chapter 3, found so uncongenial on his arrival as Governor) no doubt reflected a response characteristic of Englishmen abroad to the circumstances in which they found themselves, large numbers of them being thrown together in an isolated and restrictive colonial setting and in need of some psychological defence against a debilitating climate. Organized indulgence in distractions which they regarded as conspicuously British and to which they may have been accustomed at home (from race-meetings to bridge parties), though not particularly blameworthy in themselves, led inescapably to a kind of apartheid. Social intimacy with the local inhabitants in Aden diminished as the expatriate community – its military component in particular – expanded. In the Protectorates, on the other hand, the opposite tendency operated, as the attempt to promote federal unity and a more settled administration took its course. For this demanded closer dealings by the few British working there with a growing number of individual tribesmen than had the previous acceptance of local separatism and of a minimum of administrative intervention. To those in the Western as well as the Eastern Protectorate, Aden was a long way off, psychologically as well as physically.

Amongst the British serving in South West Arabia in a strictly military capacity,[29] it may be added parenthetically, the same syndromes were at work. Within the Aden garrison, as Trevaskis laments, most of those sent to keep the peace 'knew nothing about Aden and had no means of communicating with one Arab in a thousand', a crippling disadvantage. Present in such numbers, 'an alien soldiery were bound to excite the fiercest Arab xenophobia against themselves and against the régime which they represented'.[30] In the hinterland members of the British armed forces serving in or working with the federal forces were, like their equivalents in the Sudan Defence Force, in much closer contact with the people. They were also more directly affected by the oscillations of higher policy and in some cases (in this respect unlike their Sudan equivalents) resistant to it. To cite one example, Brigadier (as he then was) Lunt, who from 1961 to 1964 commanded what became the Federal Army, is and was at the time convinced that sensible handling of that army meant reducing the number of transient British officers whose employment higher policy enjoined and maximizing the chance for Arab officers to gain experience of responsibility and command.[31] Whether such a modification in the structure of the Federal Army would have prevented its split and partial disintegration as the final *dénouement* approached is open to question; but it might have been worth a try. Rather similarly Lunt was convinced, as were a number of Political Officers, that the whole Radfan campaign, (p. 81) involving substantial use of British troops in the hinterland, was based on a misunderstanding of the tribal scene by the policy-makers and was an expensive and ineffectual use of a sledge-hammer to crack an endemic gnat. In his view the money could have been used to much greater effect on development projects. His superior officers in Aden were more preoccupied with the problems of security in the Colony and with the continuous Aden-London debate on matters of strategy. Their priorities, as is evident from the publications of prominent military figures involved in Aden,[32] were naturally somewhat different from those concerned with the grass roots in the hinterland. Both categories may have been critical of central government policy towards South West Arabia but neither sought to examine the manner in which that policy in political and administrative terms was implemented on the ground. They fall therefore outside the scope of this chapter.

Nor can much consideration be given here to the response to the South West Arabian scene, whether they found it stimulating or insufferable, of the numbers of technical experts in sundry fields who worked there and who certainly contributed to the course of events. They represent a species not much given to recording their experiences or discussing higher policy. They were, in the epitaph accorded to them by Elizabeth Monroe, 'Englishmen who did good jobs in the fields at which they excel – on development, finance, dams, agriculture, drainage and other practical pursuits.' But, as she goes on to lament, 'too few of them could gauge the temper of the men who worked under them by speaking to them in the vernacular'. It is with those who were obliged by their politico-administrative task to 'gauge the temper' of the South West Arabians that we are primarily concerned; and to them we now revert.

Too few of those posted there for that purpose stayed long enough to make useful contributions. This was not primarily a consequence of Colonial Office policy of switching its officers from country to country: the problem arose much more from the determination of so many of those posted to this difficult place to get out of it by one means or another as soon as they could. In two years during Trevaskis' time no less than seventeen out of twenty-six political officers came and went.[33] There can be little doubt that so lamentable a turnover contributed to the failure of Britain's attempt to master the complex problems of the area. But what of those who did stay for years and put their hearts into a generally unrewarding task? What kept them at it until the assassin's bullet, retirement or final withdrawal supervened? There can be no doubt that the ethos of empire, however we define that slippery term, was (as in the Sudan) a genuine driving force. In venturing even a summary definition we are now on dangerous ground. For the absolutist concept of 'service to Queen and Country' smacks today of sentimental jingoism – a Victorian ballad unearthed only for purposes of burlesque. Yet it survived in the British psyche as a motivation openly admissible at least until World War II. It continued to be entertained, if not so openly admitted, for another decade or two, fighting a losing battle against the inroads of the powerful British penchant for self-mockery. Indeed it still exists here and there in isolated fastnesses of nostalgia. During its florescence it went hand in hand with an unquestioning assurance of the virtues of the imperial mission. To deny its potency and its merits, now that fashions have changed, is to lack a sense of history.

Admittedly, the distinction between benevolent paternalism and racial arrogance toward 'lesser breeds' is no longer widely recognized and may always have been dubious – though the behavioural distinction between the paternalist and the patronizing is genuine enough. What is beyond question true throughout the period of all three of our episodes is that amongst those in the service of a rapidly diminishing empire, while racial arrogance was increasingly sloughed off and self-mockery increasingly buttoned on, benevolent paternalism remained a powerful stimulus. More recently, since perhaps the late sixties, even the paternalist approach has been recognized as flawed, a humbler humanitarian concern for the world's underprivileged having struck root in the British *psyche*, rendered especially fertile by the admixture of uneasiness over its imperial past. But in an age when a belief in the equality of the human race was only entertained by few (and that few mostly regarded as cranks) paternalist concern for backward[34] peoples was the best the advanced ones could manage. To dismiss in retrospect the value of paternalism as an instinct for good in its day may be judged to display in itself a kind of historicist arrogance.

The point to be made here is that in the crepuscular decades we are dealing with it was certainly possible to combine a dedicated concern for the welfare of subject peoples with a lighthearted awareness of the irrationality of the whole business. The proportions of each in the mixture changed as our three episodes succeeded each other. The Sudan Political Service laughed at itself from a position, until near the end, of supreme self-confidence. Amongst representatives of the Colonial Service in South West Arabia, the best of them anyway, the two ostensibly contradictory elements – dedication and self-mockery – were in more equal balance. In the final Gulf episode a sense of the absurd had, quite properly, established a deepening salient in the disputed psychological territory. The 'Queen and Country' concept, even as a secret weapon in the battle, was distinctly on the way out. This development was neither anti-monarchist nor unpatriotic, reflecting rather a more reasoning, less emotional approach to government service overseas, as well as a recognition that the old imperialism was obsolescent. Within the shrinking phalanx of old soldiers (metaphorically speaking) who had served in all three campaigns, the old rubric retained something of its emotional sanctity. Amongst them Boustead, until he was finally retired at the age of seventy as Political Agent in Abu Dhabi, was perhaps the only one who, when he observed a Union Jack being struck at sunset, would stop in mid-stride or mid-sentence and gravely salute, without the faintest sense of behaving quaintly.

The Gulf, like South West Arabia, was not an enviable area, least of all before creature comforts were introduced, in which to serve the Crown. Nor in the earlier days was there much intimacy with the 'natives' or concern for their welfare to provide interest or inspiration. The Crown's limited requirements there virtually excluded such preoccupations and may well have encouraged the patronizing rather than the paternalist instinct. Plenty of instances of the supercilious attitude adopted in those days towards the more tiresome shaykhs can be collected by a trawl through the archives,[35] even more easily than by questioning their descendants. The seriousness, however, with which Britain's representatives addressed their task is evident from start to finish; and as the years passed a much more sympathetic relationship with the rulers and their subjects was certainly established. But whereas before World War II British objectives in the Gulf enjoyed a clear-cut simplicity, the growing ambivalence of the British role in later years – interventionism and non-interventionism jockeying for position – produced uncertainties which the single-minded colonial officer might have felt intolerable. It was perhaps as well that, in the Gulf, his place was taken by the less single-minded Foreign Office species. Even the latter found frustrating his constitutional debarment from the colonial privilege of imposing order and 'enlightened' administration by *fiat*. For if in South West Arabia the advisory nature of the Political Agent's role was often more honoured in the breach, its observance was more scrupulous in the Gulf. The tendering of advice with no overt machinery for its enforcement is the normal function of diplomacy; and one reason why diplomats rather enjoyed an off-beat posting to the Gulf was that the possibility of their advice being acted upon, of their meeting a positive response to pressure and thus of their entertaining a sense of achievement was at least higher than was the norm when serving, as Britain's world influence declined, in embassies abroad. Sitting regularly in a ruler's *majlis*, and at his right hand, could prove a rewarding as well as an entertaining experience, as long as the British representative concerned had immersed himself in the local scene and was recognized as understanding the often unstated implications of what was said. Service in the Gulf also had for some the especial attraction of rescue from the social whirligig of normal diplomacy and the prospect of leading for a time a life of their own. Latterly, it is true, the influx of other expatriates – in the armed forces, banks and business – imposed something akin to the familiar social round.[36] Nonetheless the pattern of the Political Agent's life in ordinary working hours bore a closer resemblance to that of a Chief Representative in one of the South West Arabian protectorates than to that of a diplomat in a foreign capital, with the advantage that the risk to life and limb (familiar enough in South West Arabia) was absent. All in all, a posting to the Gulf appealed more to the diplomat of a non-conformist cast of mind than to others.

Of those few who played a prominent role in all three episodes, Luce provides the most conspicuous example and best illustrates the qualities of a now vanished breed. Imperialist as he was by all his upbringing, the records disclose, as has already been said, a marked evolution in his philosophy of empire and a calculated response to changing circumstance. His reports and personal letters during his time in the Sudan are distinctly more 'serious' in their portrayal of the role of empire and more aggressively resistant to the faltering, as he saw it, of home government policies than both his private and his official accounts of the situation in South West Arabia. In these latter, while they still reveal a genuine conviction of the imperial mission and the blessings of the British way of life, the solemnity with which he confronts the policy problems at issue is matched by a sometimes hilarious feel for the tragi-comedy of seeking against increasing odds to reconcile the ideal and the possible. When it came to the Gulf, he had no difficulty in mentally adjusting to the obsolescence of the imperial mission. His task was to make the best of it in good humour, to ensure that the process was contrived as smoothly as circumstances allowed and to pursue to the maximum in doing so the interests of both parties. At no stage would he have conceded that the practice of empire in its day was not an influence for good.

But just as 'life is too serious not to be treated lightly', so too for those of his stamp was the business of governing Arab peoples. Hilarity kept breaking in. The diaries kept by his wife (a notable playwright) and published years later[37] make explicit something of the qualities in his make-up, with their combination of dedication and lightheartedness, which he characteristically never made explicit himself. One extreme illustration may perhaps be admitted. The occasion was a visit paid by Luce as Governor of Aden with Middleton, the Political Resident in the Gulf, to the remote Kuria Muria islands. Lying off the coast of South Arabia, they were presented to Queen Victoria by the Sultan of Muscat in 1854 and had barely been visited since. Being scarcely inhabited and of no conceivable value, they exercised by that very token a natural fascination. In 1959 they came mysteriously to the notice of the authorities in London and a solemn Order-in-Council decreed that their government should rest with the Governor of Aden while the Political Resident in Bahrain should be appointed Commissioner to deal with their affairs. Their joint visit by naval transport was undertaken in 1960 to make this arrangement known, if any inhabitants could be found to make it known to. The two dignitaries waded or swam ashore from a launch. A flagpole was ceremoniously erected and welfare goods were hauled through the surf in the best imperial tradition. A handful of mystified inhabitants were eventually located. The party itself only just escaped death by drowning, when being hauled back to their launch riding the breakers off the rocky coast. Margaret Luce, compelled for safety to watch the grotesque proceedings from on board, describes it graphically.[38] Luce's own oral account was superb.

Were the two qualities which we have ascribed to the last proconsuls recognized by the Arab peoples they governed? And if recognized, what response did they elicit?

Arabs everywhere, since the collapse of their own empire, had been subjected to non-Arab domination. For centuries few actively resisted it or openly resented a subordination so long experienced as to seem perhaps the natural order. Various reasons can be adduced for their resignation to it. The fact that the dominant Ottomans were, though non-Arab, at least Muslim is of course one; but by the end of the nineteenth century there were signs of developing resentment in the Arab heartlands at domination by non-Arabs. The subordination of Egypt somewhat earlier to the British, who were in addition non-Muslim, had already aroused resentment there. But in the fringe areas with which we are dealing here serious opposition to British domination, long established though that domination had been in two of them, was curiously slow in developing. For although tolerance is an Arab quality, the prolonged absence of resentment by Britain's Muslim subjects at subordination to Christian control, unless aggravated by resentments of a different nature, is remarkable. In all our three episodes, even where political opposition manifested itself, those involved rarely used Islam as a rallying cry in support of it. There were of course occasions on which the British recognized the risks of their doing so. The nervousness of the British authorities in India during the First World War, in which the Caliph of Islam sided with the Germans, is the most obvious example. The rather similar fears in the same (and other) contexts of a recrudescence of Mahdism in the Sudan have been mentioned in chapter 2. Execration of the Nazarenes in South West Arabia was a rare and localized phenomenon. Even less was it a common feature in Gulf. The principle of *jihad*, organized and forcible assertiveness of the faith, is much honoured in Islam; and it is odd that the *jihad* syndrome never seriously or openly asserted itself against the British presence in our three areas even when subjection to non-Arab and non-Muslim rule came to be widely regarded throughout the Arab world as a national humiliation.

What then were the prevailing views held in these three territories of British imperial domination, and (a rather different question) what was the general attitude towards its local exponents? And did these differ in each case? Something has already been said on the subject in chapter 5 in discussing the national characteristics of the three peoples and their respective responses to the prospect of independence. At the stage at which our first episode effectively begins (1945), hostility to the whole principle of British imperial control, however active elsewhere in the Arab world, was hardly yet formulated in any of our three fringe areas. Certainly it had not become a source of major concern to the British authorities. When it did, earlier chapters will have demonstrated that anti-imperialism took a different form, for reasons of time, place and circumstances, in each. Only in Aden did it reach violent manifestation. In the Sudan it was restrained and mannerly; in the Gulf barely even relevant.

Local attitudes to Britain's political representatives on the spot broadly followed the same pattern. Obviously those whose personalities made them misfits, or whose inclinations were against fitting in on principle, were unlikely to be regarded by the local citizenry with respect. These were certainly a small minority. What is of greater interest is the view taken of those practitioners of empire who did devote themselves to the betterment of the citizens' lot. We have already suggested that the qualities that marked the best of them in the later stages of the imperial presence were an abiding seriousness of purpose coupled with a self-critical sense of the absurdity of seeking to match the ideal with the real. Were these two creditable attributes locally recognized and, if recognized, were they given credit? Neither of them, to be sure, were consciously articulated. If the first, the good imperialists' concern for the welfare of those they governed, should perhaps have been apparent, this is less obvious in the case of the second, that element of irony which distinguished them from the earlier Curzon/Kitchener/Cromer generation with its less engaging certainties.

In attempting an answer to such questions we can of course ignore the flowery tributes to individual proconsuls on formal and social occasions dictated by Arab courtesy. And while we cannot equally ignore the unfavourable comments on the same individuals which figure prominently in the writings of contemporary or later Arab authors, most of those who have committed their views to paper are, in the nature of things, either amongst the zealous opponents of the British presence at the time or, less commendably, amongst those seeking to justify in retrospect their own personal records of resistance, or finally those born later and happy to endorse an inherited sense of resentment at the treatment of their fathers. It is advisable for the historian training his sights on such accounts to aim off for wind. The same caution may of course be necessary in the case of British memoirs of this, or any other, period: critical readers are entitled to surprise if the human instinct for self-justification has not been visibly operative. But even in these Arab accounts, which are legion, the target is generally imperialism in the abstract rather than those who served it, even if little good is said of them.

Were the views of the ordinary man in the street or the desert or the palace distinguishable from those committed to paper by politically more sensitive *literati*? The question cannot be answered with confidence. Western students of the episodes who quote remarks made to them, spontaneously or in response to questioning, may have been deceived. So indeed may Arab writers. Somewhat in line with their practice of courtesy, Arabs, the humbler ones in particular, have a reputation for answering questions with more regard for giving pleasure than for brute fact; and things said to people with influence are rightly suspect, since, as in Clough's decalogue, 'they are all From whom advancement may befall'.

By this token it may be that the Sudan Political Service were deceived into believing that they enjoyed the respect and even the affection of the ordinary Sudanese. Nonetheless the indications have hitherto been widely accepted that a warm mutual understanding existed in the Sudan to a more marked degree than in either of the other territories, South West Arabia in particular. Margery Perham, a close observer with an impeccable reputation for sympathy with the subjects of empire, declared in her Reith Lectures of 1961 that 'nowhere in any dependency in the world had relations between colonial ruler and ruled been more harmonious, more full of mutual respect'.[39]

The unquestionable seriousness of purpose may indeed have been recognized in all these territories, but this recognition was marred in South West Arabia, and in a different sense in the Gulf, by the kind of uncertainties prevalent in these two (much more than in the Sudan) about the direction in which that purpose was leading. In South West Arabia, moreover, different categories of people wanted different things from those in ostensible control. Some wanted positive signs of material progress, some were more concerned with protection from North Yemen as guaranteed (seldom effectively) by treaty, some wanted simply to be left alone. What was welcomed by one category was resisted by another: attitudes to the representatives of empire varied accordingly. In the Gulf, until oil made all things possible, improvement in material and social conditions was perhaps the universal *desideratum*, and it was widely assumed by the ordinary man that the British had the power to see that such improvements happened. In the sense that they were not the administrative authority, they could and did insist that this was not within their scope. But their disavowals were suspected of hypocrisy; and by consequence their relations with the masses, though amicable enough, lacked substance. They were of course known to have influence with the rulers and were assumed to have it with the rulers' British employees. Their 'seriousness of purpose' was doubtless judged by the uses which they were seen to put this influence. With the widening discovery of oil, that influence will have seemed to matter less, at least amongst the citizens of states where it was discovered. Oil was seen as a gift from God, its discoverers receiving little credit. But the promise it extended of a vastly easier life ahead certainly enhanced the national tolerance of the majority, if not of the politically sensitive, towards the British presence.

As for that other British characteristic, the capacity for light-hearted irony about these unfolding imperial dramas, this was something that could not, and perhaps should not, have been generally recognized. Only perhaps in the Sudan, where among the British the growing penchant for self-ridicule was less developed, might understanding of it have come easily. For the Sudanese have themselves a capacity for irony unusual in the Arab world. No-one in South West Arabia or the Gulf would have explained (to a British enquirer) his removal shortly after independence from an important administrative post in the terms chosen by a prominent Sudanese. 'My job', he said, 'was Sudanized: I was getting too friendly with the natives'.[40]

In South West Arabia the revolutionaries out for power were too absorbed in the pursuit of it to bother much about the personal qualities of those from whom they were determined to wrest it. The collaborationists (to use the term current in one theory of imperial practice) may have recognized both qualities in the make-up of the British administrator but before the end came they were too disillusioned to keep recognition of either quality intact. As for the Gulf, those encountering signs amongst Britain's representatives of shoulder-shrugging *insouciance* over the course of history either shrugged their own shoulders in mystification or, in more sophisticated cases, responded with wry understanding. A few, of course, threw stones.[41] In all three territories, it is legitimate to insert, Britain's representatives, regardless of the manner of their departure, have retained close friendships with gratifying numbers of those they once dominated, and have found no obstacle to the sharing of good-humoured reminiscences even with their old political enemies.

In all these circumstances it is not easy to present a generalized reckoning of the response of these three distinct peoples to British domination. An attempt to judge the empire, Margery Perham once wrote, would be 'rather like approaching an elephant with a tape-measure'.[42] The simile was apt enough when she used it; but bafflement at its size and shape and at its refusal to keep still was overtaken, as the great beast set about moving off, by impatience at the slowness and uncertainty of direction with which it shifted its ponderous feet. No doubt, when the dust has finally settled, a balanced reckoning will be attempted. Some of its evaporated essence, however, will then be beyond recall. Already it is difficult to identify such residue as may last amongst its erstwhile subject peoples – perhaps no more than a heightened acceptance of the rule of law and a passion for football. If that is so, it must seem an unimpressive outcome of so much effort: certainly not one that would have satisfied the French imperialist.

One of many features of Britain's policy towards her dependencies which distinguish it from that of France was her ambivalent attitude to their education. In the Sudan, it is true, the British tried hard to pursue a balanced approach in the belief that, if a reasonable number of Sudanese received a more or less British education, the experience of it would 'subdue them to the useful and the good' and prepare them by a proper degree of gradualism to qualify in due course for managing their own affairs with the British model of government implanted in their minds. British educators there, to do them justice, being more aware of the effect of their teaching than were the administrators, were less content with gradualism and more aware of the probable outcome of what educated Sudanese saw as foot dragging. Education in the Sudan may be judged to have been too narrowly based in scope but it was broad-minded in execution; and its imaginative teacher-training system was regarded in its day as a model for Africa. A respect for British education certainly survived British withdrawal.

In South West Arabia, educational effort in Aden colony was not unimpressive – even today those who benefitted by it are welcomed into employment in North Yemen and elsewhere in Arabia – but its political impact may be judged from chapter 3. In the inland Protectorates, progress was at best hesitant and not helped by the widespread local view that good education was not a necessary preparation for the good life. In the Gulf the British short-sightedly abjured almost all educational responsibility, leaving the running in the lower states to Kuwaiti money and Egyptian teachers. In Bahrain, however, where oil revenue had provided the means much earlier, education made impressive advances, generated internally.

The French, one suspects, would have handled education in all three territories very differently, had they been the imperial power there. Convinced as they were that their own interests and those of their overseas subjects lay in maximizing French cultural penetration, educational investment in their own empire was gigantic. Not even the French tax-payer, traditionally regarded in Britain as wily and evasive, queried the budgetary implications. The remotest elementary schools in, for example, the French African bush were required to follow the same curriculum as those in metropolitan France (*'nos ancêtres, les Visigoths . . .'*) and to sing the Marseillaise as a matter of course. The ultimate objective was to identify the promising, send them to the Sorbonne and turn them into black Frenchmen, qualified to play their élitist part in upholding a cultural community of interest and, by that very French token, a political understanding. A colonial subject who passed the test as an *évolué* was admitted into the French cultural hierarchy.[43] The British educational objective was quite different. It never sought to turn overseas subjects into black or brown

Englishmen: in the British view that would have risked exposing them to a cultural schizophrenia and setting up within a colony a social divide with internal barriers of a kind happily foreign to its traditions. The object was rather to prepare a subject community, without cultural disruption and at a pace Britain hoped to control, to run their own affairs, when ripe for independence, in their own way. There were, moreover, other respects in which British imperial practice was distinctly more 'liberal' than the French equivalent. In the lower reaches of the social spectrum, for example, the French treated the *non-évolués* with less sympathy, indeed with a disdain that struck observers from the rival empire with dismay.[44] This may have been French cultural snobbery: it was not racial arrogance.

Margery Perham, to quote her once more, for she studied both systems in greater detail than other contemporary observers, reached the conclusion that the British version 'was on the whole the most humane and considerate of modern colonial states and did most to prepare its subjects for self-government' (not as vainglorious a conclusion as Curzon's 'most unselfish page in history'). When she reached that conclusion, in 1961, she did not of course have the indigestible experience of South West Arabia to accommodate within her generalized judgement.

The French approach did not, to be sure, always work out as planned. But it has to be admitted that her 'secret weapon' of assimilating the *évolués* has enabled France to retain a degree of informal political influence, at least in many of her former colonial possessions, more marked than anything the British can point to in the countries of the Commonwealth. For that matter the purely emotive appeal of the French connection is a phenomenon, strange though it may look to British eyes, confidently exploited by French statesmen. As an illustration, an occasion stage-managed some years ago by President de Gaulle ranks high. With an expansive gesture he once opened an address from a balcony in Haiti to the assembled and responsive citizenry with the words '*Que vous êtes français!*' The thought – almost unthinkable for linguistic as well as philosophical reasons – of a British statesman delivering a comparable tribute ('How British you are!') to the citizens of a former British dependency would be greeted not as high policy but as low comedy.

If one further venture into the realms of comedy is permissable here, we may recall – in connection with the British penchant for self-ridicule, which is not altogether shared by the French – one of Flanders and Swann's incomparable lyrics of the sixties, entitled 'The British are best'. In their dealings with the less fortunate rest of the world, they reminded us, the British are 'clever and modest and misunderstood'. To this sally in hilarious irony British audiences responded at the time, and still do, with huge enjoyment. The hilarity, we may as well admit (since it may help to explain the lightheartedness of later British proconsuls), is backed by a secret conviction that the song's words quoted, however un-British it would be to admit it, are actually true. Or at least, so far as their old imperial behaviour is concerned, if the British were not as clever as the French, they were anyway more modest and, of course, more misunderstood.

These comparisons, frivolous or serious, with French practice are something of a diversion from our theme. Only in the case of the Sudan perhaps are they obviously relevant. But it is interesting to speculate what would have been the outcome in South West Arabia, had France, as Napoleon doubtless intended, been the imperial power there. Not, one suspects, all that different: perhaps even more violently confrontational, more Vietnamesque. What the French would have done in the Gulf is an unanswerable question, but they would certainly have made up their minds earlier and more 'logically', with less self-questioning and less deference to obsolete treaties, on their long-term objective. And they would have drafted an epitaph, justifiable or not, in more resonant terms.

In all the comparisons we have been drawing up – whether between the differing policies in our three territories or between British imperial policy as a whole and its French equivalent – the criteria used in evaluating them have been basically political ones. Little attention has been given to a quite different criterion, regarded by some commentators as deserving precedence, namely the economic consequences of British tutelage.[45] It may be argued that the exercise of empire in a deprived territory would have been more easily justified, had its effect been to raise the economy of that territory by investment and development to a point at which political independence would not be held back or ham-strung by economic non-viability. By that criterion, which ought to be more accurately measurable, how does the record look in each of our three territories?

Whether or not this was a justifiable principle, the Sudan was never regarded during the Condominium as a proper charge on the British Treasury (though for much of the period there was no scruple in debiting some accounts to the Egyptian one). It was broadly expected to pay its own way forward, with such help from loan finance as it could attract and afford. In economic terms, almost more starkly than in political terms, the Condominium started from scratch. The provision of a basic infrastructure was unhurried: for financial reasons it had to be. The concept of development grants-in-aid was still unheard of. The Colonial Development and Welfare Fund (conceived in 1929 but reaching maturity only under the Act of 1940) was a modest beginning, but the Sudan benefitted little. Five-year development plans were only introduced there in 1947. The World Bank and other supra-national funding institutions were also a post-war invention. By the end of the Condominium the Sudan's infrastructure, though still in many respects rudimentary, was sufficient to underpin a comparatively healthy economy, based of course primarily on the huge Gezira cotton scheme (put in hand by loan financed back in 1913) and on smaller state and private irrigation projects, mostly also cotton-growing. Thanks to government revenue from cotton sales a budget surplus was normal; and the rocketing of cotton prices in the years immediately before independence enabled considerable capital expenditure on development to be financed without strain. In revenue terms, however, it was virtually a one-crop economy; and though, when independence impended, the Sudan appeared economically viable, the steady downward fluctuations in world cotton prices thereafter upset that appearance and stimulated criticism of the Condominium for its failure to diversify the country's economic base. In point of fact attempts to do just that in the thirty years that have followed show how many obstacles to profitable diversification the Sudan presents. Sugar production seemed a promising investment but has not fulfilled hopes. Oil has been found but in an inconvenient area. The belief, fashionable in the seventies, that the country's central rain belt could, with generous outside capital, turn the Sudan into the breadbasket of the Middle East, now looks fanciful. And with cotton prices at rock bottom and the Gezira scheme faltering, the Sudan's economy is now desperate. But can this be blamed on its erstwhile imperial rulers?

In South West Arabia capital to invest in developing its backward hinterland was never available internally, even on the Sudan scale. Nor were the British Treasury or funds made available for development projects under the Colonial Development and Welfare Act of 1940 ever able to furnish capital in anything like the volume for which successive governors pleaded. The only serious industrial development scheme in the interior was the Abyan Cotton project (launched in 1947 with a CD & W loan of £270,000), and even that kept running into tribal problems. In the Colony itself, where government receipts and expenditure had risen by 1964 to a sizeable total, the economy was kept buoyant until independence by the huge volume of world shipping using the port,[46] by entrepôt trading activities, by the British Petroleum refinery and towards the end by the servicing of Britain's armed forces stationed there, said to have provided employment for 20,000 local civilians. To take advantage of all this, small scale manufacturing industries burgeoned healthily enough and the retail trade flourished. Wealth, to be sure, was ill-distributed, but the overall level of prosperity (and of social services) was well ahead of anywhere else in the region. There was, however, no inclination among the prosperous to share this prosperity with the hinterland, the old dichotomy remaining as sharp as ever. If Britain can take credit for the development of an ostensibly healthy economy in Aden, this was precariously based and it was obvious that little of it would survive British withdrawal, once the circumstances of that withdrawal became apparent. How much, however, would have survived, had the political policy of the successor regime been different, is open to question. If imperial rule left the rest of the country economically undeveloped, its independent successors have found little scope for improving the situation there. The People's Democratic Republic of Yemen is, and is likely to remain,[47] amongst the poorest of all Arab countries.

In the Gulf, economies had remained, before the oil explosion, at sub-sistence level and had been driven almost lower by the collapse of the pearling industry. Britain had done little in the material sense to improve things. The discovery of oil in Bahrain back in 1932, and the expectation of it everywhere else, altered the picture in almost every way but served initially as a discour-agement to further attempts of the modest kind previously initiated to provide an economic or industrial base to replace pearling. Oil revenues alone would transform the economy without local effort to secure a better livelihood for all. Some steps, with British encouragement or without, were taken to make better use of such other resources as the area possessed – experiments in agricultural extension, profitable exploitation of the seas' resources (notably prawns in the Upper Gulf), cement production and so on. Taken over from Kuwait, which no longer needed it, the curious gold trade to India – overt and legal at the Gulf end, covert and illegal at the Indian – provided an income and a livelihood for many citizens of Dubai, until it too entered the oil club. The carrying trade, of a more normal kind, had of course always been a source of income in the coastal towns up and down the Gulf, as it still is. In the smaller Trucial States, where oil was obstinately reluctant to manifest itself, ideas, mostly fanciful, to generate a local income (fish-meal factories and copper-mining, for example) were eagerly bandied but dropped as impractical. It was, however, in Bahrain, when the paucity of its oil resources became a worry, that the first serious attempts were made in the mid-sixties to identify other industrial activities which might benefit the economy and provide employ-ment. The State's aluminium industry, its slip-way and ship repair yard and later its sensationally successful offshore banking initiative were the outcome. It was not long before even the richest of the states recognized that man could not live by oil alone, that even oil was a temporary and finite asset; and the search for industrial openings, oil-based or not, engaged attention everywhere. The search, despite one or two successes, was to prove dispiriting; and the private sector has shown little inclination to invest in it. The only guaranteed income, if and when oil runs out, will come from the sensible and by now formidable investment of surplus revenues in the industrialized world. But this is to carry the story beyond independence. So far as the British were concerned in the period of their dominance, it cannot be said that they took great pains, outside the oil industry, to discover, promote and bequeath a viable economic pattern. The best defence is not that industrial development was not their concern (which perhaps is debatable) but that a non-oil-based solution to the Gulf's economic deprivation was undiscoverable (which perhaps is not).

If then, the justification for imperial tutelage is judged by the health of the economies it left behind, the record in our three territories is different in each but not notably impressive in any. In the Sudan the British tried quite hard; the subsequent collapse of the country's cotton based economy suggests that they should have made greater efforts in other directions. In South West Arabia, the demise of Aden's prosperity was no doubt foreseeable but cannot reasonably be blamed on Britain. Britain can more easily be blamed for leaving the economy of the hinterland not much more advanced than it was in 1839. As for the Gulf, they certainly left behind them a booming economy, for which they can at least take some credit. The sheer effort and dramatic adventurousness of early oil prospecting is too easily forgotten. In another and broader sense, the British contribution to strictly economic advancement was small. But if they did little in the Gulf, there was little open to the doing; and oil at least provided a retrospective alibi.

In any case, in their preparations for ceding control, the representatives of empire themselves accorded everywhere, rightly or wrongly, a much higher priority to political than to economic viability. 'Freedom rightly understood', to quote Hartley Coleridge's couplet once more, required their erstwhile subjects to be good, not rich; and good meant stable, law-abiding, reasonably if not democratically governed and governable, well-disposed to Britain and less well-disposed to the Soviet Union. Only in the Gulf – perhaps unexpectedly and undeservedly – have such British imperial aspirations been broadly fulfilled. The shaykhly system assuredly has its failings, but it incorporates a kind of democracy. Without a measure of popular consent the rulers would scarcely have retained control for (so far) nineteen years of stable independence – however large the security forces they have to prop it up and however much oil money they can deploy to take the edge off political discontent. Furthermore, despite their initial resentment at the British government's 1968 decision to leave them to make their own way, they and their subjects seem well enough disposed to post-imperial Britain. The Marxist philosophy which gripped the PDRY has made few inroads.

Hopes certainly were entertained of the Sudan. But since the legacy of empire included ten million black Southerners – unprepared, culturally antipathetic to the dominant north and politically suspicious of it – countrywide stability was in truth never on the cards. Moreover, the fall in living standards (due only in part to the drop in cotton prices) provided a growing constituency in the North for the activists of an already well-established Communist Party. Democracy was indeed put on trial[48] and summarily convicted of inadequacy. The benevolent military regime which had secured its conviction was no more successful: nor was the subsequent return to civilian rule. Numeiri's coup in

1969 produced a military dictatorship less benevolent but more determined than the first, initially with Communist support but ultimately with no support from anywhere. The political muddle that replaced Numeiri, when he was ousted with fanfares after seventeen years, had by 1989 led to yet another military take-over. The 'licence to be good', which independence would confer, had long since fallen distinctly short of British hopes.

In South West Arabia, much more dramatically than in the Sudan, independence was seized, not given. Freedom, in British eyes, was not 'rightly understood' by the triumphant National Liberation Front at all. For that matter, the federal rulers had never shown much understanding of what Britain regarded as the obligations of self-government. Their revolutionary enemies knew, to be sure, what freedom meant to them. It was an end in itself, and they took their ticket to it at gun-point unhampered by moral baggage made in England. Yet for all their intimacy with the Soviet Union, they seem increasingly disposed, so far as the old imperialists are concerned, to let bygones be bygones.[49]

One final word may be in order. If this account of the last stages of Britain's empire in the corners of the Arab World seems to have veered back and forth, from sympathy with the practitioners of empire to sympathy with their subjects, that has not been accidental. It reflects the writer's belief that most human activities – in their motivation as in their execution – are a mixture of good and bad, in part praiseworthy, in part repellent. All episodes of empire – the Roman and the Arab, no less than the British – have displayed this ambivalence. Where the British version runs a poor third, at least in its physical manifestations in the Middle East, is that it has left so much less visible behind it. '*Si monumentum requiris, circumspice*', could scarcely be inscribed as epitaph (even metaphorically) on the builders of Britain's Middle East empire, as it was on Christopher Wren. In the Sudan, it is true, the Gezira Scheme remains a conspicuous legacy of British initiative. That and a few lesser technological achievements apart, one would have to 'circumspect' hard in our three territories to detect any monuments, concrete or even abstract, of British domination. Perhaps, in a sophisticated or sophistical sense, that can be regarded as one of its virtues.

Today, Britain as a whole looks back on its moment in the Middle East with mixed sentiments, the most general being a sense of relief that it has disappeared into history – where it can be studied dispassionately and with the consuming interest that all past empires evoke. There is also in Britain's current attitudes to her imperial past a widespread, self-critical (some would say abject) repudiation of the whole complex episode, an uneasy awareness, as in T.S. Eliot's lines on the gifts reserved for age:

Of things ill done and done to others' harm
Which once you took for exercise of virtue.

But twenty years ago, when her final withdrawal from the Middle East scene was declared, sentiment in Britain was more sharply divided. Even so upolitical a poet as Philip Larkin felt passionate on the subject. 'Homage to a government' was written in January 1969. If today we do not all share his outrage at Britain's loss of imperial will-power, we can at least find his irony monumental.

> Next year we are to bring the soldiers home
> For lack of money, and it is all right.
> Places they guarded, or kept orderly,
> Must guard themselves, and keep themselves orderly.
> We want the money for ourselves at home
> Instead of working. And this is all right.
>
> It's hard to say who wanted it to happen,
> But now it's been decided nobody minds.
> The places are a long way off, not here,
> Which is all right, and from what we hear
> The soldiers there only made trouble happen.
> Next year we shall be easier in our minds.
>
> Next year we shall be living in a country
> That brought its soldiers home for lack of money.
> The statues will be standing in the same
> Tree-muffled squares, and look nearly the same.
> Our children will not know it's a different country.
> All we can hope to leave them now is money.

Notes

Introduction

1. The felicitous title, now become scriptural, of Elizabeth Monroe's masterly short book on the subject (London, 1963).
2. Some would challenge this. Halliday, for instance, quoting Minister of State Hattersley's statement in the House of Commons on 25 March 1970: 'The Sultanate of Muscat and Oman is a fully sovereign and independent State', declares 'This is an out-and-out lie' and says 'Oman was in fact a British Colony' (F. Halliday, *Arabia Without Sultans* (London, Penguin, edn, 1974), p. 280). The only counter-observation offered here is that, if Muscat and Oman was ever a colony even in Halliday's *de facto* sense, it had certainly ceased to be so by the period we are concerned with. Any British representative (the author was one) who sought in that period to tender advice to Sultan Sa'id bin Taimur on the governing of this country soon found how constitutionally (in both senses of that word) impermeable he was.
3. British Somaliland has also been disregarded here, since it was never regarded as Arab – though after its merger with Italian Somaliland into independent Somalia in 1960, the new state was admitted to membership of the Arab League.
4. *The Killearn Diaries*, ed. Trefor Evans (London, 1972), p. 349.
5. For the period of these exchanges from 1945 to March 1953, see the Robertson Papers in the Durham University Sudan Archive. Subsequent exchanges until the end of 1954 between Luce and the Sudan Agent are preserved in the former's papers, kindly put at the writer's disposal by his son, the Rt Hon. Richard Luce, MP.
6. Sir C. Johnston, *The View from Steamer Point* (London, 1964), p. 11.

Chapter 1

1. William R. Louis, *The British Empire in the Middle East, 1945–51* (Oxford, 1984), p. 34.
2. L. Carl Brown in his persuasive *International Politics and the Middle East* (London, 1984) argues that external powers have in fact never been able to manipulate the Middle Eastern Arabs to the extent that the outside world or the Arabs themselves believed, that the Middle East has always enjoyed a systemic ability to resist such manipulation and (p. 190) that no attempts to dominate the region have changed its 'stubborn penchant for kaleidoscopic equilibrium'.
3. One personal reminiscence in a book which aims to eschew them may perhaps be

allowed as illustration. Early one morning in December 1961 an abortive *coup d'état*, mounted by the off-beat Parti Populaire Syrien, broke the then tranquillity of Lebanon. Within hours the Lebanese Minister of the Interior, Kemal Joumblat, declared that it had been engineered by the British Embassy and that he had seen the Ambassador on the Embassy roof at dawn signalling to a British warship off-shore. It had fallen to the writer, as Political Officer in the Embassy, to rouse the sleeping Ambassador an hour after dawn and report that a *coup d'état* of some strange kind was going on. Also there was no British naval unit nearer than Gibraltar.

4. For a handy re-examination of Attlee's thinking on this subject see R. Smith and L. Zammetica, 'The Cold War: Clement Attlee reconsidered, 1945–47', in *International Affairs* vol. 61, no. 2, Spring 1985, pp. 237–252.

5. One of them was George Orwell, whose two-barbed prophecy of 1936 is quoted at the head of this chapter. He was writing of his experiences as a Police Officer in Burma in the twenties, which confirmed his detestation of imperialism. *Inside the Whale and Other essays* (London, Penguin edn, 1957), p. 92.

6. A useful account of this movement from the British view-point is the fifty-page FO Research Department paper 'The history of the Arab nationalist movement and the origins of the Arab League', dated 28 March 1947 (FO 371/45241, E 9471). Though the call for unification dates back at least to Sherif Husayn and the Arab Revolt, it was first formally embodied in the Arab Covenant produced at the Congress of Jersualem in December 1931. But thereafter and until Egypt saw the opportunities it offered her, the Hashemite regime in Iraq remained its most serious – perhaps its only serious – protagonist. King Abdullah of Jordan's long-cherished Greater Syria scheme was a rather different kettle of fish. A ploy of this kind promoted from either Hashemite capital – and both of them continued to pursue their own versions of it long after the establishment of the Arab League – was anathema to Ibn Sa'ud as well as to Cairo. In Britain's wartime calculations one possible advantage in the unification of the Fertile Crescent was that it might provide a solution to the Palestine problem. But the complexities of actively pro-moting the idea, given the nature of inter-Arab jealousies, dissuaded London from doing so. For a magisterial study of the whole subject see Yehoshua Porath, *The Arab Quest for Unity 1930–1945* (London, 1986).

7. The words were Lampson's from Cairo (FO 371/27045, E 6636/53/65).

8. Monroe, *Britain's Moment*, p. 92.

9. Though negotiated and initialled by the two Governments, it was angrily rejected by the Iraqi parliament (and the Baghdad public) as old imperialist wine in a new bottle. Another disillusioning experience for Ernest Bevin.

10. In the light of the opprobrium heaped on Spears by the French (both Free and Vichy) it should be stated that his close friend and Economic Adviser during his mission in Syria, Mr R. W. Tench, insists that Spears was in fact devoutly Francophile and deplored having to appear otherwise in the face of the tactics adopted by France to reimpose control in Syria and the Lebanon. Personal communication to author.

11. At the Pentagon talks in late 1947 Bevin 'was still resolutely opposed to the stationing of US forces in the Middle East'. Louis, *The British Empire*, p. 190.

12. It is arguable that the US was not as innocent of ambition in the Middle East as this brief summary suggests. The understanding struck by Roosevelt with Ibn Saʿud on board USS Quincy in February 1945 marked a calculated intrusion into British preserves. Other instances of America's undeclared readiness at this time to acquire an influential role in the region are not far to seek. For some indicators see R. F. Holland, *European Decolonization, 1918–1981* (London, 1985), pp. 52–53 and 119. America was certainly interested by this time in commercial opportunities in the Arab world and was not slow to conclude that commercial influence is barely separable in the Third World from political influence. The 'Open Door' policy promoted during the Roosevelt era was regarded in the UK with some misgivings. Barry Rubin's *The Great Powers in the Middle East, 1941–47* (London, 1980) discusses the whole subject dispassionately.

Chapter 2

1. Allenby's terms included orders for the withdrawal of all Egyptian troops from the Sudan, the announcement that the Sudan would in future be permitted to draw water from the Nile without limit, and the imposition of a £500,000 fine. The British Government itself regarded the terms of Allenby's *diktat* as excessive and shortly replaced him.
2. See L. A. Fabunmi, *The Sudan in Anglo-Egyptian Relations* (Connecticut, 1960), pp. 81–83.
3. Sir John Maffey (Governor General 1926–1934) was the protagonist of Lugardian doctrine in the northern Sudan. The experiment in its pure form did not survive his departure. His successor, Sir Stewart Symes, recognized the need to modernize the administration and put to better use the educated Sudanese, tribal or not. M. W. Daly, in his *Empire on the Nile* (Cambridge 1986), pp. 366–378, examines the history of the unsuccessful experiment under Maffey.
4. Newbold's successor Robertson wrote ten years later in a private letter to the Sudan Agent in London, 'I have never understood why Huddles[ton] and Douglas [Newbold] sent back the Congress memorandum. It was a grave mistake and the cause of many of our subsequent troubles.' Robertson to Davies, 14 June 1952. Durham Sudan Archive, file 523/3, p. 28.
5. *Tariqa*s may be described as Sufi sects established within Islam in the Sudan from the eighteenth century by religious leaders. Apart from the Khatmiyya, those with influence were the Majdhubiyya, the Idrisiyya and the Tijaniyya. (The Mahdist movement itself was of a rather different nature.) Almost everyone in the northern Sudan adhered, actively or not, to one *tariqa* or another.
6. Sudan government Security File, cited by M. O. Beshir in *Revolution and Nationalism in the Sudan* (London, 1974), p. 112.
7. The Sudan government's policy towards the South throughout the Condominium – so far as it had one – is not examined in this book. For present purposes the point is that for most of the fifty years the gulf between the two halves of the country had been considered unbridgeable. There was no ethnic, linguistic or cultural link, but only accidents of geography (the Nile) and of history (nineteenth century slave-trading and Khedivial expansion) to bring them together. Ideas were periodically

mooted by the British of detaching the South from the Sudan and merging it with one or more of three adjoining countries; namely, Kenya, Uganda, and the Belgian Congo. In setting up the Advisory Council for the North in 1944, Newbold left the issue unresolved. Only when the pace of Northern nationalist aspirations and criticism of the 'Closed Districts Order' isolation of the South became a serious embarrassment did the Sudan Government come to grips with the problem. Robertson must take much of the credit for insisting – despite the misgivings of administrators (and doubtless of missionaries) in the South – that isolation was no longer possible and that a basis for political unification had to be contrived. The watershed was in 1947. Southern hostility to the North remained (and remains) active – as the mutiny of August 1955 (see p. 45) and post-independence rebellions would make tragically manifest. For one of many studies of the Southern problem see K. D. D. Henderson *Sudan Republic* (London, 1965), pp. 152–202.

8. That this was also, surprisingly, the US view is stated by W. P. Louis, quoting a State Department analysis of March 1947, in *The British Empire*, p. 258.

9. The use of the term 'free world' exasperated some Middle Easterners for years. In 1951 a writer in an Iraqi newspaper declared: 'We do not feel ourselves to be part of the free world which they say they are defending. We are part of the oppressed world which is struggling to throw off their yoke.' Quoted in a despatch from Troutbeck, British Ambassador in Baghdad, of 13 June 1951, FO 371/91183, E 1024/359 (1951).

10. For Attlee's public revelation of this (Cabinet) decision see his statement in the House of Commons, HC Deb, 7 May 1946, cols. 883–886.

11. One of Huddleston's earlier pleas to this effect was dismissed in Olympian fashion by Killearn at a meeting with him in September 1944. See p. 3.

12. Isma'il Shereen, brother-in-law of Farouk and a top Egyptian bureaucrat who served six prime ministers until the monarchy fell and was Secretary General of Egypt's negotiating team, assured the author in January 1989 that had the 'admirable' Campbell replaced the 'offensively arrogant' Lampson two years earlier, Britain could have had a treaty without difficulty. Shereen, a pupil of J. M. Keynes at Trinity College, Cambridge, held Britain – but not Lampson – in great affection. Ibu Sa'ud, after a meeting with Farouk in January 1945, also urged on Britain a change of Ambassadors in Cairo: 'a good man would soon win the King's confidence' (Jedda telegram to FO of 2 February 1945, FO 371/45917, J 530/3/16). In the Foreign Office too there was at this time a frequently expressed wish that Lampson would 'resist the temptation to abuse the Palace in conversations which ... filter back and make the Ambassador/King relationship, never very harmonious, still worse'.

13. The appointment was not judged a success. Bevin found him 'too ready to give in when bargaining' and he was asked to retire in October. His task was in fact unenviable, as those who took it over in the next six years also found. In bargaining terms their position was always weak.

14. Students of subsequent developments in the Arab World will see this as an early example of a recurrent problem in Arab political semantics.

15. The quotation is from the report of Orme Sargent, the Permanent Undersecretary, to Bevin by letter of 9 October, FO 371/53257, J 4248/24/16 (1946).

16. FO 371/53257, J 4243/24/G16 (1946).
17. The term 'sovereignty' did not in fact figure in the final Protocol, though it had done in previous British drafts, and 'sovereignty' was, in Egyptian eyes, what the dispute was all about. Sidki evidently used the Arabic equivalent, *siada*, in his leaks in Cairo (see note 20); and since the Arabic term carries the flavour of a master-slave relationship, its use added to the uproar in the Sudan. (Attlee used the expression 'symbolic sovereignty' in his talks (see p. 29) with Sayed Abdulrahman, who said he could not understand such a term.) One of the curious features of the whole episode is that the British law officers of the Crown kept changing their minds on where sovereignty lay. Before 1946 their general view was that since 1899 it was 'shared' between Egypt and Britain. In 1946 the conclusion of their successors was that Khedivial (sole) sovereignty was unaffected by the Condominium Agreement – a judgement which imposed some restraint on Attlee and Bevin. Bevin's Private Secretary, Pierson Dixon, recorded in his diary at the time, 'There is no doubt that sovereignty has continuously been Egypt's . . . Our ancestors landed us in the soup when they failed to make Queen Victoria the co-sovereign, as they easily could have done.' A conflicting view advanced at the same time by the Ambassador in Turkey and the Legal Adviser in the Embassy in Cairo was that sovereignty had rested with the Ottoman Sultan (not the Khedive), and that in 1914 Britain had simply taken it over. Bevin himself tried to persuade Sidki that in a changed world sovereignty was anyway an academic issue. To the Egyptians it was no such thing.
18. For the full text see Cmd 7179 (Egypt No. 2) of 1947. Though Bevin and Sidki got on well enough personally, Bevin's Private Secretary looked back on the frenzy surrounding the talks as 'the worst ten days I can remember'. Sir Pierson Dixon, *Double Diploma* (London, 1968), p. 233.
19. Robertson's diary records that Huddleston saw Bevin on 22 October, and a telegram of 29 October from the Foreign Office to Khartoum, aimed at easing the outraged bewilderment there following the Sidki leaks, refers to 'the close consultations which the Foreign Secretary has had with the Governor General throughout the period of conversations with Sidki here'. FO 371/53258, J 4467/24/16 (1946). But detailed evidence for the final period is missing from the official records.
20. The usual version is that Sidki, either in his aircraft after leaving London or stumbling out of it on arrival in Cairo, spoke triumphantly to a pressman of having 'brought the Sudan back to Egypt', by having persuaded the British to accept the unity of the two countries under the Egyptian Crown. Once published, it snowballed – and certainly Sidki did nothing to stop it rolling.
21. Robertson says that a memorandum from the three of them presented to Huddleston made it clear that they 'could not possibly remain in the Sudan to force a Treaty on these terms on the Sudanese' (J. W. Robertson, *Transition in Africa* (London, 1974), p. 97). That is not quite the tenor of the memorandum as forwarded by Huddleston to Attlee on 10 November, where the critical passage reads, 'If HMG persist in acknowledging sole Egyptian sovereignty and therefore force has to be used, we want you to stay on. You have the complete confidence of the British officials in this Service and no Governor General could rival you in your influence with all classes of Sudanese.' FO 371/53260, J 4764/24/16E (1946).

22. Mekki Abbas records that he attended both a private meeting of the Advisory Council called by Huddleston, and another meeting called by Robertson, to convince Sudanese leaders that no change in the *status quo* was contemplated by the Protocol. *The Sudan Question* (London, 1952), p. 118.

23. Sidki, now standing as a Liberal with Saʿadist backing, had always been a member of minority parties. His opposition to the majority Wafd exposed him to an especial degree of the political intrigue by rival politicans, which was a feature of Egyptian political life under the monarchy. Bevin (unwisely perhaps) made no secret in his statement in Parliament on 27 January 1947 about the difficulties of negotiating with a minority government. 'If', he said, 'we can deal with a more fully representative government and if our negotiations can avoid being the subject of Egyptian party politics, there will be a much better chance of carrying them through in the right spirit.' An optimistic assessment.

24. Records of the two Cabinet discussions which followed the Sidki leak are at CM 96(46)3 and CM 97(46)1 of 14 and 18 November 1946 (CAB 126/6). The former was so drafted as to cause some confusion over who (the Prime Minister in London or the Foreign Secretary in New York) was to send Huddleston the second of the two letters; but this had no connection with the telegram of 21 November, at FO 371/53260, J 4884/16G (1946), which forbad him to use either.

25. FO 371/53262, J 5725/24/16 (1946).

26. See the Fabian Society Publication *The Sudan: The Road Ahead* (London, 1945), Research Series No. 99, which backs several horses, including the transfer of the South to Uganda, but is still 'imperialist' in Bevin's sense.

27. CP (46) 17.

28. Telegram to Attlee of 10 November from New York, FO 371/53259, J 4676/24 G 16 (1946). Orme Sargent calmed him down but admitted that 'old-type perfectionists' (like Huddleston) must give way. A new Governor General, he added, was due in Spring.

29. The manner in which Huddleston's 'retirement' took place is open to question. The FO archives, as released, contain no suggestion of summary dismissal; but his daughter, Mrs Gill Andreyev, is emphatic that he was sacked by Bevin for his resolute habit of standing up to him. What is clear from State Papers is that, following a severe bout of illness in late 1945, Huddleston expressed a desire to retire in the following July. Lengthy but vain attempts followed to identify a suitable successor and, Huddleston's health having recovered, he was asked to stay on for an additional six months, i.e. until the end of 1946. That November, following the Sidki leaks, Huddleston's gloomy prognostications and threat of resignation led to a personal letter from Attlee on 14 November saying 'HMG regard your presence in the Sudan at the moment as indispensable. Their wish is that you should continue as Governor General' – presumably until the Spring, since Orme Sargent had just reminded Bevin that Huddleston's retirement would then be due (see note 28). On 6 March 1947 Huddleston disclosed in a private letter to Luce, who was then in the UK, that Bowker, the Minister in the Cairo Embassy who had just paid a visit, 'seemed to think that I must stay on indefinitely or anyhow probably for another year, partly because of the difficulties of getting Farouk to sign a new commission' (appointing a successor). The following week,

on the other hand, Robertson wrote to the Sudan Agent on 13 March that senior staff in Khartoum all thought Huddleston should be allowed to retire 'during the current lull'. Three days later, a manuscript letter from Huddleston to Luce began, 'you will have heard the Sudan news yesterday. I heard last Sunday: a telegram to Campbell repeated to me saying they had decided to replace me by Howe: there was of course no need to consult me, but in view of all my previous discussions with the FO on the subject, I think it would have been more polite if they had, and think they have a slightly guilty conscience about it . . .' He said he proposed leaving on 5 April. (In a postscript he corrected the second sentence: the news had come in a private telegram from Campbell, the Ambassador in Cairo. This indirect method of informing him must have added to his private humiliation.) According to Mrs Andreyev he certainly believed – and so informed his wife and daughter on his arrival in London – that he had been summarily sacked by Bevin and was greatly upset; but he was too honourable a servant of the Crown to air his feelings in public. In view of what Bowker had told him the previous month, he certainly had reason to resent the Foreign Secretary's decision to replace him at short notice and the manner of conveying it to him. The shock it clearly caused his staff was obviously aggravated by the choice of his successor, though he himself sought to assure them (to quote from his letter to Luce) that the choice of Howe was probably a good thing, since he 'would be a FO servant and not an independent GG' and those in London would therefore surely believe what he reported whereas 'they, as you know, never really believed what I told them'.

Whatever the precise circumstances his treatment after seven years in an arduous post was certainly shoddy.

30. This was W. H. (later Sir William) Luce, who had long done much of the policy drafting in the Palace. He was to play a major role in all three transmission episodes studied in this book.
31. FO 371/62948, J 4840/1/G16 (1947).
32. FO 371/69157, J 1773/7/16 (1948).
33. Attorney General Shawcross delivered himself at the same time of another memorable, if irrelevant, judgement. Commenting on the argument that it was unreasonable of the Egyptians to reject the ordnance simply because it didn't go far enough, he observed: 'The maxim that half a loaf is better than no bread is not one that has any legal recognition.' FO 371/69157, J 1963/7/16 (1948).
34. FO 371/73472, J 4357 (1949).
35. FO 371/80384, JE 1059/149 (1950).
36. FO 371/80381, JE 1054/54G (1950). Slim's observation in the next sentence is at 50G in the same jacket.
37. FO 371/90152, JE 1052/14G (1951).
38. FO 371/96902, JE 1051/7 (1952).
39. FO 371/96905, JE 1051/109 (1952).
40. FO 371/96906, JE 1051/150 (1952).
41. Paragraph 14 of his Annual Review for 1953. FO 371/108311, JE 1011/1 (1954).
42. Luce's papers record that the Umma and the SRP both hastened to assure the Palace that they had only signed the agreement because Naguib's concessions over sovereignty and self-determination were too important to pass up, particularly

since Naguib's tenure was unlikely to last and no other Egyptian regime would offer such favourable terms. Once the Sudanese had their parliament, they declared, they would be able to speak with authority and get the unsatisfactory aspects of the agreement remedied.

43. FO 371/96911, JE 1051/351 (1952).
44. Robertson, *Transition*, p. 148.
45. The full text is at Cmd. 8767 of February 1953.
46. Durham Sudan Archive, Robertson papers, file 523/7.
47. Zulfakar Sabri, *Sovereignty for Sudan* (London, 1982), p. 136.
48. Sir Gawain Bell, *Shadows on the Sand* (London, 1983), p. 205.
49. Churchill's ideas were sufficiently well known in London for Robertson (on leave there) to deplore them in a letter to Luce on 14 May 1953. Nor was the possibility of giving the Sudan its independence under unilateral British arrangements abandoned in Downing Street. In the paper he prepared for Churchill on 18 March 1954, during the next clash with Howe over tactics, Selwyn Lloyd stated that a plan for doing so should be prepared since it 'might be required at any time'. FO 371/10835, JE 10124/G6 (1954).
50. As Luce put it, 'The PM is really being more of a headache to us than the Egyptians at the moment.' Letter to Sudan Agent of 19 May 1953.
51. The assembled evidence of Egyptian interference in the 'free and neutral atmosphere' was later summarized by Eden in the House of Commons in HC Deb. of 5 November 1953, cols. 319–321 and Written Answers of 13 November 1953, cols. 102–104.
52. Fabunmi, *The Sudan in Anglo-Egyptian Relations*, p. 277.
53. At this point Luce slipped out of the Palace, pushed his way through the *melée*, drove to Sayed Abdulrahman's house in Omdurman and heatedly requested him to remove his Ansar from the capital at once. Sayed Abdulrahman, though denying any responsibility for the riot, undertook to do so.
54. The main source for Churchill's interventions in 1953/1954 is Luce's private papers. FO papers do not reveal much on the subject – it would be unnatural for officials to have entered comments on the impetuosity of their Prime Minister; but there are echoes, notably over the dispute on the desirability and timing of a constitutional State of Emergency and Churchill's plan for despatching British reinforcements, in FO 371/108378, JE 1559/5G and 12/G (1954).
55. Luce to Sudan Agent, 16 February 1954.
56. *Ibid.*, 6 December 1953.
57. *Ibid.*, 30 January 1954.
58. Britain's new Trade Commissioner in Khartoum, Adams (later Sir Philip), was distinctly more critical of the Sudanisation Committee than was the Palace. The Committee had, he reported, 'been packed with NUP supporters of the meanest intelligence'. FO 371/113575, JE 1011/1 (1954). The office of the Trade Commissioner, established in 1953 as an embryo British Embassy, had D. M. Riches as its first incumbent. His reports to London surprised the FO by their criticisms of the Political Service (see p. 179).
59. Nonetheless, in answering questions at a concluding press conference, Azhari still referred to various alternative constitutional links with Egypt which were envis-

aged. The fact that two extreme pro-Egyptian ministers accompanied him to London no doubt inhibited him. FO 371/108379, JE 1059/33 (1954).

60. Private letter to Howe (in England), 30 November 1954. See also FO 371/10839, J 1059/33 (1954) for the record by the Head of the Egyptian Department at the FO of a conversation with Luce on this subject on 22 September.

61. Luce to Lampen (Davies' successor as Sudan Agent in London), 27 November 1954, and FO 371/108361, JE 10511/37 (1954). Luce's letter to Bromley of 27 October 1954 is at JE 10511/25 in the same file.

62. These words were added by Howe to Luce's draft. The extraordinary popular send-off he received in Omdurman on his final departure two days later was a personal tribute as well as a symptomatic gesture. J. R. S. Duncan, *The Sudan's Path to Independence* (Edinburgh, 1957), pp. 186–189.

63. Adams, Trade Commissioner, in his Annual Review for 1955. FO 371/119599 (1956).

64. Luce accompanied General Ahmad Muhammad to the South to supervise the surrender of the mutineers, and recorded the courageous efforts of their self-appointed leader, Rinaldo, to bring them all in. It proved an impossible task, scattered in the bush and suspicious as they were. Rinaldo's subsequent execution outraged Luce (who had left the Sudan when it took place) and did nothing to pacify the Southerners.

65. M. A. Mahjoub, *Democracy on Trial* (London, 1974), p. 56. Luce's papers indicate that the plan had been quite widely canvassed by Azhari, and that he himself had persuaded Azhari to adopt certain changes in the wording of the resolution as drafted, designed to make it less 'unconstitutional'.

Chapter 3

1. For the tribute see Gordon Waterfield, *Sultans of Aden* (London, 1968). R. J. Gavin in *Aden under British Rule 1839–1967* (London, 1975) is less impressed. Robin Bidwell in *The Two Yemens* (London, 1983) sums him up, on p. 40, as 'partly a romantic visionary and partly a shifty intriguer'. The court records of his two first (criminal) trials for misappropriation, at both of which he was acquitted, are at IOR R/20/A116 in the India Office Library. It was a third (civil) process that finally ditched him.

2. See memorandum by E. Hertsley of the FO of March 1874 on 'Turkish claims to sovereignty over . . . the whole of Arabia', IOR L/P&S/18/B8.

3. For those directed at the Persian Gulf shaykhdoms see Ch. 4. p. 100.

4. Palmerston to Hobhouse, 26 December 1838, IOR L/P&S/3/4 (Box of letters).

5. Looking back much later at this system of supervising policy in India, Lord Curzon wrote: 'Had a Committee been assembled from the padded chambers of Bedlam, they could hardly have devised anything more extravagant in its madness or more mischievous in its operation.' *British Government in India* (London, 1925), vol. 2, p. 69.

6. Palmerston to Hobhouse, 18 December 1838, IOR L/P&S/3/4.

7. Haines' detailed account is at IOR R/20/A/54.

8. Palmerston to Campbell (Consul General in Alexandria), 8 June 1838, IOR L/P&S/3/4.

9. Palmerston to Campbell, 24 May 1838, and Willoughby (Bombay) to the Secret Committee, 4 July 1839, where it is implied that the ingeniously imprecise wording was suggested by Haines. L/P&S/3/4 and 5/330.

10. Two recurrent subjects of disagreement between London and India may serve as illustrations. One was over which of them should be responsible for Aden. Transfer to London, Viceroy Canning argued in 1861, would end 'a divided and anomalous responsibility more Imperial than Indian'. London disagreed. Thereafter, in the light of Aden's increased importance after the opening of the Suez Canal, proposals for transfer were repeatedly advanced by London – in 1875, 1884, 1890, 1895–1896 and 1900 – and rejected by India. A prolonged recrudescence of the dispute from 1921 to 1926 was only settled by Cabinet intervention. (Subsequent changes are described in the text). A second constant theme of disagreement was over the extent of intervention and protection requisite in the hinterland. Despite its original lack of enthusiasm for Haines' representations on the subject, the Government of India advanced proposals for more extensive measures in 1873, 1885, 1886, 1903 and 1906. London's response on each occasion was dismissive. (Some of these instances are mentioned in the text.) What is of particular moment here is that in neither of these two recurrent debates were the interests of South West Arabia itself, let alone the need for development of the shaykhdoms, an issue.

11. For a first-hand account of the divers groups and social classes within a *dawla* see R. A. B. Hamilton, 'The social organization of the tribes of the Aden Protectorate', *Journal of the Royal Central Asian Society*, vol. 30, 1942, pp. 142–157.

12. Ingrams' expression, meant sympathetically. See his *The Yemen* (London, 1963), pp. 67–70 and *Arabia and the Isles*, 3rd edn (London, 1966), Introduction p. 20.

13. Gavin, *Aden*, pp. 203–206.

14. By the Government of India to the India Office in a letter of 9 February 1902, IOR L/P&S/18B155. The original intention was to sign Protective Treaties with the rulers near Aden, and Exclusive Treaties (i.e. those simply prohibiting dealings with anyone else) with those further afield. CO 930/19 no. 63 (1937). The distinction was later dropped.

15. See India Office Memorandum (by F. L. Bertie) of 15 September 1886, IOR L/P&S/18/B130.

16. *Ibid.*, quoting Government of India despatch of 6 August 1886.

17. Secretary of State to Viceroy, 1 April 1904, quoted in India Office Memorandum (by R. Ritchie) of 19 March 1906. IOR L/P&S/18/B155.

18. Note by Under Secretary Sir E. Lee Warner on Government of India letter of 9 August 1906. IOR L/P&S/18/B158.

19. The process was started by the Sultan of Lahej in 1728.

20. This was Muhammad Ali al-Idrisi of Asir in the north of the Yemen. Having encouraged him to mount his challenge and occupy Hodeidah, the British were prepared to ditch the family, when the war was over, in the interests of a better understanding with the Imam. The Imam however got the better of them without British intervention. Gavin, *Aden*, pp. 263–264.

21. CO 725/11/3, file no. 48004 (Pt. 1).
22. In 1921 the Viceroy's refusal to contribute more than £250,000 to the annual costs of Aden of £460,000 was resisted by Churchill as Colonial Secretary. Cabinet finally settled the dispute by a progressive reduction of the Indian contribution to a third of the total, subject to an eventual maximum of £150,000. IOR L/P&S/B462.
23. In a despatch to Bombay of 9 December 1929, Symes (the Resident) deplored the complications of divided control over Aden and the hinterland. Aden, he said, ought to become the administrative capital of the whole area (if the Protectorate was developed) as well as a metropolis. IOR R/20/E316.
24. Sir G. Clayton, *An Arabian Diary*, ed. R. O. Collins (Berkeley, California, 1969), pp. 226–247.
25. CO/725/28/14 (1934).
26. Cmnd. 4752, Treaty Series no. 34 (1934), gives the text.
27. See Reilly's detailed official report on the negotiations, CO/725/28/15 (1934)
28. This was explicitly stated by the Imam's son Husayn at a meeting in the Colonial Office in October 1937 (CO/725/48/14). The Imam, moreover, continued to deny the validity of the Anglo-Turkish Convention of 1910 on the grounds that his kingdom was not the successor state of an erstwhile Ottoman province.
29. By 1937 Hadhramis abroad were remitting as much as £630,000 a year to their homeland. IOR R/20/A/3713.
30. The figure is Ingram's own. See his *Arabia*, introduction p. 25. It excluded the residents of the Mahra Sultanate of Qishn and Socotra and the Wahidi Sultanate of Balhaf, who added, he says, about another 600 'governments'.
31. An entertaining admission of the haphazard official views of the area regarded over the years as constituting the Aden Protectorate is contained in a Colonial Office memorandum of 15 December 1937, entitled 'The Frontiers of the Aden Protectorate'. It discloses the following progressive estimates of its square mileage:

    1917   4,200 sq m (Admiralty Handbook of 1917)
    1931   9,000 sq m (Colonial Office List)
    1932   42,000 sq m (Colonial Office List)
    1937 111,000 sq m (Governor, Aden)
    Confidential Print (New Series) 1936–40, ME no. 26/52, Annex 2.
32. Properly speaking there was only one Protectorate, as Governor Hickinbotham kept insisting. The line dividing it in two was an administrative convenience, dating from 1934, to define the respective parishes of the Resident Advisers in Aden and Mukalla.
33. Reilly's despatch to Colonial Secretary of 14 February 1940, IOR C/217/40.
34. Ingrams, *Arabia*, p. 16.
35. F. Halliday, *Arabia without Sultans* (London, 1974), p. 155.
36. See CO 725/59/9 (1937) enclosing text of FO memorandum ME(O) 243 of 20 September 1937.
37. Hathorn Hall's letter of 9 March 1944 and Oliver Stanley's endorsement are at CO 725/89/2 (1944).
38. B. L. Montgomery, *Memoirs* (London, 1958), p. 436.
39. The modest recommendations of a Development Committee set up in Aden in

January 1946 for Colony and Protectorate, which deplored the lack of infrastructural services in the latter, were only submitted to the Treasury a year later – CO 725/97/4 (1947). See also minutes of the Middle East Special Committee ME (O) (49)29(1949), CAB 134/501.

40. B. Reilly, *Aden and the Yemen* (London, 1959), pp. 30–33, describes it. See also CO 725/106/7 (1951).

41. The outcome was a compromise. Air reprisals might be undertaken by the Governor but only with specific sanction of both Colonial and Foreign Secretaries. See Cabinet Papers, C(54) 212, 219 and 224 and CC(54) 45 at CAB 129/69 and CC(54) 54 at CAB 128/27, all of 1954.

42. For a fuller examination of policy after the Conservatives came to power in 1951, see P. Darby, *British defence policy East of Suez, 1947–1968* (London, 1973), pp. 46–93.

43. See Colonial Office memorandum on 'Policy in the Aden Protectorate' at CRO 725/81/8 (1942) and Hathorn Hall's letter of 6 May 1942 quoted there.

44. Hickinbotham gives his own account in *Aden* (London, 1958), pp. 164–169. Trevaskis, with whom the initiative had started, considers the proposals, as finally authorized, to have positively invited the rulers' resentment. *Shades of Amber*, pp. 44–45.

45. The initial version was drafted by Trevaskis. Under it the Presidency was to be held by one of the rulers. This was amended by Hickinbotham, who insisted that he as Governor must be its President, and the Colonial Office accepted this. The approved text also incorporated provisions for a lot of bureaucratic (British) control. This was doubtless seen as necessary if federation was to work, but the resulting proposals failed to attract the rulers. Personal communication to the author from Sir Kennedy Trevaskis.

46. The ready availability from the Imam's agents across the Yemeni border of good quality rifles – much better than those they may have already possessed – caused a fair stream of WAP tribesmen to go off and get them. A certain transfer of 'loyalties', overt or covert, was thereby inevitable. The British response was to authorize the purchase in Britain and the import into the Protectorate of further large numbers of rifles for distribution (or sale at a nominal price). The object was to discourage Protectorate subjects from seeking them from the Imam. Many were in fact re-sold by recipients at enormous profit, reputedly as far afield as Afghanistan. The Rulers themselves no doubt made a good thing of it. Whatever else may be said of British policy in this respect, it certainly caused an access of cash in these impoverished areas. Personal communication to the author from Sir Kennedy Trevaskis and Stephen Day.

47. Hickinbotham, *Aden*, pp. 182–191, especially p. 183.

48. The extent to which ATUC was politically motivated from the start is open to controversy. In the presentation of industrial grievances they were already being bear-led by the UNF in 1956 (Tel. of 26 March from Hickinbotham, CO 1015/1241). At that time all members of ATUC's executive committee were office-bearers in the UNF (Trevaskis, *Shades*, p. 98). For a more sympathetic reading see H. Lackner, *P. D. R. Yemen: Outpost of Socialist Development in Arabia* (London, 1985), pp. 29–30. D. C. Watts' 'Labour relations and tradesunionism in

Aden 1952–60' in *Middle East Journal*, vol. 16, no. 4 (1962), pp. 444–449, is a useful contemporary study. An Egyptian scholar, Gad Taha, insists that the politicization of the Unions was a direct consequence of the refusal to give Yemeni workers Adeni citizenship. See his *Siyasat Biritaniya fi janub al-Yaman* [Britain's Policy in South Yemen] (Cairo, 1969), pp. 391–393. This may be so, but what would the consequences have been if the franchise had been given them?

49. E. Macro, *Yemen and the Western World* (London, 1968), p. 119. Reilly, *Aden*, p. 41.

50. The exercise is at CO 1015/1211 (1955). In his long and, as the Colonial Office saw it, 'cantankerous' comments on the draft paper, Hickinbotham took especial exception to the deference shown to the recent report of the Committee of Enquiry into Constitutional Development in the Smaller Colonial Territories, which recognized 'no organic connection' between the Colony and the states of the Protectorate and saw the Colony's future as a separate city-state.

51. *The Times*, 19 May 1956. His statement was much criticised by Lord Listowel in the Lords on 13 June, as it is by Trevaskis, *Shades*, pp. 99–100. Gillian King contents herself with observing that its 'paternalistic tone . . . was typical of the attitude adopted by successive administrations'. See *Imperial Outpost: Aden* (London, 1964), p. 41.

52. Lord Lloyd's report on his tour, CO 1015/1213 (1926).

53. Darby, *British Defence Policy*, pp. 107–122, discusses the 'Sandys Doctrine'. For a top soldier's criticism of it see General Sir William Jackson, *Withdrawal from Empire* (London, 1986), pp. 170–174.

54. J. Kostiner, *The Struggle for South Yemen* (London, 1984), pp. 40–43, Lackner, *P. D. R. Yemen*, pp. 40–43, and Hickinbotham, *Aden*, pp. 192–200.

55. On the changing relations between the Aden authorities and the Free Yemeni opponents of the despotism of the Imam (those of them who took refuge in Aden) see J. Leigh Douglas, *The Free Yemeni Movement 1935–1962* (Beirut, 1987), especially pp. 80–82 and 163–171.

56. Hickinbotham's treatment of Sultan Ali, especially on one occasion, was distinctly insensitive. Several of his then subordinates hold the view, at least in retrospect, that Ali was the only ruler of sufficient standing and intelligence who might, if better handled and given the opportunity, have established the federation much earlier under his own control as a going concern, without alienation from Britain. A similar view has been expressed to the writer by Sir Horace Phillips, Political Secretary (a Foreign Office appointment) to the Governor from 1956 to 1960, who argues that the only sensible course would have been to bring the less extreme nationalists on board and work out a deal with them, instead of leaving them in the wilderness to be added by Nasser to his growing inventory of adherents. Other British officials in the area at the time hold the view that Sultan Ali was bent on undermining the British position from the start, SAL being constructed round him as a front for this purpose, and that he was seen through and dismissed much too late.

57. *The Observer*, 16 September 1956, Macro, *The Yemen*, p. 115, and Trevaskis, *Shades*, p. 106.

58. Those of them who found a new home in Aden itself featured in the coming years

amongst the most zealous anti-British activists there. Ali Salem al-Bidh and Faisal al-ʿAtasi were amongst the Hadhramis who were to achieve political prominence.

59. The quoted descriptions are those of Bidwell (who was a Political Officer in the Western Protectorate from 1955 to 1959), *The Two Yemens*, p. 140, and of Trevaskis (who was there from 1951 and became Governor in 1963), *Shades*, p. 134.

60. Despatch from Luce of 11 December 1956 and personal letter to Sir J. Macpherson at the Colonial Office, CO 1015/1213 (1956). As regards the Colony's future, Luce's initial view was that to give Aden independence would be 'like giving independence to Budleigh Salterton' (an innocent Devonshire township then in the public eye thanks to Noel Coward's popular play *Blithe Spirit*).

61. Save where otherwise identified, the views attributed to Luce during his governorship in Aden are derived from the records privately compiled at the time by his son, in whom he readily confided (see bibliography, Unpublished sources). Though the present writer did not see Richard Luce's compilation until 1986, his own many conversations with Sir William between 1964 and 1977 often bore upon the same points. The authenticity of the opinions attributed to him must be taken on trust.

62. For contemporary British views of King Saʿud's state of mind and his sponsorship of subversive activities in South West Arabia see CO 1015/1086 (1956).

63. London had toyed three years earlier with the idea of inviting a visit from Badr but dropped it largely as a result of protests from Hickinbotham. When, at the Imam's suggestion, he did come in 1957, Selwyn Lloyd's periodical resort to a bottle of whisky stationed beside him during the discussion aroused the horror of Trevaskis, who was present. See Trevaskis, *Shades*, p. 128.

64. Bidwell, *The Two Yemens*, p. 102. In personal communication to the author, Trevaskis has indicated that the immediate reason for his dismissal was the instruction he sent (from Italy) for the defection of his Guards. Their defection in that case would have been the cause and not the consequence of his dismissal.

65. Trevaskis, *Shades*, p. 139.

66. There had been two Township Authorities in Aden. The bigger had been promoted to Municipal Council, securing an elected majority in 1958.

67. The franchise issue was almost insoluble in a city in which over half the adult males were Yemeni immigrant workers. So far as the 1959 elections were concerned, the House of Commons was informed by Nigel Fisher on 13 November 1962 that, of the total Aden population of 220,000, 80,000 were disqualified as immigrant Yemeni workers and a further 110,000 as women and children, leaving 30,000 resident adult males. Of these, 21,500 qualified under the franchise; 26 per cent of them actually voted (HC Deb., 13 November 1962, col. 323). The second extension of tenure of the Legislative Assembly, elected as above in 1959, was necessitated by the Assembly's difficulties in reaching agreement on the franchise for the next elections, which were thus delayed till October 1964. See note 84, and also W. P. Kirkman *Unscrambling an Empire* (London, Chatto and Windus, 1960), p. 156.

68. Cmnd. 665 of February 1959 Preamble.

69. Interviewed by the author in February 1986.

70. *Aden Colony Gazette Extraordinary*, no. 41, 17 August 1960.
71. Watt, 'Labour Relations', pp. 453–455.
72. Trevaskis sadly records that, when he discussed Luce's recommendations with the Colonial Office, the latter were totally opposed to the suggestion that sovereignty over Aden should be ceded. *Shades*, p. 161.
73. Sir C. Johnston, *The View from Steamer Point* (London, Collins, 1964), p. 65. So far as the federal concept itself was concerned, the support given to it by successive Governors was not reinforced by British diplomatic missions in the area. The Cairo Embassy in particular regarded the whole ploy as a non-starter.
74. Harold Macmillan, *At the End of the Day* (London, 1973), p. 265. The Colonial Secretary, Macleod, had a deeper and more sympathetic understanding of the South West Arabian problems than that disclosed in his diary by the Prime Minister.
75. Trevaskis, *Shades*, p. 164.
76. *Ibid.*, pp. 173–174.
77. Bidwell, *The Two Yemens*, pp. 143–144; Trevaskis, *Shades*, pp. 176–178.
78. Darby, *Defence Policy*, p. 222.
79. Sandys made no bones about this when presenting the resulting draft treaty (Cmnd. 1814 of August 1962, Annex A) to Parliament. 'We are', he said, 'retaining – I should like to emphasize this – sovereignty over the whole of Aden Colony, even after its accession to the Federation'. HC Deb., 13 November 1962, cols. 245–323. The intention was also made explicit by Article 2 of the draft treaty.
80. The PSP was in fact an extension of ATUC's 'Nationalist Bureau', headed by Muhsin al-ʿAini. Kostiner, *The Struggle*, p. 47.
81. In the judgement of several outside commentators, the Legislative Council was effectively blackmailed into accepting the merger by making Aden's advance towards self-government conditional on its doing so. See Monroe, *Britain's Moment*, p. 264, and Gavin, *Aden*, p. 343. In the actual vote on the merger plan in the Aden Legislative Council, 8 opponents walked out and of the 15 who were left and who all voted in favour, 5 were British ex-officio members, 2 were European-nominated and 5 were the ministers who had helped design the plan. Thus only 3 Adeni members of Council had been converted to approval. See T. Little, *Southern Arabia* (London, 1968), pp. 86–87. There are those, Trevaskis among them, who now consider that the sensible policy for Britain would have been simply to impose a merger between Aden and the hinterland much earlier by unilateral *fiat*, thus pre-empting the farcical attempt to encourage the two to accept the idea voluntarily. This would have been an uncharacteristically bold step perhaps, but one that would at least have spared Adeni supporters of the merger proposal from ensuing embarrassment and personal danger.
82. It is now widely believed that Sallal was simply a figurehead (much like Naguib in the Egyptian revolution of 1952), adopted as a senior figure by the younger Yemeni officers primarily involved. That may be the case, but Sallal had at least a reputable past record in the Free Yemeni Movement.
83. Johnston, *The View*, pp. 111–123.
84. It is significant that when the franchise was revised in March 1964 (and the 76 per cent turn-out at the subsequent election implies acceptability of the revision) the

total number of qualified electors was in fact much smaller than in 1959, when 21,500 qualified (see note 67). Yemeni immigrants were still broadly excluded, as now were most non-Arabs. The number now qualified, according to the figures given in Keesing's Archives, 1964, col. 19995, was 12,500 adult males out of the total population of 220,000. Of that number 8,019 registered and 6,377 voted.

85. Macmillan's reference to the 'wind of change' in his speech was not in fact new. He himself had used the expression some days earlier in his African tour in Accra, having borrowed it from Douglas Home. But it was his usage of it in South Africa that caught the headlines everywhere. In point of fact the decision to get out of Africa as quickly as decency allowed appears to have been taken directly after the October 1959 General Election (Kirkman, *Unscrambling*, p. 49). The process naturally took time. Independence was obtained by Tanganyika in December 1961, by Uganda in October 1962, by Kenya in December 1963. Nyasaland was also on the point of gaining independence.

86. Johnston, *The View*, pp. 193–203. In the House of Commons debate of 13 November 1962 (see note 79) Sandys insisted on Aden's necessity as a 'vital stepping-stone on the way to Singapore' – an argument seen as dubious by Gillian King, see her *Imperial Outpost*, p. 33–35.

87. Johnston, *The View*, p. 185.

88. UNGA [United Nations General Assembly] Resolution 1949 (XVIII) of 11 December 1963.

89. Jackson, *Withdrawal*, pp. 214–223, discusses the operation in military terms and concludes that it was a success. The Commander of the Federal Army, James Lunt, who loyally conducted the first part of it, regarded the whole thing from the start as an ineffectual waste of money. Personal communication to author.

90. The most detailed Western account of the origins and early tactics of the NLF is Kostiner's *The Struggle*, pp. 53–77. See also Halliday, *Arabia*, pp. 190–207.

91. Kirkman, *Unscrambling*, p. 158, describes the exclusion of the PSP as an 'incredible piece of folly'. But would any agreement have been reached if they had been present? The memorandum which al-Asnaj sent for the occasion to Sandys flatly demanded implementation of the UNGA Resolution of 11 December 1963 (see p. 80).

92. In his report on the conference to Parliament Sandys stated that the account of it broadcast by the Fadhli Sultan on his defection to Cairo was 'completely false'. HC Deb., 7 July 1964, cols. 215–222.

93. 'Her Majesty's Government's policy is to retain the base, in agreement with the Government of the Federation of South Arabia, for so long as it is required to serve the interests which we have in common.' Healey, 30 November 1964, HC Answers to Oral Questions, col. 10.

94. D. Ledger, *Shifting Sands: The British in South Arabia* (London, 1983), p. 60, Trevaskis, *Shades*, pp. 320–321.

95. Greenwood's report to Parliament is in HC Deb., 11 December 1964, col. 1967.

96. His selection as Governor had been unsuccessfully opposed for that reason by the Foreign Office, where he was regarded as 'first-rate but the wrong fit'.

97. For the first quotation see HC Deb., 17 June 1964, col. 1405. For the second HC Deb., 16 December 1964, cols. 423–424. As regards Wilson's 'acceptability'

proviso, the problem was that, while the Federalis very much wanted the base to be maintained, the Adenis themselves didn't – though a Labour MP, Donnelly, informed the House in the June debate that he had just returned from a visit to Aden and had 'found nobody who advocated the immediate removal of the base' (cols. 1360–1361). See also Darby, *British Defence*, p. 284

98. Cmnd. 2592 of February 1965, para. 20. See HC Deb., 3 March 1965, cols. 1337–1342. If Healey does not emerge from this and the next chapter with much credit for consistency, it is worth recording that one top General, Sir John Hackett, reviewing Jackson's *Withdrawal from Empire*, describes him as 'one of the very best Secretaries of State for Defence we have had' (*The Times*, 13 November 1986).

99. This paragraph is largely based on Halliday, *Arabia*, pp. 210–213 and Kostiner, *The Struggle*, pp. 112–125.

100. Ledger, *Shifting Sands*, p. 64.

101. Sir Gawain Bell, *An Imperial Twilight* (London, 1989), p. 158.

102. The unfortunate timing was the subject of comment in *The Observer* of 3 October 1965, critical of the uncertainties in the Prime Minister's approach to the problem of South West Arabia. See Abu's cartoon (plate 6) in the same issue.

103. Darby, *British Defence*, pp. 294–296. In a sense the alternatives confronting Britain were either to concentrate its reduced defence capabilities in Europe or to maintain its world role elsewhere. Both De Gaulle's current 'Non' to Britain's application to join the European Economic Community and American and Commonwealth pressures encouraged the Labour leadership at the time to favour the second, despite the growing opposition of Labour back benchers to the maintenance of Britain's role East of Suez and despite criticism of that role in the British press. Towards the end of 1965 Treasury insistence on a reduction in overseas military expenditure became inexorable.

104. Michael Howard in 'Britain's strategic problems East of Suez', *International Affairs*, vol. 42, no. 2, April 1966.

105. Beswick's two visits were briefly reported in *The Times*, the first on 23 November 1965, the second on 22 February and 10 March 1966. The best evidence of the angry clash between the Federal rulers and Beswick on his second visit and of the horror of their (British) Federal Army staff is contained in the secret documents proudly reproduced in photostat by the Adeni historian Sultan Nagy in his *At-tarikh ol-'askari lil-yaman 1839–1967* [Military History of Yemen 1839–1967], (publisher unstated, 1976), pp. 421–423. One of the documents reproduced is a report by Col. J. F. Chaplin of the Federal Ministry of Defence, which observes: 'The fact is that, having encouraged the rulers to take an anti-Nasser line and having made them into "imperial stooges" hated by the Arab world, we are now about to go back on our word and desert them.' When the White Paper (Cmnd. 2901) was presented to Parliament in February 1966, the decisions relating to South West Arabia provoked a (Conservative) storm there too. HC Deb., 22 February 1966, cols. 250–251 and 7 March 1966, cols. 1782–1786.

106. *The Times*, 16 June 1966. For an analysis of Wilson's 'East of Suez' pronouncements and their motivations see R. F. Holland, *European Decolonisation 1918–1981* (London, 1985), pp. 274–277.

107. 65th Annual Conference [of the Labour Party] Report (1966), p. 271.
108. For details of PORF see Kostiner, *The Struggle*, pp. 136–137.
109. Ledger, *Shifting Sands*, p. 102.
110. *Ibid.*, pp. 108–117, giving a detailed and apparently eye-witness account of the UN Mission fiasco. It is worth noting that it was an Adeni, Husayn Bayoomi, who as Federal Minister of Information, refused the Mission usage of the Federal broadcasting station.
111. H. Trevelyan, *The Middle East in Revolution* (London, 1970), p. 210.
112. H. Wilson, *The Labour Government, 1964–70* (London, 1971), p. 396.
113. R. Crossman, *The Diaries of a Cabinet Minister* (vol. 2, 1966–1968) ed. Janet Morgan (London, 1976), p. 388. Crossman, though no expert on conditions in Aden, provides useful insight into the thinking of George Brown and the Cabinet. He demonstrates that, in defence planning East of Suez, a clear distinction was in their minds, from December 1966 on, between the Middle East and the Far East. Withdrawal from the former (at least from Aden) was already seen as urgently desirable, while withdrawal from the Far East was not then under consideration. See *The Diaries*, pp. 156–279.
114. Ledger, *Shifting Sands*, pp. 134–138.
115. Kostiner, *The Struggle*, pp. 131–132.
116. The Quʿaiti, Kathiri and Mahra Sultans were holding discussions on shipboard off Mukalla when the local NLF moved in. See Kelly, *Arabia*, p. 126.
117. Meccawi (see p. 86) had made a similar demand the previous December for the exclusive recognition of FLOSY in the context of the UN mission.
118. One reason given by the Government of India for rejecting London's 1874 proposal for the transfer of responsibility to the home government was that Aden was 'practically an Indian town; with the exception of the Arabs and Somalees who visit the place on business, the population is wholly Indian or engaged in Indian trade' (a remarkable exaggeration). IOR L/P&S/68/B51A.
119. Little, a balanced commentator with eye-witness experience, argues that al-Asnaj's awareness of the growing NLF threat to his own ambitions might well have made it possible for Greenwood to extract concessions from him which would have bridged the gap between al-Asnaj and the Federal rulers. Little, *South Arabia*, p. 118.
120. So the author has been assured by D. J. McCarthy, who was, during this period, successively Political Adviser to the GOC in Aden and Head of Arabian Department in the FCO.
121. For Hickinbotham's despatch and its treatment see CO 1015/1131 (CAA/164/56/01) of 1954–1956.
122. The usual argument against releasing them was that the protectorate rulers were a bunch of quarrelsome reactionaries, totally disqualified for release from outside guidance. (The Adeni nationalists' refusal to contemplate sharing power with them was based on a similar insistence on the Federalis' inability to march with the times.) Sandys himself assured the House of Commons that 'the Ministers of the Federation [were] every bit as enlightened as the political leaders in Aden colony' (HC Deb. 13 November 1962, col. 246); and there were British officials

on the spot who would have gone even further. But the Federalis, having been given a bad name, were there to be hung.

123. Crossman, *Diaries*, vol. 2, p. 283.

124. Cmnd. 3540 of February 1968, p. 14. It is not clear why the period covered did not include the actual withdrawal, completed on 29 November. Harold Wilson (*The Labour Government*, p. 445) states that the withdrawal was effected without casualties, but Trevelyan (*The Middle East*, p. 264) makes it plain that casualties continued in November, well after Crossman's diary entry of 27 October.

125. Kostiner, *The Struggle*, p. 67.

Chapter 4

1. Palmerston was in fact referring to Egypt but might well have used the same engaging simile for British objectives in the Gulf. The quotation is to be found in Cromer's *Modern Egypt* (London, 1904), vol. 1, p. 92, note 1.

2. The terms shaykhdom, emirate and state will be used synonymously throughout, as will the terms shaykh, ruler and emir. Shaykh and shaykhdom were, of course, the original British usages; they became emir and emirate on independence.

3. The words are taken from Curzon's much quoted address to the 'Chiefs of the Arab Coast' assembled to meet the Viceroy on HMS Argonaut at Sharjah in November 1903 (see plate 7). The passage containing them is reproduced in Ronaldshay's *Life of Lord Curzon* (London, 1928), p. 318.

4. Also by repeated references to Joasmee piracy in the Diaries of the Secret and Political Departments (1755–1820) of the Government of Bombay. See the Extracts therefrom at Exeter University (not held in the India Office Library). There are, it is true, more references to Joasmee piracy as a well-known fact than specific accounts of British experience of it; the source of Bombay's information is often third party, e.g. the 'prejudiced' Imam of Muscat and local sufferers from piracy. As for published British accounts, there are a number of these, the best known being perhaps Sir Arnold Wilson's *The Persian Gulf* (London, 3rd imp. 1959), pp. 192–212. Whatever the facts, there is no doubt at all that the British authorities regarded Qasimi piracy as the main threat to the freedom of navigation in the Gulf and the Indian ocean.

5. Notably by the present Qasimi ruler of Sharjah, Sultan M. al-Qasimi. See his *The Myth of Arab Piracy in the Gulf* (London, 1986). Perhaps the most telling defence of the Qawasim came from no less an authority than the Chief Secretary of the Bombay Government, who recorded in a minute of August 1819 to the Bombay Board, of which he was a member, the unpopular view that commercial disputes rather than piracy were the cause of the trouble and that the Qawasim were perhaps more sinned against than sinning. See J. G. Lorimer's *Gazetteer of the Persian Gulf, Oman and Central Arabia* (Calcutta, 1915) vol. 1, pp. 659–660. See also note 7 below.

6. See A. M. Abu Hakima, *History of Near Eastern Arabia 1750–1800* (Beirut, 1965), pp. 166–175. The difficulty in assessing the trade of the various Gulf shaykhdoms is that their ships bore no manifests.

7. In point of fact the Shaykh of Bahrain was discovered in 1820 to have been maintaining a central market for pirates' loot and for the provisioning of their ships. See FO Research Department's 1955 memorandum on Britain's Treaty Relations with Bahrain at FO 371/114606 (EA 105671). Cases of piracy all over the Gulf, indeed, were the subject of British investigation throughout the nineteenth century and later, though the involvement of the northern shaykhs themselves was never as evident as that of the early Joasmee ones.

8. This version is taken from Noam Chomsky, *Pirates and Emperors* (New York, 1986).

9. C.U. Aitchison, *A Collection of Treaties Engagements and Sanads Relating to India and Neighbouring Countries* (Delhi, 1933), p. 182. He also states, p. 198, 'The Qawasim . . . carried on a vigorous and profitable trade by sea, till in 1805 they succumbed to the influence of the Wahabis and were drawn into the piratical projects of that turbulent sect.' Aitchison was Under Secretary in the Foreign Department of the Government of India.

10. See IOR L/P&S/18/B437.

11. See Palmerston's letter to Hobhouse in India of 14 June 1839 and related correspondence in IOR L/P&S/3/4. He had indeed instructed the Consul General in Alexandria seven months earlier, when rumours of Muhammad Ali's plans to push across the peninsula to the Gulf were already causing concern, to tell him that 'any such intention could not be viewed with indifference'.

12. After the Egyptian withdrawal, however, the Imam Faysal ibn Turki, who soon recovered the Wahhabi throne, made his own attempt to bring Bahrain and Qatar under his sovereign control. This provoked the only instance of forceful British confrontation with the Wahhabis in the nineteenth century, the whole of the Persian Gulf Squadron being despatched to Bahrain to warn him off. Thereafter the Indian Government relied on diplomacy once more. But it was not until the Ottomans took steps to reassert their rights in the Imam's 'Eastern Province' by force of arms in 1871, when for other reasons as well the nineteenth century Wahhabi state was disintegrating, that the threat from that quarter to the independence of the Gulf shaykhdoms evaporated. See R. Bayly Winder, *Saudi Arabia in the Nineteenth Century* (London and New York, 1905), especially pp. 185–187 and 252–254.

13. The instructions issued by Bombay to the officer in charge of the expedition, Major General Sir William Keir Hardy, made it clear that the object was simply the destruction of the 'piratical vessels' and not occupation of Qasimi towns or territory. (Bombay's unfulfilled hope was to persuade the Turks to share in the expedition and to take charge of Ras al Khaimah after it). See Bombay Diaries, especially Diary 313 of 1819 (T313/189 in the Exeter Extracts).

14. Aitchison, *Treaties*, pp. 245–247.

15. *Ibid.*, p. 233.

16. The text of the Exclusive Agreements is in Aitchison, *Treaties*, p. 256; that of the Maritime Truce in Perpetuity on pp. 252–253. All these documents have been examined by a number of recent writers, amongst them H. M. al-Baharna in his *The Arabian Gulf States* (Beirut, 2nd ed., 1975).

17. In 1898 the India Office view was that the Ottoman claim to sovereignty over

Kuwait was 'better than ours though not effectively exercised'. Viceroy Curzon urged without success that 'the British Protectorate should be extended to Kuwait whose shaikhs have constantly asked for it for years'. IOR L/P&S/18/B120. Britain's treatment of Ottoman rights over Kuwait was in fact a shade equivocal. Although neither Britain nor Kuwait formally rejected Ottoman claims at the time, the signing of the Exclusive Agreement in 1899 (Aitchison, *Treaties*, p. 262) was kept secret.

18. The 1916 Agreement with the Shaykh of Qatar (Aitchison, pp. 258–260) secured from him adherence to all the Trucial treaties and is more comprehensive than any of those signed elsewhere.

19. The technique of investment in proposed railway construction in the Middle East as a means of securing political influence was a common feature of the policies of European powers throughout this period; and Kuwait was the obvious terminal for a railway leading to the head waters of the Gulf. It was a subject which exercised Curzon during his tenure as Viceroy, as did suspected Russian designs of advancing through Persia to the Gulf. See his Memorandum on British and rival interests in the Gulf of 19 November 1989 in IOR L/P&S/18/B120.

20. Whereas the idea, in the 1890s, of declaring Muscat a protectorate was finally abandoned on the grounds that this would conflict with the Anglo-French Declaration of 1862 (by which both agreed to respect Muscat's sovereign independence), the reason why, for instance, Kuwait's request to be taken into protection in 1897 was refused was that Britain 'did not favour more interference in Kuwait's affairs than was necessary for the maintenance of peace in the Gulf'. Lorimer, *Gazettee*, vol. 1, pp. 1021–1022. When the Secretary of State, Landsdowne, resolutely opposed Curzon's recommendations for a more forward policy, the latter's reaction (in a letter to Lord Percy of October 1902) was to write: 'When you hear a Foreign Minister say anywhere that all he wants is to defend the *status quo*, you may guess in nine cases out of ten that he has no policy at all.' Ronaldshay, *Curzon*, p. 318.

21. In Qatar's case protection against aggression by sea was explicitly written into the 1916 Agreement, as was the furnishing of Britain's good offices in the event of unprovoked aggression by land. In the early twenties the ruler of Qatar constantly sought assurance that the Agreement guaranteed him protection against moves to extend Saudi sovereignty over his territory. Good offices, he was told, entailed no more than diplomatic intervention. See R. S. Zahlan, *The Creation of Qatar* (London, 1979), pp. 62–65.

22. A study of British state papers on the subject from the thirties on shows that the implications of this special relationship was constantly re-examined over the years; and every time this curious mongrel was taken out for a run, it came back looking slightly different.

23. By the British Protectorates, Protected States and Protected Persons Order-in-Council, Statutory Instruments (1949) no. 140.

24. See, for instance, Sir W. Dale, *The Modern Commonwealth* (London, 1983), pp. 16–17.

25. The rulers themselves, once the earlier threats to their independence were removed, welcomed this disinterest. As the Political Resident Hayworth put it

when writing to the Government of India in 1927, 'The sheikhs were as anxious to keep us out of their lands as we were anxious to avoid being drawn into their quarrels on shore.' Letter quoted, with source, by R. S. Zahlan, *The Origins of the United Arab Emirates* (London, 1978), p. 68.

26. Population figures in the shaykhdoms remained more or less constant until the coming of oil, when they shot upwards. See G. Balfour-Paul, 'Kuwait, Qatar and the UAE: Political and social evolution' in *Arabia and the Gulf*, ed. I. R. Netton (London, 1986) especially fig. 11.1, p. 162.

27. Mention has not been made here of treaty measures taken by Britain in the nineteenth century to suppress, for instance, the slave trade and the import of arms. They were important but did not affect Britain's formal relationship with the shaykhdoms.

28. Foreign Office record of discussions on 3 March 1946, FO 371/20517, W 1832/152/52.

29. FO 371/19977, E 3146/2463/91. Rendel's record of conversation with Persian Ambassador on 30 May 1936.

30. Butler gave this reply on 3 February 1937. FO 371/20780.

31. 'What surprised me most in my talks with officials in Delhi was their apparent unanimity that the Persian Gulf was of little interest to the Government of India.' Report of 27 December 1937 by N. M. Butler of the British Legation in Teheran sent to discuss future arrangements in the Gulf. FO 371/21898 (1938).

32. Between 1910 and 1938 bombardment of trucial shaykhs' palaces or forts was threatened nine times and carried out twice. FO 371/21825, E 4579/573/91 (1938).

33. Despatch from Fowle to Government of India of 17 March 1935. FO 371/23180, E 3179/61/91.

34. Administrative responsibility remained with the Government of India until 1946. Policy control, however, was transferred from the India Office to the Colonial Office (after something of a battle) in 1921, reverting twelve years later to the India Office, despite the recommendations of the Warren Fisher Sub-committee of the Committee of Imperial Defence that it should go to the Foreign Office. See Zahlan, *The origins*, pp. 22–25.

35. Fowle to Secretary of State for India, 8 May 1939. FO 371/23188, E 1244/1244/19. The eventual decision to regularize the position, and the rulers' responses, are recorded at FO 371/45192, E 8527/1449/91 (1945).

36. Making good use of their 'Open Door' principle, the Americans were able, beween the two world wars, to acquire concessions in the Gulf which were to give them by 1960 the major share in the area's oil production.

37. A brief account of the development of international air routes through the Gulf is given in J. Marlowe, *The Persian Gulf in the Twentieth Century* (London, 1962) Appendix 3, pp. 249–251. For a detailed account of the establishment of imperial air traffic rights on the Arab side see Zahlan, *The Origins*, pp. 93–106.

38. Much of the debate revolved round the interpretation of the non-interference rubric by the then Political Resident, Fowle. He supported the Government of India's opposition to the urgings of home departments for a more precise definition, largely because the absence of precision enabled him to run things in his own determined way. The Middle East Sub-Committee of Imperial Defence was con-

vened in September 1935 to examine the issue but the disagreements were not resolved. Imprecision continued to prevail. See Zahlan *The Origins*, Chapter 4.

39. His mammoth report is at FO 371/98343 (1952).

40. Belgrave gives his own account of his life and achievements in Bahrain in his *Personal Column* (London, 1960).

41. Sir Rupert Hay's Annual Report on the Persian Gulf for 1951, FO 371/98323, EA 1011/1 (1952). Belgrave was less polite about the Political Residency, at any rate after Hay's time, see his *Personal Column*, p. 223.

42. There is a whole series of FO papers on the subject, including the Resident's 1948 Review of the Gulf at FO 371/74935, E 1396/1011/91 (1949). While the Secretary of State frequently urged the men on the spot to pressurize the Ruler of Kuwait into accepting a British Adviser, they kept insisting that such pressure would be ineffective. For Churchill's attempt when the Ruler came to London for the Coronation in 1953, see FO 371/114603, EA 1053/3 (1955), minute by Fry.

43. FO 371/75020, E 11470/1535/919 (1949) where a FO letter on the subject is discussed by the Chiefs of Staff on 16 September.

44. A new sentence (Art. 85 (n)) was nonetheless inserted in the Trucial States Order-in-Council in order expressly to provide for the Crown's right to set up a levy force, the Order-in-Council being re-issued complete to avoid drawing attention to the amendment. But this amendment seems to have been regarded by the Foreign Office lawyers simply as a reinsurance. They were emphatic that 'the most appropriate means of securing the legal right to establish the force was by 'sufferance' on the part of the rulers' – one of the methods by which the Crown could acquire jurisdiction under the Foreign Jurisdiction Act of 1890. See FO 371 2181/41 for a memorandum by C. M. Rose of 26 July 1950 on the whole story of the establishment of the TOL.

45. FO 371/82174, EA 2181/49 (1950), letter from PO Sharjah to PA Bahrain of 13 September.

46. FO 371/82175, EA 2181/799 (1950), tel. from Ambassador Jedda to FO of 19 December.

47. The first quotation is from the Makins Report, see note 39. The second is from a minute from Sarrell to Anthony Eden of 1 May 1952, FO 371/98343, AE 1051/58. The directive from which the other two come is at FO 371/104270, EA 1053/8 (1953).

48. FO 371/104270 (EA 1053/3), minute of 20 March 1953.

49. FO 371/91341, minute of 26 October 1951 by Furlonge submitted to Eden.

50. As early as 1949 rumours on the subject were being reported and dismissed as baseless, FO 371/74966 and 75059 of 1949. A grotesque variation on the same theme was later put about by the leading Bahraini reformist, Abdulrahman al-Bakir, in his memoirs. This was that in the early fifties Britain had been planning the unification of the Gulf states under the presidency of Abdulillah, the regent in Iraq, to be carried into effect on the establishment of the Baghdad Pact (1955). See S. K. Hashim, 'The influence of Iraq on the nationalist movements of Kuwait and Bahrain, 1920–1961' (unpublished PhD thesis, University of Exeter, 1984), p. 317.

51. The circumstances of Glubb's dismissal are objectively discussed by James Lunt

in his biography, *Glubb Pasha* (London, 1984), pp. 193–209. The newly enthroned King Husayn clearly resented the extent of Glubb's influence. No similar resentment towards Belgrave was harboured by the long-established Shaykh Abdullah in Bahrain, whatever some of his subjects felt.

52. Interpretations of the reform movement in Bahrain are not of course uniform. Belgrave's suspicions (*Personal Column*, pp. 211–223) that the reformists had the backing of the British Residency are not borne out by the Resident's despatch of 25 October 1954, FO 371/109815, EA 1013/2, or by his annual review for 1955, FO 371/12050, EA 1011/1 (1956). The British authorities would clearly have welcomed measures of reform but they did not support the reformists. Hashim, *The Nationalist Movements*, pp. 344–381, records the nationalist view of the episode. Bahrain, it should be stated, had already introduced electoral procedures at the municipal level well ahead of other Gulf states.

53. Burrows' despatch of 25 October 1954 (see note 52) covers Kuwait as well. Hashim, The Nationalist Movements, pp. 281–298, gives an account of the aspirations of the young Kuwaitis. See also R. S. Zahlan, 'The Gulf States and the Palestine Problem', *Arab Studies Quarterly*, vol. 3, no. 1, Winter 1981.

54. In 1937 the Political Resident, Fowle, had insisted that Zubara belonged to Qatar. In 1939 he gave judgement on the Hawar Islands in favour of Bahrain. His successor thought the latter judgement unsound. In any case Qatar never accepted it, any more than Bahrain accepted the earlier ruling on Zubara. See Zahlan, *Qatar*, pp. 85–90.

55. Donald Hawley, *The Trucial States* (London, 1970), pp. 289–291.

56. The only eye-witness account of this operation is in E. F. Henderson's *This Strange Eventful History: Memoirs of Earlier Days in the UAE and Oman* (London, 1988). The standard British account of the Buraimi Dispute up to the abortive 1955 Arbitration is J. B. Kelly's *Eastern Arabian Frontiers* (London, 1964). For the rival presentations at Geneva see the *Buraimi Memorials 1955* (Archive Edition, Gerards Cross, Buckinghamshire, 1987).

57. See Zahlan, *Qatar*, pp. 80–85. J. B. Kelly, *Arabia, the Gulf and the West* (London, 1980), pp. 65–69, is very critical of the Foreign Office's readiness to placate Ibn Sa'ud at the expense of Qatar and Abu Dhabi.

58. It was during this cold war period that Soviet policy in the Third World generally had adopted a more empirical, Kruschevian approach to the business of securing support from non-Communist but anti-American and anti-imperialist countries by proclaiming the possibility of different roads to socialism. Specific instances of the change in Soviet relations with the Arab World include their favourable treatment of Nasser, their assistance to the Imam in the Yemen and to the PFLO in Oman, their backing of Iraqi claims to Kuwait, and of course the switch in their attitude to Israel.

59. Al-Baharna, *Arabian Gulf States*, p. 114, citing the relevant UNESCO record of correspondence with the British Foreign Office.

60. According to Air Chief Marshall Sir David Lee's account of the operation, *Flight from the Middle East* (London, 1980), pp. 165–188, the British military authorites 'did not contemplate aggression by Iraq very seriously'. There is indeed some

doubt whether the Iraqi troop movements which followed Qassem's renewed claims of 22 and 26 June 1961 to sovereignty over Kuwait were correctly interpreted. Nonetheless, the threat certainly appeared real enough at the time, and the Ruler's request for British military protection was (so the then British Ambassador in Kuwait, Sir John Richmond, assures the author) spontaneous and genuine.

61. The views and recommendations attributed to Luce during his tenure as Political Resident in the Gulf are recalled by the author from his many conversations with Luce in Dubai and Bahrain from 1964 to 1966 and thereafter in Baghdad in September 1970 (when Luce was the author's guest) and on visits to Luce at his home in England before and after these dates. In many unpublished lectures in England from 1966 to 1968, for example to the Cambridge Middle East Centre on 11 February 1967 and the Imperial Defence College on 3 November 1968, Luce spoke openly about, for instance, his personal (but unsuccessful) advocacy over the years of 'Arabian Peninsula Solidarity' as the best formula of future stability in the Gulf.

62. It did result in the employment of Egyptian legal experts and consequently the adoption by Kuwait of French rather than British codes of law. But this, though regretted by the British, was scarcely disastrous.

63. Kuwait being now an independent state, we are no longer directly concerned in it. Independence quickly led to constitutional change there, notably in the establishment of a National Assembly in 1962.

64. Criticism was not easily disarmed. March 1965 saw the worst labour troubles, anti-ruling family in complexion, in Bahrain's history. The presence in Bahrain of British troops was, interestingly, no deterrent; and the troubles were only just controlled by the police.

65. See pp. 93–94.

66. This and the following paragraph are based on the author's own diaries as Political Agent in Dubai at the time.

67. In retrospect it is possible to feel a good deal of sympathy on both counts with Shaykh Shakhbut. Some visitors to Abu Dhabi today may suspect that he had a clearer idea of where the interests of his people lay than he was given credit for.

68. It fell to the author, as Acting Resident, to receive and act on the family's appeal.

69. See p. 86.

70. The two most explicit public statements were those made in the House of Commons by Foreign Secretary George Brown in June (HC Deb. 12 June 1967, Oral Answers col. 76) and July (HC Deb. 20 July 1967, cols. 2494–2495). Similar statements were made by Defence Secretary Healey in January (HC Deb. 19 January 1967, col. 404) and in June (HC Deb. 5 June 1962, Written Answers, col. 140). The first of these four statements, which is typical, declared, 'Our continuing presence in the Persian Gulf is required to enable us to fulfil our remaining commitments in the area and to contribute to its stability.' Corresponding assurances were conveyed to the rulers through Britain's representatives in the field.

71. The rulers had in their hands, and at least one of them showed his copy to the

embarrassed Goronwy Roberts, a recent letter from the Prime Minister assuring them that Britain's presence in the Gulf would remain for as long as it was mutually considered desirable.

72. Sir Stewart Crawford had replaced Luce in September 1966 after serving as the Middle East Undersecretary in the FCO. He was succeeded in September 1970 by Sir Geoffrey Arthur, an experienced Arabist and ideally suited to jockey the Rulers along as withdrawal neared.

73. Military expenditure on the Gulf was in fact comparatively small (some £12 million per year in foreign currency), particularly if measured against the benefits accruing to the Treasury of an assured flow of Gulf oil to the West, let alone those accruing to British oil companies involved in its extraction. The offer made by the Rulers of Dubai and Abu Dhabi at the end of January to finance the maintenance of the British military presence in the Gulf out of their own resources and with the help of other oil producing Gulf states was the subject of discourteous comment by Healey on television.

74. Some doubt continues to exist over the personal views on this issue of the party's foreign policy triumvirate – Wilson, Brown and Healey. The last two at least were understood in the Foreign Office to be opposed to precipitate withdrawal East of Suez (whatever the party's Annual Conference of 1966 may have resolved, see p. 86). It is widely believed amongst senior officials of the time that both Brown and Healey considered in 1967 (once Aden had gone) that overseas defence had taken enough cuts and that it was the turn of domestic interests to suffer in the next round of belt-tightening. In the event (on this reading) the Prime Minister defected to the home front, and 'free dentures took precedence over overseas defence'. The fact that the Gulf went first, while commitments further east lingered longer, is attributed to pressure from Commonwealth governments in the latter though in terms of British interests at the time it is arguable that the continued protection of Gulf oil, which cost the Defence budget only about a quarter of commitments further east, should logically have taken precedence. In retrospect the need for protection of the Gulf from one direction (Nasser's Egypt) can be seen as having effectively lapsed as a result of Nasser's humiliation in the June 1967 war; but no evidence is available that this changed situation in the Middle East entered into the Labour Government's calculations at the time that withdrawal from the Gulf was decided upon. Nor was it used afterwards as an additional justification for the decision.

75. HC Deb. 16 January 1968, cols. 1580–1581.

76. Many Conservative leaders condemned the wickedness of the Labour Government's decision. Most of them declared that Labour's time-table would be ignored if the Conservatives returned to power. A few went so far as to affirm that the decision would be reversed. Iain Macleod and Maudling in January 1968 in the Commons (HC Deb. 24 January, Cols. 425–426 and 25 January, Col. 643) and Heath speaking on 11 September 1968 at Inverness and on 20 February 1969 to the Monday Club, were amongst those who did. See also end of note 79 below.

77. He had been GOC Land Forces ME and Security Commander in Aden 1965–1967. It is a fascinating example of Britannia's penchant for shooting herself in the

foot that General Willoughby, though he remained on his Gulf appointment a serving officer in the British army, was (so he informed the author in March 1988) denied all access to confidential information from the Ministry of Defence on the grounds that he was employed by foreign governments. He therefore found himself unable to brief Gulf rulers on the current military capabilities of any of their potential enemies. In this respect (though in no other) the rulers would have done better to secure a Defence Adviser of almost any other nationality. General Willoughby continued his advisory role until withdrawal in 1971.

78. When the Gulf rupee was withdrawn in June 1966, currencies were introduced by Bahrain and Qatar. Dubai joined Qatar. Abu Dhabi joined Bahrain. The others used whatever came to hand. After formation of the United Arab Emirates the Union introduced its own currency, while Bahrain and Qatar retained theirs.

79. A song written at the time by a distinguished Bahraini, who has been a minister there since independence, illustrates with engaging irony the uncertainties felt, at least in Bahrain, over the prospects of union. It goes to the tune of 'Mine eyes have seen the glory of the coming of the Lord.' These are two of its verses:

Where all was once disharmony, there's been a change of heart.
The Nine Arabian Sheikhdoms met to wonder where to start.
While each one claims the others, some *in toto* some in part,
The Union marches on.

Glory, Glory, Halleluyah,
The Union marches on.

Where all was once dissension, of agreement now they speak.
The flesh is yet unwilling and the spirit somewhat weak,
But still the whispered password is relayed from creek to creek:
'The Union marches on'.

Glory, Glory, Halleluyah,
The Union marches on.

The impetus for union, as a matter of fact, dropped conspicuously for a year following Edward Heath's tour of the Gulf in late March–early April 1969, when in his discussions with the rulers he gave them the strong impression that the withdrawal decision would be reversed if his party were returned to power. See A. O. Taryam, *The Establishment of the United Arab Emirates 1950–1985* (London, 1987), p. 117. Taryam (from Sharjah) was closely involved in federal planning throughout and should know.

80. It is possible that the attitude attributed to King Faysal by the British, and by Luce in the light of his discussions in Riadh, was over-apprehensive. As early as May 1968 Faysal had declared his support without explicit reservation for the federal idea, and he certainly took steps later to encourage the project during the period when the British were still much exercised by his refusal to sanction it unless his territorial claims on Abu Dhabi were first satisfied. No doubt he saw advantage in pressing his claims in communications with the British while they

were still 'responsible' for the Gulf, since it would be harder to pursue them if and when Abu Dhabi became an integral part of an internationally recognized union on Britain's withdrawal.

81. *Arab Report and Record*, 69/2, and Anthony Parsons, *They Say the Lion: a Personal Memoir* (London, 1986), p. 137.

82. See Parsons, *They Say the Lion*, pp. 138–140, and Kelly, *Arabia*, pp. 58–59.

83. *The Times* of 4 July 1970 quotes a Foreign Office spokesman as stating that Saudi Arabia was pressing for the settlement of its frontier claims in the Buraimi area before British withdrawal.

84. In the debate on the Queen's speech, HC Deb. 6 July 1970, cols. 348–349.

85. Holland, *European Decolonization*, p. 269.

86. The advice he gave the relevant Conservative Party study group (its Commonwealth and Overseas Council) and his article 'Britain in the Persian Gulf' in *The Round Table*, no. 227 of July 1967, pp. 227–283, were characteristic.

87. See his article 'A naval force for the Gulf' in *The Round Table*, no. 326, October 1969, pp. 347–356.

88. One helpful development so far as internal security was concerned had occurred just before Luce's appointment. This was the ouster in July 1970 of the unprogressive Sultan Saʿid of Muscat and Oman by his son Qabus. This clearly reduced the *raison d'être* of the opposition movement which had been seeking Saʿid's overthrow for some years in Dhofar and which had more recently embraced the whole of the Gulf in its liberation target, as PFLOAG.

89. HC Deb., 1 March 1971, cols. 1227–1230.

90. Britain's entry into the EEC, moreover, was by now imminent and in strategic terms it was recognized that this would mean switching Britain's military potential away from wider concerns to a European focus.

91. Though they had finally expelled the Qawasim from Lingah on the Persian coast in 1887, the Persians had never seriously disputed Qasimi occupation of Abu Musa and the Tunbs for more than 200 years, until Shah Reza Khan in the 1930s had sought to assert sovereignty over them as part of his policy of promoting Iranian naval and political weight in the Gulf. Britain, under India Office pressure, had rejected his claims. The issue was not seriously pursued again by Iran until the announcement of Britain's impending withdrawal. In October 1970 the Shah formally demanded the surrender of the islands as a condition of approving a union of the Gulf states, and this demand was thereafter frequently repeated.

92. Luce found King Faysal at this stage relaxed over the Buraimi oases and focusing his further demands on the western and southern areas of Abu Dhabi territory. Shaykh Zayed, under British pressure, had offered concessions there without effect.

93. Signed with Bahrain on 15 August and with Qatar on 3 September.

94. The ten-year treaty with Kuwait had in fact expired in May 1971 without renewal. It cannot have escaped notice lower down the Gulf that Kuwait was content to face the future without one.

95. The UN sanctioned their membership on 21 September. When the Arab League accepted their applications, the only adverse vote was South Yemen's. PFLOAG

also made known its disapproval of propping up 'the frail entities set up by Britain in the Gulf'. *Arab Report and Record*, 71/471.

96. Ostensibly on the grounds that Ras al Khaimah was not given equal status in the proposed constitutional structure with Abu Dhabi and Dubai. See *Arab Report and Record*, 71/374.

97. A good example of the Shah's refusal to compromise figures in the interview published by *The Guardian* on 28 September. The fact that a group of international lawyers, commissioned by the Ruler of Sharjah the previous year to study the legal status of Abu Musa, submitted its findings in September 1971, supporting Sharjah's claim to sovereignty, was of no avail to Shaykh Khalid. See Taryam, *The UAE*, p. 186.

98. *Al Khalij* (Sharjah) published their rejections on 1 and 2 November.

99. The Iraqi condition was published by *Al-Baʻth* (Baghdad) on 7 December 1971. For the Saudi Arabian reservation see Taryam, *The UAE*, p. 190. Taryam also states on p. 216 that 'Saudi Arabia's non-recognition of the union' led her to continue dealing with its member states individually until (pp. 219–221) the agreement between King Faysal and Shaykh Zayed on 21 August 1974 on frontier demarcation finally cleared the way for the former's formal recognition of the UAE.

100. *The Times*' Middle East correspondent was on 2 December as critical as any of Britain's 'hypocrisy' in not carrying out its defence obligation right up to the last moment of their existence.

101. Thirty-three officers and fifty-five NCOs seconded from the British Army remained in the Force and took the oath of allegiance to the new state. Brigadier F. M. de Butts, erstwhile Commander of the Trucial Oman Scouts, was recruited to command it.

102. As an example of trouble during the June war, Sir Anthony Parsons, then Political Agent in Bahrain, recalls how on one of those fraught mornings, a particularly unfriendly crowd, some with rifles, converged on the Agency and were on the point of breaking in and ransacking it, when the Ruler, Shaykh Eissa, boldly and spontaneously drove unescorted into the *mêlée*, and, standing on the roof of his car, harangued the rioters until they quietly dispersed. Parsons, *They Say the Lion*, p. 131.

103. In defence of the Government of India it should be stated that whenever they did advance proposals in the nineteenth and early twentieth centuries for establishing a more thorough-going grip on the Gulf states – Curzon's being the most emphatic – it was the Imperial Government in London that held them back. Nonetheless, even Curzon's proposals did not envisage much intervention in internal affairs; nor would that have been sanctioned in London, if they had.

Chapter 5

1. Macmillan's approach is usefully discussed by Holland, *European Decolonisation*, pp. 202–213.

2. The speech was made in Cape Town to the parliament of the Union and was

designed not to set the pace for decolonization elsewhere, but to warn the South Africans against apartheid. Its effect was a good deal wider-ranging. See, for instance, Anthony Samson's *Macmillan: A Study in Ambiguity* (London, 1967), pp. 181–190. Also chapter 3, note 85.

3. D. J. Morgan, The Official History of Colonial Development, vol. 5, *Guidance Towards Self-Government in British Colonies*, pp. 96–97.

4. Initiatives envisaged personally by Churchill though not in fact taken (see Chapter 2, notes 49 and 54) did not materially upset the process.

5. Nonetheless at the meeting of Commonwealth prime ministers of February 1961, so Morgan records, 'it was considered that the Aden Protectorate was unlikely to achieve independence without Aden Colony and that *both might achieve it within the next decade*' (author's italics). *Official History*, vol. 5, p. 113.

6. *Shades of Amber*, p. 99.

7. HC Deb., 13 November 1962, col. 262.

8. By contrast the overworked Macleod, during his period as Colonial Secretary, spent hours in 1957 closeted with representatives from the Aden Government discussing what additional categories might be given the franchise and with what result. But the problem defeated him too.

9. See their submission on 'Strategic requirements in the Middle East', DO (46) 67 of 25 May 1946 in CAB 131/2, and their memorandum of 7 March 1947 protesting at Britain's deteriorating strategic position in the Middle East, DO (47) 23. Bevin pinned his faith on securing a base in Cyrenaica as a substitute for Suez, right up until 1949 when the UN decided otherwise. See Bullock, *Ernest Bevin*, pp. 250, 263, 472, 672, 678 and 724. Britain did secure certain base facilities from the independent Senussi régime in Libya, but these were no subsitute for Suez, so far as Britain's military dominance of the Middle East as a whole was concerned.

10. Reductions did not stop with Attlee's government. The proportion of Britain's GNP allocated to defence dropped progressively over the whole period of this study, from 10 per cent to 7 per cent to 5 per cent to 4.5 per cent.

11. Darby, *Defence Policy*, pp. 95–96. Sandys' endeavour could scarcely hope to appeal to the Services themselves. General Sir William Jackson's magisterial *Withdrawal from Empire: A Military View* (London, 1982), pp. 170–173, strongly criticizes the whole Sandys doctrine.

12. So far as the colonies, including Aden, were concerned, it is worth observing that the Colonial Policy Committee set up in 1955 to advise on their progress towards statehood was dissolved in 1962 on the grounds that each presented different problems and a centralized body served little purpose. Morgan, *Official History*, vol. 5, pp. 56–60.

13. Anthony Adamthwaite, 'Britain and the world: the view from the Foreign Office', *International Affairs*, vol. 61, no. 2 (1985).

14. FO 371/104190 (1953).

15. See note 41, chapter 2.

16. Bullock, *Bevin*, p. 154.

17. *Ibid.*, pp. 473–475.

18. The ambivalence in US postwar attitudes to Britain's imperial and overseas pretensions and the processes by which it was overcome are usefully discussed by G. K.

Tanham in his contribution, 'A United States view', to the special East of Suez issue of *International Affairs*, vol. 42, no. 2, of April 1966, pp. 194–206.

19. Holland, *European Decolonisation*, p. 276.
20. The behaviour in Cairo of US ambassador Caffery (and Eden's consequent dislike of him) illustrate this ambivalence. Anthony Eden, *Full Circle* (London, 1960), pp. 231, 252, 256–257.
21. Bidwell, *The Two Yemens*, p. 140. Bidwell, later turned academic, was a Political Officer in the Western Aden Protectorate from 1955 to 1959. He himself did not actually serve under Johnston.
22. In Durham University's Sudan Archive.
23. See note 29, chapter 2.
24. Huddleston to Hector McNeil, 13 November 1946, FO 371/52360, J 4860/24/16G.
25. Illustrations quoted of the resentments on Khartoum's side are drawn, during the period of Robertson's tenure as Civil Secretary, from papers in the Sudan Archive at Durham University. It would overload these footnotes to identify each specific source in full; but dates are given and they can be traced from these. For the Luce period, since his personal papers have not as yet been publicly released, illustrations drawn from them must be taken on trust. As for signs of tension at the London end, drawings on state papers will be identified in each case.
26. Minute of 15 November 1946 by Hector McNeil, FO 371/53260, J 4860/24/16G.
27. Holland, *European Decolonisation*, p. 116.
28. Sir Bernard Reilly, *Aden and the Yemen* (London, 1959).
29. All those consulted in any of these categories are listed in the bibliography and many are quoted in chapter 3.
30. We are, for instance, more indebted for one short period to Crossman's diaries than to the memoirs of Prime Minister Wilson or Foreign Secretary George Brown, whose account of his stewardship, *In My Way* (London, 1971), ignores the subject of South West Arabia altogether. No such complaint can be levied against the previous (Conservative) Prime Minister, Macmillan. His diary entries recording Cabinet support in 1962 for the merger of Aden and the Federation make no bones about British motivation, no suggestion appearing that self-interest was diluted by concern for the welfare of the people affected. In his memoirs he quotes his diary entries without inhibition. Harold Macmillan, *The End of the Day* (London, 1973), p. 265.
31. Ledger, *Shifting Sands*, p. 129.
32. Johnston, *The View*, p. 193.
33. Hickinbotham had been promoted to Government House from the Chairmanship of the Aden Port Trust, but in the sense relevant here he was an outsider. His personality may not have helped. Two of his senior subordinates have described him to the author as a total misfit.
34. 'The heroes were the British Colonial Service in the field.' Johnston, *The View*, p. 10.
35. David Holden, *Farewell to Arabia* (London, 1956), pp. 54–56.
36. Donald Foster is a case in point. See his *Landscape with Arabs* (Brighton, 1969). He attributes the expatriate life-style in Aden to the fact that the climate made life otherwise insufferable.

37. For example, one sort of inter-departmental dissension was over Aden/Yemen frontier affairs. In June 1953 the Colonial Secretary was enraged by 'the procrastination of the FO and something very like sabotage by the Air Ministry'. CO 1015/845 (1953). A similar example of the clash of priorities as between the Colonial and Foreign Secretaries over reprisal bombing across the Yemen border has already been mentioned (chapter 3, p. 64 and note 41).

38. CO 1015/685 (CAA /284/7/01). Treasury letter of 9 March 1953.

39. FO 371/120527, E 1052/7 (1956), which includes copy of the resulting CO tel. to Hickinbotham of 14 March.

40. CO 1015/1131 (CAA /104/56/01), 1956.

41. The bulky CO file – 1015/1211 (CAA /270/7/01) – recording the preparation of the original draft of that paper and the alterations made to it on its way up to the Secretary of State (Lennox Boyd) in September 1955 provides an interesting illustration of the conflict between Hickinbotham and the cautious top officials in the Colonial Office on the basic issues, i.e. of a positive push for federation of the Protectorate and of its future association with the Colony. The final amendment to the paper was the excision of a reference to the possibility of future self-determination.

42. Minute by Eden of 21 June 1956, CO 1015/1213 (CAA /270/7/01), p. 147.

43. FO 371/120527, E 1052/14G (1956).

44. Trevaskis, *Shades*, p. 161.

45. Phillips (later Sir Horace), a Foreign Office diplomat who occupied the new post in Aden of Political Secretary for the WAP from 1956 to 1959 and who may represent London thinking at the time, criticizes Trevaskis (then WAP Resident) on many counts, e.g. for failing to recognize the impact of Arab nationalism, for excessive partiality to the Sherif Husayn of Beihan and of course for resenting supervision by a FO bureaucrat unfamiliar with the niceties of tribal life up country. Personal communication to author.

46. Trevaskis dates it from 1962, *Shades*, p. 104. Bidwell in *The Two Yemens*, pp. 162–163, has some corroborative quotations that year by Labour spokesmen, though these were backbenchers. At grass roots in the Party support for al-Asnaq clearly went back to the formation of ATUC in March 1956.

47. This was David Ledger, then a Government PR man in Aden. His *Shifting Sands*, p. 225, is relevant.

48. Trevaskis' view, as expressed to the author, is that Turnbull had fallen foul of George Brown, the Foreign Secretary, during discussions in London the previous month, by rejecting George Brown's characteristic belief that a new approach to the whole problem would circumvent disaster. Other sources, including the then Commander of Land Forces in Aden, General Sir John Willoughby, confirm that Turnbull regarded his treatment by the Wilson government as painfully humiliating.

49. Kelly's *Arabia, the Gulf and the West*, to which reference has already been made, is the savagest.

50. FO 371/104270, EA 1053/3 (1953).

51. Despatch of 25 June 1953. FO 371/104270, EA 1053/7.

52. Macmillan himself attached great importance to the matter. In opposing recog-

nition of the revolutionary regime in Sanaʿa he had the support of Governor Johnston, the Colonial Office and the Ministry of Defence. The Foreign Office agreed on this issue with Luce. The US decision to recognize was mainly due to concern that Nasser, unless humoured, would choose Saudi Arabia as his next target. Macmillan, *At the End of the Day*, pp. 266–278.

53. Sir Horace Phillips, who was Luce's Deputy in Bahrain from 1962 to January 1966 after serving under him in Aden, recalls that in December 1965 Luce, on returning from discussions in London, told him in confidence that withdrawal from the Gulf was apparently already on the Government's agenda, or words to that effect. If such a decision had already been taken, it is almost inconceivable that no other senior officials in the FO at the time (many of whom the author has consulted) were aware of it. Possibly Luce had simply sensed that the Gulf would prove to be next for the chop.

54. The writings and even more the oral reminiscences of members of the Political Service who particularly relished the Sudanese make-up – K. D. D. Henderson is a case in point – provide numerous illustrations. To cite a rather different example of Anglo-Sudanese rapport at the personal level, when Province Governors were assembled in April 1954 to meet Azhari, for whose policies they entertained considerable distaste, Civil Secretary Robertson recorded in his diary that 'they all rather fell for him'.

55. Their judicial responsibilities certainly enlarged the scope of their dealings with the inhabitants but their jurisdiction covered in general only non-Arab immigrants and was, as the end approached, progressively retroceded.

56. Arnold Beichman, quoted by Johnston in *The View*, p. 28.

Chapter 6

1. Letter of 27 May 1898 to Lord Salisbury, quoted by Kenneth Rose in his *Superior Person: A Portrait of Curzon and his Circle in Late Victorian England* (London, 1969), p. 327.

2. For all the pomp and ceremony, Curzon's genuine concern for the sensitivities of the people of India and for their welfare was quickly recognized and applauded there. Ronaldshay, *Curzon*, vol. 2, *passim*.

3. The most scrupulous is perhaps Philip Woodruff's two-volume study, *The Men Who Ruled India* (London 1953 and 1954). Though himself one of them, he depicts the members of the ICS throughout its history, warts and all, without inhibition. Only when evangelical fervour overcame victorian England in the mid-fifties and bore bitter fruit in the mutiny of 1857, does he find cause for shame. James Morris' *Pax Britannica* (London, 1968), pp. 21–34, treats in particular the flamboyance of the New Imperialism of the 1890s (reflected in the Diamond Jubilee of 1897) with rather less affection.

4. One Sudanese, M. N. Nagumi (an architect), published a fulsome but spontaneous tribute to the British in the Sudan, *A Great Trusteeship* (London, 1957). No South West Arabian or Gulf citizen has done anything remotely similar. Indeed no member of the Arab intelligentsia anywhere has sought to emulate the Indian example of Nirad Chaudhuri whose recent scholarly work *Thy Hand, Great Anarch*

(London, 1987) uninhibitedly reverses the critical view in India of Britain's record in India.

5. Those not already familiar with this Egyptian national pastime or escape-valve, can find entertaining examples of it in Khalid Kishtainy's *Arab Political Humour* (London, 1987). There is less resort to it amongst other Arab peoples.

6. *Set Under Authority* is the biblical title of K. D. D. Henderson's recent book on one set of the species (London, 1987).

7. A resonant expression coined in the fifties by Sir Mortimer Wheeler, the distinguished popularizer amongst the youth of England of archaeology overseas as a means of satisfying the craving for adventure previously met by service in the outposts of empire.

8. The author was a member of the Sudan Political Service from 1946 to 1954, then narrowly escaped serving in Aden under Hickinbotham, and was later a Political Agent in the Gulf from 1964 to 1968.

9. A. H. M. Kirk-Greene, *The Sudan Political Service: a Preliminary Profile* (Oxford, 1982).

10. The average expectation of life was given by Sir Douglas Newbold (see note 12) to one prospective entrant in 1946 as fifty-two. The low figure, he explained, was due to the number of those speared by their cooks, bitten to death by rats, cut short by a variety of incurable tropical diseases, or facing other occupational hazards. In point of fact the number actually murdered over the 50 years was only five, though 27 others died, violently or not, in the course of duty.

11. Macmichael was not by any means the only 'Blue' with a First Class degree; but since the names of the others have not figured in this book, they are not mentioned here.

12. K. D. D. Henderson's full length study of Newbold's life and letters bears the title *The Making of the Modern Sudan* (London, 1953). This may be overstating his achievements, great as they were. As for inspiration, one of his remarkable practices, which continued until the eve of his death from overwork in 1946, was the writing of long personal letters, wide-ranging and witty, in the small hours after a day of prodigious industry, to dozens of members of the Service, including the most junior. Sir Charles Johnston, when Governor of Aden, once toured the Sudan with him and describes the experience as 'like travelling with one of Plato's philosophers', (*The View*, p. 192). Trevaskis, who also visited him from Aden, pays him a rather similar tribute (*Shades*, pp. 41–42).

13. One of them, in a paper significantly entitled 'Servant or saboteur: the Sudan Political Service during the critical decade, 1946–1956', describes Robertson, for example, as parochial, unimaginative, intolerant and contemptuous of the intelligence of his subordinates. He shrewdly bases this and other criticisms of the Service on quotations from its own erstwhile members, though this particular judgement (of Robertson) is not easy to reconcile with the known views of most of them. David Sconyers in the *Bulletin of the British Society for Middle Eastern Studies*, vol. 14, no. 1, 1988.

14. In his Annual Review for 1953 (FO 371/108311, JE 1011/2 (1954)) Riches referred to 'that oligarchy of officials of British nationality in contact with, rather than under the control of, HMG'; and in a letter to W. Morris of 19 February 1954

(FO 371/108378, JE 1059/39) he observed that Azhari's Government had acquired wide support because it had shown itself 'able to . . . denigrate the British administrators who have outlived their usefulness as the autocratic rulers of the country'.

15. Major C. S. Jarvis in his *Oriental Spotlight* (London, 7th ed. 1946), p. 118. Once a best-seller, its satire on Egyptian manners cannot easily be stomached by Arabophiles today.

16. Those wives, often left to sweat it out in lonely isolation, who have committed their recollections entertainingly to paper, do not suggest that their interests were given much consideration. *Sudan Tales*, compiled by Rosemary Kenrick (Cambridge, 1987).

17. But as with the Shakespearian prototype, this would have been to damn them under a misapprehension. For their verses were only composed for their own amusement – and published as an off-beat source for future students of the nature of the Condominium. See the Introduction to *Sudan Verse*, ed. K. D. D. H. and T. R. H. O. (London, 1963).

18. Amongst the pantheon of eccentrics to have entered the local folklore Wilfred Thesiger is a rare example of those recruited in the normal way. He was, however, too unusual to stay in the Service for long.

19. The same criticism can be levied of this book, which has consigned the problem of the South to a note (note 7, chapter 2).

20. Martin Daly, one of the most comprehensive in his scrutiny, is marginally less critical. But in his *Empire on the Nile* (Cambridge, 1986), which takes the story up to 1934, he finds little to commend in the Sudan Government's social, educational and judicial policies or in its reliance on biddable tribal shaykhs in preference to the emergent *effendia*.

21. Henderson, *Set Under Authority*, p. 29.

22. Dawud Abdul Latif, quoted by Francis Deng in *The British in the Sudan, 1898–1954*, ed. R. O. Collins and F. M. Deng (London, 1984), p. 233.

23. An occasion is recorded when neighbouring District Commissioners, meeting to prevent their respective tribes coming to blows over a quarrel, came to blows themselves and had to be separated by the tribesmen. And when the end came, the misery of having to abandon a people they loved to an undeserved fate caused at least one (southern) District Commissioner a nervous breakdown.

24. Hamilton, *The Kingdom of Melchior*, pp. 119–120.

25. The use of the RAF in reducing the incalcitrant to order by bombing, however scrupulous the avoidance of casualties, aroused increasing external, but much less internal, criticism. Originally used to stop tribal interference with roads and trade, it was later used to promote submission to tribal rulers – an extension of its use which Ingrams, for example, deplored.

26. Bidwell, *The Two Yemens*, p. 94. There were, of course, quite a number who adopted a more vigorous and good-humoured approach. Prominent amongst those who stayed there to the end and robustly enjoyed the whole experience were R. G. C. Young, L. J. Hobson and J. D. Ellis.

27. This was Stephen Day, now a senior diplomat.

28. At least until they were creamed off in the last few years to appointments in the

federal capital, al-Ittihad. In the Sudan inter-changeability was more of a norm and there was little hostility between periphery and centre.

29. The practise of turning British army officers into Political Agents – Hamilton was a prime example – had in later years virtually died out.

30. Trevaskis, *Shades*, p. 239.

31. Lunt had earlier reached a similar conclusion when serving under Glubb in the Arab Legion in Jordan, where MOD policy also insisted on the seconding of a high proportion of short-term British officers.

32. Two of those examining South West Arabian security as one feature in a broader strategic canvas are Air Chief Marshall Sir David Lee in his *Flight from the Middle East* (London, 1980) and General Sir William Jackson in his *Withdrawal from Empire* (London, 1986). Those involved at a rather lower level with specific military operations in the area include Colonel Julian Paget in his *Last Post: Aden (1964–67)* (London, 1969).

33. Trevaskis, *Shades* p. 109.

34. It was in the early sixties that their most appropriate nomenclature became a subject of serious debate, laughable in its way, in the British establishment. 'Backward' was replaced by 'undeveloped', 'undeveloped' soon after by 'less developed', later by 'deprived' or by the somewhat sanctimonious term 'underprivileged'. Arabic terms were found to correspond at each stage. At the British end, this was more a matter of semantic diplomacy than a change of mind; but the word has a habit of becoming flesh.

35. Rosemarie Zahlan's impressive study, *The Origins*, quotes examples.

36. Only a top proconsul as widely admired as Luce could have established, without incurring criticism from the British community, the principle of never attending drinks parties.

37. Margaret Luce, *From Aden to the Gulf* (London, 1987).

38. *Ibid.*, pp. 91–98. The specially made chair, it may be added, on which Curzon had himself been carried ashore on his visit to Bahrain in 1903 and which he left there for the edification of posterity, was not the kind of contrivance to appeal to latterday proconsuls.

39. M. Perham, *The Colonial Reckoning* (London, 1961), p. 72

40. This was Dawud Abdul Latif. Henderson, *Set Under Authority*, p. 105.

41. The prime instance was on Selwyn Lloyd's visit to Bahrain in 1956. It was not an example followed elsewhere. The politically restive, to be sure, did not share the general tolerance but their activities were not regarded as unmanageable on the South West Arabian pattern.

42. M. Perham, *The Colonial Reckoning*, p. 102.

43. Into the French political hierarchy too in certain cases, e.g. in that of Algerian deputies elected to sit in the legislative bodies in Paris, side by side with their metropolitan equivalents. There were also instances of 'black Frenchmen' appointed as colonial governors at a time when such an idea was quite foreign to British thinking.

44. Prominent Sudanese amongst them, from the author's personal experience.

45. The relative lack of interest in economic affairs shown throughout by the main Sudanese parties is a theme developed by T. C. Niblock in his *Class and Power*

in the Sudan (Macmillan, 1987). Their concentration on political affairs meant (p. 198) that 'socio-economic radicalism' was left to others, mainly the growing Communist Party in its various guises (the Movement for National Liberation and later the Anti-imperialist Front).

46. By 1964 only London, Liverpool and New York handled more than Aden's 6,000 ships bunkering there annually.

47. Oil has recently been discovered in the north-eastern desert and is now (1989) being exploited. This will help, but its location is difficult and its quantity uncertain.

48. *Democracy on Trial* was the title of the account published (London, 1974) by Muhammad Ahmad Mahjoub, a leading Umma politician when independence came – though his own life-style was not conspicuously democratic.

49. One oddity is that, though they have little enough foreign exchange, the PDRY – alone in the Middle East – spends more of it on goods from Britain than from anywhere else.

Bibliography

Unpublished sources

Public Record Office: Cabinet papers, Foreign Office papers (under FO 371), Colonial Office papers (Under CO 725, 735 and 1015), and the personal papers of Ernest Bevin.

India Office Library, especially papers in L/P&S/18; also L/P&S/3, 5, 7, 9 and 10, and R/20.

Durham University's Sudan Archive, especially the papers of Sir James Robertson.

Exeter University's Extracts from the Bombay Diaries of the Secret and Political Department, Series 1755–1820.

Diaries of Sir James Robertson.

Personal papers of Sir William Luce and records on the Sudan and Aden privately compiled from 1952 to 1960 by his son (now the Rt Hon. Richard Luce, MP).

Personal correspondence and interviews with many of those involved in each episode.

The author's own records and recollections of the Sudan (1941–1954), the Trucial States (1964–1966), Bahrain (1966–1968) and Iraq (1969–1971).

Published sources

Government publications

(Note: the following documents have not been listed individually but are identified, as appropriate, in the text and notes.

British Government publications: Command Papers, Statutory Instruments, British Information Services pamphlets, *Hansard*, etc.

Sudan Government publications: the Sudan Government Gazette and related documents published locally (Condominium period) and the Republic of Sudan Gazette (post-Condominium).

Aden Government Gazette

Persian Gulf Gazette (1953–1971)

Books and pamphlets

Abbas, Mekki. *The Sudan Question* (London, 1952).

Abdullah, M. Mursi. *United Arab Emirates: a Modern History* (London, 1978).

Abdulrahim, Mudaththir. *Imperialism and Nationalism in the Sudan* (Oxford, 1965).

Abu Hakima, A. M. *History of Eastern Arabia: the Rise and Development of Bahrain and Kuwait* (Beirut, 1965).

Aitchison, C. V. *A Collection of Treaties, Engagements and Sanads Relating to India and Neighbouring Countries*, vol. 11 (Delhi, 1933).

Anon. '*General handbook on Aden Colony and the Protectorate*', Intelligence Branch, BFAP, January, 1959.

Anthony, J. D. *The Arab States of the Lower Gulf: People, Politics, Petroleum* (Washington DC, 1975).

al-Baharna, H. M. *The Arabian Gulf States: Their Legal and Political Status and Their International Problems*, 2nd revised edn. (Beirut, 1975).

Bartlett, H. Moyse. *The Pirates of Trucial Oman* (London, 1960).

Bashir, M. O. *The Southern Sudan: Background to Conflict* (London, 1968). *Revolution and Nationalism in the Sudan*, 2nd edn. (London, 1977).

Belgrave, Charles. *Personal Column* (London, 1960).

Bell, Sir Gawain. *Shadows on the Sand* (London, 1983). *An Imperial Twilight* (London, 1989).

Berque, J. *Egypt: Imperialism and Revolution* (London, 1972).

Bidwell, Robin. *The Two Yemens* (London, 1983).

Boustead, Hugh. *The Wind of Morning* (London, 1971).

Brown, George. *In My Way: the Political Memoirs* (London, 1971).

Bulloch, J. *The Gulf: a Portrait of Kuwait, Bahrain and the UAE* (London, 1984).

Bullock, Alan. *Ernest Bevin: Foreign Secretary, 1945–1951* (London, 1983).

Busch, B. C. *Britain and the Persian Gulf, 1894–1914* (Berkeley, 1967).

Clayton, Sir Gilbert. *An Arabian Diary*, ed. Collins, R. O. (Berkeley, 1969).

Collins, R. O. and Deng, F. M. *The British in the Sudan, 1898–1956* (London, 1984).

Cottrell, A. M., ed. *The Persian Gulf states* (Baltimore, 1980).

Cromer, Earl of [Evelyn Baring]. *Modern Egypt*, 2 vols. (London, 1908).

Crossman, R. *The Diaries of a Cabinet Minister*, vol. 2, *1966–68*, ed. Janet Morgan (London, 1976).

Curzon, G. N. *Persia and the Persian Question* (London, 1892, new edn. 1966).

Dale, Sir William. *The Modern Commonwealth* (London, 1983).

Daly, M. W. *Empire on the Nile: The Anglo-Egyptian Sudan 1898–1934* (Cambridge, 1986).

Darby, Philip. *British Defence Policy East of Suez, 1947–1968* (Oxford, 1973).

Darwin, John. *Britain, Egypt and the Middle East: Imperial Policy in the Aftermath of War* (London, 1981).

Dixon, Sir Pierson. *Double Diploma* (London, 1968).

Douglas, J. Leigh. *The Free Yemeni Movement, 1935–1962* (Beirut, 1987).

Duncan, J. S. R. *The Sudan: a Record of Achievement* (Edinburgh and London, 1952). *The Sudan's Path to Independence* (Edinburgh and London, 1957).

el-Ebraheem, H. A. *Kuwait and the Gulf* (London, 1980).

Eden, Anthony. *Full Circle* (London, 1960).

Evans, Trefor, ed. *The Killearn Diaries* (London, 1972).

Fabunmi, L. A. *The Sudan in Anglo-Egyptian Relations* (London, 1960).

Foster, Donald. *Landscape with Arabs* (Brighton, 1969).

Gavin, R. J. *Aden Under British Rule, 1839–1967* (London, 1975).

Graham, G. S. *Great Britain in the Indian Ocean: A Study of Maritime Enterprise, 1810–1850* (Oxford, 1967).

Halliday, Fred. *Arabia Without Sultans* (London, 1974).

Hamilton, J. C. de A., ed. *The Anglo Egyptian Sudan from Within* (London, 1935).

Hamilton, R. A. B. *The Kingdom of Melchior: Adventure in South West Arabia* (London, 1949).

Hashim, S. K. *The Influence of Iraq on the Nationalist Movements of Kuwait and Bahrain.* Unpublished PhD thesis, University of Exeter, 1984.

Hawley, Donald. *The Trucial States* (London, 1972).

Hay, Sir Rupert. *The Persian Gulf States* (Washington DC, 1959).

Heard-Bey, Frauke. *From Trucial States to United Arab Emirates* (London, 1982).

Henderson, Edward. *This Strange Eventful History: Memoirs of Earlier Days in the UAE and Oman* (London, 1988).

Henderson, K. D. D. *The Making of the Modern Sudan: the Life and Letters of Sir Douglas Newbold* (London, 1953).

   Sudan Republic (London, 1965).

   Set Under Authority (Castle Cary, 1987).

Hickinbotham, Sir Tom. *Aden* (London, 1958).

Holden, David. *Farewell to Arabia* (London, 1966).

Holland, R. F. *European Decolonisation: an Introductory Survey* (London, 1985).

Holt, P. M. and Daly, M. W. *The History of the Sudan* (London, 4th edn., 1988).

Ingrams, Harold. *The Yemen* (London, 1963).

   Arabia and the Isles (London, 3rd edn., 1966).

Jackson, Gen. Sir W. *Withdrawal from Empire* (London, 1986).

Johnston, Sir Charles. *The View from Steamer Point* (London, 1964).

Kelly, J. B. *Eastern Arabian Frontiers* (London, 1964).

   Britain and the Persian Gulf, 1795–1880 (Oxford, 1968).

   Arabia, the Gulf and the West (London, 1980)

Kerr, Malcolm. *The Arab Cold War 1958–1964* (Oxford, 1965).

King, Gillian. *Imperial Outpost – Aden: Its Place in British Strategic Policy* (Oxford, 1964).

Kirk, G. *Survey of International Affairs, 1939–1946: The Middle East in the War* (Oxford, 1952).

Kirkman, W. P. *Unscrambling an Empire: a Critique of British Colonial Policy, 1956–66* (London, 1966).

Kostiner, J. *The Struggle for South Yemen* (London, 1984).

Lackner, Helen. *PDR Yemen: Outpost of Socialist Development in Arabia* (London, 1985).

Ledger, David. *Shifting Sands: the British in South Arabia* (London, 1983).

Lee, Air Chief Marshal Sir David. *Flight from the Middle East: a History of the Royal Air Force in the Arabian Peninsula and Adjacent Territories* (London, 1980).

Little, Tom. *Southern Arabia* (London, 1968).

Litvak, R., S. Chubin, and A. Plascov. *Security in the Gulf*, 4 vols (Aldershot, 1982) (reprinted as Adelphi Library vol. 7).

Long, David. *The Persian Gulf: an Introduction to its Peoples, Politics and Economics* (Boulder, revised ed., 1978).

Lorimer, J. G. *Gazetteer of the Persian Gulf, Oman and Central Arabia*, vol. 1 (*Historical*), vol. 2 (*Geographical and Statistical*) (Calcutta, 1908–1915).

Louis, William Roger. *The British Empire in the Middle East, 1945–51* (Oxford, 1984).

Luce, Margaret. *From Aden to the Gulf: Personal Diaries, 1956–66* (Salisbury, 1987).

Lunt, James. *The Barren Rocks of Aden* (London, 1973).

MacMichael, H. A. *The Anglo-Egyptian Sudan* (London, 1934).

Macmillan, Harold. *At the End of the Day, 1961–63* (London, 1973).

Macro, Eric. *Yemen and the Western World* (London, 1968).

Mahjoub, M. A. *Democracy on Trial* (London, 1974).

Marlowe, John. *The Persian Gulf in the Twentieth Century* (London, 1962).

Monroe, Elizabeth. *Britain's Moment in the Middle East* (London, 2nd edn., 1981).

Morris, James. *Pax Britannica: The Climax of an Empire* (London, 1968).

Nagy, Sultan. *At-tarikh al-askari lil-yaman 1839–1967* [Military History of the Yemen, 1839–1967] (publisher unstated, 1976).

Netton, I. R. ed. *Arabia and the Gulf: from Traditional Society to Modern States* (London, 1986).

Niblock, T. C. *Class and Power in the Sudan* (London, 1987).

Nagumi, M. N. *A Great Trusteeship* (London, 1957).

Paget, J. *Last Post: Aden, 1964–67* (London, 1969).

Parsons, Anthony. *They Say the Lion: a Personal Memoir* (London, 1986).

Perham, Margery. *The Colonial Reckoning* (London, 1961) Reith lectures.

Pridham, B. R., ed. *Contemporary Yemen: Politics and Historical Background* (London, 1984).

Qasimi, Sultan M. *The Myth of Arab Piracy in the Gulf* (London, 1986).

Reilly, Sir Bernard. *Aden and the Yemen* (London, 1959).

Risso, Patricia. *Oman and Muscat: an Early Modern History* (London, 1986).

Robertson, Sir James. *Transition in Africa* (London, 1974).

Ronaldshay, Earl of [Lawrence J. L. Dundas] *The Life of Lord Curzon* (London, 1928).

Rose, Kenneth. *Superior Person: a Portrait of Curzon and his Circle in Late Victorian England* (London, 1969).

Sabri, H. Zulfaker. *Sovereignty for Sudan* (London, 1982).

Sampson, Anthony. *Macmillan: a Study in Ambiguity* (London, 1967).

Shibeika, Mekki. *The Independent Sudan* (New York, 1959).

Sidki, Ismail. *Mudhakarati* (Memoirs) (Cairo, 1950).

Taha, Gad. *Siyasat Biritania fi janub al-Yaman* (Britain's policy in South Yemen) (Cairo, 1979).

Taryam, A. O. *The Establishment of the United Arab Emirates* (London, 1987).

Trevaskis, Sir Kennedy. *Shades of Amber* (London, 1968).

Trevelyan, Humphrey. *The Middle East in Revolution* (London, 1970).

Waterfield, Gordon. *Sultans of Aden* (London, 1968).

Wilson, Sir Arnold. *The Persian Gulf* (London, 3rd edn., 1959).

Wilson, Harold. *The Labour Government, 1964–70: A Personal Record* (London, 1971).

Wilson, K. M., ed. *Imperialism and Nationalism in the Middle East* (London, 1983).

Winder, R. Bayly. *Saudi Arabia in the Nineteenth Century* (London and New York, 1965).

Woodruff, Philip. *The Men who Ruled India*, vol. 1, *The Founders*, vol. 2, *The Guardians* (London, 1953 and 1954).

Woodward, Peter. *Condominium and Sudanese Nationalism* (London, 1979).

Zahlan, Rosemarie S. *The Origins of the United Arab Emirates* (London, 1978). *The Creation of Qatar* (London, 1979).

Articles and pamphlets

Adamthwaite, Anthony. 'Britain and the world, 1945–49: the view from the Foreign Office'. *International Affairs*, vol. 61, no. 2, Spring 1985.

Anon. 'The Sudan: the road ahead', Fabian Society, Research Series no. 99, September 1945.

Anon. 'Britain and Egypt 1914–51', RIIA Information Paper no. 19, London, 3rd edn., 1952.

Buchan, Alistair. 'Britain in the Indian Ocean', *International Affairs*, vol. 42, no. 2, April 1966.

Hamilton, R. A. B. 'The social organization of the tribes of Aden Protectorate', *Journal of the Royal Central Asian Society*, vol. 30, 1952.

Holden, David. 'The Persian Gulf: after the British Raj', *Foreign Affairs*, July 1971.

Howard, Michael. 'Britain's strategic problem East of Suez', *International Affairs*, vol. 42, no. 2, April 1966.

Ingrams, Harold. 'The progress towards independence of Aden and the Aden Protectorate', *Journal of the Royal Society of Arts*, vol. 111, 1962–1963.

Luce, Sir William. 'Britain in the Persian Gulf', *The Round Talbe*, no. 227, July 1967. 'East of Suez', *Journal of the Royal United Service Institution*, March 1969. 'A naval force for the Gulf', *The Round Table*, no. 326, October 1969.

Sconyers, David. 'Servant or saboteur: the Sudan Political Service during the crucial decade', *British Society for Middle East Studies Bulletin*, vol. 14, no. 1 (1985). 'Hurrying home: Sudanisation and national integration, 1953–1956', *British Society for Middle East Studies Bulletin*, vol. 15, nos. 1 and 2 (1988).

Smith, M. and Zammetica, J. 'The Cold War: Clement Attlee reconsidered', *International Affairs*, vol. 61, no. 2, Spring 1985.

Sorensen, R. 'Aden, the Protectorates and the Yemen', Fabian International and Commonwealth Bureaux pamphlet, July 1961.

Standish, J. F. 'British maritime policy in the Persian Gulf', *Middle Eastern Studies*, vol. 3, no. 4, July 1967.

Tanham, G. K. 'A United States view'. *International Affairs*, vol. 42, no. 2, April 1966.

Trevaskis, Sir Kennedy. 'The future of South Arabia', British Commonwealth Union pamphlet, no. 459, September 1965.

Watt, D. E. 'Labour relations and trades unionism in Aden, 1952–60', *Middle East Journal*, vol. 16, no. 4, Autumn 1962.

Zahlan, Rosemarie S. 'The Gulf States and the Palestine Problem, 1936–1948', *Arab Studies Quarterly*, vol. 3, no. 1, Winter 1981.

Comparative chronology

For Period A (up to 1945) only basic items are listed. The crucial Period B (1945–1972) is shown in greater detail. Entries in Period C (1973 on) include only significant post-withdrawal developments.

Period	UK (and Colonies)	Sudan (Egyptian items bracketed)	South West Arabia	The Gulf	Elsewhere (Middle East)
A 1. Up to 1914	*Period of Establishment of Empire* East India Company founded (1600)				*India.* East India Company assumes control of Bombay (1688)
				Political Resident established in Bushire (1778)	*Egypt.* Napoleon occupies Egypt (1798) British forces remove this French threat to Indian possessions (1800)
				Destruction of Ras al-Khaimah (1819)	
		Ottoman/Egyptian conquest begins (1821)		First Trucial Treaties (1820)	
			British occupy Aden (1839)		*Egypt.* Muhammad Ali withdraws troops from Arabia (1841)
					Yemen. Ottoman reoccupation (1849)
				Treaties of Perpetual Peace (1853)	
	India Office/Government of India replaces East India Company (1858)				

Comparative chronology (*cont*)

Period	UK (and Colonies)	Sudan (Egyptian items bracketed)	South West Arabia	The Gulf	Elsewhere (Middle East)
	British Occupation of Egypt (1882)	Mahdi's revolt begins (1881) Gordon killed (1885) Battle of 'Kerreri (1898) Anglo-Egyptian Condominium established (1899)	Protective Agreements in hinterland begin (1886) Anglo-Ottoman frontier delimitation begins (1902)	Exclusive Agreements (1892) Viceroy Curzon's visit to Shaykhdoms (1903) Political Agencies in Kuwait and Bahrain set up (1904)	*Egypt.* Suez Canal opened (1869) *Turkey.* Young Turks revolution (1908)
2. 1914–1918	*World War I*	Rehabilitation of Mahdi's son (Sayed Abdulrahman)	Turkish troops advance to Lahej (1915) First re-distribution of responsibilities between India and Home Departments (1917)		*Yemen.* Imam sides with Turks and Germany. *Palestine.* Balfour Declaration (1917) *Turkey.* Collapse of Ottoman Empire (1918)

Period	UK (and Colonies)	Sudan (Egyptian items bracketed)	South West Arabia	The Gulf	Elsewhere (Middle East)
3. 1918–1939	*Inter-War period*	(Britain declares Egypt independent sovereign state) (1922)			San Remo Agreement on Middle East Mandates (1922)
		(High Commissioner Stack assassinated in Cairo) (1924)			*Hejaz.* Ibn Sa'ud ousts King Husayn (1924)
		Allenby's *diktat* curtails Egyptian presence (1924) Gezira Cotton Scheme formally opened (1925)			
			Lahej Pact between Western rulers (1929)	Belgrave appointed Adviser to Ruler of Bahrain (1926)	*Iraq.* Anglo-Iraqi Treaty prepares for end of Mandate (1930)
			Anglo-Yemeni Treaty of Sana'a (1934)	Oil production starts in Bahrain (1932)	*Saudi Arabia.* Kingdom declared (1932)
					Ethiopia. Italian invasion (1935)
		Anglo-Egyptian Treaty leaves Sudan issue unresolved (1936)	Aden becomes Crown colony. Protectorates transferred to Colonial Office (1937)		*Palestine.* Arab revolt (1936)
			Advisory Treaties begin (1937)		

Comparative chronology *(cont)*

Period	UK (and Colonies)	Sudan (Egyptian items bracketed)	South West Arabia	The Gulf	Elsewhere (Middle East)
			'Ingram's Peace' in EAP (1937)		
		Graduates' Congress founded (1938)			*Palestine.* White Paper rejected (1939)
3. 1939– 1945	*World War II*		Hathorn Hall replaces Reilly as Governor (1940)	Intended transfer of Resident to Bahrain postponed (1939)	
		Congress Memorandum rejected by Newbold (1942)	Tradesunionism legalized (1942)		
		Egypt reasserts Unity of Nile Valley (1943 on)			
		Ashiqqa and Umma parties established (1943/44)			
		Advisory Council for Northern Sudan established (1944)			Arab League established (1945)

Period	UK (and Colonies)	Sudan (Egyptian items bracketed)	South West Arabia	The Gulf	Elsewhere (Middle East)
B. 1945–1972 *Period of imperial relinquishment*					
Year					
1945	Labour Government elected (August)	(Egypt requests revision of 1936 Treaty) (December)			
1946		Bevin announces No change without consulting Sudanese (March)		Oil production starts in Kuwait (and Saudi Arabia)	
		(Anglo-Egyptian negotiations in Cairo begin) (April)		Political Residency transferred to Bahrain	
		Sidki/Begin Protocol drawn up and leaked (October)			*Egypt.* Sidki replaced by Noqrashi (November)
1947	British Raj in India ends (June)	Egypt refers Sudan issue to United Nations (January)	Aden Legislative Council inaugurated (January)	Foreign Office assumes control	*India and Pakistan* become independent (June)
	Announcement of intention to relinquish Palestine Mandate (September)	Huddleston replaced (April)	Abyan Cotton scheme inaugurated		*Palestine.* United Nations votes for Partition (November)
		Draft Constitutional Ordinance submitted to Co-domini (June)			
		Egypt sends London counter-proposals (November)			

Comparative chronology (*cont*)

Period	UK (and Colonies)	Sudan (Egyptian items bracketed)	South West Arabia	The Gulf	Elsewhere (Middle East)
1948					*Iraq.* Anglo-Egyptian Treaty of Portsmouth signed but rejected in Iraq (January)
					Yemen. Imam Yahia assassinated (February)
	Palestine Mandate surrendered (May)	Constitutional Ordinance promulgated, without Egyptian agreement (June)			*Palestine.* Mandate ends. State of Israel proclaimed (May). First Arab–Israeli war follows
		Legislative Assembly elections, boycotted by Unionists (November)			
1949				Britain publicly defines shaykhdoms as British Protected States.	*Saudi Arabia.* Frontier claim against Abu Dhabi advanced in maximum form.
				Oil production starts in Qatar	
1950				Nationalist stirrings in Kuwait and Bahrain intensify.	*Egypt.* Wafd returns to power (January)
				Trucial Oman Levies	

Period	UK (and Colonies)	Sudan (Egyptian items bracketed)	South West Arabia	The Gulf	Elsewhere (Middle East)
		Legislative Assembly passes self-government resolution (by one vote) (November)			
1951	Bevin replaced by Morrison as Foreign Secretary (March)	Constitutional Amendment Committee appointed (April)	Anglo-Yemeni *modus vivendi* Agreement (January)		*Iran.* Musaddeq regime begins (April)
	General Elections. Conservatives to power (October)	Egypt abrogates 1936 Agreement. Farouk declared King of Sudan (October)			*Jordan.* King Abdullah assassinated (July)
		Constitutional Amendment Commission breaks up (November)			
		Eden declares self-government to proceed end 1952, self-determination to follow (November)			

Comparative chronology (*cont*)

Period	UK (and Colonies)	Sudan (Egyptian items bracketed)	South West Arabia	The Gulf	Elsewhere (Middle East)
1952		Naguib secures agreement of all Sudanese parties on future of Sudan (August–September)	British Petroleum licensed to build refinery in Aden (July) New 'Forward Policy' in Protectorate takes shape	Trucial States Council (of Rulers) set up Makins' review of policy in the Gulf	*Egypt.* Black Friday in Cairo. Nahas dismissed (January) *Egypt.* Revolution. Naguib to power (July)
1953	Churchill seeks US backing for Britain's Middle East policies (January) Breakdown of Suez Canal talks (May)	Anglo-Egyptian Agreement on Sudan signed (February) Self-government Statute promulgated (March) Robertson retires (April) Legislative Assembly elections, NUP winning (November)	Aden College opened. Aden Broadcasting Service inaugurated	Political Agencies in Dubai (for Trucial States) and Qatar opened	*Iran.* Musaddeq ousted (August) *Saudi Arabia.* Death of Ibn Sa'ud (November)

Period	UK (and Colonies)	Sudan (Egyptian items bracketed)	South West Arabia	The Gulf	Elsewhere (Middle East)
1954			Governor's first attempt to promote Federation (January)		
				Higher Executive Committee set up by Bahrain nationalists	
		Ansar riot delays opening of parliament for 14 days (March)			
		Sudanisation Committee reports (June) followed by exodus of British officials	BP Refinery in Aden completed (July)		
	Anglo-Egyptian Agreement on evacuation of Suez base signed (October)	Azhari visits London (November)			
		Naguib's ouster offends Sudanese (November)			*Egypt*. Naguib's final ouster. Nasser takes full control (November)
1955	Knox Helm replaces Howe (March)		United National Front formed		*Iraq, Turkey*. Turco-Iraqi Pact (signed February) becomes Baghdad Pact on UK joining it (April).
					Yemen. Imam Ahmad temporarily ousted (April)

Comparative chronology (*cont*)

Period	UK (and Colonies)	Sudan (Egyptian items bracketed)	South West Arabia	The Gulf	Elsewhere (Middle East)
			Trades Unions proliferate		
			Aden Legislative Council enlarged and partially elected (July)		
	General Elections. Conservatives retain power. Eden replaces Churchill as Prime Minister (June)	Parliament requests Co-domini to put self-determination process into motion (August)			
		Mutiny of Equatorial Corps (August)			
			Colonial Office produces Long Range Policy paper on Aden and Protectorates (September)		
				Saudi detachment dislodged from Buraimi with help of Trucial Oman Scouts (October)	
		British and Egyptian military complete withdrawal (November)			
		Departure of last Governor General (15 December)			
		Parliament adopts independence resolutions (19 December)			

Period	UK (and Colonies)	Sudan (Egyptian items bracketed)	South West Arabia	The Gulf	Elsewhere (Middle East)
1956	Anglo-French invasion of Suez (October)	Sudan becomes independent Republic (1 January) Azhari's Government defeated. Abdullah Khalil takes over (July)	Aden trades unions establish Congress (ATUC) (March) Governor's second attempt to promote Federation (April) Lord Lloyd's policy declaration in Aden (May) Luce replaces Hickinbotham (August) Aden hit by closure of Suez Canal (October on)	Selwyn Lloyd visits Bahrain. His motorcade stoned (April)	*Egypt, Saudi Arabia, Yemen.* Jedda Military Pact signed (April) *Egypt.* Nasser nationalizes Suez Canal Company (July) *Egypt.* Anglo-French invasion (October)
1957	Macmillan replaces Eden as Prime Minister (January) Sandys' Defence White Paper (conscription to end, Armed Forces to be progressively cut) (February)		United Nationalist Front breaks up.		*USA.* Eisenhower Doctrine announced (January) *Muscat and Oman.* Imam of Oman revolts against Sultan (July)

Comparative chronology (*cont*)

Period	UK (and Colonies)	Sudan (Egyptian items bracketed)	South West Arabia	The Gulf	Elsewhere (Middle East)
				Trucial Oman Scouts begin assistance to Sultan of Muscat against rebel Imam (Autumn)	
1958					*Egypt*-Syria. Union announced and joined by Yemen as UAS (February)
			British Forces in Arabian Peninsula become independent command (April)		
			Declaration of Emergency in Aden, following Yemeni incursions (May)		
			Sultan Ali of Lahej dismissed (July)		*Iraq*. Revolution and overthrow of monarchy (July)

Period	UK (and Colonies)	Sudan (Egyptian items bracketed)	South West Arabia	The Gulf	Elsewhere (Middle East)
		Breakdown of Umma/PDP coalition. Gen. Abboud takes power (November)	Six WAP rulers announce decision to federate (July) Serious riots in Aden (October)		*Lebanon/Jordan.* US marines come to aid of President, British troops to aid of King Husayn (August)
1959	Cyprus declared independent (February) General Elections. Conservatives retain power (October)		New Aden Constitution promulgated (January) Aden Legislative Assembly election, boycotted by UNF/ATUC (January) Federation of Emirates of the South inaugurated (February) Emergency lifted (October)	Trucial Oman Scouts assist in conclusive battle against Omani rebels (January)	*Muscat and Oman.* Final suppression of Imam's revolt (April)
1960			Five more States join Federation (April)		

Comparative chronology (*cont*)

Period	UK (and Colonies)	Sudan (Egyptian items bracketed)	South West Arabia	The Gulf	Elsewhere (Middle East)
	Independence of United Somalia (July)		Industrial Relations ordinance (requiring compulsory arbitration) issued (August)		
			Luce succeeded by Johnston (September)		
1961			HQ BFAP becomes HQ Middle East Command	Middleton succeeded by Luce (June)	
				Kuwait becomes independent (June)	
			Federal and Adeni Ministers meet Colonial Secretary Macleod and agree on principle of merger (July)	Kuwait, threatened by Iraq, invokes British protection (July)	
					Egypt, Syria, Yemen. Syria breaks away from Egypt. UAS abolished (October)
			Protectorate Levies merged with Federal Army (November)	Political Agency established in Abu Dhabi (November)	
	Independence of Tanganyika (December)				

Period	UK (and Colonies)	Sudan (Egyptian items bracketed)	South West Arabia	The Gulf	Elsewhere (Middle East)
1962	Independence of Uganda (December)		ATUC sets up Peoples' Socialist Party (PSP) Sandys' first conference with South West Arabian ministers (July) Prospective merger of Aden and Federation approved by Aden Legislative Council (September)	Oil production starts in Abu Dhabi Constitution promulgated in Kuwait (December)	*Yemen.* Imam Ahmad dies (September). Imam Badr ousted by Sallal's *coup.* Yemen Arab Republic established (September)
1963	Central African Federation (imposed 1953) abolished		Merger of Aden and Federation takes effect (January) Tenure of existing Aden Legislative Council renewed for 12 months (January) Formation of National Liberation Front (as rival of PSP) announced (March)		*Yemen.* Severs diplomatic relations with Britain (February)

Comparative chronology (*cont*)

Period	UK (and Colonies)	Sudan (Egyptian items bracketed)	South West Arabia	The Gulf	Elsewhere (Middle East)
			New Franchise Bill approved by Aden Legislative Council (March)		
	Independent Federation of Malaysia approved (June)		Johnston replaced by Trevaskis (July)		
	Douglas Home replaces Macmillan as Prime Minister (October)		Committee of 24 mission refused entry to Aden (November)		
			Attempted assassination of Governor at Aden airport (December)		
	Independence of Kenya and Zanzibar (December)		United Nations General Assembly Resolution 1949 calls for abrogation of constitution. British withdrawal, general elections on basis of universal franchise (December)		
1964			Radfan operation (January to June)		

Period	UK (and Colonies)	Sudan (Egyptian items bracketed)	South West Arabia	The Gulf	Elsewhere (Middle East)
			Sandys' Constitutional Conference in London ('Independence not later than 1968') (July)		
	General Elections. Labour take power (October)	Abboud removed. Civilian government restored (October)	Legislative Council elections in Aden (October)		*Saudi Arabia.* Faysal replaces deposed Sa'ud as King (November)
			Colonial Secretary Greenwood visits Aden (November–December)		
1965			Turnbull replaces Trevaskis (January)		
			Federalist Baharoon replaced as Aden Chief Minister by anti-federalist Meccawi (March)	Deposition of Shaykh Saqr of Sharjah (April)	
			NLF outlawed by Governor (June)	Arab League mounts anti-British operation in Trucial States (May–June)	
				Nine Gulf rulers meet for first time (July)	

259

Comparative chronology (*cont*)

Period	UK (and Colonies)	Sudan (Egyptian items bracketed)	South West Arabia	The Gulf	Elsewhere (Middle East)
	US and Commonwealth urge Prime Minister to maintain East of Suez role		Greenwood (in Aden) sets up working party to prepare for Constitutional Conference in December (July)		
			Murder of Sir A. Charles (Speaker of Aden Legislative Council). Meccawi dismissed. Direct rule reimposed (September)		*Yemen.* Nasser–Faysal agreement on withdrawal of troops from Yemen (August)
			Lord Beswick visits Aden and reassures Federal leaders (November)	Death of Shaykh Abudllah as-Salem, ruler of Kuwait (November)	*Saudi Arabia.* Faysal establishes Islamic Pact (as counter to Nasser) (December)
1966			Front for the Liberation of South Yemen set up under Nasser's patronage (January). NLF opt out		
	Defence White Paper presented by Healey declares intention of evacuating Aden (February)		Lord Beswick on second visit announces intention of abandoning Aden (February)	Build-up of British military facilities in Bahrain of Sharjah proceeds	*Yemen.* Nasser declares intention of retaining Egyptian forces in Yemen (despite August 1965 undertaking) (February)

Period	UK (and Colonies)	Sudan (Egyptian items bracketed)	South West Arabia	The Gulf	Elsewhere (Middle East)
	Merger of Colonial Office and Commonwealth Relations Office (August)			Luce retires (July) succeeded by Crawford (September)	
				Deposition of Shaykh Shakhbut of Abu Dhabi. Shaykh Zayed takes over (August)	
	Labour Party Conference declare for complete military withdrawal East of Suez (October)		Britain appeals to United Nations for good offices (December)		
1967			UN 3-man Mission to Aden ends in fiasco (April)		
			Shakleton sent to Aden as Special Envoy (April)		
	King Faysal appeals to Wilson for maintenance of military presence in Aden (May)		Turnbull replaced by Trevelyan (May)		
			Mutiny in Federal Army (June)	Anti-British demonstrations in Bahrain (June)	*Palestine/Israel.* Six-Day Arab–Israeli War (June) King Faysal reconciled with Nasser
			Federation disintegrates. NLF progressively take over inland states		

Comparative chronology (*cont*)

Period	UK (and Colonies)	Sudan (Egyptian items bracketed)	South West Arabia	The Gulf	Elsewhere (Middle East)
	Supplementary Defence Policy statement implies approaching run down East of Suez (July)				
			Trevelyan offers talks to Nationalist groups (September)		
			FLOSY force (PORF) meet NLF in battle (September–October)		*Egypt/Yemen.* Egyptian troops withdrawn from Yemen (October)
	Foreign Secretary announces readiness to talk with NLF in Geneva (7 November)		Britain advances date for withdrawal to end November (2 November)	Minister of State Goronwy Roberts visits rulers with reassurances of continued protection (November)	
			Federal Army declares for NLF (6 November)		
	Devaluation of sterling (18 November)		Last British troops and High Commissioner leave Aden (29 November)	British Military HQ transferred to Bahrain	
			People's Republic of South Yemen (PRSY) established under NLF. Qahtan ash-Sha'abi President		
1968	Announcement of plans for withdrawal East of Suez (16 January)		Talks on unity with Yemen Arab Republic begin	Goronwy Roberts returns to announce withdrawal in three years time (January)	

Period	UK (and Colonies)	Sudan (Egyptian items bracketed)	South West Arabia	The Gulf	Elsewhere (Middle East)
	Commonwealth Relations Office merges with Foreign Office as FCO (October)			Nine rulers meet and agree on principle of Union (February)	*Indian Ocean.* Soviet naval presence established (April) *Iraq.* Ba'th Party seizes power (July)
1969		Political parties in increasing disarray. Nimeiri seizes power and imposes military rule (May)	Ash-Sha'abi ousted by extreme leftists under Salem Rubai'a (June)	Oil production starts in Dubai Sixth (and last) meeting of all nine rulers breaks up inconclusively (October)	*Libya.* Monarchy overthrown by Qadhafi (September)
1970				United Nations 'Ascertainment' resolves Iranian claim to Bahrain (April) Bahrain and Qatar progressively lose interest in Union project (May on)	

Comparative chronology (*cont*)

Period	UK (and Colonies)	Sudan (Egyptian items bracketed)	South West Arabia	The Gulf	Elsewhere (Middle East)
	General Elections. Conservatives to power (June)			Shaykh Zayed rebuffed by King Faysal on Frontier issue (May)	
	Luce appointed by Foreign Secretary to examine policy options in the Gulf (July)				*Muscat and Oman.* Sultan Sa'id deposed and replaced by Qaboos (July)
				Luce's first tour of the area on behalf of Foreign Secretary (August)	
				Crawford succeeded by Arthur (August)	
					Egypt. Death of President Nasser (September)
				Shah steps up insistence on Iranian sovereignty over Abu Musa and Tunb islands (October)	
			PRSY changes name to People's Democratic Republic of Yemen (PDRY), implying claim to dominate YAR (November)		
1971	Douglas Home announces government policy on withdrawal from the Gulf (March)			Adherence to previous British Government's timing of withdrawal announced (March)	

Period	UK (and Colonies)	Sudan (Egyptian items bracketed)	South West Arabia	The Gulf	Elsewhere (Middle East)
		Short lived success of anti-Nimeiri coup.		Bahrain becomes independent sovereign state under new Agreement with Britain (August)	
				Qatar follows suit (September)	
				Sharjah announces agreement with Iran on Abu Musa Island (23 November). Shah effectively withdraws opposition to Union of Emirates.	
				Union of Arab Emirates (Abu Dhabi, Dubai, Sharjah, Ajman, Umm al-Qaiwayn, Fujayrah) announced (25 November)	
				Iranian troops land on Abu Musa and the Tunbs (30 November)	*Iraq* breaks relations with Britain; *Libya* nationalises British oil interests (December)
				UAE formally inaugurated (2 December). Treaty of Friendship with Britain signed (3 December)	

Comparative chronology *(cont)*

Period	UK (and Colonies)	Sudan (Egyptian items bracketed)	South West Arabia	The Gulf	Elsewhere (Middle East)
1972		Nimeiri achieves settlement with south	PDRY and YAR abandon talk of Union and are effectively at war.	Ruler of Sharjah assassinated by ex-Ruler Saqr (January) Ras al-Khaimah joins UAE (February) Political Residency withdrawn (26 March)	*Iraq.* Treaty of Friendship with Soviet Union signed (April) 51 per cent participation by Arab governments in oil companies becomes general
C. 1973–1986	*Political developments since Britain's final withdrawal* Nimeiri gets constitution written. Sudan Socialist Union (SSO) set up as single party (1973)			Bahrain experiments with elective parliament (repealed two years later) (1973)	Third Arab–Israeli War (1973) Massive increase in crude oil prices imposed by OPEC (1973) *Oman.* Dhofar rebellion ends (1975) *Saudi Arabia.* Assassination of King Faysal (1975)

Period	UK (and Colonies)	Sudan (Egyptian items bracketed)	South West Arabia	The Gulf	Elsewhere (Middle East)
					Lebanon. Civil War starts (1975)
		Exiles launch unsuccessful attacks from Libya and Ethiopia (1976)		Kuwait suspends elective parliament (1976)	
		Sudan/Egypt sign Military Defence Pact against Libya (1977)	YAR President al-Hamdi assassinated on eve of union talks (1977)		
			YAR President al-Qashmi assassinated (1978)		Egypt/Israel. Camp David Agreement (1978)
			NLF execute PDRY President Salim Rubai'a (1978)		Iran. Revolution ousts Shah (Winter 1978–79)
			Deposition of President Abdul Fattah Isma'il (1979)		Afghanistan. Soviet invasion (1979)
			Fighting between YAR and PDRY ends with Kuwaiti mediation	UAE Federal National Council submits memorandum on extension of elective principle, etc. (1979)	Saudi Arabia. Seizure of the Great Mosque at Mecca by rebels (1979)
			Presidency of less dogmatic Ali Nasser Muhammad begins (1980)		Iraq. Iraq–Iran War begins (1980)

Comparative chronology (*cont*)

Period	UK (and Colonies)	Sudan (Egyptian items bracketed)	South West Arabia	The Gulf	Elsewhere (Middle East)
				Kuwait's second experiment with elective parliament (1981)	*Egypt.* Assassination of Sadat (1981)
					Lebanon. Israeli invasion (1982)
				Establishment of Gulf Co-operation Council between all Gulf States plus Saudi Arabia and Oman (1981)	
					Saudi Arabia. Death of King Khaled. King Fahd succeeds (1982)
					Palestine/Israel. Reagan's proposals for Middle East settlement rejected by Israel (1982)
			Oil discovered in YAR (1984)		
		Numeiri overthrown by opposition political parties (1985)			
			Ali Nasser Muhammad overthrown in PDRY civil war (1986)	Kuwait again suspends elective parliament (1986)	

Index

Index